# Crucial
# Issues
## in Education

# Crucial
# Issues
## in Education
### Fifth Edition

## Henry Ehlers
*University of Minnesota, Duluth*

HOLT, RINEHART AND WINSTON, INC.
New York   Chicago   San Francisco   Dallas
Atlanta   Montreal   Toronto

Copyright © 1955, 1959, 1964, 1969, 1973 by Holt, Rinehart and Winston, Inc.
All rights reserved
Library of Congress Catalog Card Number: 73-187
**ISBN: 0-03-005681-0**
Printed in the United States of America
3  4  5  6    090    9  8  7  6  5  4  3  2  1

# Preface

This is the fifth edition of a series of anthologies which, since 1955, have tried to report the pros and cons on major issues in contemporary education. It is not the function of this anthology to provide clear-cut answers to any of the problems raised, or to decide the "right side" or the "wrong side" of a disputed area. Rather, each chapter presents claims and counterclaims, assertions and denials, proofs and disproofs, conflicting values and rival hypotheses. Each chapter may be viewed as a dialogue among some of the outstanding minds of our time. To gain the most from this anthology, the reader should strive not merely to understand the opposing points of view, but also to clarify his own attitudes and beliefs.

Not every issue in this anthology will seem equally crucial to every reader. Accordingly, you, the reader, should ask yourself at the very start, "What issues are most crucial to *me*?" Peruse the book hurriedly, study the general contents carefully, and decide which topics you would like to study in greatest detail. What issues would you add to—or drop from—this anthology? What criteria would you use to determine whether an issue is significant or trivial, whether a discussion is constructive, or whether it is merely a form of emotional release?

The book demands that you exercise your critical faculties, and you are encouraged to exercise them, first of all, on the anthology itself.

Why should we read *both* (or several) sides of a disputed issue? The reason is clear. We are so comfortable with ourselves and with the prejudices which make us what we are, that we are loath to read anything that might upset these cherished beliefs. As scholars, however, we must abide by the Socratic maxim, "The unexamined life is not worth human living." This may also be translated, "The unexamined belief is not worth human holding." A careful study of opposing viewpoints will generally help to clarify an issue and to replace emotional outbursts by rational understanding. The net result is a restructuring of our original beliefs which have now become more comprehensive and more precise. The net result should be an increase in personal esteem and self-confidence because our beliefs, and the personality they reflect, are now maintained with understanding and integrity.

An open society is progressive and dynamic precisely because different individuals and organizations are permitted to defend their opposing viewpoints with passionate intensity before the court of public opinion. Hopefully, these controversial issues may some day be resolved in a manner reasonably satisfactory to all, but the process of arriving at a viable position is one of tension, not rest. For, as Ralph Waldo Emerson wrote in his essay, *Intellect*,

> God offers to every mind its choice between truth and repose. Take what you please—you can never have both. Between them, as a pendulum, man oscillates. He in whom the love of repose predominates will accept the first creed, the first philosophy, the first political party he meets—most likely his father's. He gets rest, commodity and reputation: but he shuts the door of truth. He in whom the love of truth predominates will keep himself aloof from all moorings, and afloat. He will abstain from dogmatism, and recognize all the opposite negations between which, as walls, his being is swung. He submits to the inconveniences of suspense and imperfect opinion, but he is a candidate for truth, as the other is not, and respects the highest law of his being.

Now for a few brief acknowledgements. In putting this book together, the joy of learning has far exceeded the labor of writing; so my first thanks go to the authors whose works are used, and to the publishers whose permissions are found in the footnotes accompanying each selection. Next, let me thank the late Gordon C. Lee for his work as coeditor of the second and third (1959 and 1964) editions. For their very great help in "liberalizing a liberal," and thus in making the substance of this fifth edition considerably different from the previous editions, I am especially indebted to Professors Walter Feinberg (University of Illinois, Urbana), John Paul Strain (University of Redlands, California), and Donald R. Warren (University of Illinois, Chicago). For their more detailed criticisms of the several manuscript versions of this fifth edition, I am grateful to my two Duluth colleagues, Professors Dean A. Crawford and A. Dean Hendrickson, and to the editorial adviser for Holt, Rinehart and Winston, Inc., Professor R. Freeman Butts (Teachers College, Columbia University). For their constant and ever-willing service, my librarian friends both here and at the University of Washington, Seattle, must not be forgotten. For the many nitty-gritty details that go into writing a book, I am again indebted to Mrs. Jo Ann Larson, not only for her proficiency as a typist, but also for her ability to decipher illegible scribbling. Finally, for her constant patience with a husband who, on numerous occasions, while sitting across a dining room table, was a thousand miles distant in thought, I thank my wife.

Henry Ehlers

*Duluth, Minnesota*

# Contents

# Crucial Issues
# in Education

CHAPTER

# 1

# Equalize Educational Opportunity

# A. Are Color Barriers Diminishing?

## 1.1 INTRODUCTION

Democracy is a form of society whereby men and women may gain confidence in themselves and in their fellow humans, and thereby move from force to persuasion, from restriction to liberty, from blind obedience to creative effort. Unlike dictatorial forms of government, democracy has everything to gain and nothing to lose from the intelligence of its citizens. In the words of James Madison:

A popular government without popular information or the means of acquiring it, is but a Prologue to a Farce or a Tragedy, or, perhaps both. Knowledge will forever govern ignorance; and a people who mean to be their own Governors must arm themselves with the power which knowledge gives.[1]

In any society progress depends on developed leadership. True leadership must be renewed from the ranks of the unknown, not from the small group of families already famous and powerful. If one class possesses all the wealth and education while the laboring class remains both poor and ignorant, labor will inevitably be servile to capital, and our society will be divided into distinctive, permanent classes. But if education is widely and equally diffused according to ability rather than wealth, children of all classes may attain their maximum potential, and society as a whole will gain from the fuller use of its human resources.

Democracy holds that there is no safe repository of the ultimate powers of society except in the people themselves. If the people make mistakes, the remedy is not to take the power away from them, but to help them in forming their judgment through better education and more open communication. In his First Inaugural Address, Abraham Lincoln expressed democracy's faith in the people as follows:

[1] James Madison, Letter to W. T. Barry, Aug. 4, 1822, in *The Complete Madison: His Basic Writings,* Saul K. Padover, ed., New York: Harper & Row, Publishers, 1953, p. 337.

4 / **Equalize Educational Opportunity**

Why should there not be a patient confidence in the ultimate justice of the people? Is there any better or equal hope in the world? . . . Truth and justice will surely prevail by the judgment of the great tribunal of the American people.

Democratic education should develop citizens who are "easy to lead, but difficult to drive; easy to govern, but impossible to enslave."[2] It should make them easy to lead by bringing out latent talent and leadership, conceived in cooperative terms. It should make them impossible to enslave—and, we would add, intolerant of enslavement—because their education will have emphasized individual self-reliance, free expression, and unthwarted communication.

The democratic citizen will admit that, in specialized areas, there are authorities whose technical knowledge may greatly influence decisions concerning public policy. But in a free society, the citizen should never relinquish his personal freedom, autonomy, and moral dignity. External guidance may be a means, but self-direction is an end in itself. The mature man wants self-confidence, courage to face all difficulties, and the consciousness of being man in the fullest sense of the word.

Such a man is possessed by the wish to see the same inner strength develop in others. As he himself abhors alien rule, neither does he wish to rule over others. He is pleased to see life unfolding itself free and strong in his fellow humans. He finds himself happiest in a circle of equals, not surrounded by slaves. In education, his aim is not to exact submissive obedience, but to foster young individuals who in due course will themselves be able to form their own lives with freedom and responsibility.[3]

Such is the democratic ideal which moved our society to broaden suffrage from the wealthy 10 percent or 20 percent to all male adults, to women, and then to all men and women over 18 years of age. It is the ideal which inspired our schools in their effort to mold immigrants from various European nationalities throughout the nineteenth and early twentieth centuries. It is the ideal of *liberty, equality* and *fraternity* which has motivated social progress since 1789.

But this ideal is far from realization: The African American, the American Indian and, more recently, the Puerto Rican, the Chicano, and other non-White and non-Christian groups, have not been accorded a full and honored place in the American community. Since the first step in dealing with any issue is to understand it, Section A of this chapter tells of progress made and of problems encountered.

[2] Lord Henry Peter Broughton, Speech in House of Commons, January 29, 1828.
[3] Alf Ross, *Why Democracy?* Cambridge, Mass.: Harvard University Press, 1952, p. 104. Compare Harry A. Overstreet, *The Mature Mind*, New York: W. W. Norton & Company, Inc., 1949.

Those who say that no progress has been made should know the attitudes which antedated the Civil War. In 1856, speaking for a majority of the United States Supreme Court, Chief Justice Roger B. Taney described the situation as follows:

> This unfortunate class [the black people] have, with the civilized and enlightened portion of the world, for more than a century, been regarded as an inferior order and unfit associates for the white race, either socially or politically, having no rights which white men are bound to; and [hence] that the Negro might justly and lawfully be reduced to slavery for his benefit.

These attitudes persisted far beyond the Civil War. The opening sentence of the chapter "Racial Segregation in Education" in the first edition of *Crucial Issues in Education* began with these words:

> Within the memory of some people still alive [in 1955], there was a time when human beings were bought and sold as chattel property, when men honestly affirmed that dark-skinned people had neither souls nor intellects, and that Negroes were incapable of rational, moral action or of intellectual achievement.

Certainly we cannot take much pride in the progress we have made: Nevertheless, an honest reading of the history of the past may help give us hope for the future, and spur our continued efforts to realize the democratic ideal.[4]

---

[4] Because of lack of space, this chapter deals exclusively with Blacks, and says nothing about other minority groups. Our concluding chapter on Values has one selection by an Indian, Harold Cardinal. For an understanding of what is now the largest immigrant group, read Wayne Mosquine, ed., *A Documentary History of Mexican Americans*, New York: Praeger, 1971.

# 1.2 FOUR STAGES OF BLACK REVOLT
## Kenneth S. Tollett

As a black man, my personality, my character, my motivation, and my philosophical perspectives have been forged and shaped by various persons and by conflicting, sometimes contradictory, forces and experiences.

Three persons played important roles in my life: my paternal grandfather, my father, and my mother.

My grandfather was born shortly after the Civil War. Exposed to the ravages and barbarities of the post-Reconstruction betrayals of blacks, he detested and distrusted all whites. He was an Afrophile and an Anglophobe. He often recalled the glories of a grand African history. He taught me to hate and suspect all white people. His endlessly repeated advice was, "Never trust a white man!"

My father counseled against involvement in politics and freewheeling social intercourse. Physical strength and courage, hard work, self-reliance, and frugality were his means of self-preservation, self-realization, and self-defense. White people were not so much to be hated as to be socially avoided. He quietly and firmly warned that, whether you were white or black, if you were destitute you were likely to be mistreated. Grandpa's rhetoric was fine, but from the early Depression he had to live with his son, my father, for nearly twenty years until his death. So my father held that hard work was more satisfying than hot talk, and that white people were not all bad.

My mother was all tender loving care—insisting upon regular Sunday School and church attendance; forgiving or overlooking my faults and those of my three older brothers; praising, encouraging, and attending our efforts in play, school, and sports. Life and people were a joy; they were to be loved and appreciated, not hated or self-righteously judged.

So in my most formative years I was taught to hate and avoid white folk by my grandfather, to learn and earn by my father, and to love and forgive by my mother.

My grandfather's many stories of the atrocities perpetrated by whites against blacks in the South inspired in me an enduring interest in history and politics. Grandpa always said that the black man must learn both of these

Kenneth S. Tollett, Review of *Black Protest Thought in the Twentieth Century*, edited by August Meier, Elliott Rudwich, and Francis L. Broderick, Indianapolis: Bobbs-Merrill, 1970. The review is reprinted, with permission, from the November/December 1971 issue of *The Center Magazine*, a publication of the Center for the Study of Democratic Institutions in Santa Barbara, California.

Kenneth S. Tollett, former dean of Texas Southern University Law School and Visiting Fellow at the Center, is Distinguished Professor of Higher Education at Howard University.

subjects carefully or he would be duped by the chicanery and deception of whites. Although at the time I doubted many of the stories he told me about Africa's past glorious achievements, I have since learned that one of the places he talked about was probably Timbuktu, which did have a highly developed civilization and culture. My grandfather, more than anyone else in my life, I believe, inoculated me against an inferiority complex because I was black.

Yet, much as I loved and admired my grandfather, his life during the time I knew him was a living testimony to the limitation of black nationalism and chauvinism. This was not so much because of any frailties of his position or character, but because of the economic realities of the Depression. He was a railroad porter and was laid off shortly after the Depression started. He never worked regularly the rest of his life. He was a militant talker, but had to be housed, fed, and clothed by my hard-working, soft-talking, but tough, father. Still, Grandpa demonstrated the validity of Jean-Paul Sartre's notion that blacks may have to go through an antiracist racism in order to free themselves fully from the dehumanization of white racism.

Although my father's counsel of self-reliance, hard work, and learning, like that of Booker T. Washington, was not ideologically pleasing to my youthful mind which had been somewhat radicalized by Grandpa's hot talk, yet my father's example prepared me for life; it gave me a direction in which I could go and a method by which I could get there.

Mother's love and tolerance helped me to live with, even sympathize with, both Grandpa's detestable whites and my fellow demoralized and alienated blacks. [But I never could . . .] understand how the United States could have had the gall to claim it was fighting that war for democracy and to free mankind from racism. Black American soldiers in that war, including two of my older brothers, seemed to me to manifest the utter absurdity and self-contradiction of America's stated aims. Because our efforts and those of the allies in general received almost universal support, I concluded that all wars are inherently and absurdly vicious, insane, destructive, and immoral.

My religious mother led me to take seriously very early the teachings of the Bible, particularly the Gospels. But I soon learned that, although in Sunday School I was told that God was no respecter of persons and that God is love, blacks and whites did not worship together in the same church. Also during the war every church service was punctuated with imprecations against the Axis. So I appreciated the beauty, love, and power of the concept of Christianity. But I also realized that it was rarely practiced by anyone, that religion and the church were not to be counted on for the salvation of man.

These memories and feelings were stirred anew upon reading *Black Protest Thought in the Twentieth Century*, edited by August Meier, Elliott Rudwich, and Francis L. Broderick (Bobbs-Merrill). The book deals with black protest in its four successive stages: (1) the transition from accommodation to protest; (2) legal protest; (3) nonviolent direct action; and (4) black power. Although the book's editors are white, the speeches, documents, and writings are principally the products of blacks.

[1] Booker T. Washington, in his "The Atlanta Exposition Address" of 1895, ushered in the philosophy of accommodation with the frequently quoted statement, "In all things that are purely social, we can be as separate as the fingers, yet one as the hand in all things essential to mutual progress."

One cannot be sure whether Booker T. Washington, as a temporary measure, was pragmatically and realistically acquiescing to a remorseless, rampant, violent racism in order to forestall widespread murder and brutalization of blacks, or whether he thought that if blacks proved themselves economically, socially, and morally, whites would ultimately approve and accept them. Booker T. Washington was driven by an ambivalent faith in the decency and good sense of whites, some of whom, of course, recognized and were repelled by the almost uncontrollable savagery of the Ku Klux Klan rabble.

What was wrong with Booker T. Washington was not that he urged economic, social, and moral development of blacks, but that he thought these virtues would be recognized and rewarded by whites. The fundamental fact in Washington's time, as also today, is that the black man's basic difficulty in this country is not his economic, social, or moral deficiency, but the callous, dehumanizing racism of whites.

Of course Booker T. Washington did not go unanswered. Black militants like W. E. B. DuBois . . . [and] William Monroe Trotter . . . thought Booker T. Washington should have condemned the "idea of reducing a people to serfdom to make them good."

Accommodation failed. The lesson to be learned from it is that blacks should never acquiesce in the dilution of their constitutional and civil rights. Indeed, nothing less than full manhood should be accepted. That was the position of W. E. B. DuBois and of the N.A.A.C.P. which he was instrumental in founding.

[2] The second stage in black protest thought was the era of legal recourse, resort to the courts to fight racist laws and to insist on the enforcement of constitutional rights. In 1905, led by W. E. B. DuBois, the all-black Niagara Movement was formed to oppose Washington. Segregation, the separate-but-equal doctrine, and disfranchisement laws were categorically denounced. Although Washington's opposition to this group undermined their movement, the black radicals in it together with prominent white progressives and socialists formed the National Association for the Advancement of Colored People in 1909.

The N.A.A.C.P.'s strategy was based on the proposition that the enforcement of constitutionally declared rights should bring full personhood and equal citizenship to blacks.

The fratricidal Civil War ended the institution of slavery. The Thirteenth

Amendment, ratified in 1865, reaffirmed the Emancipation Proclamation and constitutionally freed the slaves. The Fourteenth Amendment, in 1868, granted citizenship to all persons born or naturalized in the United States. It also especially provided for the protection of freedmen by prohibiting the abridgement of privileges or immunities of citizens and the denial to any person within a state the equal protection of the laws. The Fifteenth Amendment, ratified in 1870, prohibited the denial or abridgement of the rights of citizens to vote on account of race, color, or previous condition of servitude. Some civil-rights acts were enacted by Congress to enforce these constitutional amendments.

The goal of the N.A.A.C.P., through its legal strategy, was to get these amendments enforced, make the spirit of the Reconstruction civil-rights acts a living reality, and enact additional federal legislation to halt lynching. This was thought to be pretty radical stuff.

The N.A.A.C.P. won two early legal victories. In 1915 the Supreme Court overruled the "grandfather's clause" used in several Southern state constitutions to disfranchise blacks. This victory was circumvented and frustrated by discriminatorily administered literacy tests for voting, by poll taxes, and by all-white Democratic primaries.

In 1917, the Court held unconstitutional municipal ordinances which ordained residential segregation. That victory, too, was frustrated by private restrictive covenants. Through the N.A.A.C.P.'s persevering litigation and legislative campaigns, all of these legally sanctioned circumventions and frustrations were overcome by the late nineteen-sixties.

The N.A.A.C.P.'s greatest victory came in 1954 when the Supreme Court held that separation of the races in education was inherently unequal. There was much rejoicing and some felt that perhaps a new day had dawned for blacks that would bring about the realization of their full, equal citizenship and manhood in the United States.

The failure of the national government and the states to implement this great decision led to frustration and to disenchantment with the gradualist litigation strategy of the N.A.A.C.P. The N.A.A.C.P.'s tactics had its critics almost from the start. A. Philip Randolph and Chandler Owens, editors of the militant monthly, *The Messenger*, thought that protest-by-litigation was too tame and almost irrelevant to the more important and pressing economic and labor needs of the black masses. Randolph claimed in 1919 that capitalism was the cause of lynchings. Marcus Garvey and his Universal Negro Improvement Association said the solution to the problems of black lynchings, peonage, and disfranchisement was to establish "a nation in Africa where Negroes will be given the opportunity to develop by themselves. . . ."

Also, intellectuals and artists in the Harlem Renaissance asked whether it would be better to conform to surrounding white culture (which, to some, seemed implicit if blacks accepted the legitimacy and propriety of enforcing formally declared constitutional and legal rights), or to develop a unique black culture as Langston Hughes wrote in *The Nation* in 1926 when he said he wanted to be "a Negro poet . . . for no great poet has ever been afraid of being himself."

The Depression led to a preoccupation with economic solutions such as self-help, sporadic flirtation with communism by a very few blacks, and reconsideration of the relative merits of the tactics of integration or separation, violence or nonviolence. During World War II, A. Philip Randolph called for a march on Washington to end discrimination in the expanding defense industries and to integrate the armed services. The Congress on Racial Equality (CORE) was created in 1943 with one purpose—"to eliminate racial discrimination"—and one method—"interracial nonviolent direct action."

[3] In Montgomery in 1955, one year after the great Court victory and ten years after the war, more direct and some would say militant action had already begun in the now famous bus boycott which opened the third era of black protest, the era of nonviolent direct action.

Martin Luther King began his rise to leadership in the black struggle and the civil-rights movement. Gradualism and legalism had accomplished much, but not enough. Young people, particularly on college campuses, wanted to step up the pace of the civil-rights struggle. They wanted freedom now, not tomorrow, not next week, certainly not next year.

Martin Luther King's strategy was based upon the redemptive power of love and suffering. He believed that nonviolent direct action would expose the moral bankruptcy of a racist society. He thought that a vigorous and virtuous militant but nonviolent protest by blacks would redeem the whites, help them see the light, and recognize the humanity of blacks.

Demonstrations captured public attention in the United States in the late nineteen-fifties and early nineteen-sixties. They precipitated the most far-reaching legislative and executive initiatives since the Civil War, including the Civil Rights Acts of 1957 and 1960. The former created the Civil Rights Commission and the latter attempted to strengthen the voter protections of the former. The great Civil Rights Act of 1964 dealt with many matters treated previously by Reconstruction legislation including public accommodations, a provision held unconstitutional in the civil-rights cases in 1883. The most comprehensive federal legislation dealing with the franchise was enacted in the Voting Rights Act of 1965.

Thus, nonviolent direct action supplemented, stimulated, and expanded the formal declaration of legal rights. It did have some redeeming effect. It did raise consciousness and it did result in legislative victories more far-reaching than the judicial successes of the N.A.A.C.P. However, the N.A.A.C.P.'s legal staff played an important part in drafting and adopting the civil-rights acts of the nineteen-fifties and nineteen-sixties. These acts, like the Supreme Court's Brown decision, intensified the revolution of rising expectations.

[4] More importantly, a number of blacks were disturbed when they saw how young blacks who participated in peaceful direct action were electrically shocked with cattle prods, beaten by police, and otherwise brutalized in the demonstrations and school integration efforts of this period. So there grew up a reaction to the passive nonviolent resistance. And the shooting of Medgar Evers during his march through Mississippi in 1966 gave rise to the fourth era, that of black power, which still has not run its course, although it may have led to one partially counterproductive cul-de-sac in the Black Panther Party.

Black power, say Meier, Rudwich and Broderick, "first articulated a mood rather than a program—disillusionment and alienation from white America, race pride, and self-respect, or 'black consciousness.'"

Programmatically it means political power and independent action; economic institutions, enterprises, and turf owned, controlled, and run by blacks; educational institutions—elementary, secondary, and higher—controlled and run by blacks; and cultural self-appreciation and self-definition. Throughout, a strain of separation puts into bold relief the complexity, ambiguity, and paradox of black thought and action.

Initially a separatist, Booker T. Washington was an accommodationist and conservative. Separatists today are presumably uncompromising radicals and nonaccommodationists. Early the N.A.A.C.P. and its strategy were considered radical and integrationist. Today its legalism and integrationism are considered accommodationist and conservative, if not cowardly reactionary, by young turks. Some aspects of nationalism, which could also almost be characterized as chauvinism in the social, political, economic, and cultural milieux, are espoused by almost all blacks except for a benighted few.

My past has enabled me to understand and sympathize with some aspects of every phase of black protest thought and action. Yet, I have to conclude that, although hatred of whites and glorification of blacks may be mentally liberating in a transitional period, it is not a very useful or productive emotion. A measure of separation may be necessary for blacks to find and accept themselves. A lot of integration is necessary for whites to find and accept blacks. Much pride, some anger, more self-respect and self-reliance, but most of all love and the recognition of the dignity and integrity of all human beings are what is most needed if the American Dream is to become a reality for blacks and whites, Jews and Gentiles, Catholics and Protestants, Democrats and Republicans.[1]

---

[1] *EDITOR'S NOTE*: Professor Tollett described four successive stages of black protest. The last two stages, which dominate Negro thinking in the 1960s and 1970s, are represented in the next four selections.

---

# 1.3 THREE MYTHS CONCERNING BLACK AMERICANS
## Martin Luther King, Jr.

Throughout slavery the Negro was treated in a very inhuman fashion. He was a thing to be used, and not a person to be respected. The famous Dred Scott decision of 1857 well illustrated the status of the Negro during slavery. With this decision the Supreme Court of the United States said in substance that the Negro is not a citizen of the United States—that he is merely property, subject to the dictates of his owner. And it went on to say that the Negro had no rights that the white man is bound to respect. . . .

While living with the conditions of slavery, and then later with humiliating patterns of segregation, many Negroes lost faith in themselves. Many came to feel that perhaps they were inferior; perhaps they were less than human.

But then something happened to the Negro. Circumstances made it possible and necessary for him to travel more—the coming of the automobile, the upheavals of two world wars, the great depression. So his rural plantation background gradually gave way to urban industrial life. His cultural life was gradually rising, too, with the steady decline of crippling illiteracy. He watched with a deep sense of pride the great drama of his independence taking place on the stage of African history. And all of these forces conjoined to cause the Negro to take a new look at himself.

Negro Americans all over began to re-evaluate themselves, and the Negro came to feel that he was somebody. His religion revealed to him that God loves all of His children, and that all men are made in His image, and that the basic thing about a man is not the specifics but the fundamentals—not the texture of his hair, nor the color of his skin, but his eternal dignity and worth. . . .

The mind is the standard of a man, and with this new sense of self-respect, a new Negro came into being with new determination to struggle, to suffer, and to sacrifice in order to be free. . . .

[We shall pass over the insufferable economic, housing and educa-

Martin Luther King, Jr., "The Future of Integration," in *Issues of 1968*, William W. Boyer (ed.), Lawrence: University of Kansas Press, 1968. Reprinted by permission of Joan Davis. Copyright © 1968 by the Estate of Martin Luther King, Jr.

For a more adequate statement of the philosophy of nonviolence, read Martin Luther King, Jr., *Stride Toward Freedom*, New York: Harper & Row, Inc., 1968, pp. 101–107, 178–186. For another Christian view, read Thomas Merton, "Blessed are the Meek: The Roots of Non-Violence," *Fellowship* 33: 18–22, May 1967, and Mulford Q. Sibley, "Nonviolence and Revolution," *The Humanist* 27: 3–6, November–December 1968. For a brief exposition of Mahatma Gandhi's theory of nonviolence, read E. A. Burtt, *Man Seeks the Divine*, New York: Harper & Row, Inc., 1964, p. 454–460.

tional problems, and the angry explosions of bitterness that have characterized so many Negro ghettos during the past few years.]

I am still convinced that non-violence is the most potent weapon available to oppressed people in their struggle for freedom and human dignity. I am still convinced that violence creates many more social problems than it solves. And if the Negro in America succumbs to the temptation of using violence as his problematic strategy, unborn generations will be the recipients of a long and desolate night of bitterness. And our chief legacy to the future will be an endless strain of meaningless chaos.

So I will continue to raise my voice against violence, against riots, because they tend to intensify the fears of the white majority, while relieving their guilt. And we need a method that will somehow disarm the opponent, expose his moral defenses, and at the same time work on his conscience.

But after saying this, I must say that it would be an act of moral irresponsibility for me to condemn riots and not be as vigorous in condemning the continued existence of intolerable conditions in our society, which cause people to feel so angry and bitter that they conclude they have no alternative to get attention but to engage in this kind of violence. . . .

In order to develop the kind of action programs [which will bring Negroes into the mainstream of American culture] . . . we must get rid of two or three myths that are still being disseminated around our society. One is what I refer to as the "myth of time." I am sure you have heard this notion. It is the notion that only time can solve the problem. And I know there are those sincere people who say to civil rights leaders and persons working for civil rights, "You are pushing things too fast; you must slow up for a while." And then they have a way of saying: "Now just be nice and be patient and continue to pray, and in a hundred or two hundred years the problem will work itself out, because only time can solve the problem."

Well, I think there is an answer to that myth. And it is that time is neutral. Time can either be used constructively or destructively. . . . And it may well be that we may have to repent in this generation, not merely for the vitriolic words and violent action of the bad people, but for the appalling silence and indifference of the good people who sit around and "wait on time."

Somewhere, we must come to see that human progress never rolls in on the wheels of inevitability. It comes through the tireless effort and the persistent work of dedicated individuals who are willing to be co-workers with God. Without this hard work, time itself becomes an ally of the primitive forces of social stagnation.

And there is another myth that is disseminated a great deal. It is the notion that legislation has no role to play in establishing justice and in moving toward an integrated society. The argument here is that you must change the heart of man and you cannot change the heart through legislation. You cannot legislate morals. I would be the first one to say that hearts must be changed.

I said earlier that I am a Baptist preacher. That means that I am in the heart-changing business. . . .

But after saying that, I must point out the other side. It may be true that morality can not be legislated. But behavior can be regulated. It may be true that the law cannot change the heart. But it can restrain the heartless. It may be true that the law can not make a man love me. But it can restrain him from lynching me, and I think that is pretty important, also. And so while the law may not change the hearts of men, the law can change the habits of men if it is vigorously enforced. . . .

Another myth surrounding us is what I call an exaggerated use of the "boot-strap" philosophy. People say to the Negroes: "You must lift yourself by your own boot straps." So often I hear people saying: "The Irish, Italians —and they go right down the line of all other ethnic groups—came to this country and faced problems. They had difficulties, and yet they lifted themselves by their own boot straps. Why can't and why won't the Negro do this?"

It does not help the Negro for unfeeling, insensitive whites to say to him that ethnic groups that voluntarily came to this country 150 years ago have now risen beyond the Negro, who has been here more than 344 years but was brought here in chains involuntarily. The people who project this argument never seem to realize that no other ethnic groups have been slaves on American soil. They do not stop to realize that America made the Negro's color a stigma.

Making color a stigma had the support of the semantics or linguistics structure, so to speak. Even the language conspired to give the Negro the impression that something was wrong with his color. Open *Roget's Thesaurus* and you will see the 120 synonyms for "black." All of them are low and degrading, or represent smut or dirt. Then look at the 130 synonyms for "white." They are all high, noble, chaste, pure. So in our society when somebody goes wrong in the family, you don't call him a "white sheep"; you call him a "black sheep." If you tell a lie, it's better to tell a "white lie" than a "black lie," because a white lie is a little better. If you know something about somebody and you use that as a means of bribing him for money, and you would expose him if you don't get it, you don't call it "whitemail"—you call it "blackmail." Now this is a bit humorous, but it is a fact of life.

Many things conspired to make the Negro feel that he was nobody because of his color. But the other thing that refutes this myth is the notion that anybody, any ethnic group, lifted itself totally by its own boot straps.

The Negro was freed from the bondage of physical slavery in 1863 through the Emancipation Proclamation. But the Negro was not given any land to make that freedom meaningful. . . . In 1863 America just said, "You are free"; and he was left penniless, illiterate, with nothing.

Here is the story that is not often told. At the same time America refused to give the Negro any land, by Act of Congress she was giving away millions of acres of land in the West and the Midwest, which meant that America was willing to undergird her white peasants from Europe with an economic floor. Not only did the nation give the land, it built land-grant colleges to teach these people how to farm. It provided county agents to further expertise in farming. It provided low interest rates so that they could mechanize their farms. And today many of these people are being paid through federal subsidies *not* to farm.

These are the very people who, in many instances, are saying to the Negro that he should lift himself by his own boot straps. I guess this is all right to say to a man that he should lift himself by his own boot straps, but it is a cruel jest to say to a bootless man that he should lift himself by his own boot straps. . . .

I conclude by saying our goal is freedom. . . .

We are going to win our freedom, because both the sacred heritage of our nation and the eternal will of the Almighty God are embodied in our echoing demands.

And so I can still sing, "We shall overcome."

# 1.4 FREEDOM NOW—FOR ALL MEN, EVERYWHERE!
## Stokely Carmichael and Malcolm X

Some white Americans can afford to speak softly, tread lightly, employ the soft-sell and the put-off—or is it put-down?—because they own the society. For us to adopt their methods of relieving our oppression is certainly ludicrous. We blacks must respond in our own way, on our own terms, in a manner that fits our temperaments. The definition of ourselves, the road we pursue, and the goals we seek, are our responsibility. It is clear that society is capable of, and willing to, reward those individuals who do not forcefully condemn it—to reward them with prestige, status, and material benefits—

This selection consists of two short excerpts. The first is from Stokely Carmichael: *Stokely Speaks: Black Power Back to Pan-Africanism,* Copyright © 1965 by Stokely Carmichael. Reprinted by permission of Random House, Inc.

The second excerpt is from *The Autobiography of Malcolm X,* with the assistance of Alex Haley (1964). Introduction by M. S. Handler, 1965, New York: Grove Press (paperback), 1966. Extracts from pages 272–275, 310–311, 366–377. By permission. This is one of the greatest autobiographies ever written. It will stand comparison with such books as St. Augustine's *Confessions.* Every twentieth century educator should read it.

but these crumbs of corruption will be rejected. As a people we have absolutely nothing to lose by refusing to play such games. Anything less than clarity, honesty, and forcefulness perpetuates the centuries of sliding over, dressing up, and soothing down the true feelings, hopes, and demands of an oppressed black people. Mild demands and hypocritical smiles mislead white America into thinking that all is fine and peaceful; they lead white America into thinking that the path and pace whites choose for dealing with racial problems are acceptable to the masses of blacks. It is far better to speak forcefully and truthfully. Only when one's true self, black or white, is exposed, can society proceed to deal with the problems from a position of clarity, and not from one of misunderstanding.

Thus, we have no intention of engaging in the meaningless language so common to discussions of race in the world today: "Things were and are bad, but we are making progress." "Granted, your demands are legitimate, but we cannot move hastily. Stable societies are best built slowly." "Be careful that you do not anger or alienate your white allies. Remember, after all, you are only 10 per cent of the population."

We reject the language and the views, whether expressed by blacks or by whites. We leave them to others to mouth, because we don't feel that this rhetoric is either relevant or. useful. Rather we suggest a more meaningful language—that of Frederick Douglass, a man who understood the nature of protest in society:

> Those who profess to favor freedom, yet deprecate agitation, are men who want crops without ploughing up the ground. . . . Power concedes nothing without demands—it never did and it never will. . . . The limits of tyrants are prescribed by the endurance of those whom they oppress.

He was a slave.

Black power, to us, means that black people see themselves as a part of a new force, sometimes called the Third World; that we see our struggle as closely related to liberation struggles around the world. We must hook up with these struggles. . . .

## MALCOLM X

Human rights! Respect as *human beings*! That's what America's black masses want. That's the true problem. The black masses want not to be shrunk from as though they are plague-ridden. They want not to be walled up in slums, in the ghettoes, like animals. They want to live in an open, free society where they can walk with their heads up, like men, and women! . . .

[Before my conversion to the Islamic religion,] because I had been a hustler [i.e., a dope peddler,] I knew better than all whites knew, and better than nearly all of the black "leaders" knew, that actually the most dangerous black man in America was the ghetto hustler.

Why do I say this? The hustler, out there in the ghetto jungles, has less respect for the white power structure than any other Negro in North America. The ghetto hustler is internally restrained by nothing. He has no religion, no concept of morality, no civic responsibility, no fear—nothing. To survive, he is out there constantly preying upon others, probing for any human weakness like a ferret. The ghetto hustler is forever frustrated, restless and anxious for some "action." Whatever he undertakes, he commits himself to it fully, absolutely.

What makes the ghetto hustler yet more dangerous is his "glamor" image to the school-dropout youth in the ghetto. These ghetto teen-agers see the hell caught by their parents struggling to get somewhere, or see that they have given up struggling in the prejudiced, intolerant white man's world. The ghetto teen-agers make up their own minds they would rather be like the hustlers whom they see dressed "sharp" and flashing money and displaying no respect for anybody or anything. So the ghetto youth become attracted to the hustler worlds of dope, thievery, prostitution, and general crime and immorality. . . .

Actually, America's most dangerous and threatening black man is the one who has been kept sealed up by the Northerner in the black ghettoes—the Northern white power structure's system to keep talking democracy while keeping the black man out of sight somewhere, around the corner. . . .

[During the period when I was a Muslim,] I said to Harlem street audiences that only when mankind would submit to the One God who created all—only then would mankind even approach the "peace" of which so much *talk* could be heard. . . . but toward which so little *action* was seen.

I said that on the American racial level, we had to approach the black man's struggle against the white man's racism as a human problem, that we had to forget hypocritical politics and propaganda. I said that both races, as human beings, had the obligation, the responsibility, of helping to correct America's human problem. The well-meaning white people, I said, had to combat, actively and directly, the racism in other white people. And the black people had to build within themselves much greater awareness that along with equal rights there had to be the bearing of equal responsibilities.

I knew, better than most Negroes, how many white people truly wanted to see American racial problems solved. I knew that many whites were as frustrated as Negroes. . . .

I tell sincere white people, "Work in conjunction with us—each of us working among our own kind." . . . Let sincere whites go and teach non-violence to white people!

We will completely respect our white co-workers. They will deserve every credit. We will give them every credit. We will meanwhile be working among our own kind, in our own black communities—showing and teaching black men in ways that only other black men can—that the black man has got to help himself. Working separately, the sincere white people and sincere black people actually will be working together.

In our mutual sincerity we might be able to show a road to the salvation of America's very soul. It can only be salvaged if human rights and dignity, in full, are extended to black men. Only such real, meaningful actions as those which are sincerely motivated from a deep sense of humanism and moral responsibility can get at the basic causes that produce the racial explosions in America today. Otherwise, the racial explosions are only going to grow worse. Certainly nothing is ever going to be solved by throwing upon me and other so-called black "extremists" and "demagogues" the blame for the racism that is in America.

Sometimes, I have dared to dream to myself that one day, history may even say that my voice—which disturbed the white man's smugness, and his arrogance, and his complacency—that my voice helped to save America from a grave, possibly even a fatal catastrophe.

The goal has always been the same, with the approaches to it as different as mine and Dr. Martin Luther King's non-violent marching, that dramatizes the brutality and the evil of the white man against defenseless blacks. And in the racial climate of this country today, it is anybody's guess which of the "extremes" in approach to the black man's problems might *personally* meet a fatal catastrophe first—"non-violent" Dr. King, or so-called "violent" me.[1]

---

[1] *EDITOR'S NOTE*: Malcolm X was assassinated on February 21, 1965; Martin Luther King, Jr. was assassinated on April 4, 1968.

Shortly before his death, in a speech entitled "The Ballot or the Bullet," Malcolm X declared:

> Our gospel is black nationalism. We're not trying to threaten the existence of any organization, but we're spreading the gospel of black nationalism. Anywhere there's a church that is also preaching and practicing the gospel of black nationalism, join that church. If the NAACP is preaching and practicing the gospel of black nationalism, join the NAACP. If CORE is spreading and practicing the gospel of black nationalism, join CORE. Join any organization that has a gospel that's for the uplift of the black man.—*Malcolm X Speaks*, New York: Merrit Publishers, 1965, p. 41.

Even as fear and hatred tend to generate fear and hatred, so tolerance tends to increase tolerance and understanding. For a summary of three opinion polls, for three successive decades, showing a continuous advance in the support of desegregation by United States whites, read Andrew M. Greeley and Paul B. Sheatsley, "Attitudes toward Racial Integration," *Scientific American* 225: 13–18, December 1971.

Concerning Negro attitudes, read William Brink and Louis Harris, *Black and White: A Study of U.S. Racial Attitudes Today*, New York: Simon and Schuster, 1969; and *Racial Attitudes in America*, John C. Brigham and Theodore A. Weissbach (eds.), New York: Harper & Row, Publishers, Inc., 1972. These attitudes are not significantly different in 1973 from what they were in 1968, when David

Ginsberg, Executive Director, National Advisory Commission on Civil Disorders, reported that:

. . . the urban riots of the 1960s are a form of social protest by noncriminal elements and are justified as such by a majority of Negroes . . . [and suggesting] that short of massive suppression of millions, future riots can be prevented only by transforming the Negro slums and the institutions and attitudes that have made them.

An extensive poll of Negro and white attitudes showed that

the majority of Negroes still desire integration and conciliation with whites, but that a substantial minority seem to have lost faith in the American system and are looking increasingly to militant leaders who advocate violence and separatism. Approximately 200,000 Negroes (6 percent—almost 15 percent in the Negro ghettos) favor a "separate black nation here" and feel so little a part of American society that they favor withdrawing allegiance from the United States and establishing a separate national entity. While 39 percent of the Negroes favor "laws and persuasion" to gain their rights and 38 percent favor "nonviolent protests," a substantial 15 percent believe they should "be ready to use violence."

On a more optimistic note, the survey also showed that 75 percent of the Negroes approved of the NAACP, 75 percent approved of Martin Luther King, 50 percent approved of Roy Wilkins, and 14 percent approved of Stokely Carmichael and H. Rap Brown. Although whites have a strong tendency to blame conditions of Negroes on Negroes themselves, 62 percent of the whites questioned said that Negroes have a right to live anywhere. (See *The New York Times*, July 28, 1968, p. 1 (col. 8), p. 48.)

In another survey, Caplan and Paige report that Negro riots are the result of

blocked opportunity. . . . Negroes who riot do so because their conception of their lives and their potential has changed without commensurate improvement in their chances for a better life. . . . Negroes are still excluded from economic opportunity and occupational advancement, but they no longer have the psychological defenses or social supports that once encouraged passive adaptation to this situation. The result has been the most serious domestic violence in this country.—Nathan S. Caplan and Jeffery M. Paige, "A Study of Ghetto Rioters," *Scientific American* 219: 15–21, August 1968.

For a more recent survey of Negro attitudes, read "The Black Mood: More Militant, More Hopeful, More Determined." A *Time-Louis Harris Poll* summarized in *Time* 54: 8–9, April 6, 1970.

# 1.5 AFRICAN HISTORY: 1400–1900
## Basil Davidson and Malcolm X

## DAVIDSON

A gap in social and technical development may always have existed, no doubt, between those who lived close to the cradles of ancient civilization [the Africans] and those who lived far from them [the Europeans]. . . . [The] main consequence of a good deal of recent research into Southern and Central and East African history—over the past thousand years or so—is precisely to suggest that the gap was once a relatively narrow one, and not always to Europe's advantage either.

Writing in 1067, the mediaeval Arab scholar El Bekri described the court of the king of Ghana such as the Arabs knew it from their penetration and eventual conquest of that country. "When he gives audience to his people," wrote El Bekri, "to listen to their complaints and set them to rights, he sits in a pavillion around which stand his horses caparisoned in cloth of gold; behind him stand ten pages holding shields and gold-mounted swords; on his right hand are the sons of the princes of his empire, splendidly clad and with gold plaited into their hair. . . ." A barbaric king and a barbaric kingdom? But were they more barbaric or less civilized than the king and kingdom that William of Normandy had conquered the year before? Were they not, conceivably, less barbaric and more civilized?

When the Portuguese adventurers first rounded the Cape of Good Hope they were certainly as much concerned with "the mystic powers of persons and things" as the most superstitious native of any part of Africa. Their ignorance of the Eastern world was no smaller than East Africa's ignorance of Europe and was quite possibly greater. They were astonished to find the harbours of the East Coast—of what are now Mozambique and Tanganyika and Kenya—the goal and shelter of long-range ocean shipping; and when they sailed for India it was with pilots whose navigational equipment was, in

This selection consists of two excerpts. The first is reprinted from Basil Davidson, "The Fact of African History: An Introduction," *Africa South,* Vol. 2, No. 2, January–March 1958, pp. 44–49. By permission of the author.

This article is reprinted in full in *The Epic of Modern Man,* edited by L. S. Stavrianos, New York: Prentice-Hall, 2d edition, 1971, pages 59–62.

The second excerpt is by Malcolm X from *Malcolm X: The Man and His Times,* edited by John Clarke, New York: Macmillan, 1969, pages 322–328. By permission.

Although this selection deals with Negro history *during the period preceding the twentieth century,* we should realize that few, if any, Americans were *aware* of this history until after Malcolm X. For this reason, we place this selection here rather than at the beginning of the chapter.

some ways, better than their own. The superiority of the society of Lisbon over the society of Kilwa and Mombasa was not, in those days, by any means obvious. The one certain superiority of those Europeans was in cruelty and aggressiveness.

Yet three hundred and fifty years later, in the hey-day of Victorian rediscovery, the gap had grown immensely wide—so wide, indeed, that it became easy for Europeans to wonder (as many still do) whether Negroes did not after all belong to an inferior species. There is little mystery about the reasons for this widening of the gap: while Europe, freeing itself from mediaeval limits, plunged into commercialism and industrialism and won its great technical superiority over the rest of the world, much of Africa lay fettered in the oversea slave trade. The one went forward, the other went back, and the gap, narrow enough in 1500, grew into a gulf.

Historians and archaeologists are now building new bridges of explanation across that gulf. . . .

What appears to emerge from the present state of knowledge is nothing like a state of savage chaos, but, on the contrary, the long-enduring growth and development of an African Metal Age—beginning over two thousand years ago and producing, for example, the Monomotapa culture of what were Rhodesia and Mozambique in the 15th century—that went through many phases and vicissitudes, but showed remarkable flexibility of invention and resource. It is certain that there developed down the East Coast, sometime after the discovery of the trading use of the monsoon winds in the first century A.D., a flourishing and stable *African* trade with Arabia, Persia, India, Indonesia and China. It is probable that while the Arabs became the intermediaries and chief carriers in this trade, they were no more the originators of it in Africa than they were in India or China. They established trading posts as far south as Sofala, at points where African kingdoms already existed or subsequently grew. Behind these coastal kingdoms, in the hinterland of Africa, there was meanwhile developing a network of Metal Age polities whose growth was increasingly stimulated by the coastal and oversea demand for gold, ivory and iron. These African goods were exchanged by Africans—through Arab and Indian intermediaries—for Indian textiles, Indonesian beads, and Chinese porcelain. Only when the Portuguese arrived to monopolize this trade, and rapidly destroy it, did these coastal and inland civilizations enter their decline. The hand of the European guided, as it came about, not away from chaos, but towards it.

And what continually surprises, in reviewing the evidence so far available, is the *coherence* of these African cultures. Already it is possible to glimpse connections, whether by cultural drift, migration, or trade, between the early kingdoms of Uganda, for example, and those of Rhodesia; between Zimbabwe and the coastal cities as far north as Gedi, sixty miles beyond Mombasa; between the wooden cities of West Africa and the stone cities of Monomotapa. All these links between African societies of the past, whether immediate or remote, have the same kind of coherence and suggestion of common origin, native origin, as those which gave the Indo-European tribes their historical affinity as they spread across the northern world. We are clearly in the presence of a large segment of the human story: of another contribution to the proof of that unity-in-diversity which scientists otherwise ascribe to all branches of *homo sapiens*.

## MALCOLM X

[White anthropologists] say that we're Negro, and they say that Negro means black; yet they don't call all black people Negroes. You see the contradiction? Mind you, they say that we're Negro, because Negro means black in Spanish, yet they don't call all black people Negroes. Something there doesn't add up.

And then to get around it they say mankind is divided up into three categories—Mongoloid, Caucasoid, and Negroid. Now pick up on that. And all black people aren't Negroid—they've got some jet black ones that they classify as Caucasoid. But if you'll study very closely, all of the black ones that they classify as Caucasoid are those that still have great civilizations, or still have the remains of what was once a great civilization. The only ones that they classify as Negroid are those that they find with no evidence that they were ever civilized; then they call them Negroid. But they can't afford to let any black-skinned people who have evidence that they formerly occupied a high seat in civilization, they can't afford to let them be called Negroid, so they take them on into the Caucasoid classification.

And actually Caucasoid, Mongoloid, and Negroid—there's no such thing. These are so-called anthropological terms that were put together by anthropologists who were nothing but agents of the colonial powers, and they were purposely given that status, they were purposely given such scientific positions, in order that they could come up with definitions that would justify the European domination over the Africans and the Asians. So immediately they invented classifications that would automatically demote these people or put them on a lesser level. All of the Caucasoids are on a high level, the Negroids are kept at a low level. This is just plain trickery that their scientists engage in in order to keep you and me thinking that we never were anything, and therefore he's doing us a favor as he lets us step upward or forward in his particular society or civilization. I hope you understand what I am saying.

### Ancient Black Civilizations

Now, then, once you see that the condition that we're in is directly related to our lack of knowledge concerning the history of the black man, only then can you realize the importance of knowing something about the history of the black man. The black man's history—when you refer to him as the black man you go way back, but when you refer to him as a Negro, you can only go as far back as the Negro goes. And when you go beyond the shores of America you can't find a Negro. So if you go beyond the shores of America in history, looking for the history of the black man, and you're looking for him under the term "Negro," you won't find him. He doesn't exist. So you end up thinking that you didn't play any role in history.

But if you want to take the time to do research for yourself, I think you'll find that on the African continent there was always, prior to the discovery of America, there was always a higher level of history, rather a higher level of culture and civilization, than that which existed in Europe at the same time. At least five thousand years ago they had a black civilization in the Middle East called the Sumerians. Now when they show you pictures of the Sumerians they [whites] try and make you think that they were white people. But if you go and read some of the ancient manuscripts or even read between the lines of some of the current writers, you'll find that the Sumerian civilization was a very dark-skinned civilization, and it existed prior even to the existence of the Babylonian empire, right in the same area where you find Iraq and the Tigris-Euphrates Rivers there. It was a black-skinned people who lived there, who had a high state of culture way back then.

And at a time even beyond this there was a black-skinned people in India, who were black, just as black as you and I, called Dravidians. They inhabited the subcontinent of India even before the present people that you see living there today, and they had a high state of culture. The present people of India even looked upon them as gods; most of their statues, if you'll notice, have pronounced African features. You go right to India today—in their religion, which is called Buddhism, they give all their Buddhas the image of a black man, with his lips and his nose, and even show his hair all curled up on his head; they didn't curl it up, he was born that way. And these people lived in that area before the present people of India lived there. The black man lived in the Middle East before the present people who are now living there. And he had a high culture and a high civilization, to say nothing about the oldest civilization of all that he had in Egypt along the banks of the Nile. And in Carthage in northwest Africa, another part of the continent, and at a later date in Mali and Ghana and Songhai, and Moorish civilization—all of these civilizations existed on the African continent before America was discovered. . . .

When you read the opinions of the white scientists about the pyramids and the building of the pyramids, they don't make any secret at all over the fact that they marvel over the scientific ability that was in the possession of those people way back then. They had mastered chemistry to such an extent that they could make paints whose color doesn't fade right until today. . . .

[In short, insofar as the word "Negro" has taken on the meaning "inferior," we] were scientifically produced by the white man. Whenever you see somebody who calls himself a Negro, he's a product of Western civilization—not only Western civilization, but Western crime. The Negro, as he is called or calls himself in the West, is the best evidence that can be used against Western civilization today. One of the main reasons we are called Negro is so we won't know who we really are. And when you call yourself that, you don't know who you really are. You don't know what you are, you don't know where you came from, you don't know what is yours. As long as you call yourself a Negro, nothing is yours. No languages—you can't lay claim to any language, not even English; you mess it up. You can't lay claim to any name, any type of name, that will identify you as something that you should be. You can't lay claim to any culture as long as you use the word "Negro" to identify yourself. It attaches you to nothing. It doesn't even identify your color.

If you talk [to whites] . . . they call themselves white, don't they? Or they might call someone else Puerto Rican to identify them. Mind you how they do this. When they call him a Puerto Rican, they're giving him a better name. Because there is a place called Puerto Rico, you know. It at least lets you know where he came from. So they'll say whites, Puerto Ricans, and Negroes. Pick up on that. That's a drag, brothers. White is legitimate. It means that's what color they are. Puerto Rican tells you that they're someone else, came from somewhere else, but they're here now. Negro doesn't tell you anything. I mean nothing, absolutely nothing. What do you identify it with? —tell me—nothing. What do you attach it to, what do you attach to it?— nothing. It's completely in the middle of nowhere. And when you call yourself that, that's where you are—right in the middle of nowhere. It doesn't give you a language, because there is no such thing as a Negro language. It doesn't give you a country, because there is no such thing as a Negro country. It doesn't give you a culture—there is no such thing as a Negro culture, it doesn't exist. The land doesn't exist, the language doesn't exist, and the man doesn't exist. They take you out of existence by calling you a Negro. And you can walk around in front of them all day long and they act like they don't even see you. Because you made yourself non-existent. It's a person who has no history; and by having no history, he has no culture.

Just as a tree without roots is dead, a people without history or cultural roots also becomes a dead people. And when you look at us, those of us who are called Negro, we're called that because we are like dead people. We have nothing to identify ourselves as part of the human family.

# 1.6 THE NATIONALIST VS. THE INTEGRATIONIST
## Charles V. Hamilton

[In May, 1972,] a National Urban League analysis of three national surveys of school busing found that only 52 per cent of blacks favor busing, although the proportion of blacks who say they oppose busing has declined from 41 per cent in 1970 to 34 per cent in 1972. . . . [This Survey is an indication of] two major strands in black political thinking: integrationist and nationalist. This distinction might be an oversimplification, of course, but it is nonetheless helpful to understanding the new tensions that exist among blacks.

The integrationists insist that the earlier struggles to overcome *de jure* segregation must be continued beyond merely declaring segregation unconstitutional. There is very heavy reliance on an interpretation of the Constitution that argues that officials must take affirmative action to insure that there will be integration of the races. This means busing of school children if necessary; it means deliberately placing blacks in public housing projects in all-white neighborhoods if necessary. In other words, the integrationist position is that there cannot be exclusive reliance on *voluntary* action of private citizens if a meaningful amount of racial integration (in schools, in housing, on jobs) is to occur in this country.

The nationalists, on the other hand, are much more inclined to form all-black organizations and to push for goals that emphasize, in their view, the consolidation of black control over institutional policies. This spans a wide range of concerns, including busing, child adoption, scatter-site housing and community control of schools and the police. . . .

The nationalists . . . feel that busing will not solve educational problems for the mass of black children. Some nationalists welcomed a recent controversial article on busing by Prof. David J. Armor reporting findings that showed no significant improvement in academic achievement for black students who were bused. The nationalists prefer to concentrate on establishing alternative semiprivate schools in black communities that would experiment with new curricula and teaching techniques; as one spokesman put it, "schools that convey to our children that peculiarly black culture and spirit combined with solid academic standards." They also prefer to push for effective community-controlled public schools. . . .

Excerpt from Charles V. Hamilton, "The Nationalist vs. the Integrationist," *New York Times Magazine*, October 1, 1972 (Section 6, Part 1, pp. 36–51). © 1969–1972 by the New York Times Company. Reprinted by permission.
    Professor of political science at Columbia University, Charles V. Hamilton is author of *The Black Preacher in America* (New York: Morrow, 1972).

The two attitudes have also been focused by the issue of child adoption. Last May the National Association of Black Social Workers, in its fourth annual convention in Nashville, Tenn., condemned the placement of black children with white families for either foster care or adoption. The group called such placements "a growing threat to the preservation of the black family." . . .

Bayard Rustin of the A. Philip Randolph Institute [representing the integrationists] takes exception to this position. "It is not," he said, "interracial adoptions which threaten the stability of the black family but rather the absurdities of our welfare system and a black unemployment rate in excess of 10 per cent." While recognizing the existence of racial prejudice and discrimination, Rustin believes that "poverty, and all the evils attached to it, is not due solely or even largely to racism, but to an economic system already weighted to those with wealth and power." As an integrationist (as the category is used here), he is opposed to all-black organizations. "Separatist organizations are further weakened by their need to adopt unrealistic and sometimes irresponsible public positions in order to justify their existence. This often takes the form of unsound criticism of their own profession, as, I believe, is the case in the adoption resolution."

Another issue of profound disagreement between integrationists and nationalists concerns the merger of school districts. The N.A.A.C.P. Legal Defense & Educational Fund brought a suit in Richmond, Va., calling for the merger of the predominantly black school district of that city with two surrounding predominantly white suburban school districts. To some in the nationalist camp, this was a major mistake. A black economist, David H. Swinton of the Black Economic Research Center in New York, sees such a merger, if it were to occur (the case was won by the N.A.A.C.P. Fund in the Federal District Court, reversed by the Court of Appeals, and is being appealed to the Supreme Court), as jeopardizing the eventual control by blacks of the city school system. Swinton says, "This includes the power to make the major decisions about curriculum, personnel and general educational policy. Perhaps of almost equal importance is control over the economic power represented by the budget of a large school district. . . ."

The integrationists are not persuaded by these arguments. They believe that, in the words of one prominent integrationist, the "real way blacks gain power ultimately is to be where the decisions are made, and this is not done by isolating oneself." Bayard Rustin has stated it this way:

"Those who support community control because they believe it will give minorities a measure of self-government, a 'piece of the action,' see only half of the picture. For inherent in the concept is the surrender of the suburbs to white domination. Blacks, in other words, will have the ghetto, with its drug addiction, soaring crime rate, high unemployment, and deplorable housing. Whites will keep the suburbs, where job opportunities are expanding, the air is unpolluted, housing is decent, and schools provide superior education.

Separatism, no matter what form it takes or how slickly it is packaged, has always worked to the detriment of the black man." . . .

[But Swinton and other nationalists reply that segregation] is clearly only a symptom of the lack of effective power in the black community. It is not itself the cause of the myriad problems confronting the black community in the area of education and elsewhere. To attack the symptom may do nothing at all to eradicate the disease. . . . The true cause of the black problem is the lack of basic economic, political and social power, as is indicated by the black people's inability to take the decisions and allocate the resources that are required to deal with the black situation. This lack of power results from white dominance of the instruments and processes of power." . . .

[Some] black nationalists call the integration movement basically a pleading-beggar movement. Blacks pleaded with whites to take them into their schools, their neighborhoods, restaurants, churches, etc. And this begging approach could only create a paternalistic relationship between black and white. If the integrationists responded that they were only seeking their constitutional rights, the nationalists' retort would be that in the final analysis constitutional rights could only come from political power, not from benevolent handouts.

The traditionally understood integration movement was, in a profound sense, demeaning to many black nationalists. Not so much in the goals it sought (freedom from racial segregation and discrimination), but in some of the methods it used. Many nationalists felt it was fundamentally demeaning to have whites in leadership positions in black civil-rights organizations. . . .

If the nationalists were able to work their will and have their way, their programs would range all the way from starting an entirely new, sovereign nation, the Republic of New Africa, carved out of five Southern states, to flying the black, red and green liberation flag over schools in black communities as was done recently in Newark, N.J. In general, nationalist groups would like to insure that such institutions as schools, police and health facilities in black communities are controlled by blacks; that is, no final decisions affecting their operation would be taken by any but black people acting in official capacity. This means that they would staff these facilities, whenever possible, with blacks—teachers, policemen, social workers, etc. They are immediately aware, of course, that this puts them in direct conflict with existing public-service unions. They would also require black control over the allocation of tax funds for the various agencies. (The integrationists see this goal as the most utopian of all.)

The nationalists would base electoral representation on the proportion of blacks in the population. A statement issued at the black political convention held in Gary, Ind., last March, read: "We want the establishment of Black Congressional representation in proportion to our presence in the national population. We are at least 15 per cent of the population. Through constitutional amendment—or any other means necessary—we ought to have a minimum of 66 Representatives and 15 Senators; that until such time as the House and Senate represent black people fairly, our due seats are to be filled by persons elected at-large by the national black community. The same principle should obtain for state and local governments."

The nationalists would "see to it that no cable television comes into our communities unless we control it," and they would have at least two more black persons appointed to the Federal Communications Commission.

If the nationalists had their way, there would be a publicly funded, black-controlled agency like the Tennessee Valley Authority "to function as a planning, coordinating, and management structure for a rural industrial development program in the Black Belt." They would establish a National Commission/Foundation for Black Education, funded from private and public sources, to develop and encourage national and local research, planning and experimentation toward the creation of new models of black education at all levels.

The problems the integrationists have with these points relate not only to whether they are politically feasible. Integrationists simply do not believe that such matters as economic development and educational improvement should be dealt with on the basis of race. Thus, they question not only the gall but the goals of the nationalists. And in spite of occasional attempts to unite the two camps politically, it is unlikely that this will happen in any permanent sense.

At the Gary convention, for example, the 3,000 delegates held together for a time under the banner of "Unity Without Uniformity" until antibusing and anti-Israel resolutions (nationalist sponsored) were introduced and adopted. But even without these, it was clear that the N.A.A.C.P. and some other groups and prominent spokesmen could not accept the generally nationalist tone of the convention. In fact, in May, the N.A.A.C.P. withdrew its affiliation. . . .

In addition to having basically different orientations toward goals and tactics, the two groups have rather seriously divergent views about each other. The integrationists see the nationalists as unwilling to compete in the open market, as being insecure in competition with whites. This, they say, explains in large part the demand for black-studies programs in colleges and universities just at the time when vastly increased numbers of black students are entering predominantly white schools, the thinking being that such programs are academically easier. They see the nationalists as frustrated and disappointed with the pace of civil-rights progress, largely from a lack of historical perspective. If the nationalists had greater knowledge of history, they would know that major changes have occurred. Since much of the nationalist thrust comes from younger people, the integrationists accuse them of not knowing very much, if anything, about the struggle before Watts or the assassination of Malcolm X or the rise of the Black Panthers—all mid- to late-nineteen-sixties phenomena.

The integrationists are also prone to see many nationalists as hustlers, out to line their own pockets off the "new industry of blackness." And in the process, they accuse the nationalists of being not only hypocritical, but mostly rhetorical, not substantive, capable only of posturing, not producing. They do not understand "real power"; they engage largely in symbols—in clothing, hair styles, handshakes and speech.

Finally, the integrationists constantly point out that the nationalists naively give aid and comfort to racial bigots and conservatives. For example, Gov. George Wallace could only be pleased by an antibusing resolution passed by blacks. And when the black group, the National Economic Growth and Reconstruction Organization (NEGRO), supported the residents of Forest Hills, Queens, against a low-income housing project being built there, integrationists accused the group of being used by forces of racial bigotry. Nationalism, the integrationists point out, can create strange political bedfellows in the racial struggle, as black nationalists line up with Southern segregationists and Northern conservatives like Senator James Buckley.

The nationalists, on the other hand, are convinced that because the integrationists rely so heavily on money furnished by whites, the integrationists have no real voice of their own. They are controlled.

The nationalists see the integrationists as being overly impressed with whites and too willing to go to whatever lengths necessary to "prove" themselves to whites.

Above all, the integrationists are perceived as possessing a great deal of self-hate, which, again, is a form of adopting a characteristic of the larger society, that is, rejection of blacks.

If the nationalists are considered naive in politics, they, in turn, view the integrationists as too idealistic about human beings. The integrationists' alliance with white liberals (whom the nationalists see as insultingly paternalistic) is one that overlooks the fact that all people operate on the basis of self-interest, not altruism. The nationalists want the integrationists to realize that the white liberal is no better, in the end, than the white conservative—the end constituting the lack of willingness to relinquish power to black people. . . .

These differences can show up in everyday life as well as in theoretical discussions. In one desegregated elementary school in a New York suburb not too long ago the white teacher was having a discussion with her fifth-grade class. The topic was how the children were going to spend their upcoming winter vacation. A substantial portion of the white children were from middle-class families whose parents were taking them to Florida to escape the dreary New York February weather. Most of the black children were from lower-class families who lived in a nearby public-housing project, and some were bused from another part of town.

The discussion from the white students was spirited and full of exciting accounts of flight plans, hotel reservations, Florida beaches and play areas. The black students sat silently. When a visiting black parent, who had observed the session, spoke to the teacher afterwards, the teacher was quite elated over the lively discussion and enthusiasm of the students. The parent, however, complained that that session was precisely the kind of insensitive education to which she felt the black students should not be exposed. The teacher was puzzled and hurt; she saw or heard nothing wrong or offensive in the discussion at all. The parent explained that the black children were totally excluded because their parents could not afford to take them on expensive vacations. Their sense of inferiority was reinforced, and they were made to feel that watching television and running the halls of the housing project during the week while their parents worked could not match the glamour and thrills of a week's vacation in the Florida sun. The teacher explained that she was unaware of the race of those students who did and did not participate. This episode, to the parent, was an example not of the admirable trait of color-blindness but of the insensitivity of the educational system to the needs of the black children, and it was further evidence of the dubious benefits of integration on both racial and class bases.

Strong exception to this view was taken by a black integrationist parent who also observed the class. Rather, she thought this was exactly the kind of educational experience to which the black children should be exposed. It broadened their vision; it introduced them to other worlds. "We Negroes must stop being so sensitive. Our children need those wider contacts. The parents can't give it to them, and that is just why school integration is important."

Thus, one parent saw the class as stifling, parochial and harmful. The other saw it as enlightening, stimulating and helpful. . . .

The two groups broadly described here simply have little, if any, common ground to share over the basic issue, say, of dispersal of the black community—in housing or school attendance. Nationalists firmly believe that blacks can begin to consolidate their political power only if they remain geographically consolidated. Integrationists believe in "breaking up the ghetto." (Indeed, the debate extends to the different uses of terms: The nationalists see a "black community" that should be strengthened and controlled by blacks; the integrationists see a "black ghetto" that should be broken up and integrated into the mainstream.)

Some doubt that a *rapprochement* can ever be worked out between the two groups; I believe, however, that if both groups are as politically sophisticated as each claims to be, they should be able to unite around ideologically neutral issues. . . .

It is very clear, for instance, that one need not be a nationalist or an integrationist to know that the black community must be cleansed of the plague of narcotics. There ought to be consensus and cooperation on this issue, because it is certain that there will be neither effective community control nor successful integration as long as drugs remain a pervasive problem in black communities.

The same is true with tackling the problem of finding more jobs for able-bodied people. Both groups are coming to see public welfare in its present form as little more than the mechanism for perpetuating a dependent populace. Increased employment in the public and private sectors should be a goal permitting cooperation. Substantially improved health care is another area. There should be no ideological hang-ups over this issue.

Whether one is a nationalist or an integrationist, it is difficult to perceive *any* effective political leverage as long as black voter-registration and turn-out rates remain abysmally low. The political interests of both groups, it would seem, would be served by cooperating and dealing with this problem.

# 1.7 BUSING: WHO'S BEING TAKEN FOR A RIDE?
## Nicolaus Mills

[By sorting out five myths and fictions which have surrounded the busing issue, this article would hope to help] put the school bus issue in perspective.

1) *Busing goes against tradition and represents a break with past approaches to improving education*: The fact [is that] . . . consolidation and the need for improved education are at the root of busing. . . .

Nicolaus Mills, "Busing: Who's Being Taken for a Ride?" *Commonweal* 96: 55–60, March 24, 1972. By permission of the publisher.
Nicolaus Mills is a consultant at the ERIC Information Retrieval Center on the Disadvantaged at Teachers College, Columbia. This article is based on a longer study done for the Center.

Because the busing issue takes on different dimensions with each passing year, and because it will undoubtedly continue to be headline news throughout the 1970s, this anthology will not attempt to recount the particular skirmishes that occurred in 1970, 1971 or 1972. For a readable impartial pro-con story of the situation in 1971, read "The Agony of Busing Moves North," *Time* 98: 57–74, November 15, 1971. For pros and cons concerning progress in the South, read John C. Walden and Allen D. Cleveland, "The South's New Segregated Academies," *Phi Delta Kappan* 53: 234–239, December 1971, *versus* John Egerton, "Report Card on Southern School Desegregation," *Saturday Review* 55: 41–48, April 1, 1972. And there are many other such articles, most of which will be outdated by 1974 or 1975. So, on this issue, which is so newsworthy, it is impossible to prepare a group of pro-con statements which will not very soon be out of date.

It is well, however, to take note of the manner in which emotional attitudes prevent rational thought. So we include this article by Nicolaus Mills describing five widely entertained beliefs ("myths") which have very little basis in fact.

The extent of busing, no less than its history, goes against the assumptions which are generally made about it. As *New York Times* education writer Gene Maeroff recently noted, "Busing for desegregation is still only a small part of all school busing. For millions of American children who live too far from any school to walk, the institution known as the neighborhood school is not and never has been a reality."

The most recent surveys put the number of students bused at 42.2 percent of all pupils in the United States. Other statistics are as follows:

| | |
|---|---|
| Number of children bused to school | 19.6 million |
| Cost of busing (including replacement) | $1.5 billion |
| Busing costs in states as percentages | |
| of total education outlays | 0.7 to 6.9 percent |
| Number of buses | 256,000 |
| Number of drivers | 275,000 |
| Miles traveled per year | 2.2 billion |

These figures make school busing the greatest single transportation system in the country. They reflect not only the quality of school busing, however, but also its breadth, the fact that 80 percent of the school districts in the country maintain one or more vehicles for pupil transportation, with fleets in the largest districts including more than 500 vehicles and the average fleet at 15 vehicles. . . .

2) *Busing is the exception and the neighborhood school is always the most desirable*: With the number of bused school children now 19.6 million and the percentage of bused children at 42.2 percent, it is no longer possible to regard busing as unusual. . . . All across the country the neighborhood school has become an educationally less viable institution for reasons generally having nothing to do with desegregation.

Since the end of World War II, the number of school districts in the country has, for example, dropped from over 100,000 to 17,153. In addition, new forces have helped spur the growth of pupil transportation. Cities and suburban areas have shown a willingness to transport children, even though public transportation systems are often available to them, and the states themselves have increasingly asserted leadership in pupil transportation programs. . . .

The parochial schools of this country, which have continually gone to court in order to have their students transported at public expense, provide perhaps the best-known example of the close ties between busing and special education. They have continually argued that their viability depends on pupil transportation, and they have been instrumental in getting state school boards to transport nonpublic school students at public expense. Four states, Delaware, New Jersey, New York and Wisconsin, have Constitutions which authorize such transportation, and a number of other states have statutory provisions for school boards to transport nonpublic school students at public expense.

Busing in urban areas also has been and is being used to deal with the opposite population problem rural areas have—overcrowding. In cities where shifts in population have made it impossible for neighborhood schools to cope with an influx of students, busing to less crowded areas has been adopted. St. Louis provides a classic case of this. There busing was used as an alternative to having double-sessions, which would have set one set of children free in the morning and another set in the afternoon. For those transported, the benefits of the program were obvious, but they were not the only beneficiaries. As a report to the Superintendent of St. Louis schools emphasized "reduction of class size, through bus transportation and other expediencies . . . made it possible for *nontransported as well as transported* children residing in the districts of these seriously overcrowded schools to suffer minimal education loss." . . .

3) *The decision to bus has, until recently, not been guided by social beliefs or principles*: The history of pupil transportation offers the most conclusive refutation of this notion. The growth of pupil transportation is inseparable from the belief that education is required for the social welfare of the country and offers a chance for individual social advancement. Ironically, it is the South which provides the most dramatic case of bus transportation's being used to support a set of social values. The dual school system of the South would not have been possible without an elaborate pupil transportation system. As G. W. Foster, a former consultant to the Office of Education and a professor of law, has noted, "In dual school systems it has been customary in many instances for separate buses to travel the same roads, one to pick up Negroes for the Negro school and the other to take whites to a different school. . . . What busing to achieve desegregation has done is not to introduce social values to the concept of pupil transportation but introduce social values that stir opposition. . . .

[This opposition consists in opposition to the ideals of our own Constitution as interpreted by the United States Supreme Court since 1954. Thus, in the McKlenburg case, 1971, Chief Justice Warren Burger declared:]

All things being equal, with no history of discrimination, it might well be desirable to assign pupils to schools nearest their homes. But all things are not equal in a system that has been deliberately constructed and maintained to enforce racial segregation. . . .

4) *Riding on the school bus is bad for children*: There are certainly occasions when long-distance riding places a hardship on students, and the courts have been especially sensitive to this problem in ordering busing. Except when busing involves desegregation, this problem is rarely raised, however. . . .

[The] attitude of the South towards busing is most revealing when one considers its reputed bad effects: As the U.S. Civil Rights Commission has noted, in the South "in many cases, busing was the exclusive privilege of white children—black children often were required to walk considerable distances. No complaints then were heard from whites of any harmful [busing] effects." Indeed, rather than being bad for children, busing per se has shown itself a safety factor as well as a health factor.

5) *Busing is invariably a financial burden on a community*: In a number of instances racial busing certainly has introduced expenses which a community was avoiding when it had segregated schools. But it cannot be assumed that increased busing—racial or otherwise—is automatically a drain on a community. The busing which eliminated the one-room schoolhouse was a financial saving for the community, and busing for desegregation purposes is often the same. In the case of a dual school system, busing not only eliminates overlapping bus routes but the kinds of inefficiencies the Civil Rights Commission found in Alabama when it discovered, for example, that black students in Selma, seeking to attend trade school, were bused 50 miles to Montgomery to a nearly all-black trade school rather than allowed to attend an all-white trade school in Selma. . . .

[An example in the North] of the economy of busing is to be found in New York City, where Dan Dodson, professor of education at New York University, has proposed a plan that would involve busing 215,000 students in order to achieve desegregation. In his plan a large share of the cost would be made up for by the use of under-utilized schools in areas outside Manhattan.

"It is quite obvious that busing per se has been widely accepted by the parents of the nation's children as an essential component of an education system," Donald Morrison, president of the National Education Association, has written. . . . [and he continues:]

> The current controversy over school busing is surprising to those of us who have devoted our lives to public education. The school bus has been a major factor in improving the educational opportunity of hundreds of millions of American children during the last half century.[1]

---

[1] *EDITOR'S NOTE*: In an anthology which attempts to be reasonably impartial on controversial issues, it may be well to cite a statement made by Charles Silberman in 1964. It will be noted that this article does not deal directly with busing, but it does deal with the issue whether busing of deprived children to schools in more affluent neighborhoods is good for the deprived child. Admitting that *talented* Negro youth gain much by being bussed to schools which challenge their abilities, this does not prove that *general* busing, purely on the basis of race, is justified:

> Large-scale transfers of Negro children to schools in white neighborhoods . . . raise questions whose answers are by no means obvious. Should the Negro children be put in heterogeneous classes in the new school, in which case they tend to perform at the

bottom of the class if the school draws from middle-class and upper-class families? Or should they be put in homogeneous classes, i.e., classes grouped according to academic ability—in which case they are again segregated in the new school? The latter seems pointless: nothing is gained by transporting youngsters several miles in order to keep them segregated. Yet dumping youngsters who are reading several years below grade level, as the New Rochelle experience suggests, is not likely to enhance the former group's ego nor lead to meaningful encounters between the two races—Charles E. Silberman, *Crisis in Black and White*, New York: Random House, Inc., 1964, p. 300.

# B. Are There Tax and Economic Barriers?

## 1.8 FINANCING SCHOOLS: PROPERTY TAXES AND EQUAL EDUCATIONAL OPPORTUNITY
### Arthur E. Wise and Harold Howe II

**WISE**

On August 30, 1971, the Supreme Court of California announced what may become as historic a decision as *Brown vs. Board of Education*. In *Serrano vs. Priest*, the court tentatively concluded that the state's public school financing system denies children equal protection guaranteed under the Fourteenth Amendment, because it produces substantial disparities among school districts in the amount of revenue available for education. The problem to which the case was addressed can be simply stated by an example. The Baldwin Park school district expended only $577.49 to educate each of its pupils in 1968–69, while the Beverly Hills school district, in the same county, expended $1,231.72 per pupil. The principal source of this inequity was the difference in local assessed property valuation per child: In Baldwin Park the figure was $3,706 per child, while in Beverly Hills it was $50,885—a ratio of 1 to 13. Furthermore, Baldwin Park citizens paid a school tax of $5.48 per $100 of assessed valuation, while Beverly Hills residents paid only $2.38 per $100—a ratio of more than 2 to 1. [See Chart]. . . .

The idea that the unequal allocation of educational resources within a state might be unconstitutional was first suggested only during the mid-1960s. It was not that the allocation of educational resources among school districts within a state suddenly became unequal in the mid-1960s, nor were these

Arthur E. Wise and Harold Howe II, "Financing Schools: Property Tax is Obsolete," *Saturday Review* 54: 78–88, 95, November 20, 1971 (two articles). © 1972 by Saturday Review, Inc. Used with permission.

Arthur E. Wise, Associate Dean of the Graduate School of Education at the University of Chicago, is the author of *Rich Schools, Poor Schools: The Promise of Equal Educational Opportunity*, 1969, one of the earliest and most influential studies in the field.

Harold Howe II, former United States Commissioner of Education, is vice president in charge of education and research at the Ford Foundation.

## Comparison of Tax Rates and Expenditure Levels
## in Selected Counties in California (1968-1969)

| County | ADA | Assessed Value per ADA | Tax Rate | Expenditure per ADA |
|---|---|---|---|---|
| Alameda | | | | |
| Emery Unified | 586 | $100,187 | $2.57 | $2,223 |
| Newark Unified | 8,638 | 6,048 | 5.65 | 616 |
| Fresno | | | | |
| Coalinga Unified | 2,640 | $ 33,244 | $2.17 | $ 963 |
| Clovis Unified | 8,144 | 6,480 | 4.28 | 565 |
| Kern | | | | |
| Rio Bravo Elementary | 121 | $136,271 | $1.05 | $1,545 |
| Lamont Elementary | 1,847 | 5,971 | 3.06 | 533 |
| Los Angeles | | | | |
| Beverly Hills Unified | 5,542 | $ 50,885 | $2.38 | $1,232 |
| Baldwin Park Unified | 13,108 | 3,706 | 5.48 | 577 |

Some districts with low expenditures per child in Average Daily Attendance (ADA) have correspondingly low tax rates, but in many other cases the opposite is true. Often districts with very low expenditures per ADA have unusually high tax rates, as a result of their limited tax base, while the tax rate is comparatively low in "wealthy" districts.—*Table and text adapted from the decision of the California Supreme Court in* Serrano vs. Priest.

inequities suddenly discovered. Rather, the inequities in school finance were, for the first time, viewed in the light of the then prevailing egalitarian thrust of the U.S. Supreme Court.

The Court, under Chief Justice Earl Warren, had been embarked on a campaign of guaranteeing fundamental rights to dispossessed minorities and had precipitated broad social change. In 1954, the Supreme Court declared that, at least as far as race is concerned, public education is a right that must be made available equally. Beginning in 1956, the Court began to attack discrimination based on wealth in a series of cases concerned with rights of defendants in criminal cases. In 1962, the Court moved to eliminate geographic discrimination by requiring legislative reapportionment. By 1966, the wealth discrimination argument had been extended to voting rights in a case that eliminated the poll tax. . . .

[In *Serrano,* California's Supreme Court declared:] "If a voter's address may not determine the weight to which his ballot is entitled, surely it should not determine the quality of his child's education."

This analysis is consistent with the more egalitarian proposition that the quality of a child's education may not be a function of local wealth or of how highly his neighbors value education. In other words, it would prohibit variations in the number of dollars spent on any child by virtue of his place of residence. It would apparently permit variations based on educationally relevant characteristics of the child. . . .

The next months, indeed years, will be a time of substantial confusion in the history of American public school finance. A principal outcome of *Serrano* will be to free legislatures from the strictures of the past to experiment with new models of school finance. Efforts at reform will be aided by a growing discontent with the local property tax.

In sum, *Serrano*-type lawsuits are designed to attack our school finance systems that effectively deliver more educational resources to children in wealthy communities and less to children in poor communities. The suits have as their objective squaring the reality of school finance schemes with the rhetoric of equality of educational opportunity.

## HOWE

It is an article of faith in America that every citizen should have an equal chance. We pride ourselves on a system of government and an open society designed to turn this principle into a fact of life. Any informed American knows, however, that all people do not have an equal chance in the United States. Wealth still gives special privilege; race confers abiding handicaps; inappropriate distinctions are made on the basis of sex. Our society is not wide open to people who are different, who speak another language, who are somehow out of the mainstream of the middle-class culture.

And nowhere are our ideals of equality further from reality than in the way we finance our schools. But it is possible that revolutionary change may be just over the horizon. It may be that the early 1970s will turn out to be the time in which these inequalities become a major issue in every legislature in the land. On August 30, 1971, the Supreme Court of the State of California decided by a majority of 6 to 1 that the system of financing schools in California through local property taxes violates the equal protection clause of the Fourteenth Amendment to the U.S. Constitution.

The court declared:

> We have determined that this funding scheme invidiously discriminates against the poor because it makes the quality of a child's education a function of the wealth of his parents and neighbors. Recognizing as we must that the right to an education is a fundamental interest which cannot be conditioned on wealth, we can discern no compelling state purpose necessitating the present method of financing.

As an educator rather than a legal specialist, I read the decision as a powerful argument indeed. It casts a shadow over the legality of the entire system of financing public education and clearly documents the inequalities that characterize present practice. It finds that the efforts of the state at equalization are "inadequate to offset the inequalities inherent in a financing system based on widely varying local tax bases." It sets aside—as unrealistic for poor school districts—the argument that a district that wants to can have good education by taxing itself adequately: ". . . affluent districts can have their cake and eat it too; they can provide a high-quality education for their children while paying lower taxes. Poor districts, by contrast, have no cake at all." It argues that fortuitous location of highly assessed commercial properties in a school district creates imbalances that ought to be irrelevant in planning educational financing.

Up to World War II, we were trying to get every youngster into school. Since then, we have become more concerned with whether the school he enters gives the pupil a fair chance. Numerous studies have documented the failure of the schools to serve poor children adequately, particularly blacks, the Spanish-speaking, and American Indians.

The federal government has financed special add-on programs on behalf of those groups of young people who seem to be especially ill served by the schools. The landmark Elementary and Secondary Education Act of 1965 recognizes the inequalities in American education and provides special funds to schools where there are concentrations of poor people. The Headstart, Upward Bound, and Follow Through programs have similar objectives. But federally financed programs, which have attracted so much attention in recent years, pay for only a very small part of U.S. education. At present, only about 7 percent of all school funds come from the federal government. The bulk comes from state authority—about 40 percent directly, and some 55 percent from local property taxes levied by localities that are creatures of the state. While there are differences among the states, in general they leave it to local boards to raise through property taxes the money needed to run their schools.

This local system means that a youngster's chance for a quality education depends in a very large measure on the accident of where he lives and attends school. Disparities among states have attracted some notice in recent years as wealthier states have received migrations of poorly educated children from poorer states. (A child who happens to be born in Mississippi receives an elementary school education that costs annually about $521. If he lives in New York State, his citizenship brings him, on the average, the advantages of what $1,370 can buy in the way of good educational service.) Less well known is the equally glaring gap between have and have-not areas within states, even comparatively wealthy states. . . .

The California decision has exposed these inequities to the full glare of national publicity and, in effect, has redefined the rules of the game in the annual legislative battles over educational appropriations.

But the California decision leaves unanswered the question of how schools are to be financed. It simply says that the present system is not legally acceptable. The California legislature has the job of designing a new system that will give children the equal protection of the laws. . . .

Seventeen years have passed since the Supreme Court handed down the *Brown* decision, and the schools are still in the process of desegregation.

Educators and laymen concerned about the schools should get to work now to ensure that no such anguished chasm develops between the promise of the California doctrine and its fulfillment.[1]

---

[1] *EDITOR'S NOTE:* For an excellent summary of the ten or twenty legal precedents for *Serrano* and a good overview of the Coleman Report, the New York City More Effective Schools Project, and other experimental programs, read Ferdinand P. Schoettle (Professor of Law, University of Minnesota), "The Equal Protection Clause in Public Education," *71 Columbia Law Review* 1355–1419, December 1971.

In a 1972 article "Full State Funding of Education," Richard A. Rossmiller (University of Wisconsin) not only reviews *Serrano v. Priest* (487 P.2nd 1241) but also discusses two more recent decisions dealing with tax equalization via state funding: *Van Dusartz v. Hatfield* (334 F. Supp. 870) and *Rodriguez v. San Antonio Independent School District* (337 F. Supp. 280). Looking ahead, Professor Rossmiller examines three general models for possible state funding:

1. Complete state funding with no provision for local school taxes.

2. Full state funding with the state providing a basic flat grant per pupil and permitting local school districts to supplement state revenue by up to 20 percent with revenue obtained from a local tax levy.

3. Percentage equalizing with the state providing a basic flat grant per pupil and permitting the school district to supplement this basic grant with a local tax levy. In this model, however, the state will provide additional funds to compensate for deficiencies in a local district's tax base relative to other districts in the state. This will be accomplished by establishing a guaranteed tax base and supplementing local tax revenue with additional state aid so that each district that levies a given tax rate is assured of receiving the same amount of revenue per pupil.

—Richard A. Rossmiller, "Full State Funding of Education," in *Six Crucial Issues in Education,* edited by David T. Tronsgard, Executive Secretary, NASBE, 1972, pp. 2–28 (good bibliography). Copies of this booklet may be obtained from: National Association of State Boards of Education, 2480 West 26th Avenue—Suite 215-B, Denver, Colorado 80211.

---

# 1.9 THE SCHOOLS AND EQUAL OPPORTUNITY
## Christopher Jencks, and others

### Poverty and Inequality

[Most] Americans define poverty in relative rather than absolute terms. Public-opinion surveys show, for example, that when people are asked how much money an American family needs to "get by," they typically name a figure about half what the average American family actually receives. This has been true for the last three decades, despite the fact that real incomes (incomes adjusted for inflation) have doubled in the interval.

During the Depression the average American family was living on about $30 a week. A third of all families were living on less than half this amount, which made it natural for Franklin Roosevelt to speak of "one-third of a nation" as ill-housed, ill-clothed, and ill-fed. By 1964 mean family income was about $160 a week, and the Gallup poll found that the average American thought a family of four needed at least $80 a week to "get by." Even allowing for inflation, this was twice what people had thought necessary during the Depression. Playing it safe, the Johnson administration defined the poverty line at $60 a week for a family of four, but most people felt this was inadequate. By 1970 inflation had raised mean family income to about $200 a week, and the National Welfare Rights Organization was trying to rally liberal support for a guaranteed income of $100 a week.

These changes in the definition of poverty were not just a matter of "rising expectations" or of people's needing to "keep up with the Joneses." The goods and services that made it possible to live on $15 a week during the

This article is based on research done by Christopher Jencks and his colleagues at the Center for Educational Policy Research, Harvard University, with the support of the Carnegie Corporation of New York. The research group started in 1968 by reexamining the data on the effects of schooling gathered by the Equality of Educational Opportunity Survey (EEOS), whose most famous product was the *Coleman Report*. It also reanalyzed Project Talent's longitudinal study of students in 100 high schools as well as many smaller studies. In addition, Jencks reviewed, and in some cases reanalyzed, data on adult occupational status and income gathered by the United States Bureau of Census, by the National Opinion Research Center, and many smaller studies. The complete results are presented in *Inequality: A Reassessment of the Effect of Family and Schooling in America* by Christopher Jencks and Marshall Smith, Henry Acland, Mary Jo Bane, David Cohen, Herbert Gintis, Barbara Heyns, and Stephan Michelson (New York: Basic Books, 1972). A brief summary is found in the *Saturday Review* 55: 37–42, September 16, 1972. This excerpt © 1972 by *Saturday Review* and used by permission of the author.

Professor of Education at Harvard, Christopher Jencks is coauthor, with David Riesman, of *The Academic Revolution*, New York: Doubleday, 1968.

Depression were no longer available to a family with the same real income ($40 a week) in 1964. Eating habits had changed, and many cheap foods had disappeared from the stores. Housing arrangements had changed, too. During the Depression many people could not afford indoor plumbing and "got by" with a privy. By the 1960s privies were illegal in most places. Those who still could not afford an indoor toilet ended up in buildings that had broken toilets. For these they paid more than their parents had paid for privies.

Examples of this kind suggest that the "cost of living" is not the cost of buying some fixed set of goods and services. It is the cost of participating in a social system. It therefore depends in large part on how much other people habitually spend to participate in the system. Those who fall far below the norm, whatever it may be, are excluded. Accordingly, raising the incomes of the poor will not eliminate poverty if the cost of participating in "mainstream" American life rises even faster. People with incomes less than half the national average will not be able to afford what "everyone" regards as "necessities." The only way to eliminate poverty is, therefore, to make sure everyone has an income at least half the average.

Arguments of this kind suggest not only that it makes more sense to think of "poverty" as a relative rather than an absolute condition but that eliminating poverty, at least as it is usually defined in America, depends on eliminating, or at least greatly reducing, inequality.

## Schooling and Opportunity

Almost none of the reform legislation of the 1960s involved direct efforts to equalize adult status, power, or income. Most Americans accepted the idea that these rewards should go to those who were most competent and diligent. Their objection to America's traditional economic system was not that it produced inequality but that the rules determining who succeeded and who failed were often unfair. The reformers wanted to create a world in which success would no longer be associated with skin color, economic background, or other "irrelevant" factors, but only with actual merit. What they wanted, in short, was what they called "equal opportunity."

Their strategy for achieving equal opportunity placed great emphasis on education. Many people imagined that if schools could equalize people's cognitive skills this would equalize their bargaining power as adults. Presumably, if everyone had equal bargaining power, few people would end up very poor.

This strategy for reducing poverty rested on a series of assumptions that went roughly as follows:

1) Eliminating poverty is largely a matter of helping children born into poverty to rise out of it. Once families escape from poverty, they do not fall back into it. Middle-class children rarely end up poor.

2) The primary reason poor children cannot escape from poverty is that they do not acquire basic cognitive skills. They cannot read, write, calculate, or articulate. Lacking these skills, they cannot get or keep a well-paid job.

3) The best mechanism for breaking this "vicious circle" is educational reform. Since children born into poor homes do not acquire the skills they need from their parents, they must be taught these skills in school. This can be done by making sure that they attend the same schools as middle-class children, by giving them extra compensatory programs in school, by giving their parents a voice in running their schools, or by some combination of all three approaches.

Our research over the last four years suggests that each of these assumptions is erroneous:

1) Poverty is not primarily hereditary. While children born into poverty have a higher than average chance of ending up poor, there is still an enormous amount of economic mobility from one generation to the next. A father whose occupational status is high passes on less than half his advantage to his sons, and a father whose status is low passes along less than half his disadvantage. A family whose income is above the norm has an even harder time passing along its privileges; its sons are typically only about a third as advantaged as the parents. Conversely, a family whose income is below average will typically have sons about a third as disadvantaged as the parents. The effects of parents' status on their daughters' economic positions appear to be even weaker. This means that many "advantaged" parents have some "disadvantaged" children and vice versa.

2) The primary reason some people end up richer than others is not that they have more adequate cognitive skills. While children who read well, get the right answers to arithmetic problems, and articulate their thoughts clearly are somewhat more likely than others to get ahead, there are many other equally important factors involved. The effects of I.Q. on economic success are about the same as the effects of family background. This means, for example, that if two men's I.Q. scores differ by 17 points—the typical difference between I.Q. scores of individuals chosen at random—their incomes will typically differ by less than $2,000. That amount is not completely trivial, of course. But the income difference between random individuals is three times as large and the difference between the best-paid fifth and the worst-paid fifth of all male workers averages $14,000. There is almost as much economic inequality among those who score high on standardized tests as in the general population.

3) There is no evidence that school reform can substantially reduce the extent of cognitive inequality, as measured by tests of verbal fluency, reading comprehension, or mathematical skill. Eliminating qualitative differences between elementary schools would reduce the range of scores on standardized tests in sixth grade by less than 3 percent. Eliminating qualitative differences between high schools would hardly reduce the range of twelfth-grade scores at all and would reduce by only 1 percent the disparities in the amount of education people eventually get.

Our best guess, after reviewing all the evidence we could find, is that racial desegregation raises black elementary school students' test scores by a couple of points. But most of the test-score gap between blacks and whites persists, even when they are in the same schools. So also: Tracking has very little effect on test scores. And neither the overall level of resources available to a school nor any specific, easily identifiable school policy has a significant effect on students' cognitive skills or educational attainments. Thus, even if we went beyond "equal opportunity" and allocated resources disproportionately to schools whose students now do worst on tests and are least likely to acquire credentials, this would not improve these students' prospects very much. . . .

## Equal Opportunity and Unequal Results

The evidence we have reviewed, taken all together, suggests that equalizing opportunity cannot take us very far toward eliminating inequality. The simplest way of demonstrating this is to compare the economic prospects of brothers raised in the same home. Even the most egalitarian society could not hope to make opportunities for all children appreciably more equal than the opportunities now available to brothers from the same family. Looking at society at large, if we compare random pairs of individuals, the difference between their occupational statuses averages about 28 points on the Duncan "status scale" (the scale runs from 0 to 96 points). The difference between brothers' occupational statuses averages fully 23 points on this scale. If we compare men's incomes, the difference between random pairs averaged about $6,200 in 1968. The difference between brothers' incomes, according to our best estimate, probably averaged about $5,700. These estimates mean that people who start off equal end up almost as unequal as everyone else. Inequality is not mostly inherited: It is re-created anew in each generation.

We can take this line of argument a step further by comparing people who not only start off in similar families but who also have the same I.Q. scores and get the same amount of schooling. Such people's occupational statuses differ by an average of 21 points, compared to 28 points for random individuals. If we compare their incomes, making the additional assumption that the men have the same occupational status, we find that they differ by an average of about $5,300, compared to $6,200 for men chosen at random.

These comparisons suggest that adult success must depend on a lot of things besides family background, schooling, and the cognitive skills measured by standardized tests. We have no idea what these factors are. To some extent, no doubt, specialized varieties of competence, such as the ability to hit a ball thrown at high speed or the ability to persuade a customer that he wants a larger car than he thought he wanted, play a major role. Income also depends on luck: the range of jobs available when you are job hunting, the amount of overtime work in your plant, good or bad weather for your strawberry crop, and a hundred other unpredictable accidents.

Equalizing opportunity will not, then, do much to reduce economic inequality in America. If poverty is relative rather than absolute, equalizing opportunity will not do much to reduce poverty, either.

## Implications for Educational Policy

These findings imply that school reform is never likely to have any significant effect on the degree of inequality among adults. This suggests that the prevalent "factory" model, in which schools are seen as places that "produce" alumni, probably ought to be abandoned. It is true that schools have "inputs" and "outputs," and that one of their nominal purposes is to take human "raw material" (*i.e.,* children) and convert it into something more "useful" (*i.e.,* employable adults). Our research suggests, however, that the character of a school's output depends largely on a single input, the characteristics of the entering children. Everything else—the school budget, its policies, the characteristics of the teachers—is either secondary or completely irrelevant, at least so long as the range of variation among schools is as narrow as it seems to be in America.[1]

## Implications for Social Reform

Then how *are* we to affect adult life? Our findings tell us that different kinds of inequality are only loosely related to one another. . . . [This] means that inequality in one area does not dictate inequality in other areas.

To begin with, genetic inequality is not a major obstacle to economic equality. It is true that genetic diversity almost inevitably means considerable variation in people's scores on standardized tests. But this kind of cognitive inequality need not imply anything like the present degree of economic inequality. We estimate, for example, that if the only sources of income inequality in America were differences in people's genes, the top fifth of the population would earn only about 1.4 times as much as the bottom fifth. In actuality, the top fifth earns seven times as much as the bottom fifth.

Second, our findings suggest that psychological and cultural differences between families are not an irrevocable barrier to adult equality. Family background has more influence than genes on an individual's educational attainment, occupational status, and income. Nonetheless, if family background

---

[1] *EDITOR'S NOTE*: "The point is not that schools make *no* difference. Mosteller and Moynihan comment sharply: 'Children don't think up algebra on their own. . . . But given that schools have reached their present levels of equality, the observed variation [in resources] was reported [in a survey done by the RAND Corporation for the President's Commission on School Finance] . . . to have little effect on school achievement.' Thus none of the major studies, nor any of the handful of social scientists who fully comprehend their statistical intricacies, offers reason to expect that changing the way our schools are financed will have more than a trivial effect on what children learn in them."—Chester E. Finn, Jr., and Leslie Lendowsky, "Serrano vs. the People," *Commentary* 44: 68–72, September 1972.

were the only source of economic inequality in America, the top fifth would earn only about twice as much as the bottom fifth.

Our findings show, then, that inequality is not determined at birth. But they also suggest that economic equality cannot be achieved by indirect efforts to manipulate the environments in which people grow up. We have already discussed the minuscule effects of equalizing school quality. Equalizing the amount of schooling people get would not work much better. Income inequality among men with similar amounts of schooling is only 5–10 percent less than among men in general. The effect is even less if we include women.

If we want to eliminate economic inequality, we must make this an explicit objective of public policy rather than deluding ourselves into thinking that we can do it by giving everyone equal opportunity to succeed or fail. If we want an occupational structure which is less hierarchical and in which the social distance between the top and the bottom is reduced, we will have to make deliberate efforts to reorganize work and redistribute power within organizations. . . .

In America, as elsewhere, the long-term drift over the past 200 years has been toward equality. In America, however, the contribution of public policy to this drift has been slight. As long as egalitarians assume that public policy cannot contribute to equality directly but must proceed by ingenious manipulations of marginal institutions like the schools, this pattern will continue. If we want to move beyond this tradition, we must establish political control over the economic institutions that shape our society. What we will need, in short, is what other countries call socialism. Anything less will end in the same disappointment as the reforms of the 1960s.[2]

---

[2] *EDITOR'S NOTE*: Some of the conclusions of the Jencks report were anticipated in the *Coleman Report*. In the mid–1960s, Congress directed the United States Commissioner of Education to examine "the lack of availability of equal educational opportunities for individuals by reason of race, color, religion, or national origin in public educational institutions." The results were published in *Equality of Educational Opportunity* (Washington, D.C., 1966), more commonly known as the *Coleman Report*, for Dr. James Coleman, principally responsible for its design.

To the surprise of many educators, the *Coleman Report* disclosed that achievement disparities among pupils attending the same school were far more pronounced than variations in the level of student achievement from one school to another. (On this point, the Coleman report anticipated the Jencks report.) The *Coleman Report* stated:

. . . despite the wide range of diversity of school facilities, curriculum, and teachers, and despite the wide diversity among student bodies in different schools, over 70 percent of the variation in achievement for each group is variation within the student body. . . .

Schools bring little influence to bear on a child's achievement that is independent of his background and general social context; and . . . this very lack of an independent effect means that the inequalities imposed on children by their home, neighborhood, and peer environment are carried along to become the inequalities with which they confront adult life at the end of school.

The *Coleman Report* also addressed itself to the relationship of school-related variables to achievement, and distinguished three major variables: (1) facilities, curriculum, and other characteristics of the school itself; (2) teacher characteristics; and (3) student body characteristics. And it found that (3) was more important than either (2) or (1). The rank order of importance was (3), then (2), then (1).

---

# 1.10 SCHOOLING AND INEQUALITY: THE SOCIAL SCIENCE OBJECTIVITY GAP
## Henry M. Levin

---

[In the book *Inequality* (briefly summarized in Selection 1.9 above) Christopher Jencks (and his colleagues)] notes two concepts of equality: equality of opportunity and equality of results. He suggests that most people are willing to accept a world with unequal incomes and status if they believe that these differences are based on such merits as ability, training, industriousness, and so on. Most people regard equality of opportunity to compete for life's unequal rewards as a social objective, and schools represent a major instrument to attain that goal. Accordingly, Jencks weighs the relative importance of inequalities in school resources, genetic endowments, and family backgrounds—and, surprisingly, finds that they are not strongly related to economic outcomes. They do not account for a person's income in his adult life.

The authors proceed to draw two major conclusions from their analyses. First, since inequalities in schooling, test scores, and family background do not appear to be strongly related to differences in income, "equality of opportunity" in an economic sense already exists. While we should attempt to make schools more pleasant places for young people, we should not view them as important social instruments for obtaining equality of results. Second, as long

Henry M. Levin, "Schooling and Inequality: The Social Science Objectivity Gap," (A review of the complete Jencks report with its charts and tables) *Saturday Review* 55: 49–51, November 11, 1972. Excerpt used by permission of *Saturday Review* and the author.

Henry M. Levin holds joint appointments in the departments of education and economics at Stanford University.

as the available economic and occupational roles provided by society are so unequal, large inequalities in economic outcomes will persist. Therefore, Jencks and his colleagues argue that, if we wish to reduce large inequalities in income between rich and poor—the top fifth of the population receives seven times what the bottom fifth receives—we should redistribute income directly by increasing the taxes of the rich and raising the minimum incomes provided for the poor.

The second conclusion seems eminently reasonable from a technical point of view. If we wish to improve the distribution of income, we should adopt policy measures that affect income directly. Yet, if the nature of our society is such that the present, large inequalities in income have existed for almost fifty years, it is difficult to believe that there is a powerful enough political coalition to effect a major redistribution. (Witness the recent decision by Congress to postpone welfare reform for several years.)

We might consider whether the competition for the present unequal rewards is a fair one, as Jencks and his coauthors imply. This is the single most crucial finding of the book, since it represents the basis for the authors' derogation of social policies aimed at improving equality of opportunity. Stated explicitly, the lack of relationship between family background, schooling, and test scores with income leads to the conclusion that policies to alter schools and family background will have little impact on eliminating economic inequalities.

Certainly, Jencks's assertion that the advantages with which one starts life have little to do with one's economic success seems to defy empirical verification for both the very poor and the very rich, although it may reflect accurately substantial mobility in the middle class. Surveys of the poverty population suggest that the "permanently poor" (in contrast with the transient poor, such as students, or the elderly who are living on pensions and social security payments) were themselves born into impoverished households and have low educational attainments. The very rich also seem to be able to sustain their position from generation to generation. Only the tumultuous economic upheaval associated with the Great Depression provided any appreciable movement from riches to rags, and only the calamity of World War II seemed to provide any appreciable movement from rags to riches over the last half-century. To assert that the forces of luck and other random factors give the children of the poor about the same chance in life as the children of the rich is in substantial conflict with this evidence.

In addition, many previous studies by economists on the subject have found that both schools and family background appear to have substantial effects on earnings. How is it possible, then, that Jencks's conclusions are in such sharp contrast to those of other researchers? The answer seems to lie in differences in interpretation and in the treatment of the data. For example, some differences that Jencks interprets as small ones would not seem trivial to other observers. Even according to the findings presented in the book, an extra year of elementary or secondary schooling appears to boost future income by about 4 per cent, an extra year of college by about 7 per cent, and a year of graduate school by about 4 per cent. According to these data a comparison of high school graduates and college graduates, who were otherwise identical, would show the college graduates earning about 30 per cent more than their less-educated peers. Jencks apparently believes that such differences are small, but two men separated by such income disparities might not agree. Thus, part of the conflict appears to revolve around the rather subjective issue of what magnitudes are important.

Clearly, the more serious discrepancies between Jencks and other researchers appear to be due to differences in the statistical treatment of data. The book's principal finding on the inefficacy of schools is that test scores, family background, and related factors account for only 12–15 per cent of differences in income. In contrast, other studies have found that from one-third to one-half of the variance in income can be explained by these and similar influences; according to their results, we should seriously consider the policy implications of improving the distribution of schooling.

It is not difficult to find the sources of the differences between these studies and that of Jencks. In fact, the *Inequality* study omitted data that would have improved considerably the amount of variance in income inequality. The most notable of these omissions include data on age and place of residence.

Ordinarily, when economists attempt to explain the determinants of income or earnings, they are concerned with *real* difference, not just artificial differences that are due to variations in price levels. Much of the differences in income among the various regions of the United States is really attributable to differences in the cost of living. The U.S. Bureau of Labor Statistics found that in 1970 the annual costs of a four-person urban family at an intermediate standard of living varied from about $9,200 in Austin, Texas, to over $12,000 in the New York area and almost $13,000 in Honolulu. There are also large differences within metropolitan areas and regions. Thus, much of what appear to be differences in income among a national population are really due to differences in price levels and do not represent differences in *real* incomes. In order to adjust for these effects, other studies have done their analyses within regions or have adjusted the data for the place of residence. Jencks's failure to do this resulted in a substantial overstatement of the "unexplained" variance in income relative to that of other studies.

A second omission that biases Jencks's results is the failure to include the age of the income recipient. Persons with the same educational and family background show large differences in their income over the life cycle. In the early stages of a career incomes rise briskly as individuals advance through on-the-job training, experience, and occupational upgrading. Peak earnings and advancement are reached at about forty-five to fifty years of age, and at this point many workers and self-employed professionals begin to withdraw from the labor market through early retirement or a reduction of hours worked. Thus, earned incomes decline considerably over the latter segment of the life cycle. Since Jencks's income data are based upon white, nonfarm men, twenty-five to sixty-four years of age, they include large components of income differences that are due to this normal life-cycle phenomenon. His failure to adjust the estimates for the age of the worker will serve to increase the amount of "unexplained" variations in income. Researchers usually treat this adjustment as a matter of standard procedure.

Finally, the fact that Jencks's data include income from property, social security, pensions, and other sources also tends to weaken the relationship between schooling, family background, and income. The statistical treatment in *Inequality* uses virtually the same variables to explain the income of the fully productive worker as it does the one who is retired and receives only a pension or social security payments. It uses the same attributes to explain the 15–20 per cent of income that is derived from nonproperty sources such as rents, dividends, and interest, even though such income is not derived from employment. Thus, the statistical formulation itself does not lend itself to explaining components of income that have little to do with individual labor-market productivity. Jencks does not take these important adjustments into account.

Further, the Jencks approach to explaining differences in income does not take noncognitive personality traits into account—even though recent research has found that schools and family appear to have a greater impact on the development of attitudes and values such as independence and conformity than on test scores. Such attributes appear to play an important role in determining social and economic outcomes. Jencks agrees that noncognitive traits ". . . play a larger role than cognitive skills in determining economic success or failure." Yet he omits such effects because of his stated inability to assess and measure them.

The result of all these omissions is to understate seriously the ways in which incomes vary systematically with differences in schooling and family background. If Jencks had corrected the data for such idiosyncrasies and if he had included data on place of residence, age, and noncognitive attributes, his formulation would probably have explained from three to four times as much of the inequality in income as did the more naïve formulation he actually used.

In a sense this example illustrates the fragility of social-science research in complex areas where theories are mere speculations and the techniques of analysis are subject to wide differences in application, usage, and interpretation. Jencks concluded that, because such a small portion of the variance in income was explained statistically by the family-background, schooling, and test-score variables, differences in income must be due primarily to differences in luck and competences that are not related to an individual's educational and family experiences. Yet the obvious alternative explanation is that the omission of important variables, as well as problems in the quality of the data, were the culprits and that differences in family and schooling do indeed affect economic success of adults.

Though Jencks gives the impression that his results are derived strictly from his statistical model and social-science methodology, in fact, the application of that model and its methodology are based upon numerous judgments and opinions. The omission of important variables because of "ignorance of their effects," the casual ordering of the variables, assumptions of linear relationships and normal distributions, the scavenging and use of data collected for other purposes and the questionable treatment of their measurement errors, as well as the ambiguity of many of the results, means that the actual findings and interpretations are at least as much a product of the value perspectives and opinions of the researcher as they are of this methodology and data. Unfortunately, the values and biases of the researcher are built into his procedures and interpretations at every stage.[1]

---

[1] *EDITOR'S NOTE*: To the above statement by Professor Levin, Mary Jo Bane and Christopher Jencks responded promptly. We cite only the opening paragraph of their reply:

Henry Levin . . . seems to have misread our book *Inequality* in one important respect. The book does not say, nor do the authors believe, that America provides children with equal opportunity. On the contrary, we offer a mountain of evidence that opportunity is now highly unequal. What seems to have confused Levin—and many others—is that we also provide evidence that making opportunity more equal would not make distribution of income appreciably more equal. This does not mean we ought to forget about equal opportunity; it just means that equal opportunity will not produce anything like equal results.—*Saturday Review of Education* 55: 24–25, January 1973.

---

# 1.11 SCHOOLS AND INEQUALITY
## James W. Guthrie and others

Societies that have persisted longest throughout history appear to be those that have avoided vast social and economic differences among major segments of their populations. Clearly the relative success of the United States in avoiding such extremes has been fostered significantly by the past successes of our schools. Today, however, because of a shortage of resources and an inappropriate distribution of the resources that are available, schools are no longer as successful as they once were. The preservation of equal opportunity and the reality of an open society wherein individuals rise or fall in accord with their interests and abilities demands a restructuring of present arrangements for the support and provision of school services. . . .

Persons suffering from educational handicaps are caught in a downward-spiraling cycle of despair. On one hand they are tempted on almost every side by the advantages that can be achieved with the assistance of good schooling. On the other hand, their own pursuit of such objectives is frequently brought to an abrupt halt by the inadequacy of their education. For them as individuals the goals of our society become relatively meaningless. At best they are left to experience frustration and defeat. At worst, they may be propelled into a life of crime and decadence. From the perspective of the entire society, this human wastage is a double burden. Not only do the undereducated not contribute their share, but also everyone else is deprived of the benefits of those individuals who, if properly schooled, could have contributed more than their share. We have long since passed the point in our development where we can tolerate vast numbers of unskilled and underdeveloped individuals. . . .

[To cite only one of several studies, in 1965] Hanoch used the "one in one thousand sample" from the 1960 census to estimate income returns from schooling for American males by age, race, and region while holding constant other influential variables. Even when he employed the most stringent of statistical controls to separate other-than-school influences, Hanoch found a

Reprinted from *Schools and Inequality* by James W. Guthrie, George B. Kleindorfer, Henry M. Levin, and Robert T. Stout, by permission of the MIT Press, Cambridge, Mass., 1971. Foreword by John W. Gardner. Excerpts from pages 156, 157, 97–108, 91, xiv. By permission. Footnote references here omitted.

The four authors are from Berkeley, Stanford, and Claremont, California. In preparing this study, they were assisted by twenty or thirty other scholars from all parts of the country.

Not included in our excerpt is the portion of the book which deals with the question "What Parts (What Aspects) of Schools Make a Difference?" Contrary to the Jencks report, these studies show that "what a child brings to school" is only one of several important factors that make a very considerable difference.

strong correspondence between schooling and earnings. For example, among white males in the North, ages thirty-five to forty-four, the estimated effect on earnings of going beyond elementary school is substantial. High school graduates were receiving almost $1,300 more and college graduates $3,100 more than elementary school graduates. The average earnings for all northern males in this category was $6,300 in 1959, so these educational differences are significant. . . .

[Other studies have analyzed] what portion of an individual's earnings is uniquely attributable to education . . . [and what portions] are due to differences in ability, motivation, social class, and so on. Denison estimates that only 60 percent of the differences in individual earnings that correspond to differences in schooling is attributable to schooling itself, and 40 percent is due to the superior earnings attributes on other dimensions of persons with higher levels of schooling. More recent studies suggest that Denison understates the significance of schooling. In fact, two statistical studies that have examined the relative effects on income of both educational attainment and IQ [the type of studies underscored in the Jencks study] report that the introduction of the latter measure [the IQ factor] into the analysis does not reduce the discernible impact of schooling. . . .

[Furthermore, abundant] evidence supports the view that education affects [not only] earnings and income, [but also] occupational choice, intergenerational mobility, political participation [and other noneconomic factors which relate to attainment and success]. . . .

That schooling has an effect on earnings is substantiated by numerous studies. Better schools have higher persistence rates (fewer dropouts) and higher student achievement. Both of these schooling outcomes have been shown to be related to higher earnings or greater economic opportunity. Even when adjustments are made for individual ability and other intervening influences, the payoffs from schooling persist. Also, studies that have related school expenditures to student earnings support the view that investment in the quality of schooling is likely to improve individuals' productive capacities and earnings opportunities. While there are differences between studies in their findings on the relative magnitude of the schooling-earnings effect, virtually all studies on the subject, nevertheless, acknowledge a significant connection. There are probably few social science hypotheses that have been tested so intensively and produced such consistent findings. . . .

[As Horace Mann said,] "Education prevents being poor." . . . [On the basis of such evidence, we] contend that under present circumstances the general tendency is for children from wealthy homes to have high-quality educational services available to them, whereas their peers from less fortunate circumstances have access only to low-quality educational services.

# C. Are There Intellectual Barriers?

## 1.12 INTRODUCTION

Our pluralistic society comprises citizens with a wide variety of cultural backgrounds, and we know that cultures and languages differ greatly. To emphasize this point, we open Section C with Dorothy Seymour's "Black Children, Black Speech."

We also know that most people like to think of themselves and their own culture as superior to all others, even though such attitudes seldom bear close scrutiny. A generation ago, J. B. S. Haldane stated the predominant scientific view on the subject with the following example:

> We are so accustomed to hearing of the superiority of Europeans that it is perhaps worth quoting from the [Black] Moorish writer, Said of Toledo, when Toledo was in Moorish hands. Describing the people who lived north of the Pyrenees, he said: "They are of cold temperament and never reach maturity. They are of great stature and of a white color. But they lack all sharpness of wit and penetration of intellect." We must remember that seven hundred years ago such a point of view had at least an empirical justification, for at that time trigonometry was being studied in Toledo, while in Europe a man was regarded as learned if he had got as far as the fifth proposition of the First Book of Euclid.[1]

In twentieth century America, whites have found equally good reasons to assert their superiority. It was a fact that the I.Q. tests administered in World War II showed that Blacks scored on the average about 15 points lower than whites. And this was interpreted to mean that Blacks naturally (i.e., genetically) lacked the ability to reason or to comprehend.[2]

However, "average" is a very tricky word, and we must use it cautiously. Recall the elderly judge who, on his retirement, bragged, "During my twenty-five years on the bench, I have sent to the gallows about twenty men who should have been set free. But, on the other hand, during this same period I set free another twenty men who should have been sent to the gallows. So, *on the average*, my judgment has been quite fair."

[1] J. B. S. Haldane, *Heredity and Politics*, New York: Norton, 1938, pp. 138–139.
[2] Carleton Putnam, *Race and Reality*, Washington, D.C.: Public Affairs Press, 1967.

When we examine the I.Q. scores of *all* Black Americans examined in World War II, we find indeed that they *average* about fifteen points below other groups. But when we study the average I.Q. scores of Negro children in Northern cities whose parents had migrated from the South to the North, we find that their average I.Q. scores have gone up about ten points in twenty years.[3]

But after lying dormant for ten or fifteen years, the argument that whites are genetically superior to Blacks in intellectual ability has again become a topic for discussion. The selection by Lee Edson, "What is 'Jensenism'?" tells how the debate made headline news. The remaining selections consist of a series of commentaries on the issue.

[3] For further treatment of this point, read Allison Davis, "Cultural Factors in Remediation," in *The Body of Knowledge Unique to the Profession of Education*, Wilma A. Bailey (ed.), Washington, D.C.: Pi Lambda Theta, 1966; Otto Klineberg, "Negro-White Differences in Intelligence Test Performances," *American Psychologist* 18: 198–203, April 1963 (good bibliography).

# 1.13 BLACK CHILDREN, BLACK SPEECH
## Dorothy Z. Seymour

"Cmon, man, les git goin'!" called the boy to his companion. "Dat bell ringin'. It say, 'Git in rat now!' " He dashed into the school yard.

"Aw, f'get you," replied the other. "Whe' Richuh? Whe' da' muvvah? He be goin' to schoo'."

"He in de' now, man!" was the answer as they went through the door.

In the classroom they made for their desks and opened their books. The name of the story they tried to read was "Come." It went:

Come, Bill, come.
Come with me.
Come and see this.
See what is here.

Dorothy Z. Seymour, "Black Children, Black Speech," *Commonweal* 95: 175–178, November 19, 1971. By permission of *Commonweal*.

Dorothy Z. Seymour is an editorial specialist in linguistics for an educational publisher.

See also "Postscript on Black English" in *The History of English Syntax* by Elizabeth Closs Traugott, New York: Holt, Rinehart and Winston, Inc., 1972, pp. 187–198; J. L. Dillard, *Black English: Its History and Usage in the United States*, New York: Random House, Inc., 1972.

The first boy poked the second. "Wha da' wor'?"
"Da' wor' *is,* you dope."
"*Is?* Ain't no wor' *is.* You jivin' me? Wha' da' wor' mean?"
"Ah dunno. Jus' *is.*"

To a speaker of Standard English, this exchange is only vaguely comprehensible. But it's normal speech for thousands of American children. In addition it demonstrates one of our biggest educational problems: children whose speech style is so different from the writing style of their books that they have difficulty learning to read. These children speak Black English, a dialect characteristic of many inner-city Negroes. Their books are, of course, written in Standard English. To complicate matters, the speech they use is also socially stigmatized. Middle-class whites and Negroes alike scorn it as low-class poor people's talk.

Teachers sometimes make the situation worse with their attitudes toward Black English. Typically, they view the children's speech as "bad English" characterized by "lazy pronunciation," "poor grammar," and "short, jagged words." One result of this attitude is poor mental health on the part of the pupils. A child is quick to grasp the feeling that while school speech is "good," his own speech is "bad," and that by extension he himself is somehow inadequate and without value. Some children react to this feeling by withdrawing; they stop talking entirely. Others develop the attitude of "F'get you, honky." In either case, the psychological results are devastating and lead straight to the dropout route.

It is hard for most teachers and middle-class Negro parents to accept the idea that Black English is not just "sloppy talk" but a dialect with a form and structure of its own. Even some eminent black educators think of it as "bad English grammar" with "slurred consonants" (Professor Nick Aaron Ford of Morgan State College in Baltimore) and "ghettoese" (Dr. Kenneth B. Clark, the prominent educational psychologist).

Parents of Negro school children generally agree. Two researchers at Columbia University report that the adults they worked with in Harlem almost unanimously preferred that their children be taught Standard English in school.

But there is another point of view, one held in common by black militants and some white liberals. They urge that middle-class Negroes stop thinking of the inner-city dialect as something to be ashamed of and repudiated. Black author Claude Brown, for example, pushes this view.

Some modern linguists take a similar stance. They begin with the premise that no dialect is intrinsically "bad" or "good," and that a non-standard speech style is not defective speech but different speech. More important, they have been able to show that Black English is far from being a careless way of speaking the Standard; instead, it is a rather rigidly-constructed set of speech patterns, with the same sort of specialization in sounds, structure, and vocabulary as any other dialect.

## The Sounds of Black English

Middle class listeners who hear black inner-city speakers say "dis" and "tin" for "this" and "thin" assume that the black speakers are just being careless. Not at all; these differences are characteristic aspects of the dialect. The original cause of such substitutions is generally a carryover from one's original language or that of his immigrant parents. The interference from that carryover probably caused the substitution of /d/ for the voiced *th* sound in *this*, and /t/ for the unvoiced *th* sound in *thin*. (Linguists represent language sounds by putting letters within slashes or brackets.) Most speakers of English don't realize that the two *th* sounds of English are lacking in many other languages and are difficult for most foreigners trying to learn English. Germans who study English, for example, are surprised and confused about these sounds because the only Germans who use them are the ones who lisp. These two sounds are almost nonexistent in the West African languages which most black immigrants brought with them to America.

Similar substitutions used in Black English are /f/, a sound similar to the unvoiced *th,* in medial word-position, as in *birfday* for *birthday*, and in final word-position, as in *roof* for *Ruth* as well as /v/ for the voiced *th* in medial position, as in *bruvver* for *brother*. These sound substitutions are also typical of Gullah, the language of black speakers in the Carolina Sea Islands. Some of them are also heard in Caribbean Creole.

Another characteristic of the sounds of Black English is the lack of /l/ at the end of words, sometimes replaced by the sound /w/. This makes word like *tool* sound like *too*. If /l/ occurs in the middle of a Standard English word, in Black English it may be omitted entirely: "I can hep you." This difference is probably caused by the instability and sometimes interchangeability of /l/ and /r/ in West African languages.

One difference that is startling to middle-class speakers is the fact that Black English words appear to leave off some consonant sounds at the end of words. Like Italian, Japanese and West African words, they are more likely to end in vowel sounds. Standard English *boot* is pronounced *boo* in Black English. *What* is *wha*. *Sure* is *sho*. *Your* is *yo*. This kind of difference can make for confusion in the classroom. Dr. Kenneth Goodman, a psycholinguist, tells of a black child whose white teacher asked him to use *so* in a sentence—not "sew a dress" but "the other *so*." The sentence the child used was "I got a *so* on my leg."

A related feature of Black English is the tendency in many cases not to use sequences of more than one final consonant sound. For example, *just* is pronounced *jus'*, *past* is *pass, mend* sounds like *men* and *hold* like *hole. Six* and *box* are pronounced *sick* and *bock*. Why should this be? Perhaps because West African languages, like Japanese, have almost no clusters of consonants in their speech. The Japanese, when importing a foreign word, handle a similar problem by inserting vowel sounds between every consonant, making *baseball* sound like *besuboru*. West Africans probably made a simpler change, merely cutting a series of two consonant sounds down to one. Speakers of

Gullah, one linguist found, have made the same kind of adaptation of Standard English.

Teachers of black children seldom understand the reason for these differences in final sounds. They are apt to think that careless speech is the cause. Actually, black speakers aren't "leaving off" any sounds; how can you leave off something you never had in the first place?

Differences in vowel sounds are also characteristic of the non-standard language. Dr. Goodman reports that a black child asked his teacher how to spell rat. "R-a-t," she replied. But the boy responded "No ma'am, I don't mean rat mouse, I mean rat now." In Black English, *right* sounds like *rat*. A likely reason is that in West African languages, there are very few vowel sounds of the type heard in the word *right*. This type is common in English. It is called a glided or dipthongized vowel sound. A glided vowel sound is actually a close combination of two vowels; in the word *right* the two parts of the sound "eye" are actually "ah-ee." West African languages have no such long, two-part, changing vowel sounds; their vowels are generally shorter and more stable. This may be why in Black English, *time* sounds like *Tom, oil* like *all*, and *my* like *ma*.

## Language Structure

Black English differs from Standard English not only in its sounds but also in its structure. The way the words are put together does not always fit the description in English grammar books. The method of expressing time, or tense, for example, differs in significant ways.

The verb *to be* is an important one in Standard English. It's used as an auxiliary verb to indicate different tenses. But Black English speakers use it quite differently. Sometimes an inner-city Negro says "He coming"; other times he says "He be coming." These two sentences mean different things. To understand why, let's look at the tenses of West African languages; they correspond with those of Black English.

Many West African languages have a tense which is called the habitual. This tense is used to express action that is always occurring, and it is formed with a verb that is translated as *be*. "He be coming" means something like "He's always coming," "He usually comes," or "He's been coming."

In Standard English there is no regular grammatical construction for such a tense. Black English speakers, in order to form the habitual tense in English, use the word *be* as an auxiliary: *He be doing it. My Momma be working. He be running.* The habitual tense is not the same as the present tense, which is constructed in Black English without any form of the verb *to be*: *He do it. My Momma working. He running.* (This means the action is occurring right now.)

There are other tense differences between Black English and Standard English. For example, the nonstandard speech does not use changes in grammar to indicate the past tense. A white person will ask, "What did your brother say?" and the black person will answer, "He say he coming." "How did you get here?" "I walk." This style of talking about the past is paralleled in the Yoruba, Fante, Hausa, and Ewe languages of West Africa.

Expression of plurality is another difference. The way a black child will talk of "them boy" or "two dog" makes some white listeners think Negroes don't know how to turn a singular word into a plural word. As a matter of fact, it isn't necessary to use an s to express plurality. For example, in Chinese it's correct to say "There are three book on the table." This sentence already has two signals of the plural, *three* and *are*; why require a third? This same logic is the basis of plurals in most West African languages, where nouns are often identical in the plural and the singular. For example, in Ibo, one correctly says *those man*, and in both Ewe and Yoruba one says *they house*. American speakers of Gullah retain this style; they say *five dog*.

Gender is another aspect of language structure where differences can be found. Speakers of Standard English are often confused to find that the nonstandard vernacular often uses just one gender of pronoun, the masculine, and refers to women as well as men as *he* or *him*. "He a nice girl" and even "Him a nice girl" are common. This usage probably stems from West African origins too, as does the use of multiple negatives such as "Nobody don't know it."

Vocabulary is the third aspect of a person's native speech that could affect his learning of a new language. The strikingly different vocabulary often used in Negro Nonstandard English is probably the most obvious aspect of it to a casual white observer. But its vocabulary differences don't obscure its meaning the way different sounds and different structure often do.

Recently there has been much interest in the African origins of words like *goober* (peanut), *cooter* (turtle), and *tote* (carry), as well as others that are less certainly African, such as *to dig* (possibly from the Wolof *degan*, "to understand"). Such expressions seem colorful rather than low-class to many whites; they become assimilated faster than their black originators do. English professors now use *dig* in their scholarly articles, and current advertising has enthusiastically adopted *rap*.

Is it really possible for old differences in sound, structure, and vocabulary to persist from the West African languages of slave days into present-day inner city Black English? Easily. Nothing else really explains such regularity of language habits, most of which persist among black people in various parts of the Western Hemisphere. For a long time scholars believed that certain speech forms used by Negroes were merely leftovers from archaic English preserved in the speech of early English settlers in America and copied by their slaves. But this theory has been greatly weakened, largely as the result of the work of a black linguist, Dr. Lorenzo Dow Turner of the University of Chicago. Dr. Turner studied the speech of Gullah Negroes in the Sea Islands off the Carolina coast and found so many traces of West African languages that he thoroughly discredited the archaic-English theory.

When anyone learns a new language, it's usual to try speaking the new language with the sounds and structure of the old. If a person's first language does not happen to have a particular sound needed in the language he is learning, he will tend to substitute a similar or related sound from his native language and use it to speak the new one. When Frenchman Charles Boyer said "Zees ees my heart," and when Latin American Carmen Miranda sang "Souse American way," they were simply using sounds of their native languages in trying to pronounce sounds of English. West Africans must have done the same thing when they first attempted English words. The tendency to retain the structure of the native language is a strong one, too. That's why a German learning English is likely to put his verb at the end: "May I a glass beer have?" The vocabulary of one's original language may also furnish some holdovers. Jewish immigrants did not stop using the word *bagel* when they came to America; nor did Germans stop saying *sauerkraut.*

Social and geographical isolation reinforces the tendencies to retain old language habits. When one group is considered inferior, the other group avoids it. For many years it was illegal to give any sort of instruction to Negroes, and for slaves to try to speak like their masters would have been unthinkable. Conflict of value systems doubtless retards changes, too. As Frantz Fanon observed in *Black Skin, White Masks*, those who take on white speech habits are suspect in the ghetto, because others believe they are trying to "act white." Dr. Kenneth Johnson, a black linguist, put it this way: "As long as disadvantaged black children live in segregated communities and most of their relationships are confined to those within their own subculture, they will not replace their functional nonstandard dialect with the nonfunctional standard dialect."

Linguists have made it clear that language systems that are different are not necessarily deficient. A judgment of deficiency can be made only in comparison with another language system. Let's turn the tables on Standard English for a moment and look at it from the West African point of view. From this angle, Standard English: (1) is lacking in certain language sounds, (2) has a couple of unnecessary language sounds for which others may serve as good substitutes, (3) doubles and drawls some of its vowel sounds in sequences that are unusual and difficult to imitate, (5) lacks a method of forming an important tense, (6) requires an unnecessary number of ways to indicate tense, plurality and gender, and (7) doesn't mark negatives sufficiently for the result to be a good strong negative statement.

Now whose language is deficient?

How would the adoption of this point of view help us? Say we accepted the evidence that Black English is not just a sloppy Standard but an organized language style which probably has developed many of its features on the basis of its West African heritage. What would we gain?

The psychological climate of the classroom might improve if teachers understood why many black students speak as they do. But we still have not reached a solution of the main problem. Does the discovery that Black English has pattern and structure mean that it should not be tampered with? Should children who speak Black English be excused from learning the Standard in school? Should they perhaps be given books in Black English to learn from?

Any such accommodation would surely result in a hardening of the new separatism being urged by some black militants. It would probably be applauded by such people as Roy Innis, Director of C.O.R.E., who is currently recommending dual autonomous education systems for white and black. And it might facilitate learning to read, since some experiments have indicated that materials written in Black English syntax aid problem readers from the inner city.

But determined resistance to the introduction of such printed materials into schools can be expected. To those who view inner-city speech as bad English, the appearance in print of sentences like "My mama, he work" can be as shocking and repellent as a four-letter word. Middle-class Negro parents would probably mobilize against the move. Any stratagem that does not take into account such practicalities of the matter is probably doomed to failure. And besides, where would such a permissive policy on language get these children in the larger society, and in the long run? If they want to enter an integrated America they must be able to deal with it on its own terms. Even Professor Toni Cade of Rutgers, who doesn't want "ghetto accents" tampered with, advocates mastery of Standard English because, as she puts it, "if you want to get ahead in this country, you must master the language of the ruling class." This has always been true, wherever there has been a minority group.

The problem then appears to be one of giving these children the ability to speak (and read) Standard English without denigrating the vernacular and those who use it, or even affecting the ability to use it. The only way to do this is to officially espouse bi-dialectism. The result would be the ability to use either dialect equally well—as Dr. Martin Luther King did—depending on the time, place, and circumstances. Pupils would have to learn enough about Standard English to use it when necessary, and teachers would have to learn enough about the inner-city dialect to understand and accept it for what it is—not just a "careless" version of Standard English but a different form of English that's appropriate in certain times and places.

Can we accomplish this? If we can't, the result will be continued alienation of a large section of the population, continued dropout trouble with consequent loss of earning power and economic contribution to the nation, but most of all, loss of faith in America as a place where a minority people can at times continue to use those habits that remind them of their link with each other and with their past.[1]

---

[1] EDITOR'S NOTE: Every language contains many subtleties of voice, tense, pronunciation, and grammatical structure, and we are almost totally ignorant of the manner in which children come to understand these subtleties. Hence, says Charles Read:

To attribute the children's accomplishment *a priori* to exceptional general intelligence or an exceptional environment merely begs the important question. The children had tacitly acquired a knowledge of phonological relations of which their parents [and teachers] were themselves unaware. What the children had learned was not related in any obvious way to what they had heard or seen. The important theoretical question is how pre-school children can learn abstract relations of this sort. Until we have serious evidence bearing on this question, we can not assume that general intelligence must be the major factor in acquiring the knowledge that makes spelling possible. . . . Whatever variations there may be in individual development, the crucial conclusion remains that children can (and to some degree, must) make abstract inferences about the sound system of their language before they learn to read and write.

The educational importance of this conclusion seems clear enough, at least in general. We can no longer assume that a child must approach reading and writing as an untrained animal approaches a maze—with no discernible prior conception of its structure. We can not asssume, in the essentially digestive metaphor that Paulo Freire rightly ridicules, that the child is an empty vessel, mentally inert although physically so dynamic, waiting to be filled with adult spellings. Evidently, a child may come to school with a knowledge of some phonological categories and relations; without conscious awareness, he may seek to relate English spelling to these in some generally systematic way. If this inference is correct, some long-neglected questions turn out to be crucial for understanding and facilitating the process of learning to read: what levels of phonological analysis do individual children tacitly control at various stages of development; how do these analyses relate to the lexical representations that generally correspond to standard spelling; and how can reading instruction build on this relationship, while encouraging children to extend and deepen their notion of the sound system of the language? Detailed answers to these questions are not at all obvious; in fact, it is difficult to devise means of acquiring some answers, since children's [thought processes are not directly observable.]"—Charles Read (University of Wisconsin), "Pre-School Children's Knowledge of English Phonology," *Harvard Educational Review* 41: 32–33, February 1971. Copyright © 1971 by President and fellows of Harvard College.

In a study confined to British *whites*, Basil Bernstein compared children from upper class homes with children from lower class homes, and found that children from these two occupational and social classes employed two forms or types of language. One form is called *restricted* and the other form is called *elaborated*. . . . A child who has learned a restricted language at home is likely to have difficulty in school, where an *elaborate* language is used and taught by the teacher; and the difficulty of the child is likely to increase as he goes further in school, unless he learns the elaborate language that is expected in the school. On the other hand, the child who had had experience with an elaborate language from his earliest years has a relatively easy time in school, because he must simply go on developing the kind of language and related thinking which he has already started.

See Basil Bernstein, "Language and Social Class," *British Journal of Sociology* 11: 271–276, 1960; "Social Class and Linguistic Development: A Theory of Learning," in A. H. Halsey, J. Floud, and C. A. Anderson, eds., *Economy, Education and Society*, New York: The Free Press (Crowell-Collier and Macmillan, Inc.), 1961, pp. 288ff.; "Social Class, Linguistic Codes and Grammatical Elements," *Language and Speech* 5: 221–240, October–December 1962.

Here is a brief summary of Bernstein's views by Stones:

Bernstein considers the language of the . . . [culturally deprived] family a linguistically *restricted code*. He considers that of the middle class an *elaborated code*. He suggests the main attributes of the restricted code are its syntactical crudity, its repetitiveness, its rigid and limited use of adjectives and adverbs, short, grammatically simple, often unfinished sentences, and above all, much of the meaning is implicit and dependent upon a commonly held system of speech habits.

The elaborated code is a much more flexible instrument. It has an accurate grammar and syntax. It employs a range of subordinate clauses unknown to the restricted code. It makes much more widespread and flexible use of conjunctions, prepositions, adjectives, and adverbs. It is much more discriminating and it has a much greater potentiality of abstraction. It also differs from the restricted code in that the pronoun *I* is used frequently, reinforcing the personal and individual nature of the language.

Bernstein illustrates the nature of the restricted code for the learning child. He gives an imaginary example of two conversations on a bus. A mother has a child sitting on her lap.

First conversation: [restricted code]
Mother:   Hold on tight.
Child:   Why?
Mother:   Hold on tight.
Child:   Why?
Mother:   You'll fall.
Child:   Why?
Mother:   I told you to hold on tight, didn't I?

Second conversation: [elaborated code]
Mother:   Hold on tightly, darling.
Child:   Why?
Mother:   If you don't you will be thrown forward and you'll fall.
Child:   Why?
Mother:   Because if the bus suddenly stops you'll jerk forward on to the seat in front.
Child:   Why?
Mother:   Now darling, hold on tightly and don't make such a fuss.

As can be seen in the restricted code the symbolic function is slight; the words have little more than signal significance. . . . Later, when he enters school, the language of the [culturally disadvantaged] child acts as a filter to restrict what gets through from the teacher (an elaborated code user) to the elements of the restricted code.

Following from this Bernstein concludes that the problems facing a . . . [culturally deprived] child in a school situation aimed at improving his language skills will be very different from that of a middle-class child. The latter has merely to *develop* his linguistic skills, the former has to *change* them. This makes it extremely difficult for the user of a restricted code to schematize the learning he is asked to make, since it is presented in the unfamiliar forms of the elaborated code.

—E. Stones, *An Introduction to Educational Psychology,* London: Methuen & Company, Ltd., 1966, pp. 186–187. By permission of Methuen & Company, London.
    E. Stones is Lecturer in Educational Psychology at the University of Birmingham.

# 1.14 WHAT IS "JENSENISM"?
## Lee Edson

[In February, 1969, the] *Harvard Educational Review*, a 30-year-old scholarly journal published by Harvard graduate students, came out with an article by Jensen entitled: "How Much Can We Boost I.Q. and Scholastic Achievement?" The detailed scientific paper, the longest ever printed in the review, begins with an appraisal of the alleged failure of compensatory education programs such as Head Start, a project to help preschool ghetto youngsters overcome years of cultural deprivation in order to catch up with middle-class youngsters in school readiness. The article goes on to state that these programs seek, in effect, to raise children's academic achievement by increasing their I.Q.'s. Jensen then examines the entire concept of the I.Q.: "what makes it vary from one individual to another; what can change it, and by what amount." In the process he says that Negroes as a group—as opposed to any single individual Negro—test out poorly compared with whites or Orientals on that aspect of general intelligence that involves abstract reasoning and problem-solving. And he adds that this ability (which he equates with the ability measured by I.Q. tests) is largely inherited, a matter of genes and brain structure, and therefore no amount of compensatory education or forced exposure to culture is going to improve it substantially.

Jensen emphasizes in his article, that the "particular constellation of abilities we call 'intelligence,' and which we can measure by means of 'intelligence' tests," is only a part of the whole spectrum of human abilities—and that it "has been singled out from the total galaxy of mental abilities as being especially important in our society mainly because of the nature of our traditional system of formal education and the occupational structure with which it is coordinated." He points out that, "as far as we know, the full range of human talents is represented in all the major races of man." But such statements did little to lessen the impact of the article's conclusions about I.Q. and race. The magazine had hardly hit the academic mailboxes when a sound truck manned by members of the Students for a Democratic Society roared through the Berkeley campus, blaring: "Fight racism. Fire Jensen." Jensen's normally sparse scholarly mail grew fat with hate literature. He was accused

Lee Edson (journalist), "Jensenism–the Theory that I.Q. is Largely Determined by the Genes," *New York Times Magazine*, August 31, 1969. © 1969–1972 by the New York Times Company. Reprinted by permission.

This short summary by Edson should be supplemented by reading the original Jensen article and various reactions to it in the *Harvard Educational Review*, Vol. 39, No. 1 and No. 2, Winter and Spring 1969. Both issues are now combined as a special issue.

Arthur Robert Jensen is Professor of Psychology, University of California, Berkeley.

of being a fascist, a white supremacist, of having black ancestry and hating it. He received postcards emblazoned with the Nazi swastika; one had a single hand-scrawled word: "Death." A group of aroused left-wing students invaded his classroom and he had to lecture in secret locations; crank callers engaged him on the phone, and he was forced to summon the Berkeley campus security forces to protect his files from being raided. At night the lights burned bright in his office to discourage looters. One fearful assistant quit her job.

In the academic and political worlds the furor has become ever more intense. Not since Darwin's theory of evolution, as one writer put it, has so much fiery discussion and violent opposition been generated over a treatise. A Congressman put all 123 pages of the article into the Congressional Record, and segregationists took to citing the article in court as the word of science. Lengthy reviews of the article were printed almost everywhere in intellectual circles. At Columbia University's Teachers College the article became required reading in some classes, and at the University of Minnesota a psychology professor, in as irrelevant a reaction as one could find, offered $100 to anyone who could predict a man's intelligence by looking at his features. . . .

Jensen concentrated at first on individual differences in verbal learning in college students, but in 1962 he became interested in testing children. He developed a series of tests which could be used in any language, directed at discovering how fast children learn. He tested Mexican-American youngsters and then went on to test Negro and white children in Oakland, Richmond and other Bay Area cities. He found that he was measuring two different sets of learning abilities—what he now calls Level 1, associative learning, and Level 2, conceptual learning and problem-solving ability. The first ability involves simply the retention of input and the capacity to repeat it; the second involves the student's ability to manipulate and transform material.

For example, one of Jensen's Level 1 tests is made up of a series of pictures of common objects (or the objects themselves in miniature) which the child is asked to recall by name after they're shown one by one and removed from sight. Negroes and whites who may differ in I.Q. by as much as 20 points score equally on this test. In a Level 2 test, the examiner groups the different objects in categories—say, furniture, animals, clothing and food. Then he mixes them again and they are presented in random order, one at a time. After the child has seen all the objects again, he is asked to name as many as he can remember. This is done a number of times. The white children catch on and soon recall the objects by their categories; they call them off in groups and thus remember more individual objects. The Negro children by and large don't do this, or they group the objects on a functional basis; they relate apples and horses for instance. They fail to make use of the group concept as a memory device, but call off the objects more or less in the order they saw them, and they don't remember as many.

In the first and second grades there is no significant difference in the amount of recall or in the amount of "clustering," as it is called, but in the fourth and fifth grades the difference appears and Negro children in general start to fall behind white children as the conceptual material gets more difficult. In short, Jensen concludes that Level 1 ability is distributed about equally in all races while Level 2 is distributed unevenly. Jensen contends that for Level 2 abilities to develop requires not merely learning ability but also certain inherited neural structures in the brain. "Without them, the learning of abstract concepts doesn't develop," he says.

Jensen drew this conclusion slowly. In the tests themselves, he made sure that the children knew the names of each object and each category. He also investigated the role of motivation and found that both Negro and white children do better when well motivated but not enough better to change the scores significantly. (Oriental children, incidentally, stay the same; they are apparently already motivated to do their best.)

Jensen found that scores on the category lists correlated with I.Q. differences among the youngsters. He concluded that Level 2 is "pretty much what we mean by I.Q."

Then Jensen reviewed all the published papers dealing with genetic differences. He found Burt's study on twins and was amazed at the lack of attention given to it by social scientists in America. . . . Psychologist Sir Cyril Burt and geneticist J. A. Shields studied 100 pairs of identical twins in England who were reared apart from each other. It was found that the separated twins were, on the average, only six points apart in I.Q. By contrast, any two people in the total population, chosen at random, will be on the average 18 points apart. Nonidentical siblings reared in the same household are on the average 12 I.Q. points apart.

"If you look at studies of adopted children," Jensen says, "you find that their intelligence relates more closely to their natural parents than to their adoptive parents. And if you add this to 100 other twin and kinship studies over the last 25 years over four continents and a wide range of environmental conditions, you have a strong body of evidence for the heritability of I.Q. In short, the closer people are related, the more similar are their I.Q.'s."

The second line of evidence of the heritability of intelligence, Jensen says, comes from the studies of the relationship between intelligence and socioeconomic status dating back to the work of Alfred Binet 70 years ago. We know that people in the upper classes generally have higher I.Q.'s than those in lower classes. Some people like to read an environmental cause into this. But, in fact, studies indicate otherwise. Regardless of the social class in which an adopted child is reared, for example, the child's I.Q. will correlate better with that of his natural parents than that of his adoptive parents. If a child's natural parents have high I.Q.'s it is most likely that he will also have a high I.Q. even if he is raised by low-I.Q., lower-class adoptive parents. The environment is not the deciding factor.

How does all this evidence tie up with racial differences? "First," Jensen says, "it should be noted that race is not an abstract Platonic essence—it is actually a 'breeding population,' as the geneticists term it; the population is not closed, but there is a well-known probability of greater mating within this population than outside it. As a result, the frequency of genes for white skin or dark skin differs in the different groups. It is true that there are extremely few if any Negroes of pure African descent in the United States today; but this doesn't change the genetic analysis of a particular population or affect the opportunity to study it by methods that have worked in other genetic fields."

Social scientists have been studying racial differences for many years, Jensen says, citing some 400 major studies. "All of them point out—unhappily perhaps—that in the standard distribution of I.Q. throughout the population the Negro is 15 points lower than the white. Only 3 per cent of the Negro population exceed an I.Q. of 115; in the white population 16 per cent exceed 115. In the white population 1 per cent exceed 140; a sixth of that exceed 140 in the Negro population. A similar percentage prevails at the lower end of the distribution. In fact it may even be worse in the retarded area. A long-term study by researchers at Johns Hopkins, conducted in one rural county of Maryland, showed that 31 per cent of the Negro males tested between the ages of 40 and 44 were mentally retarded—that is, they had I.Q.'s under 70. This was true of only 1.5 per cent of the tested white males of the same age."

Jensen asks: "Is this genetic in origin or caused by environment? I think it must be genetic to a very large extent. When you control samples of white and black population for social class differences, you still have major differences in I.Q. between them—from 15 points on the average to 11 points over the various social classes. In other words, across the same occupational category and income bracket, you still find this striking fact—children of Negroes in the highest income class of our society will average lower in I.Q. than white children of the lowest class; this is backed up by a great deal of data, including that obtained in studies conducted by the Federal Government. You couldn't predict such results from purely environmental theory, and it would be highly improbable to assume that the entire influence was due to subtle factors of early prenatal and postnatal environment. It is more likely—though speculative of course—that Negroes brought here as slaves were selected for docility and strength rather than mental ability, and that through selective mating the mental qualities never had a chance to flourish.

"In the famous Coleman study, the American Indians come out lower on all environmental indices than do American Negroes; yet the Indians score higher on I.Q. and scholastic achievement. So do disadvantaged children of the island of Taiwan. In fact, they do as well as children of white middle-class parents in the United States.

"Remember—we're talking of populations here, not of individuals. There are Negro geniuses, and certainly many greatly talented figures among Negroes, and race should not stand in the way of hiring, promotions or providing awards. But in large groups, one is compelled to say that on the basis of these studies improved environment is not likely to change the fundamental intelligence of large groups of individuals to a substantial extent—no matter how romantic the environmentalists want to be."

Jensen grants that some extremely deprived children can have their I.Q.'s raised by markedly changing their environment. He mentions the classic and dramatic case of Isabel, studied by Kingsley Davis of the University of California. An illegitimate child, she was reared for her first six years in a dark attic by a deaf-mute mother. When found, she was unable to speak, and tests showed that she had an idiot's mentality. But in two years in a good home with lots of attention her mental age jumped up to the average of her age group, and she could perform normally in school. But, as Jensen points out, her I.Q. didn't increase further than this average value. "You can boost an I.Q. in an enriched environment, but once its genetic potential is achieved —once the threshold environment capacity is reached—you cannot improve I.Q. any further. I am afraid there is nothing you can do to create an Einstein without the right kind of genes."

# 1.15 INTELLIGENCE AND GENES
## David C. McClelland and Richard J. Light

### McCLELLAND

There has always been a tendency on the part of certain people who are good at manipulating symbols to use this capacity to exclude other people from positions of power in society. For example, to insure their dominant position, the Chinese intelligentsia invented a language, Mandarin Chinese, that could be learned by only a very small part of the population. . . .

At one time, in order to get into the Chinese civil service, a person had to pass some extremely rigorous and extensive examinations. Of course, only

This selection consists of two excerpts. The first is by David C. McClelland, "I.Q. Testing and Assessing Competence." This article first appeared in *The Humanist*, January–February 1972. The second is from Richard J. Light, "Intelligence and Genes," and appeared in the same issue of *The Humanist*. Both are reprinted by permission.

David C. McClelland, Professor of Psychology in the Department of Social Relations at Harvard University, is the author of *The Achieving Society* (1961, 1967), and with W. G. Winter of *Motivating Economic Achievement* (1969).

Richard J. Light is Associate Professor, Laboratory of Human Development, Harvard Graduate School of Education. He is also Assistant Director of the Institute of Politics, John F. Kennedy School of Government at Harvard, and Chairman of a Faculty Study Group on Statistical Methods for Educational Evaluation.

See also Jerome Kagan, "The Magical Aura of the IQ," *Saturday Review*, 54: 92–93, December 4, 1971.

certain people in certain families had the leisure time necessary to learn the rules of the games being tested and to develop their playing skills. In our own society, the so-called intelligence movement has been extended to an extraordinary number of things. We demand good performance on similar tests as an important qualification for all sorts of jobs and positions. Consequently, we also discriminate against people who haven't had the chance to learn the games that have been selected. We can look at this practically, moreover, and ask the businessman's utilitarian question: "So what, so if you play chess and these other wonderful games so beautifully—what does that mean? What else can you do?" As far as I can determine, the justification for the use of the tests is almost completely circular. There is no evidence that they predict anything more useful than one's ability to take other intelligence tests. Yes, they may also predict grades, but grades, of course, involve the same kinds of tests. I'd like to give a simple example of how the system works.

I have been serving as a member of a governor's commission appointed to deal with the problem of discrimination in the civil service of Massachusetts. To determine a person's qualifications for a job in the civil service, Massachusetts uses an intelligence-scholastic-aptitude type of test for all positions except maybe that of janitor. We have been especially concerned with the one that must be passed to become a policeman. An applicant has to play the analogies game; a typical item is the following: "Lexicon is to dictionary as policeman is to (check one of the four alternatives)." Now in order to qualify to be a cop, you have to score 70 on this test. (Where they get the number 70, I don't know, and they don't know. It's just one of those games that they play.) But if you're a black resident of Roxbury, chances are you haven't been exposed to words like "pyromaniac," "lexicon," and so on. There are several consequences of this simple fact.

First, by definition, a person is less intelligent if he can't play the game these people have made up. He doesn't know the words or the rules. Second, as a result, the person naturally doesn't qualify to be a cop or anything else in Massachusetts, and there is therefore a high and significant correlation between intelligence and occupational level. We've all seen tables showing that people in lower occupations have lower I.Q. scores, while those in higher occupations have higher scores. This guy who can't be a policeman because he can't play the I.Q.-test game is contributing to those tables. He can't do the intelligence test, so all he can be is a janitor, whereas people who play the games well can become policemen and enter higher-level jobs. The test itself thus becomes part of an élitist mechanism to discriminate against the disadvantaged.[1]

---

[1] EDITOR'S NOTE: For a 75-year history of tests and a defense of the view that they have been used to benefit the advantaged and to control the disadvantaged, read Clarence J. Karier, "Testing for Order and Control in the Corporate Liberal State," *Educational Theory* 22: 154–180, Spring 1972.

## LIGHT

At least three questions generally arise in discussions of I.Q. tests. One is precisely what such tests measure. A second is how social stratification is related to I.Q. scores, and what are the consequences of these relationships. The third question—the one I intend to focus on here—concerns the potential role of genetic differentiation in I.Q.'s within and between social groups.

In 1925, Karl Pearson, one of Britain's most creative and methodologically sophisticated statisticians, wrote about Jewish immigrants: "Taken on the average, and regarding both sexes, this alien Jewish population is somewhat inferior both physically and mentally to the native population." The context of Pearson's assertion was that this alleged inferiority was genetic. In both America and Britain today, however, it is quite well known that Jews score as high on intelligence tests as the majority non-Jewish population.

Prior to 1960, Catholics in America scored lower than non-Catholics on standardized intelligence tests. In the 1930's, a genetic explanation was put forth to account for the observed differences. Since 1960, however, the distribution of intelligence-test scores for American Catholics has duplicated the non-Catholic score distribution almost exactly.

These two historical examples illustrate that a genetic explanation for differences of intelligence-test scores between social groups can be mistaken.

Consider now two research findings relating genes and intelligence. First, there exist four studies of identical twins reared apart—one conducted in America, two in England, and one in Denmark. These four studies, involving a total of 122 twin pairs, showed essentially that identical twins reared apart had much more similar I.Q. scores than pairs of children selected at random. Since identical twins share the same genes, the studies imply that genetic variation explains some intelligence variation (the data suggest approximately 75 per cent).

A second group of five studies examined pairs of unrelated foster children raised in the same families. They found that a relatively low proportion (approximately 25 per cent) of I.Q.-score variation was explained by environmental factors: Foster children score only slightly closer together than pairs of children selected at random. If pairs of unrelated foster children raised in the same family are presumed to be exposed to similar environments, and if environmental effects are very "important," then I.Q. scores for each pair of these children should be quite close together. They are not.

We thus have two sets of conflicting findings. History tells us that two social groups who at one time had a lower mean I.Q. than that of the "general population" no longer lag behind. More specifically, the genetic explanations for these gaps have been discredited. Yet at the same time, evidence from the twin studies indicates that a large genetic component of intelligence in fact exists. What can we reasonably conclude?

I believe that only three conclusions are warranted. First, intelligence (as measured very specifically by I.Q.-test scores) appears to be somewhat heritable: That is, a genetic component to intelligence exists. Second, we have no way of estimating with reasonable scientific accuracy the true proportion of variation in I.Q. scores explained by genetic factors. The statistical procedures used in the twin studies do not represent intellectual development as a dynamic process, over time, but provide only a snapshot at a single point in time. In addition, it is important to remember that heritability is not a single fixed number for all people, but varies among populations because it depends upon the social structure within the population. Third, any assertion that observed differences between social groups' mean I.Q. scores are largely genetically based simply has no foundation in data.

Why can't the estimate I mention in conclusion two be made more definitively? Because I.Q. tests given to twin pairs, and to children generally, can lead to misestimates of heritability. The additive linear statistical model used to estimate heritability does not allow for changes due to outside stimulative factors in a child's I.Q. performance over time. It simply has no way of detecting such factors. For example, imagine that a mother has two children. Suppose that it was possible to measure their "intelligence genes" at birth, and that child A's genetic I.Q. capacity was 99, and child B's was 101 —a small but real genetic difference. Now, assume that the mother, like many mothers, enjoys interacting with the more verbal, more responsive, "brighter" child. When she talks to this "brighter" child, she is reinforced by his response; he in turn is reinforced by her response; and so on. The opposite happens with the less "bright" child; he is less reinforced. It is then possible that the observed I.Q.'s for these two children when they are, say, six years old will differ by more than two points. In this event, a tiny genetic effect will have been magnified substantially by an environmental effect. Measuring children's I.Q. at a single point in time does not enable us to identify such features of children's growth and development; yet such features probably have an impact upon the formation of intelligence.

Why can't the assertion I refer to in conclusion three be made more definitively? Because the *interaction* between genetic endowments and environments can lead to incorrect explanations of performance differences between social groups. For example, imagine that a large group of fat people and a large group of thin people are born at a certain point in time, and that the two groups have identical distributions of intelligence genes. Suppose also that in general fat people are treated less well than thin people. We may then find such differential treatment reflected in the groups' intelligence scores. Specifically, we may find that fat people have a lower mean I.Q. than thin people. Further, this may be construed as a genetic effect due to fatness or thinness.

But this genetic-difference interpretation would be wrong. What has happened is that a genetic-environmental interaction (the way society reacts to fat people versus thin people) has transformed what is really an environmental factor into a seemingly consistent genetic difference between social groups. Thus, in terms of heritability estimates, the heritability of intelligence might be accurately estimated as high for fat people, high for thin people, and there would still be a difference between the mean I.Q. scores of the two groups.

The implication of these arguments is simply that the development of human intelligence is a complex time-dependent process. We do not understand very well how I.Q. tests reflect a genetic component of intelligence, as any genetic component will interact with a person's environment. Further, differences in I.Q.-score distributions between social groups can be artificially created by the genetic-environmental interaction operating over time. There is an illusory attractiveness in the "simple explanation" that the existence of genetic differences in intelligence *within* social groups implies genetic differences *between* social groups. The difficulty with such simple explanations is that history often proves them wrong. Electrical engineers have found that they need detailed time-dependent models to describe complex circuit and network behavior. Surely we need models at least as sensitive when we try to describe even more complex human behavior.

# 1.16 TREATING INTELLIGENCE TESTS INTELLIGENTLY
## Arthur R. Jensen

## THE CASE FOR I.Q. TESTS

[Many] arguments against I.Q. tests ignore a large number of scientifically established facts. Below I have listed some of these that seem most germane; except the first, all items are amply substantiated by research published in the scientific journals. . . .

Excerpts from "The Case for I.Q. Tests: Reply to [David C.] McClelland" and "The Ethical Issues" by Arthur R. Jensen. These articles first appeared in *The Humanist,* January–February 1972 and are reprinted by permission.

Arthur R. Jensen is Professor of Educational Psychology and Research Psychologist in the Institute of Human Learning, University of California, Berkeley. Selections 1.14–1.18 may be viewed as pro and con responses to his epoch-making article "How Much Can We Boost I.Q. and Scholastic Achievement?" (*Harvard Educational Review* 39: 1–123, 1969). In June 1969, *HER* published a special issue, *Environment, Heredity and Intelligence,* which consists of the lengthy Jensen article, plus seven responses to it, plus a concluding reply by Jensen. This *HER* special issue and the January-February 1972 issue of *The Humanist* are highly recommended as supplementary reading for Section C of Chapter 1.

1. The level of technology needed to maintain the standard of living enjoyed in North America and Europe, given their present populations, demands that a substantial proportion (say, 15 per cent) of the population possess a high level of the kind of mental ability measured by intelligence tests. We could get along without this kind and amount of intelligence in the population only if we drastically reduced population size and returned to a simple agrarian way of life or became hunters and gatherers of food, as in primitive societies. The present population could not be sustained without the technology (food production, transportation, health services, sanitation, and so on) and the kinds of brains needed to maintain it. Thus, to denigrate intelligence is to abandon civilization as we know it.

2. Intelligence tests do, in fact, predict socially and occupationally significant criteria. I.Q. is in a sense a measure of a person's ability to compete successfully in the world of work in all known civilized societies. When the "man in the street" is asked to rank various occupations in order of their "prestige," "desirability," and so on, it turns out that the rank order of the average I.Q. of persons in those occupations closely corresponds to the rank order of their desirability. For example, most of the practical business executives to whom McClelland refers have an average I.Q. that places them above approximately 96 per cent of the rest of the population.

3. Persons would still differ in intelligence even if there were no intelligence tests. Any merit system based on performance reveals these differences. I.Q. tests reveal the same differences to the extent that the performance involves mental capabilities. They are not intended to predict performance based on physical capacities or on special talents such as artistic and musical ability. Bright persons and dull persons were recognized long before intelligence tests came into existence, and there has always been a marked relationship between mental characteristics and occupational attainments. Throwing out intelligence tests will not improve a person's intelligence or reduce differences between persons, just as throwing away the thermometer will not cure a patient's fever.

4. The use of intelligence tests in the armed forces shows that they are highly correlated with the kinds and levels of skills for which men can be trained and the time they need to achieve certain levels of skill. Reversing the assignments of recruits in mental Categories I and IV would guarantee the greatest snafu in military history.

5. Intelligence tests do not reflect only the accidents of cultural and social privilege; they get at some quite basic biological capacity underlying the ability to reason, to organize and utilize one's knowledge, and so on. Hereditary or genetic factors account for more of the I.Q. differences among persons than do cultural and environmental factors. In the white European and North American populations, where this has been studied most extensively, it has been found that genetic factors are about twice as important as environment as a cause of individual differences in I.Q.

6. Intelligence is positively related to other nonintellectual traits of

personality and character that are also involved in competing successfully for what most persons in our society—rich or poor, black or white—regard as the "good things in life."

7. Various intelligence tests differ in their degree of "culture loading." Contrary to popular belief, blacks perform *better* on the *more* culture-loaded than on the more culture-free tests. (The opposite is true for other minorities.) Blacks also do better on verbal than on nonverbal tests. Thus, on some non-verbal I.Q. tests, about 85 per cent of American blacks score below the average for whites, while the culturally very different Arctic Eskimos score on a par with white norms. This shows that higher scores on these tests do not depend upon having experienced a white, middle-class American background.

8. Just as no one has been able to make up a test of mental ability that favors younger children (say, 10-year-olds) over older children (say, 12-year-olds), so no one has been able to make up a test that favors persons of low socioeconomic status over persons of middle- and upper-class status. If the reasons for social-class intelligence differences were due to status-biased content, it should be possible to make tests that reverse the differences. Yet, despite many attempts, no one has succeeded in devising such tests.

9. Language and dialect do not have the importance in intelligence tests attributed to them by popular belief, especially where nonverbal I.Q. tests are used. Urban black children tested on the Stanford-Binet I.Q. Test by a black tester using ghetto dialect do not score appreciably higher than when the test is administered in standard English. Children who are born deaf, though scoring poorly on verbal tests because of their severe language deprivation, score no differently from children with normal hearing on the nonverbal tests.

10. College aptitude tests, such as the S.A.T., predict college grades for blacks as well as for whites, for rich as well as for poor. The tests are color-blind. Black individuals and white individuals, rich or poor, with the same I.Q. can be expected to perform equally well in school or on the job—insofar as the job depends upon intellectual ability. In predicting a person's scholastic performance, knowledge of his race or social class adds little or nothing to what is predicted by his I.Q. . . .

## THE ETHICAL ISSUES

The range of ethical issues concerning research and research applications in human genetics is so great that I will not even attempt to review it here. It involves diverse questions about raising human embryos in "test tubes," the use of artificial insemination in human research, the cross-fostering of fetuses, and direct alteration of chromosomes and genes by what is now called genetic surgery, and goes all the way to questions of eugenics and population quantity and quality control.

But the most frequently heard objection to further research into human genetics, particularly research into the genetics of behavioral characteristics, is that the knowledge gained might be misused. I agree. Knowledge also, however, makes possible greater freedom of choice. It is a necessary condition for human freedom in the fullest sense. I therefore completely reject the idea that we should cease to discover, to invent, and to know (in the scientific meaning of that term) merely because what we find could be misunderstood, misused, or put to evil and inhumane ends. This can be done with almost any invention, discovery, or addition to knowledge. Would anyone argue that the first caveman who discovered how to make a fire with flint stones should have been prevented from making fire, or from letting others know of his discovery, on the grounds that it could be misused by arsonists? Of course not. Instead, we make a law against arson and punish those who are caught violating the law. The real ethical issue, I believe, is not concerned with whether we should or should not strive for a greater scientific understanding of our universe and of ourselves. For a scientist, it seems to me, this is axiomatic.

An important distinction, often not made or else overlooked, is that between scientific research and the specific use of the research findings in a technological application with a highly predictable outcome. The classic example is the atomic bomb. Should Einstein have desisted from the research that led to $e = mc^2$? Nuclear physics can, of course, be misused. But it need not be. For it can also be used to cure cancer and to provide electric power. Moral decisions involve the uses of knowledge and must be dealt with when these are considered. Before that, however, my own system of values holds that increasing knowledge and understanding is preferable to upholding dogma and ignorance.

In a society that allows freedom of speech and of the press, both to express and to criticize diverse views, it seems to me the social responsibility of the scientist is clear. He must simply do his research as competently and carefully as he can, and report his methods, results, and conclusions as fully and as accurately as possible. When speaking as a scientist, he should not introduce personal, social, religious, or political ideologies. In the bizarre racist theories of the Nazis and in the disastrous Lysenkoism of the Soviet Union under Stalin, we have seen clear examples of what happens when science is corrupted by servitude to political dogma. . . .

[Professor Dwight Ingle in *Perspectives in Biology and Medicine* (1967, page 10)] has written:

"Knowledge can be misused, but this does not excuse efforts to block inquiry and debate or to deny laymen in a democratic society the right to know. Closed systems of belief can also be misused, and ignorance is a barrier to progress. All possible causes for people's being disadvantaged should be investigated, and hopefully the application of knowledge to their advancement will be guided by moral principle." In my view, society will benefit most if scientists treat these problems in the spirit of scientific inquiry rather than as a battlefield upon which one or another preordained ideology may seemingly triumph. . . .

In recent years, however, we have witnessed more and more the domination of ideologically motivated environmentalist dogma concerning the causes of large and socially important differences in average educational and occupational performance among various subpopulations in the United States, particularly those socially identified as racial groups. For example, the rate of occurrence of mental retardation, with I.Q.'s below 70 plus all the social, educational, and occupational handicap that this implies, is six to eight times higher in our Negro population than in the rest of the population. According to research sponsored by the National Institutes of Health, as many as 20 to 30 per cent of the black children in some of our largest urban centers suffer severe psychological handicaps. Yet the Government *has* not supported, *does* not, and *will* not, as of this date, support any research proposals that could determine whether or not any genetic factors are involved in this differential rate of mental handicap. To ignore such a question, in terms of our present knowledge, I submit, may not be unethical—but it is, I believe, short-sighted, socially irresponsible, and inhumane.

More important than the issue of racial differences per se is the probability of dysgenic trends in our urban slums. The social-class differential in birthrate appears to be much greater in the Negro than in the white population. That is, the educationally and occupationally least able among Negroes have a higher reproductive rate than their white counterparts, and the most able segment, the middle class, of the Negro population have a lower reproductive rate than their white counterparts. If social-class intelligence differences within the Negro population have a genetic component, as in the white population, this condition could both create and widen genetic intelligence differences between Negroes and whites. The social and educational implications of this trend, if it exists and persists, are enormous. The problem obviously deserves thorough investigation by social scientists and geneticists and should not be ignored or superficially dismissed because of well-meaning wishful thinking. I find myself in agreement with Professor Dwight Ingle, who has said, "If there are important average differences in genetic potential for intelligence between Negroes and non-Negroes, it may be that one necessary means for Negroes to achieve true equality is biological." The possible consequences of our failure to seriously study these questions may well be viewed by future generations as our society's greatest injustice to Negro Americans. . . .

[We conclude with a statement by Harvard geneticist Carl Jay Bajema:] "Each generation of mankind faces anew the awesome responsibility of making decisions which will affect the quantity and genetic quality of the next generation. A society, if it takes its responsibility to future generations seriously, will take steps to insure that individuals yet unborn will have the best genetic and cultural heritage possible to enable them to meet the challenges of the environment and to take advantage of the opportunities for self-fulfillment present in that society."


# 1.17 INTELLIGENCE: GENETIC AND ENVIRONMENTAL INFLUENCES
## Robert Cancro, J. McV. Hunt and Girvin E. Kirk

---

## CANCRO

[There] is substantial disagreement among experts as to the definition of intelligence and appropriate methods of measuring it. Clearly, intelligence will be defined differently in different cultures according to the values of that

This selection consists of three excerpts. The first and third are from Robert Cancro, "Genetic Contributions to Individual Differences in Intelligence: An Introduction," in Robert Cancro (Professor, Department of Psychiatry, University of Connecticut School of Medicine), editor, *Intelligence: Genetic and Environmental Influences*, New York and London: Grune and Stratton, 1972, pp. 59–64.

The middle excerpt is from another selection in the same anthology, "Social Aspects of Intelligence: Evidence and Issues" (pages 262–306 at 269–271) by J. McV. Hunt (Professor of Psychology, University of Illinois, Champaign) and Girvin E. Kirk (Research Assistant Professor, Department of Educational Psychology, University of Illinois, Champaign). By permission. Footnote and bibliographical references here omitted.

Before proceeding with this selection the reader should clearly distinguish two terms: *genotype* and *phenotype*. *Genotype* signifies those traits or characteristics that are programmed into an individual at the time of conception. *Phenotype* signifies the traits or characteristics of an individual which develop during growth and *after* interaction of the genotype with a physical and social environment. Experimental psychology can deal only with phenotypes, never with genotypes. Genotypes are hypothetical constructs.

Failure to distinguish genotypes from phenotypes gives rise to arguments such as the following [words in brackets added by the editor]:

1. If [all] differences in mental abilities are inherited [i.e., if there is no essential difference between a genotype and a phenotype], and
2. If success requires those abilities, and
3. If earnings and prestige depend on success,
4. Then social standing (which reflects earnings and prestige) will be based to some extent on inherited differences between people."

The final qualifying "to some extent" prevents this argument from being completely speculative and nonempirical. Nevertheless, the argument is set forth as if founded on scientific evidence, and as if logically cogent and valid, by R. J. Herrnstein, "I.Q.," *Atlantic* 228: 43–64, September 1971.

particular culture. It is not a unitary trait, nor is it as highly visible as eye color. Intelligence is a construct, and the presence of an underlying reality is inferred by the observer. This in no way eradicates the actual and real effect of genes on individual differences in that trait. The only way we can deny a significant genetic contribution to intelligence is by denying the very existence of the trait itself. However politically palatable this pseudoposition may be, it is not scientifically tenable. If we define intelligence as a complex trait which is measured, to some practical degree, by IQ tests, we can avoid much of the fruitless debating that has so obscured this subject. . . .

As Dobzhansky has emphasized, . . . . a heritability measure is only useful as long as the environment is relatively constant.

A difficult problem, which is more than semantic, is that the term environment is used to include everything from the concentration of electrolytes in contact with the genome to the sociocultural milieu in which an infant develops. The term environment simultaneously covers a range of variables from disciplines as diverse as biochemistry and cultural anthropology. This leads to much confusion since constructs from very different universes are mixed as if they were interchangeable. . . .

One can speculate that as the environment—broadly defined—is made more constant for all, the variation between individuals will be increasingly a function of their genotypes. In this sense a perfectly "equal" environment might be the least democratic condition of all. A distinction that may be helpful can be drawn between the equivalence of the actual versus the evocativeness of the environment. The identical environment may not be equally evocative for two different people. Equal opportunity for these two individuals would *not* be accomplished through exposure to the identical environment but rather through exposure to equally evocative environments. Implicit in this approach is the desire, conscious or otherwise, to homogenize the population and erase individual differences. The expressed goal of many workers is to equalize performance. An alternative is to diversify the range of skills that is valued and rewarded by society, but this approach is usually disregarded. There is a danger that education will attempt to shape men to meet the demands of society rather than try to modify society to meet the range of individual human differences. While we speak of maximizing each individual's potential, operationally this often means minimizing his individual difference from that neo-Platonic ideal—the "modal" man. . . .

We should also consider the popular lay misconception that genes determine the trait in an inevitable manner; e.g., if you have a certain genetic make-up, you will have brown eyes. While this is true in practical terms, it is because the range of environments to which the particular genotype will be exposed is very narrow. In other words, the environment with which the genotype will interact is so probable that the phenotype can be predicted from an earlier knowledge of the genotype with great accuracy. Obviously, the same seed grown under very different conditions of temperature, barometric pressure, or sunlight would develop quite differently. The variation in environmental circumstances must be great enough to have an effect. Most genotypes can withstand some variation in the environment without being affected. The important considerations are the degree of environmental fluctuation and the developmental stage at which the exposure to the altered conditions occurs. The product of the interaction of the genotype with the *most probable environment* is highly predictable. As the probability of exposure to a particular environment decreases, there is a concomitant increase in the probability of an alteration in the final phenotype when exposure to that unlikely environment occurs. It is only through carefully controlled research that these outcomes can be predicted and environments selected so as to influence the phenotype. . . .

There are also population genetic considerations that should be included in studying intelligence. The expression "like produces like" is an oversimplification, but offspring are more likely to be similar rather than dissimilar to their parents on any genetically loaded trait. For this reason it is biologically sound as well as empirically true to say that the best predictor of an unborn child's IQ is the IQ of its biological parents independent of who rears the child. . . .

[Geneticists] subscribe to a polygenic theory of intelligence. There is no single gene for the measure called IQ, let alone for the broader construct of intelligence. Yet, that does not mean that the frequency of particular genes in a given population pool may not be directly related to the performance of that population on tests of intelligence. Even a primitive knowledge of genetics leads one to expect real differences in gene distributions between population pools on any given trait that is genetically loaded. Races are, by definition, gene pools that differ from each other in a statistically significant way. Therefore, we should expect significant racial differences on a variety of traits. This does not mean that the groups are innately different in the sense of immutability nor that one is superior in an absolute sense. It does mean that at a given time on a given trait there are differences between the gene pools that contribute to the phenotypic expression of that trait. Different groups, be they races or nationalities, have undergone different selection pressures of a variety of types. For example, the selection pressures in the arctic region were very different from those in the temperature or tropical zones. Cultural factors also play a role in population selection. If particular gene pools have been selectively bred for certain culturally valued traits, it comes as no surprise that these traits are more heavily represented in the population that has selectively bred for them. This very population, however, given a different selection pressure for an appropriate length of time, will become a radically different gene pool. It is in this sense that most geneticists believe that all human gene pools are potentially equal.

One tragic error that frequently intrudes in the mind of man is the confusion of difference with relative inferiority. As indicated earlier in this chapter, man has a long history of treating individual differences as undesirable and of attempting to eradicate them. This characteristic continues to make itself manifest. Superiority can only be defined (and arbitrarily at that) in an operational context. Even more important is the geneticist's realization that diversity between gene pools is biologically useful and, therefore, to be encouraged. Even if a particular group differs at a certain time from the other groups in its average level of performance on a particular trait measure, it does not mean that any given individual performance can be predicted. Nor does it mean that the group cannot achieve equal performance on that trait measure should it be willing to sacrifice the potential benefits of its genetic differences.

An example of difference in IQ test performance between two groups may help to illuminate some of the values and limitations of this measure in predicting the actual performance of these groups in real life. Italians and Jews, as groups, respectively score significantly below and above the mean on IQ tests. Does this result mean that Jews are smarter than Italians? Or is this the wrong question to ask of the data? The result certainly does mean that Jews, as a group, perform better on IQ tests and will, as a group, do better at those tasks that correlate highly with IQ. As would be expected, a study of the roster of scientists—particularly physicists—who have received the Nobel Prize reveals a disproportionately high representation by Jews. The excellence of Jews on tests of abstraction, and thereby in mathematics and those sciences closely related to it, cannot be explained adequately in cultural terms alone. Nor should we be surprised to find the values of a culture are determined, at least in part, by the historical strengths of that particular people. There have been relatively few great Italian mathematicians and physicists, as would be predicted from the group performance on IQ tests. However, it would be false to say that Italians represent an inferior gene pool for intelligence, particularly since their contributions to Western culture are second to no group. The population of that small peninsula has not only made unique contributions to culture in the past but continues to do so to this very day. In a variety of fields, including painting, sculpture, writing, music, architecture, and design, the Italian influence has been strongly present. These are all intellectual activities and are the product of intelligence, but they are not so highly correlated with IQ tests. The lessons to be drawn from this example are clear. IQ test performance is not the alpha and the omega of intelligence, but it can be valuable when properly used. When used improperly, we must blame the man and not the measure. The inferences that can be drawn from differences in group performance are real but limited. The need to reward a greater variety of talents is quite pressing in a technologically advanced society where the tendency is to selectively reward the individual who is outstanding in his ability to abstract. . . .

# HUNT AND KIRK

## Amount of Environmental Influence on IQ

The most relevant evidence known to us concerning the issue of how much influence the environment can have on the IQ comes from studies by Dennis (1966) and Skeels (1966). In the study by Dennis (1966), which should be more widely known, the Goodenough Draw-a-Man Test was given to good-sized samples of typical children, 6 to 9 years of age, living in normal family environments in some fifty cultures over the world. The variations in mean Draw-a-Man IQs for these samples extended from a high of 124 to a low of 52. Mean IQs of 124 were found for suburban children in America and England, for children in a Japanese fishing village, and for Hopi Indian children. In each of these four cultures children grow up with continual contact with representative, graphic art. The low mean IQ of 52 came from a sample of children in a nomadic Bedouin tribe of Syria and the mean IQ of 53 from a nomadic tribe in the Sudan. It should be noticed in this connection that the Muslim religion prohibits contact with graphic art. Yet, even among groups of Arab Muslim children, the mean IQs for the Draw-a-Man Test ranged from 52, for the children of Syrian Bedouins who had almost no contact with graphic art, to 94, for the children of Lebanese Arabs in Beirut who have repeated contact with the graphic art of Western civilization— even that including television.

It is likely that the Draw-a-Man IQ calls for a less complex set of abilities, as these are described by factor analysis (Guilford, 1967), than does the IQ derived from either the Stanford-Binet battery or the Weschler-Bellevue battery. For American children, nevertheless, IQs from the Draw-a-Man Test correspond about as well with IQs from either of these two standard measures of intelligence as the two standards do with each other.

It should be noted that the variation of 72 points in mean Draw-a-Man IQs holds for children reared in environmental circumstances quite normal for their various cultures. Moreover, the 72 points of variation in mean IQs from such typical groups of children fall only about 18 points short of the range of individual IQs (that between 60 and 150), which includes all but a fraction of 1 percent of individuals above the pathological bulge at the low end of this distribution. Thus, variation in mean IQ associated with circumstances of rearing has a range nearly equal to that variation for individual differences in the IQ which is commonly attributed largely to genetic variation.

While Jensen (1969) acknowledged that "extreme sensory and motor restrictions in environments such as those described by Skeels and Dye (1939) and Davis (1947), in which the subjects had little sensory stimulation of any kind and little contact with adults (p. 60)" result in large deficiencies in IQ, he minimized their importance for class differences and race differences. In favor of his view that the environment has little permanent effect on the IQ, he notes that the orphanage children of Skeels and Dye gained in IQ from an average of 64 at an average age of 19 months to 96 at 6 years of age as a result of being given "social stimulation and placement in good homes at between two and three years of age (p. 60)." He notes further that when these children were followed up as adults, they were found to be average citizens in their communities, and their own children had an average IQ of 105 and were doing satisfactorily in school. They actually had a median educational attainment of twelfth grade. Four had one or more years of college work; one received a bachelor's degree and went on to graduate school.

Neglected in Jensen's (1969) report are two points of importance for interpretation. Neglected first is the fact that most of these children were well under 2 years of age when they were transferred from the orphanage to the institution for the mentally retarded. At this age the children of the poor typically average approximately 100 in DQ or IQ. It is between the age of about 18 months and the age of 5 or 6 years that the IQs of children of the poor, both black and white, drift downward (Gray & Klaus, 1970; Klaus & Gray, 1968). As long as conditions that fail to foster psychological development persist but for a short or limited time, the very plasticity of early child development permits considerable recovery when development-fostering circumstances are provided. Neglected also in Jensen's report are the results of the follow-up for the Skeels-Dye children who were left in the orphanage. When the study began, these children had a mean IQ of 87. Retested after periods varying from 20 to 43 months, all of them showed decreases that ranged from 8 to 45 points, and five of the decreases exceeded 35 points. The median of ultimate educational attainment for this contrast group proved to be less than the third grade. At the time of the follow-up, one had died in adolescence following continued residence in a state institution for the mentally retarded; five were still wards of state institutions; and all but one of the remaining six were employed in work calling for only the lowest of skills. One gleans from these studies by Skeels and Dye (1939) and Skeels (1966) that persisting environmental circumstances can make a tremendous difference. The effects of circumstances are reversible early in life; but as given circumstances endure, their effects become more and more difficult to change. This principle holds for a variety of organisms and a variety of different kinds of circumstances. . . .

## CANCRO

There are enormously important ethical and social implications to our present-day understanding of the role of genetics in the determination of human behavior. The most powerful emotional argument against any form of genetic intervention is that man must not meddle in this delicate system. Yet, the medical advances of the last generation, e.g., antibiotics, plus the social legislation that has been passed has resulted in a radical alteration of the gene pool. Many individuals who are presently alive and actively contributing offspring to the gene pool would have been dead prior to the remarkable developments of twentieth-century medicine and/or the more liberal social legislation. We must recognize that we are in fact influencing the gene pool in very real ways. For example, keeping schizophrenics out of the hospital and encouraging them to socialize and "lead normal lives" is producing an increased number of offspring and thereby increasing the incidence of schizo-phrenia in the future generations. Once we recognize that we are in fact meddling with the system, we are compelled to examine in a critical manner the ways and results of our interventions. Any thoughtful consideration of these issues leads one to recognize the enormous importance of rational and humane genetic counseling for the future of our species.

In conclusion, we must avoid the Scylla of making all groups the same —be it through genetic and/or environmental manipulation—on any given trait while ignoring the human and social cost. If we believe in the value of group differences, we will not try to remove them. We must also avoid the equally dangerous Charybdis of self-righteous neglect of genetic counseling. This recognition of man's responsibility to plan and shape his destiny does not alter the fact that equality of opportunity is not negotiable, nor is a decent standard of living for all. America is too strong economically to tolerate the present extent and level of poverty. Morality alone dictates the implementation of certain social changes. These changes must be brought about because it is the morally correct thing to do, independent of their im-pact on IQ test performance. The existence of genetic contributions to indi-vidual and group differences in IQ does not justify discrimination in any form. There are measurable differences in the mean IQ of white groups from differ-ent national backgrounds. These groups represent slightly different population pools—both genetically and environmentally. Given the identical environ-ment, the groups may still show different relative strengths. This is the diver-sity that has been needed for evolution to progress, and we have no reason to believe that conditions have changed to the point where this diversity is no longer essential.

We must also identify and reward talents that are not uncovered by IQ tests but which can be of equally great value to our society. In a technologi-cally advanced society, such as ours, it is primarily the individuals with IQs over 115 who are highly rewarded. In the white population this group is less than 17 percent of the total. When 83 percent of the white population is "disadvantaged" vis-à-vis the prestigious positions in society, the exact per-centage for blacks or Orientals becomes of questionable value. There are those who believe that the abilities measured on IQ tests represent the pinnacle of human evolution. It logically follows from their view that man as a species should try to maximize this variable. Others feel that the evolution of man is far too complex and on too broad a front to permit any single trait measure to be anything more than misleading.[1]

---

[1] *EDITOR'S NOTE:* In the same anthology (p. 34) Lloyd G. Humphreys declares "It is safe to conclude that no amount of training will transform a chimpanzee into a human being intellectually, or a Mongoloid into a genius, but present data does not allow much more specific inferences than these." But David Wechler (p. 55) asserts that ". . . one does not throw out the baby with the bath water. The I.Q., whatever its defects, is still one of the most useful measures of intelligence available to us."

---

## 1.18 I.Q. TESTS: BUILDING BLOCKS FOR THE NEW CLASS SOCIETY
### David Kolodny and Noam Chomsky

**KOLODNY**

In the following article Noam Chomsky discusses the controversial views of Harvard Professor Herrnstein [whose basic argument is given in the introduction to Selection 1.17 by Cancro and others, and whose views concerning race are quite similar to those of Professor A. R. Jensen, explained in Selection 1.14 and elsewhere, above.]

Class subordination and social privilege have never been the most promising subjects for ethical defense. Historically the defenses that have been mustered, and which could be espoused with any presentable show of disinterest or conviction, have turned out to be very few, and by now rather ancient. But since every system of social inequality craves to be legitimized, the same time worn apologia of privilege have had to be perennially resur-

Excerpt from Noam Chomsky, "I.Q. Tests: Building Blocks for the New Class System," *Ramparts* 11: 24–30, July 1972, and from David Kolodny's introduction to that article. Copyright, Noah's Ark, Inc. (for *Ramparts* Magazine), 1972. By permission of the editors.

David Kolodny is the editor of *Ramparts*.

Noam Chomsky is Professor of Linguistics, M.I.T. For an overview of his philosophy, read John R. Searle, "Chomsky's Revolution in Linguistics," *New York Review of Books* 18: 16–24, June 29, 1972. (Good bibliography.)

rected. And in each case an attempt is made to draw renewed conviction from the particular epoch's most vital springs of faith.

Thus, in orthodox times the social order is sanctified by its conformity to the Divine Order, a sanctity which has been considered useful at one time or another by both the pedigreed noble and the successful bourgeois, by the annointed and the elect.

In a period (like our own) when rationalism casts doubt on divine testimonials on behalf of the ruling class, a substitute is usually found in science. Privilege is now shown to be in conformity with the Natural Order rather than the Divine. Class subordination is no longer "what God decreed," but "what Nature intended."

For those on top, whether their endorsement comes from science or religion, the main thing is that authority is on the side of power. Of course for people (like ourselves) who consider themselves hardheaded, the appeal to science has always been more persuasive, since any subjective inclination of the privileged in favor of the status quo will presumably be tested against objective data.

Aristotle, for instance, considering whether slavery was really natural and just, appealed to the evidence of biology: "all tame animals are better off when they are ruled by man; for then they are preserved. Again, the male is by nature superior, and the female inferior; and the one rules and the other is ruled," and he concludes, "this principle, of necessity, extends to all mankind."

The Greeks generally at this time relied on an objective criterion to indicate the naturally subordinate. The *barbaros*, meaning those people who did not speak Greek, were set off almost as a distinct species by their deficient linguistic ability. Greek speaking served as a kind of I.Q. test for them, and those who flunked it were fair game to be conquered and enslaved.

An appeal to science was also made by Thomas Hobbes in his defense of absolutist government and total submission to established power. These were necessary, he argued, as the only viable alternative to the intolerable state suffered by people lacking such an authority. So that we should not have to rely on his own speculative assessment of the dire alternative to absolutist rule, Hobbes resorted to what we now call anthropology, citing empirical data gathered by observers in the field: "The savage people in many places of America, except for the government of small families, the concord whereof depends on natural lust, have no government at all and live at this day in that brutish manner as I said before."

In the 19th century, Charles Darwin's depiction of Survival of the Fittest gave a tremendous scientific boost to those who wished to believe that the people on the top in society were there because they deserved to be. In Bertrand Russell's words, Darwin's model was popularly pictured as "a global free competition, in which victory went to the animals that most resembled successful capitalists."

Of course nowadays the self-serving interpretations and anecdotal methods that used to pass for science would influence no one. Today we give credence only to what impresses us as hard data, and we look for the authenticating signs: everybody recognizes that laboratories are scientific, and everybody knows that numbers are precise. It is natural then that the current attempts to legitimize class subordination and social privilege should employ these present day talismans of scientific authority as they are applied in the study of human psychology. So we have appeals first to the principles of behaviorist psychology, whose identification with the laboratory is so complete because they never found much in reality outside of it; and second to the statistics of the I.Q. which being numerical are thought to transform the amorphous concept of intelligence into something quantifiably precise.

Appeals to one or both of these are the basis of the new genre of scientific apologia for established privilege and the status quo. Although white racial chauvinism is not flatly expounded in the more respectable of the various arguments, it is always present. And it is clear that in the consciousness and unconsciousness of white America there exists a longing to have the socially repressed ugliness of candid racism vindicated and unleashed by prestigious professors using two dollar words. There is the feeling that if debator's points could be won in a few university classrooms, the great historical imperatives of racial justice that are straining and testing American society will somehow be eased, and continued suppression of black people will suddenly be morally sanctioned and socially tenable.

It is odd that these academicians and others ever got the idea in the first place that the roots of the intractable racial conflict in America could be searched out by probing for a statistical margin of racial difference. The manifest social reality that stares us in the face is just the opposite. It is precisely the tension between *equality* and inequity that is so agonizing and explosive. Hobbes understood the dynamic of equality and social conflict far better than today's computerized numerologists: *"From this equality of ability* arises equality of hope in the attaining of our ends. And therefore if any two men desire the same thing, which nevertheless they cannot both enjoy, they become enemies . . . and from hence it comes to pass that . . . if one plant, sow, build, or possess a convenient seat, others may probably be expected to come with forces united to dispossess and deprive him, not only of the fruit of his labor, but also of his life or liberty. And the invader again is in the like danger of another."

## CHOMSKY

Professor Herrnstein claims that "the gradient of occupations" is "a natural measure of value and scarcity," and that "the ties among I.Q., occupation, and social standing make practical sense." This is his way of expressing the familiar theory that people are automatically rewarded in a just society (and more or less in our society) in accordance with their contributions to social welfare or "output." The theory is familiar, and so are its fallacies.

To assume that society's rewards go to those who have performed a social service is to succumb to essentially the same fallacy (among others) involved in the claim that a free market leads to the optimal satisfaction of wants. In fact, when wealth is badly distributed, a free market will tend to produce luxuries for the few who can pay, rather than necessities for the many who cannot. Similarly, given great inequalities of wealth, we will expect to find that the "gradient of occupations" by pay is a natural measure, not of service to society but of service to wealth and power, to those who can purchase and compel. The ties among I.Q., occupation, and social standing that Herrnstein notes make "practical sense" for those with wealth and power, but not necessarily for society or its members in general.

The point is quite obvious. Herrnstein's failure to notice it is particularly surprising given the data on which he bases his observation about the relation between social reward and occupation. He bases these judgments on a ranking of occupations which shows, for example, that accountants, specialists in public relations, auditors, and sales managers tend to have higher I.Q.'s (hence, he would claim, receive higher pay, as they must if society is to function effectively) than musicians, riveters, bakers, lumberjacks and teamsters. Accountants were ranked highest among 74 listed occupations, with public relations 4th, musicians 35th, riveters 50th, bakers 65th, truck drivers 67th, and lumberjacks 70th. From such data, Herrnstein concludes that society is wisely "husbanding its intellectual resources" and that the gradient of occupation is a natural measure of value and makes practical sense.

Is it obvious that an accountant helping a corporation to cut its tax bill is doing work of greater social value than a musician, riveter, baker, truck driver, or lumberjack? Is a lawyer who earns a $100,000 fee to keep a dangerous drug on the market worth more to society than a farm worker or a nurse? Is a surgeon who performs operations for the rich doing work of greater social value than a practitioner in the slums, who may work much harder for much less extrinsic reward? The gradient of occupations that Herrnstein uses to support his claims surely reflects, at least in part, the demands of wealth and power; a further argument is needed to demonstrate Herrnstein's claim that those at the top of the list are performing the highest service to "society," which is wisely husbanding its resources by rewarding accountants and public relations experts and engineers (e.g., designers of anti-personnel weapons) for their special skills. Herrnstein's failure to notice what his data immediately suggest is another indication of his uncritical and apparently unconscious acceptance of capitalist ideology in its crudest form. . . .

The situation is reminiscent of 19th century racist anthropology. Marvin Harris notes:

Racism also had its use as a justification for class and caste hierarchies; it was a splendid explanation of both national and class privilege. It helped to maintain slavery and serfdom; it smoothed the way for the rape of Africa and the slaughter of the American Indian; it steeled the nerves of the Manchester captains of industry as they lowered wages, lengthened the working day, and hired more women and children. . . .

The 19th century racist anthropologists were no doubt quite often honest and sincere. They may have believed that they were simply dispassionate investigators, advancing science, following the facts where they led. Conceding this, we might nevertheless question their judgment, and not merely because the evidence was poor and the arguments fallacious. We might take note of the relative lack of concern over the ways in which these "scientific investigations" were likely to be used. It would be a poor excuse for the 19th century racist anthropologist to plead, in Herrnstein's words, that "a neutral commentator . . . would have to say that the case is simply not settled" (with regard to racial inferiority) and that the "fundamental issue" is "whether inquiry shall (again) be shut off because someone thinks society is best left in ignorance." The 19th century racist anthropologist, like any other person, is responsible for the effects of what he does, insofar as they can be clearly foreseen. If the likely consequences of his "scientific work" are those that Harris describes, he has the responsibility to take this likelihood into account. This would be true even if the work had real scientific merit —in fact, more so in that case.

Similarly, imagine a psychologist in Hitler's Germany who thought he could show that Jews had a genetically determined tendency toward usury (like squirrels bred to collect too many nuts) or a drive toward anti-social conspiracy and domination, and so on. If he were criticized for even undertaking these studies, would it be sufficient for him to respond that "a natural commentator . . . would have to say that the case is simply not settled" and that the "fundamental issue" is "whether inquiry shall (again) be shut off because someone thinks society is best left in ignorance?" I think not. I think that such a response would have been met with justifiable contempt. At best, he could claim that he is faced with a conflict of values. On the one hand, there is the alleged scientific importance of determining whether in fact Jews have a genetically determined tendency toward usury and domination (an empirical question, no doubt). On the other, there is the likelihood that even opening this question and regarding it as a subject for scientific inquiry would provide ammunition for Goebbels and Rosenberg and their henchmen. Were this hypothetical psychologist to disregard the likely social consequences of his research (or even of his undertaking such research) under existing social conditions, he would fully deserve the contempt of decent people. Of course, scientific curiosity should be encouraged (though fallacious argument and investigation of silly questions should not), but it is not an absolute value. . . .

In fact, it seems that the question of the relation, if any, between race and intelligence has very little scientific importance (as it has no social importance, except under the assumptions of a racist society). A possible correlation between mean I.Q. and skin color is of no greater scientific interest than a correlation between any two other arbitrarily selected traits, say, mean height and color of eyes. The empirical results, whatever they might be, appear to have little bearing on any issue of scientific significance. In the present state of scientific understanding, there would appear to be little interest in the discovery that one partly heritable trait correlates (or does not) with another partly heritable trait. Such questions might be interesting if the results had some bearing, say, on hypotheses about the physiological mechanisms involved, but this is not the case. Therefore the investigation seems of quite limited scientific interest, and the zeal and intensity with which some pursue or welcome it cannot reasonably be attributed to a dispassionate desire to advance science. It would, of course, be foolish to claim, in response, that "society should not be left in ignorance." Society is happily "in ignorance" of an infinitude of insignificant matters of all sorts. And, with the best of will, it is difficult to avoid questioning the good faith of those who deplore the alleged "anti-intellectualism" of the critics of scientifically trivial and socially malicious investigations. On the contrary, the investigator of race and intelligence might do well to explain the intellectual significance of the topic he is studying, and thus enlighten us as to the moral dilemma he perceives. If he perceives none, the conclusion is obvious, with no further discussion.

As to social importance, a correlation between race and mean I.Q. (were this shown to exist) entails no social consequences except in a racist society in which each individual is assigned to a racial category and dealt with not as an individual in his own right, but as a representative of this category. Herrnstein mentions a possible correlation between height and I.Q. Of what social importance is that? None, of course, since our society does not suffer under discrimination by height. We do not insist on assigning each adult to the category "below six feet in height" or "above six feet in height" when we ask what sort of education he should receive or where he should live or what work he should do. Rather, he is what he is, quite independent of the mean I.Q. of people of his height category. In a non-racist society, the category of race would be of no greater significance. The mean I.Q. of individuals of a certain racial background is irrelevant to the situation of a particular individual, who is what he is. Recognizing this perfectly obvious fact, we are left with little, if any, plausible justification for an interest in the relation between mean I.Q. and race, apart from the "justification" provided by the existence of racial discrimination.

# CHAPTER

## 2

# Make
# Education
# Relevant

# 2.1 INTRODUCTION:
## RELEVANT—TO EACH INDIVIDUAL STUDENT

This chapter is related (i.e., relevant) to Chapter 1, and also to Chapter 4. We treat it separately because the slogan "Make Education Relevant" is widely proclaimed today. But the term is quite meaningless until we ask "Relevant—to Whom?" or "Relevant—to What?" and, even then, we find a wide variety of answers. This chapter then consists of a series of selections explaining what "Make Education Relevant" means to persons viewing the educational picture from different points of view.

Our introductory remarks will reemphasize an old truism, namely, that we do not teach *classes* (of students); we teach individual *students* (who happen to come to us in groups, or in classes). This is a simple truth, but it is basic.

Let us begin by viewing the problem, not from the point of view of the individual, but from that of society as a whole.

Civilization requires that men *not* all be alike, but that different men cultivate their diverse talents to form a variety of men, each with a unique or special type of excellence. To appreciate the importance of diversity, consider three famous geniuses: Paganini, Newton, and Napoleon. Week after week, year after year, Paganini practiced his violin fifteen hours a day (yes, 15!) until he displayed a virtuosity never before known to man. Newton worked fifteen to twenty hours a day, scarcely stopping to eat. Napoleon, in the heat of a military campaign, would go for three or four days with no more than three or four hours of sleep. In hydrostatics a force is concentrated on a piston of a small area in order to produce great pressures. So each of these three men concentrated their tremendous energies on a special area of art, of science, and of public affairs; and each became a world renowned genius.

But can you picture Napoleon or Newton practicing the violin 15 hours a day? Can you imagine Paganini or Newton becoming enthusiastic about, or even involved in, a military campaign? Can you envision Paganini or Napoleon developing new systems of abstract mathematics, or conducting painstaking experiments in optics or alchemy? The point of these examples should be obvious: Genius takes many forms. Hence, any educational curriculum designed especially for one type of excellence is almost certain to be unsuited for other types.

What applies to men of genius applies also to men of talent, to men of normal ability, and to men of less than average ability. Booker T. Washington was right when he said that American society will not prosper until it puts worth and dignity into the common occupations of men. And John Kenneth Galbraith was also right when he noted that the shift from an agrarian to an industrial civilization has meant a shift from a pyramid-shaped social structure (with only a few places at the top for the aristocracy) to a vase-shaped social structure (where the great bulk of occupations are now in the fat middle-class areas):

> In the early stages of industrialization, the educational requirement for industrial manpower was in the shape of a very squat pyramid. A few lawyers, engineers, bookkeepers, timekeepers, clerks, and the like were needed in or by the office. The wide base reflected the large requirement for repetitive labor power for which even literacy was something of a luxury. To this pyramid the educational system conformed. Elementary education was provided for the masses at minimum cost. . . .
> By contrast the manpower requirements of the industrial system are in the shape of a tall urn. It widens out below the top to reflect the need of the technostructure for administrative, coordinating and planning talent, for scientists and engineers, for sales executives, salesmen, those learned in the other arts of persuasion and for those who program and command the computers. It widens further to reflect the need for white-collar talent. And it curves in sharply toward the base to reflect the more limited demand for those who are qualified only for muscular and repetitive tasks and who are readily replaced by machines.
> This revision of educational requirements is progressive. The top of the urn continues to expand while the bottom remains the same or contracts.[1]

But being in the middle "large" part of the vase does not mean being alike. There is as great a diversity of talent as there is diversity of genius. A major failing of our schools today is that, although we have excellent curricula for the *academically* talented—for those who are to become doctors, lawyers, engineers, and members of other so-called "higher" professions—we do not have enough variety and diversity for the great majority—for the many students whose special talents are not so pronounced as to be readily detected. And it is these students—the great majority—for whom the "assembly line" treatment is so often used as an excuse for genuine education.

In today's world there are no longer five or ten "higher" professions, nor are there five or seven "liberal" arts. There are some 30,000 different occupations in contemporary American society, each of which may be, and should be, meaningful and worthwhile, each of which should enable the person who performs it both to find gratification in his work and to find moral dignity in his contribution to society. But today, it is simply untrue to say that *all* who complete high school are mature and educated; for it is all too evident that many high school graduates do not have mature minds; they have not cultivated social graces, and they seem to lack the determination and the self-discipline that are prerequisites of excellence.

The strength of democracy derives from the fact—if it is a "fact" and

---

[1] *The New Industrial State*, copyright © 1967, 1971 by John Kenneth Galbraith. Reprinted with permission of Houghton Mifflin Company.

not simply an unrealized "ideal"—that no artificial barrier, such as race, creed, ideology, or economic status, shall stand in the way of a youth of talent or genius, from any group in our society. Democracy does not mean mediocrity: it does not mean the emphasis of *equality* to the neglect of *quality*. It means, rather, and most especially in the field of education, that all students, however varied their talents and however diverse their abilities, receive as much help as possible to further develop their varied talents and thus to contribute to the making of a glorious civilization.

During the 1960s some of the most widely read critics of American education have been emphasizing the points we have just stated. But these ideas are far from new. To show how old they are, we turn to an old fable, *The Animal School*. The version we use here was written about 1920 by Dr. G. H. Reavis, then Assistant Superintendent of the Cincinnati Public Schools. But earlier versions, in somewhat modified forms, are in print. This fable was widely read in the 1920s and 1930s.

## The Animal School

Once upon a time, the animals decided they must do something heroic to meet the problems of "a new world," so they organized a school.

They adopted an activity curriculum consisting of running, climbing, swimming, and flying. To make it easier to administer the curriculum, all the animals took all the subjects.

The duck was excellent in swimming, in fact better than his instructor; but he made only passing grades flying and was very poor in running and climbing. The school then assigned him extra work in these two subjects until his web feet were badly worn and he was only average in swimming. But average was acceptable in school, so nobody worried about that except the duck.

The rabbit started at the top of the class in running, but had a nervous breakdown because of so much make-up work in swimming.

The squirrel was excellent in climbing until he developed frustration in the flying class where his teacher made him start from the ground up instead of from the treetop down. He also developed "charlie horses" from overexertion and then got C in climbing and D in running.

The eagle was a problem child and was disciplined severely. In the climbing class he beat all the others to the top of the tree, but insisted on using his own way to get there.

At the end of the year, an abnormal eel that could swim exceedingly well and also run, climb, and fly a little had the highest average and was valedictorian.

The prairie dogs stayed out of school and fought the tax levy because the administration would not add digging and burrowing to the curriculum. They apprenticed their child to a badger and later joined the groundhogs and gophers to start a successful private school.

What is the moral of this fable for educators? When it comes to playing the violin, a violinist is superior to a scientist, superior to a statesman, superior to a general, etc. When it comes to physics, a physicist is superior to an artist or an architect. And so it is for every developed specialized ability. But in school, where such varied abilities are not yet developed, only students who are strong in academic aptitude are rated as superior. And we must pause to ask ourselves, why has the nonacademic student been treated so shabbily in our schools?

To consider only the recent history of this problem: During the post-Sputnik era, every effort was made to find and to encourage potential scientists. However, as we strove thus to keep ahead of Russia in our air-space programs, we learned that good marks in school did not always correlate with creative ability. Indeed, some of the more creative individuals were turned off by classroom procedures designed almost exclusively to help students pass college entrance examinations. Careful study of such students has led to a major reassessment of thinking with respect to the use and misuse of intelligence tests. For example:

> Guilford and Allen . . . selected some 28 dimensions of the mind which they felt were relevant to success on the job in the physical sciences. Then they prepared plain English descriptions and also a sample item of a best test for each of these 28 intellectual characteristics. A sizable number of scientists on the job were interviewed by Allen, after which he asked them to arrange these 28 characteristics in terms of importance on their job. The 28 characteristics were arranged in rank order according to their judged importance by the total group of scientists. Traditional intelligence tests have included about 5 or 6 of these characteristics, such as general reasoning, vocabulary ability, number ability, memory for ideas, ability to visualize spatially, and perhaps perceptual speed. All but one of these traditional intelligence factors ranked below 20th in the list. In other words, 19 of the 20 intellectual characteristics ranking at the top on the job in science were *non-intelligence intellectual characteristics*. Some examples are intellectual flexibilities, fluencies, originality, penetration, redefinition ability, sensitivity to problems.[2]

If the lock-step system of classroom teaching was bothersome to creative individuals, it was devastating and tragic for the so-called "non-learner." J. W. Getzels offers this analysis of the so-called "apathetic student":

> It is often said that the lower class child fails in school because he is apathetic or aggressive. Without denying this, some would turn it around and raise the further question whether he is not also increasingly apathetic and aggressive

[2] Calvin W. Taylor, "A Tentative Description of the Creative Individual," *A Source Book for Creative Thinking*, S. J. Parnes and H. D. Harding, eds., New York: Charles Scribner's Sons, 1962. By permission. See also Calvin W. Taylor, "Be Talent Developers," *Today's Education* 57: 33–36, December 1968.

See also E. Paul Torrance, *Guiding Creative Talent*, Englewood Cliffs, N.J.: Prentice-Hall, Inc., 1962; Banish Hoffman, *The Tyranny of Testing*, New York: Crowell-Collier and Macmillan, Inc., 1962.

in school because he fails. For what can be more tormenting than to be faced day upon day with a situation you cannot handle and yet may not leave on pain of severe punishment? Insofar as the preschool experiences of the lower class child have not prepared him for school, school can only be a source of frustration: he is neither ready to do what is required nor can he escape. The reaction to this type of frustration is hopelessness and rage. In school, the hopelessness is manifested in apathy, i.e., psychological withdrawal from the source of frustration, and the rage in aggression, i.e., physical attack upon the source of frustration. Ultimately, not only does this failure lead to dropping-out with consequent unemployability, but the patterns of apathy and aggression maintained over the compulsory school years often become stabilized into deep-seated maladjustment and delinquency.[3]

In attempting to adapt classroom procedures to suit the needs of the poor and the needy, of children from deprived racial and cultural minority groups, of middle-class and upper-class students of low academic interest and ability, we have come more and more to realize the folly of rigid classroom procedures and of inflexible academic requirements. In spite of our loudly proclaimed ideal of "education for *all* American youth" we have, as a matter of fact, developed a system tailored to less than half of our student population. Says Benjamin Bloom:

We have for the past century conceived of mastery of a subject as being possible for only a minority of students. With this assumption we have adjusted our grading system so as to certify that only a small percent of students (no matter how carefully selected) are awarded a grade of A. If a group of students learns a subject in a superior way (as contrasted with a previous group of students) we still persist in awarding the A (or mastery) to only the top 10 or 15 percent of the students. We grudgingly recognize that the majority of students have "gotten by" by awarding them grades of D or C. Mastery and recognition of mastery under the present relative grading system is unattainable for the majority of students—but this is the result of the way in which we have "rigged" the educational system. . . . [rigged] on the assumption that there is a standard classroom situation for all students. . . We persist in asking such questions as: What is the best teacher for the *group*? What is the best method of instruction for the *group*? What is the best instructional material for the *group*?
One may start with the very different assumption that individual students may need very different types and qualities of instruction to achieve mastery. . . . [and] define quality of instruction in terms of the degree to which the presentation, explanation, and order of elements of the task to be learned approach the *optimum for a given learner*. . . . [Some] students will need more concrete illustrations and explanations than will others; some students may need more examples to get an idea than do others; some students may need

---

[3] J. W. Getzels, "Pre-School Education," *Teachers College Record* 48: 218–228, December 1966. (Contains good bibliography.)

more approval and reinforcement than others; and some students may even need to have several repetitions of the explanation while others may be able to get it the first time. . . . The main point to be stressed is that the quality of instruction is to be considered in terms of its effects on *individual* learners rather than on random *groups* of learners.[4]

We conclude these introductory remarks by noting what students themselves have to say about relevance in education. In response to the question, "What could schools do to educate you in ways that no other agencies could or should?" students answered (in paraphrase):

1. Put what we learn in school into a framework or system which will help us understand it better. (Youngsters think disconnected, unassociated content falls into the category of useless baggage.)

2. Teach us "fundamentals." Nowhere except in school are you likely to gain the tools you need for thinking and serving.

3. Give us opportunities and materials in school to help us inquire, discover, and probe meaning. Getting meaning is perhaps the most important thing schools can do to help us.

4. Stop attempting to compete with and to destroy what we learn elsewhere. Instead, seek to coordinate what we are taught in school with what we learn outside school.[5]

[4] Benjamin Bloom, excerpt from "Learning for Mastery," *Evaluation Comment*, May 1968, Vol. 1, No. 2. By permission. These ideas are expanded in *Handbook on Formative and Summative Evaluation of Student Learning*, by Benjamin S. Bloom, J. Thomas Hastings, and George F. Madaus, New York: McGraw-Hill, 1971, Chapter 3, pp. 43–60, "Learning for Mastery."

Another cause of student failure has been dramatized in a study by Robert Rosenthal and Lenore Jacobson in *Pygmalion in the Classroom: Teacher Expectations and Pupils' Intellectual Development*, New York: Holt, Rinehart and Winston, 1968. Pros and cons concerning the validity of the Rosenthal-Jacobson expectancy theory may be found in *Pygmalion Reconsidered*, edited by Janet D. Elashoff and Richard E. Snow, and published by the Charles A. Jones Publishing Company, Worthington, Ohio, 1971. This booklet, one of a series of ten sponsored by the National Society for the Study of Education, would make an excellent supplement to this chapter.

[5] Ronald C. Doll (Richmond College, The City University of New York), "Alternative Forms of Schooling," *Educational Leadership* 29: 391–393, February 1972. See also Harry S. Broudy, *The Real World of the Public School*, New York: Harcourt Brace Jovanovich, Inc., 1972, Chapter VII, "The Fallacy of Misplaced Relevance."

# A. Relevant–To Whom?

## 2.2 RELEVANT—TO NONACADEMIC STUDENTS
### K. Patricia Cross

John Gardner (1961) has asked, Can we be equal and excellent too? We might paraphrase the question and ask, Can we be *different* and excellent too? . . . Surely quality education consists not in offering the same thing to all people in a token gesture toward equality but in maximizing the match between the talents of the individual and the teaching resources of the institution. . . .

There must be no compromise on quality of performance, but it is essential to permit wide individual variation in choice of subjects. This reversal in the emphasis of the educational task is not only more humane but also more realistic. Once we get out of school, we choose the areas in which we will display our competencies. Only in school do we require students to display—more or less publicly—their weaknesses. Human dignity demands the right to be good at something. Indeed, a healthy society is built upon the premise that all citizens will contribute their best talents. The social necessity of emphasizing quality of performance and deemphasizing area of performance has been eloquently expressed by John Gardner (1961): "An excellent plumber is infinitely more admirable than an incompetent philosopher. The society which scorns excellence in plumbing because plumbing is a humble activity and tolerates shoddiness in philosophy because it is an exalted activity will have neither good plumbing nor good philosophy. Neither its pipes nor its theories will hold water." . . .

One of the unintentional lessons learned by low-ability students is that failure is always reaching out to envelop them. The picture is not unlike that of a strong and a weak swimmer thrown into downstream currents above a waterfall. The strong swimmer soon swims to calm waters and begins to focus

K. Patricia Cross, *Beyond the Open Door*, San Francisco and London: Jossey-Bass, 1971. Consulting editor: Harold L. Hodgkinson. Excerpts from pp. 12–26 and 160–165. By permission.

K. Patricia Cross and Harold L. Hodgkinson are at the University of California, Berkeley.

his attention on how fast he can swim, while the weak swimmer is dragged into such swift currents that his only concern is to keep himself from going over the waterfall. In the language of psychology, the strong swimmer becomes achievement-motivated while the weak swimmer becomes fear-threatened. Future learning is structured differently for the two swimmers. . . .

Some basic research in psychology has implications for understanding the phenomenon of passivity in learning. Seligman (1969) and his colleagues made laboratory dogs "passive" to new learning experiences and then experimented with procedures that would make them into "active" learners again. In a sense this is our goal for New Students [i.e., students of low academic achievement or ability]—to take students whose natural curiosity and bent for learning have been stifled through past experiences with education and make them want to learn again. Although dogs are not people, the parallels to human learning and to failure-threatened personalities make for fascinating speculation and the generation of some testable hypotheses. Seligman and his colleagues conducted a standard conditioning experiment. Their naïve dogs behaved just as the dogs in the Psychology 100 textbooks do. In these experiments, the dog was placed in a box with an electric grid on the floor. The lights dimmed, ten seconds later the shock came on, and the dog howled and ran around showing fear and lack of purposive behavior. During this random activity, the dog managed to throw himself over the barrier and out of the box, at which point he escaped from shock and the lights went on again. The next time the lights dimmed, the dog started his fear reaction, the shock came on, and the escape from the box and the shock was more rapid and purposeful than before. With repeated trials, the dog finally jumped over the barrier as soon as the lights dimmed, thus avoiding the shock altogether.

But Seligman found that the reaction was very different for dogs who had previously been shocked in the box *while in a harness* that prevented escape. Twenty-four hours later, these dogs entered the conditioning experiment "knowing" that nothing they did would terminate the shock. Struggling in the harness had no effect. When they were later put in the box *unharnessed* and free to learn to escape just as the naïve dogs had been, they howled for just a few seconds when the shock came on and then settled down and took the shock. After several trials, the dogs ceased even to try to escape and became passive or helpless.

The situation is analogous to that of a young student who tries hard in the beginning but who finds that he never gets rewarded by an *A*, the teacher's approval, or classmates' admiration. In other words, his efforts, like those of the dog struggling in the harness, are futile. After repeated experience, he does learn something—that the result of trying is failure. The resultant personality characteristic would appear to be passivity in learning. . . .

The relationship between personal problems and low academic achievement can be regarded as cause or effect or both. . . . Whichever came first—the poor school performance or the personal problems—once the cycle starts, it tends to reinforce itself. Personal problems can lead to poor school performance, which in turn may lead to problems of self-doubt and self-dissatisfaction, which, added to the further burden of poor grades, may increase personal insecurity. While the schools cannot be expected to solve the personal and home problems of students, they can offer personal counseling for a period in life that many young people find quite difficult. Most important, schools can begin to make some of the fundamental changes that would remove the fear-of-failure and personal-threat syndrome from the educational experience. . . .

[What are the characteristics of low-academic-ability students? Most of them] are positively attracted to careers and prefer to learn things that are tangible and useful . . . [They] prefer watching television programs to reading; they prefer working with tools to working with numbers; they feel more competent in using a sewing machine than in reciting long passages from memory . . . [and they] possess a more pragmatic, less questioning, more authoritarian system of values than [academically talented] students. . . .

Many educators as well as the general public are still thinking of New Students [i.e., students of low academic ability] largely in ethnic terms. . . . [But] educational problems are not color-bound. Two thirds of the community colleges surveyed in the spring of 1971 stated that less than one fourth of the students enrolled in "remedial" classes were members of ethnic minorities . . . [We must abandon] the fallacy of assuming that traditional education has served the privileged classes well and the disadvantaged poorly. It would be more accurate to acknowledge that education has served young people with abilities and interests that are developed through traditional academic discipline-bound curricula. The concept of *academic* talent as *the* talent worthy of cultivation and encouragement represents a perspective that is too narrow to provide a base for the development of a new education for the egalitarian age. . . .

New Students—those in the lowest third academically—are telling us in a variety of ways that traditional education must be redesigned for the egalitarian era. They drop out of our traditional schools; they quit listening to lectures; they fail to put forth their best effort; they score low on conventional tests designed to reflect the heart of the traditional academic curriculum; they get low marks for their school performance; their interests, leisure-time activities, and hobbies are "nonacademic"; they fail to develop self-confidence, and they tell us they are nervous and tense in class. They are caught in the impossible bind of wanting to be successful but knowing that they will be required to display the style and values that traditional education will certify.

In moving from the meritocratic era in education to one of egalitarianism, we have not faced up to the fact that equality of educational opportunity requires more than guarantees of equal access to postsecondary education. Access to education that is inappropriate for the development of individual talents may represent nothing more than prolonged captivity in an environment that offers little more than an opportunity to repeat the damaging experiences with school failure that New Students know so well. John Gardner (1961) has described the situation forthrightly: "In the case of the youngster who is not very talented academically, forced continuance of education may simply prolong a situation in which he is doomed to failure. Many a youngster of low ability has been kept on pointlessly in a school which taught him no vocation, exposed him to continuous failure and then sent him out into the world with a record which convinced employers that he must forever afterward be limited to unskilled or semi-skilled work. This is not a sensible way to conserve human resources" (p. 80).

Neither is it a sensible way to develop individual talents. In a society as complex as ours we need to encourage diversity, and yet we seem unable to move away from our unproductive preoccupation with wanting all children to learn the same things at the same rate. We are in the grip of a "deficiency" conception of New Students. From nursery school to college, we give more attention to correcting the weaknesses of New Students than to developing their strengths.[1]

---

[1] *EDITOR'S NOTE*: A major reason for student unrest is the awareness by many youth that they are not to be allowed to enter the mainstream of American life and culture. In an excellent analysis of contemporary youth (*Youth and Dissent*, New York: Harcourt Brace, Jovanovich, 1971), Kenneth Keniston distinguishes three types of contemporary youth (pp. 325–332): (1) The Solidly In, (2) The Tenuously In, and (3) The Excluded. It should be obvious that the above selection by K. Patricia Cross was a recommendation that our schools should do more to help those who are excluded, or nearly excluded, from entrance into the mainstream of American life. Selection 2.4 by Grant Venn and Donald E. Super will reemphasize this point.

---

# 2.3 RELEVANT—TO YOUTH OF THE 1970s
## Jonathan Kozol

---

[It is laudable to feel sympathy toward the alienated and the dispossessed. But it is of no real help to downtrodden people to] build the core of their life-style around the simulation of essential impotence: with competence admitted only

Jonathan Kozol, *Free Schools*, Boston: Houghton Mifflin Co., 1972, Excerpts from pp. 59–61, 117–118. Copyright © 1972 by Jonathan Kozol. Reprinted by permission of the publisher.
Jonathan Kozol won the National Book Award for *Death at an Early Age*, Houghton Mifflin, 1967.

in those areas of basic handiwork and back-to-nature skill in which there is no serious competition from the outside world inasmuch as there is neither function, use nor application in the social interlock in which we are obliged to live. "Wow!" I hear some of these Free School people say. "We made an Iroquois canoe out of an oak log!" Nobody, however, needs an Iroquois canoe. Even Iroquois do not. The Iroquois can buy aluminum canoes if they should really need them. They don't, however. What they need are doctors, lawyers, teachers, organizers, labor leaders. The obvious simulation-character of the construction of an Iroquois canoe by a group of well-set North American children and adults in 1972 is only one vivid and easily identifiable portion of the total exercise of false removal from the scene of struggle which now typifies the counter-culture. There may be some pedagogic value or some therapeutic function in this form of simulation for the heartsick or disoriented son or grandson of a rich man. It does not, however, correspond to my idea of struggle and survival in the context of the streets and cities that I know.

In the face of many intelligent and respected statements, writings, essays on the subject of "spontaneous" and "ecstatic" education, it is simple truth that you do not learn calculus, biochemistry, physics, Latin grammar, mathematical logic, constitutional law, brain surgery or hydraulic engineering in the same spontaneous and organic fashion that you learn to walk and talk and breathe and make love. Hours and seasons, months and years of long, involved and—let us be quite honest—sometimes non-utopian labor in the acquisition of a single unit of complex and intricate attainment go into the expertise that makes for power in this nation. The poor and black, the beaten and despised, cannot survive the technological nightmare of the next ten years if they do not have this kind of expertise in their own ranks. . . .

[The] children of the black and poor ought to be able to know, and ought to be able to believe, right from the first, that the struggle for liberation does not need to end with sickness in the mountains or with steel helmets in Chicago or with a T-group in Manhattan. It can also end with personal strength, political passion, psychological leverage and the deepest kind of moral and imaginative power. . . .

It is in this context, then, that sane and sober parents of poor children in such cities as my own draw back in hesitation, fear or anger at the often condescending if, in the long run, idealistic statements and intentions of those who attempt to tell them to forget about English syntax and the preparation for the Mathematics College Boards but send away for bean seeds and for organic food supplies and get into "group-talk" and "Encounter." It seems to me that the parents are less backward and more realistic than some of their white co-workers are prepared to recognize. It seems to me that a tough, aggressive, skeptical and inventive "skill" like beating out a tough and racist and immensely difficult examination for the civil service, for City College or for Harvard Law School, rings a good deal more of deep-down revolution than the handlooms and the science gadgets and the gerbil-cages that have come, in just five years, to constitute an Innovative Orthodoxy on a scale no less totalitarian than the old Scott Foresman reader.

To plant a bean seed in a cut-down milk container and to call this "revolution" is to degrade and undermine the value of one of the sacred words. To show a poor black kid in East St. Louis or in Winston-Salem or in Chicago how to make end runs around the white man's college-entrance scores—while never believing that those scores are more than evil digits written on the sky— to do this, in my scale of values, is the starting-point of an authentic revolution. It is not to imitate a confrontation, but to engage in one. It is not to speak of doing "our own thing," but rather to do one thing that really matters and can make a visible difference in the lives of our own brothers in the streets that stand about our school. Harlem does not need a new generation of radical basket-weavers. It does need radical, strong, subversive, steadfast, skeptical, rage-minded and power-wielding obstetricians, pediatricians, lab technicians, defense attorneys, Building Code examiners, brain surgeons. Leather and wheat germ may appear to constitute a revolution in the confines of a far-removed and well-protected farm or isolated commune ten miles east of Santa Barbara or sixteen miles south of Santa Fe; but it does not do much good on Blue Hill Avenue in Boston on a Sunday evening if a man's pocket is empty and his child has a fever and the buses have stopped running.

There has to be a way to find pragmatic competence, internal strength and ethical passion all in the same process. This is the only kind of revolution that can possibly transform the lives of people in the land in which we live and in the time in which we are now living.

# B. Relevant–To What?

## 2.4 RELEVANT—TO CAREERS OR JOBS
### Grant Venn and Donald E. Super

---

**VENN**

[*Some Facts About Traditional Education:*]   First, in the past, the great majority of the people spent most of their lives doing mean, manual work, often for more than ten hours a day, six or more days a week. Even children were involved in full-time manual work. The average man had little, if any, use for education; in fact, he had little time or energy even for reading. What reading was done was mainly in connection with the church and the religious activities of the family.

Second, there was little reading material available, and what was available was too expensive for most people. Even libraries were primarily started as resources for the educated and as recreation for the general public.

Third, the relationship between education and work was not even a concept for argument. Education was for those who did not work, for those in law, religion, education, philosophy, logic, and so on. This concept is so much a part of our ethic that in 1962 while I was with the Selection Division of the Peace Corps I had an experience which should be related here. One question on a form to be filled out by all volunteers was, "What kind of work does your father do?" One young man responded by writing, "My father no longer works; he is now a minister, but he used to work as a carpenter." . . .

[*The Importance of a Job in Today's World*]   Today the forces of in-

This selection consists of excerpts from two sources. The first is from Grant Venn, *Man, Education and Manpower*, Washington, D.C.: National Association of School Administrators (NEA), rev. ed. 1970, pp. 85, 35–37, 11, 39, 63–64, 58–59, 106, 80–81. Footnote references here omitted. By permission of the American Association of School Administrators, 1801 No. Moore, Arlington, Va. 22209.

Grant Venn, since 1966, has been Associate Commissioner of Education, U.S. Office of Education, Department of Health, Education and Welfare, Washington, D.C.

The second excerpt is from Donald E. Super, "The Changing Nature of Vocational Guidance," in *Issues in American Education*, edited by Arthur M. Kroll, New York: Oxford University Press, 1970, pp. 139–155. By permission of publisher and author. Copyright © 1970 by Oxford University Press.

Author of *The Psychology of Careers* (1957), Donald E. Super is Professor of Psychology and Education, Teachers College, Columbia University, New York.

dustrialism and technology have altered the meaning of the word *work* and man's relation to the world of work. The displacement of muscle power by the automated machine makes possible the production of vast surpluses of goods; abundance has replaced scarcity.

The blue-collar to white-collar shift in the employment force signifies that the primary function of work today is to secure the distribution of goods, not the production of goods. In 1900, for example, 70 percent of the nation's labor force was engaged in production, compared with less than 40 percent today. And only a very small percentage of the present labor force is engaged in what earlier centuries would call "hard work."

This situation leads to the problem at hand. As Gerard Piel points out, any hard work that a machine can do (and that includes virtually all such work) is better done by a machine; "hard" these days means mostly boring and repetitive, whether in the factory or the office. But the instinct for workmanship, the need to feel needed, the will to achieve are deeply felt in every human heart. "They are not," says Piel, "universally fulfilled by the kind of employment most people find." Indeed, with the enactment of social legislation such as workman's compensation and unemployment relief and with the steady downgrading of manual occupations, work itself is no longer an absolute necessity for subsistence or a means of gaining status. *In the place of work we have substituted "the job."* A man's occupation in American society is now his single, most significant, status-conferring role. Whether it be high or low, a job status allows the individual to form some stable conception of himself and his position in the community.

The social and psychological effects of joblessness are painfully apparent in America today. They can be seen in the faces of those standing in line for relief checks; none of them may be starving, and there may be work around the home that could keep them busy, but without a job they are lost. Tens of thousands of jobless youths cast about at loose ends, with 80 to 90 percent of the juvenile cases in the courts coming from their ranks. Job discrimination creates a hard knot of frustration in the Negro, frustration that explodes in bitter racial conflict. Also included in this group is the middle-aged woman whose children are grown and who now wishes to get a job. There still may be plenty of work around the home and the family may not need the money, but she feels a need for new identifications found only in holding a job. This crucial importance of the job to the individual in American society must be borne in mind in any discussion of man, his work, and his education. Statistical compilations of the effect of technology on the labor market can be compelling, but for millions of Americans the problem of joblessness is real and personal. . . .

*Youth without jobs.* Important as a job may be to adults, it is no less important to the young person leaving school. For him it is initiation into the adult world. Here again things have changed, for although the psychological and social significance of initiating youth into adulthood has been recognized by every society, it seldom has involved getting a job. In primitive societies initiation often took the form of a prolonged, formal test of physical endurance. Knighting and the sacrament of confirmation performed a similar function in medieval society. In more recent times, American youngsters looked upon shoes or their first pair of long pants as a symbol of adulthood. Some girls had a formal coming-out to mark their adulthood; for most, marriage was the turning point. But *not* work. Work was something they experienced long before adulthood, whether in the form of helping on the farm or being put into a factory at the age of ten. A child's capacities were not left idle when the family subsistence depended upon these resources.

But modern society increasingly denies opportunities for work during youth. There are no fires to build, wood to chop, or cows to milk for most young boys and girls. A boy may mow the lawn or wax the car, a girl may vacuum the rugs or wash dishes, but little formal work awaits them until they get a job. Since the modern economy hires only mature workers, and since adults themselves measure status in terms of jobs, a job becomes the symbol of acceptance into the adult world. Neither religious ceremonies (which come too early), nor marriage (which for many comes too late), nor school graduation ceremonies (a good excuse for new clothes and a round of parties) rank even close to a job as an initiation symbol.

This is not to suggest that something is wrong with the value system of American youth. These are simply the values of the adult world, and every young person has always looked forward to becoming an adult and doing things adults do. Today, this means getting a job, the assumption of an occupational status. The big difficulty is that when young men and women leave school, they find there are no jobs for them.

There are now more than one million young men and women under twenty-two who have left school and are not working. At any given time 30 percent of the high school dropouts will be unemployed; even high school graduates average 15 percent unemployed. The figure for college dropouts is considerably lower, but they share the same problem as those who have dropped out of the system earlier: there is little room in the labor market for the undereducated, unskilled young worker. Instead of initiation they find rejection. . . .

[These facts have great importance to education; and] the questions that become more pertinent every day are: What must the schools be doing for the one-third of today's youth who are handicapped in finding employment and who encounter serious problems in making the transition from school to work? And what is the school's role in preparing the needed manpower in a society that by 1975 will find only 5 percent of the work force engaged in unskilled work? . . .

Peace Corps and Vista are two types of experiences available for youth. However, these "volunteer" activities will provide opportunities only to those who can afford one or two years of "financial irresponsibility" and will consequently attract mainly those youth who are economically secure. Job Corps will meet the needs of a very small number of those with whom we are concerned. Neighborhood Youth Corps offers larger-scale possibilities, but its eligibility requirements are too often high, and many of its job offerings have been largely "make-work" with no future. Both these programs, however, have offered models which may well help to provide answers to the problems of locked-out youth. *The combination of work-for-pay, skill development and education if it can lead to job placement with career-ladder possibilities, seems to offer the most promising solution to the needs of this growing number of youth for which the traditional system offers small promise.*

Jobs, however, are hard to come by for youth from ghetto areas, areas which are producing the greatest numbers of dropouts and delinquents. *This existing and projected lack of meaningful employment opportunities for large numbers of youth growing into adulthood is perhaps the major domestic problem in America today.*

The school must share the responsibility not only for training for jobs, but also for *job development* and *job placement*. . . .

[Attitudes towards jobs are as important as jobs themselves. The First (1968) Annual Report of the National Advisory Council on Vocational Education put the matter this way:]

At the very heart of our problem is a national attitude that says vocational education is designed for somebody else's children. This attitude is shared by businessmen, labor leaders, administrators, teachers, parents, students. . . .

The attitude infects the Federal government, which invests $14 in the Nation's universities for every $1 it invests in the Nation's vocational education programs. It infects State governments, which invest far more in universities and colleges than they do for support of skill training for those whose initial preparation for the world of work precedes high school graduation. It infects school districts, which concentrate on college preparatory and general programs in reckless disregard of the fact that for 60 percent of our young people high school is still the only transition to the world of work. It infects students, who make inappropriate choices because they are victims of the national yearning for educational prestige.

The attitude must change. The number of jobs which the unskilled can fill is declining rapidly. The number requiring a liberal arts college education, while growing, is increasing far less rapidly than the number demanding a technical skill. In the 1980s it will still be true that fewer than 20 percent of our job opportunities will require a four-year college degree. In America every child must be educated to his highest potential, and the height of the potential is not measured by the color of the collar. Plumbers, carpenters and electricians make more than many school superintendents and college presidents; only the arrogant will allow themselves to feel that one is more worthy than the other. . . .

[However, in most American schools today, the] election of a vocational program, since it is not the approved form of preparation for further liberal or professional studies, will often severely limit the student's chances of getting into college. For many students a vocational program in high school represents a closed-end track: since this form of education occupies an ambiguous, peripheral position on all educational levels, there is no clear and acknowledged path to specific occupational goals running up through the secondary and collegiate levels. Vocational subjects may be elected at any stage from the tenth grade on, but there is no logical progression leading to a post-high-school or collegiate degree or potential further study. . . .

[It] is time that we ended the artificial cleavage between vocational education and so-called academic education. All of our citizens require education to function effectively as citizens and to realize their potentials as human beings. Moreover, we know that literacy and the basic skills which should be developed in any educational process are also necessary for people to learn work skills properly and to advance in their jobs.

We also regard it as nonsense to have an imaginary line separate the individual's academic education and his participation in his life's career. Academic education would be enhanced, not compromised, if vocational preparation were introduced into our general school system. Moreover, an increase in vocational education might help to end the false hierarchy of values which educators have consciously or unconsciously introduced through their treatment of vocational education, the notion that preparation for a life career is a second-class activity for second-class citizens. [Stanley Ruttenberg] . . .

The first revolution in American education was a revolution in *quantity*. Everyone was to be provided the chance for an education of some sort. That revolution is almost won in the schools and is on its way in higher education. The second revolution is *equality* of opportunity. That revolution is underway. The next turn of the wheel must be a revolution in *quality*. [Francis Keppel]

The debate continues over the question of equality, which is really far from being achieved, and certainly the debate has really yet to begin on the definition of quality. Quality is the issue around which the schools of tomorrow must be discussed.

The question of quality revolves around the concept that education must prepare students for the kind of world in which they will be living as adults. If education does not do this, it will fail in its purpose, no matter how "well educated" our citizens become, no matter what level of educational attainment is reached.

In the world which is already upon us, the goal of education must be to develop individuals who are open to change, who are flexible and adaptive, who have learned how to learn, and are thus able to learn continuously. Only such persons can constructively meet the perplexities of a world in which problems spawn much faster than their answers. The goal of education must be to develop a society in which people can live more comfortably with *change* than with *rigidity*. In the coming world the capacity to face the new appropriately is more important than the ability to know and repeat the old. [Carl Rogers]

Perhaps one answer to how to teach people to adjust to change and to continue learning would be to have youth participate earlier in the processes of our society rather than exclude them from the real activities of our culture until after they have completed school. . . .

In the future the nature of work will become more and more the basis for man's place in society, a way to determine his self-worth and dignity, the way in which he contributes to society, and the way in which his unique talents contribute to the total pool of manpower skills that advance society and the general welfare. Work will continue to become less and less a process of producing goods, less and less a necessity in order to live, less and less a repetitive application of energy.

The old concept of work as the curse of mankind will be replaced by a concept of work as the way in which the individual can become most creative and contributory. Individuals will be able to choose work suited to their talents, interests, and desires. If this is true, then work as a part of education, and education as a part of man's work success, points to an early and developing marriage of convenience and choice between the two—not a union of force demanded by the economics of the times.

## SUPER

[*"Careers" versus "Jobs."* Because of the relative stability of occupations in preindustrial societies, the word career] has come to be almost a synonym for occupation, and the connotation is one of a person entering an occupation, finding in it a major means of self-actualization, and staying in it for the balance of his working life. This is a concept which has validity for a number of people, including physicians who typically remain in medicine from medical school until retirement and businessmen who climb from the position of junior executive toward, if not to, that of president of the corporation. But these careers with continuity and self-fulfillment possibilities, these *stable* and *conventional careers,* as they have come to be called in occupational sociology, characterize only about half of our working population. The other half (and hence the emphasis in my talk) have *unstable* or *multiple-trial* careers. That is, they occupy, during the course of their working lives, a series of unrelated and often depersonalized positions, and the continuity in their careers is not that of [a] field [of] work, it is that of a person working. Another way of putting it is to say that whereas about half of our labor force has what might be called a life work, the other half has a *life of work*. . . .

Perhaps stable and conventional careers *are* the most desirable, in view of the fact that they provide greater continuity, make possible more detailed and more effective planning, provide a sounder basis for family financing, and tend to permit self-fulfillment. They may, therefore, be desirable goals for all, just as the taking on and achievement of middle-class values seems, despite their defects, a legitimate goal of education in a society such as ours. But the fact of desirability for all does not mean attainability for all, at least not so long as our economy is based in part on a large number of jobs which can be filled by semi-transient, easily replaced, anonymous workers.

Stabilized neither by their own investment in the acquisition of a skill, nor by the challenge of their work, nor by the rewards of their efforts, large numbers of the semiskilled and unskilled move from job to job in search of better working conditions, of work which provides more assurance of continuity, or better outlets for ability and interest. But workers who can be let go when a job is finished or an order is filled, and who can easily be replaced when production is to be resumed, cannot have stable or conventional careers unless the productive and distributive systems are organized to provide them continuity. For most unskilled and semiskilled workers, including office clerks, and for increasing numbers of young people for whom automated business and industry have no place, a career with middle-class stability and continuity is a will-o'-the-wisp. The reality, for the 50 or 70 percent, is discontinuity, uncertainty, and change.

[*Guidance for Discontinuity*]   If more than half of our students are to have discontinuous careers . . . and if the unpredictables of automation mean that change and uncertainty are to characterize the lives of an even greater percentage, what then becomes of career guidance? Do we declare that it is for the elite only, and let placement in a job when available and needed take its place for the 50 percent, for the majority of the future? Or do we, recognizing the facts of career patterns, develop a type of career guidance and of vocational education which recognizes the continuity of the individual and seeks to help him find this continuity even in the midst of change?

To do the former, and guide only the elite, will hardly satisfy us in this day and age. . . . [What we need today is a better understanding of the unstable and multiple-trial work patterns which seem to be the only career patterns available to the great majority of modern men.]

[We need a better] understanding of what discontinuity and change in a rapidly evolving economy means in the way of adaptability and retraining. The obsolescence of the methods of production and distribution, and even of the very scientific principles upon which some methods are based, calls for expanding the scope and duration of education on a scale such as has never until recently been dreamed of, for varieties of occupations such as we have never seen, and for education continuing or resumed at times and over a longer period of time than any but a few scholarly professional men have ever experienced. . . .

[Most of all, we must rid ourselves of the idea that nonacademic students do not need academic subjects. Or perhaps it would be] better to say that we must recognize that the academic subjects taught in high school are *not* academic, but basic. Please do not mistake me, I am no Essentialist, no academic snob or cultural ethnocentric who thinks that those who are not interested in learning what he learned, in the way in which he learned it, are unworthy of a teacher's attention. What I mean is that linguistic and arithmetic skills, and scientific, economic, political, and social understanding, are essential vocational skills for all students. This is so even for those who will leave school before graduation (whether in order to escape from school or in order to go to work), *especially* for those who will drop out or who will not continue beyond high school. For these are the students who, pursuing discontinuous careers, will need to know when to change and how to change, and who will need the skills and understanding which make possible quick training for, or adaptation to, a new type of work. For those who need retraining for a new type of work, languages, mathematics, and natural sciences often prove to be basic vocational skills.

---

*EDITOR'S NOTE*: The U.S. Office of Education personnel have identified 15 major occupational clusters around which career education should revolve. These are:

| | |
|---|---|
| Business and Office | Fine Arts and Humanities |
| Marketing and Distribution | Consumer and Homemaking |
| Communication and Media | Transportation |
| Construction | Agri-Business and Natural Resources |
| Manufacturing | Marine Science |
| Health | Environmental Control |
| Hospitality and Recreation | Public Services |
| Personal Services | |

Professor Bill Wesley Brown believes that students at the Elementary grade level should be made well acquainted with each of these fifteen general career areas; that Junior High School students should be making a definite career choice in one or two of these areas; and that Senior High School students should be taking general courses appropriate to one or two of the areas, and should also be taking more specialized courses preparing for more definite careers within the area. For more on this topic, read Bill Wesley Brown (Professor of Industry and Technology, Chico State College, Chico, California), "Career Education" in *Six Crucial Issues in Education*, edited by David T. Tronsgard, Executive Secretary, NASBE, pp. 93–112. Copies of this 114-page booklet may be obtained from: National Association of State Boards of Education, 2480 West 26th Avenue, Suite 215–B, Denver, Colorado 80211.

---

# 2.5 RELEVANT—TO FUTURE EXPECTATIONS
## W. R. Wees

Survival schooling, extended as a descriptive term from primitive to modern education, is a name that we may now apply to that practice of education which undertakes to force upon each new generation only what the old one knows, to keep it in the grip of the same time. Perhaps this was all right for the Eskimos before the white man came. Perhaps it was all right when I was a boy . . . [when the] faith of our fathers was still holy faith (as with Stefansson's Eskimos) and all was right with the world. But is the type of schooling that shackles the future to the past ever all right? It becomes more and more evident that each generation must explore and "learn" a new environment. . . .

[Here are some examples of traditional "survival schooling":]

In the fourth century, Donatus wrote a grammar text that started out and continued in this fashion:

| | |
|---|---|
| How many parts of speech are there? | eight. |
| What are they? | noun, pronoun, verb, adverb, participle, conjunction, preposition, and interjection. |
| What is a noun? | a part of speech with case, signifying a body or thing particularly or commonly. |
| How many attributes have nouns? | six. |
| What are they? | quality, comparison, gender, number, figure, case. |

Nobody would have much difficulty in seeing the similarity between Donatus' teaching method and the "objective" tests and examinations so popular in schools today. An objective test runs like this:

Underline the correct answers to the following questions:

1. How many parts of speech are there?     five     nine     eight
2. In the sentence, "The dog runs," what part of speech is dog?     noun     verb     adverb
3. What is the gender of "dog"?     masculine     feminine     neuter
   etc., etc., etc.

The one difference between Donatus' method and modern "objective"

From *Nobody Can Teach Anyone Anything: What Our Schools Are Doing TO Our Children, Not FOR Them* by W. R. Wees. Copyright © 1971 by W. R. Wees. Reprinted by permission of Doubleday & Company, Inc. Excerpts from pp. 4, 6–8, 20–36, 51, 193–199.

After many years as a teacher, beginning in a one-room rural school, W. R. Wees is now a member of Canada's educational "establishment" at Toronto.

multiple-choice testing is that now the child has only to say "Tick-tack-toe, around I go" and can still be right one time out of three.

The similarity can be carried further into modern times by anyone who might wish to amuse himself by comparing Donatus, programmed learning-teaching machines, and computers used as teaching tools.

For readers in the lower middle ages of their lives and up, Priscian's method of teaching literature in the sixth century may be of interest. Here is a sample from his textbook on the first book of the *Aeneid*:

| | |
|---|---|
| What part of speech is "arma"? | a noun |
| Of what sort? | common |
| Of what class? | abstract |
| Of what gender? | neuter |

etc., etc.

Until quite recently, Shelley's "To a Skylark" would, most likely, have been pulled apart in the same way, word by word, line by line, until the poor bird lay there on the teacher's desk, dead or dying, without a feather on him.

I am reminded of a superior type of teaching friend of mine who insists that "the whole art of teaching is the art of questioning"—questioning, of course, to elicit previously taught "right" answers. In some teachers' colleges, this method is called "the Socratic method." Socrates would willingly die all over again at such malignment. In his teaching he was trying to get people to think their way through to the answers, to invent them, not simply to repeat them back to him. . . .

Survival schooling, the kind of schooling that was organized into the system and forced upon the child, represents the hegemony of the past in the confederation of the past, present, and future, which is the life of the child. When I tell a child what I know, I can tell him only what was. . . . [The child] lives in the present, by the past, and for the future. And that which we live for, that future time, whether the next moment or the years to come, must be the concern of education, as it is the urgent concern of every child.

When we think of the child set in these time relationships, we see him now as all that he has been, a product of his own past. He is what he has done. We could turn Ulysses' famous statement around and paraphrase it to read "All that he has done is part of him."

But even as we are looking at him, the child, who has turned his has-beens into what he is, turns the future into now and drops it back into his past. The infant, agile on his hands and knees, grips the chair rungs, stands, gains equilibrium, takes a step and falls into his mother's arms. He has turned the future into now and made it a part of him. Now he is looking for new futures.

As the child develops his language power his future thinking becomes clearer to us. The future is what he does not know. All the little question-mark words are continually on his tongue: What? Why? How? When? Where? And even, So what? At the same time he goes to work on the unknowns on his own, exploring, adventuring. Young Billy, not yet at school, becomes fascinated with numbers and their relationships. One day, as he goes exploring in his mind, his mother hears him say, "Well! If 20 and 20 make 40, 19 and 21 must make 40 too." He has made the unknown known.

To make the unknown known, to turn the future into now, is the urgent need of every child. And for each unknown that he makes known to himself he advances his power to know and do. The urgency to make the unknown known is the dynamic of growth. And the increasing power to do it is growth itself.

Growth is change. Probing those future moments, days, and (as he grows) finally years, to turn their darkness into the light of knowledge, the child changes himself. As he changes himself he changes in his concept of his world. Carrying his concepts into action he also changes the world about him, creating a new environment. The cycle of change is thus cumulative in speed and in complexity. . . .

*It is not the role of the teacher today, as it has been in the past, to recite answers and force the child to memorize them. Instead, the teacher must provide the means by which the child himself will find the answers.* . . .

In the new kind of classroom that is beginning to be seen across the country the children glory in the freedom of their minds. Their minds are doing what their minds were made for: Finding out what they did not know, creating new ideas and concepts, generating their own power. . . .

In the thinking school where children make their own ideas, concepts, things, the phenomenon that is perhaps most rewarding to the observer is the way in which the children build their own value systems, with human values at the core. In making things the maker forgets himself, and self-forgetfulness is the only viewpoint from which one fully sees other people. Working cooperatively with other children toward achievement of a common goal the child learns to respect the other children for their contributions.

In the thinking school the child works fearlessly. He has no fear of being wrong because he is his own evaluator, helped along by the other children. The teacher helps when he is asked for his opinion and even then usually turns the evaluation back to the child himself. Because he knows that the teacher respects him for the person that he is (whatever he is) he grows in self-respect, from which flows respect for others.

In a workshop classroom I have yet to see anything but politeness in our children, a politeness based on respect and self-respect. The kinds of environment these children will build around themselves need not cause anxiety. On the contrary, they could create the environment that will awaken humaneness in humanity living in an anxious world. . . .

Studying man's search for what is good, philosophers identify three sets of values. The first set they call the psychological values, which turn out to be biological, the life preservers such as nourishment, security, sleep, and sex. The second set—logical, aesthetic, ethical, economic, and religious values—

they call the historical values. The third set are the axioms—the triad of good-ness, beauty, and truth, which from ancient times, have been the *axioma,* forms of worthiness that are self-evident.

Within these sets of categories the child must eventually find his values. At the start, however (except for the life-preserving values), they aren't there. The children can make them live only as they formulate their own value sys-tems, as they grow.

The purpose of childhood is to give the child time to develop, to organ-ize, and to co-ordinate all the complex organs of his body and complex func-tions of his mind. At some point along the way, we say, "He is now a man; she is a woman." But the child must grow so that he can say to himself, "I am not just a man; I am my own man." The significant aspects of growth toward becoming one's own man can be recapitulated briefly thus: (1) growth in self-respect, (2) growth in companionship with others, (3) growth toward inde-pendence, and (4) growth in the ability to evaluate one's growth and the products of one's mind. . . .

[Stated somewhat less briefly,] these are the changes we must make:

(a) Instead of demeaning the child because he is small, ignorant, and bad we respect him both for the person that he is and for the person that he can become. In our respect for him, the child's self-respect and respect for others bloom.

(b) Instead of individualizing education as we have always done (lock-ing each child up in a compartment of silence to listen to us), we socialize it. It has been said that education is the pursuit of truth in the company of friends. And when I go into one of those new schools in which children work together to achieve common learning goals the most heartening thing I see is their competency in working and in being together. They are creating social order as they grow.

(c) Instead of smothering the child's mind in answers and curricula, we alert it to questioning and finding out. For the verbose artificiality that we call teaching we substitute a real world of people and things. After all, there are only four sets of relationships that man's mind can perceive: the relation-ships between people and people, people and things, things and things, and man himself to all three. Out of his perception of these relationships the child must create his own real world. In that real world of his own creation the child finds his independence in thought and judgment.

(d) For the continual evaluation by the teacher, right and wrong, good and bad, sin and righteousness, we substitute the child's evaluation of himself and of the products of his mind. And believe me, when we do, we'll find that in evaluating his own values, nobody can be more severe than the child himself. . . .

John Holt says that creativity and intellect are the same thing. To this I would add the word "thought." Creativity means putting perceptions together in new ways (new, at least, to the person who is doing it) and this is exactly what thought is. Putting things together in new ways is to create new relationships among them, to make a new ordering of perceptions, a new form. To think is to create, and to create is to make new knowledge for the person thinking.

Should we then not set as our overall aim, something that takes this into account? Try the following: *The whole purpose of education is to nurture the child's power of thought. . . .*

The way we must go at it is summed up aphoristically by a graduate student in education, who said the other day: "Schooling is what you *get*; education is what you *do*."[1]

---

[1] *EDITOR'S NOTE*: No one will deny that we should prepare a child for the world in which *he* is to live, and not for the one in which his ancestors lived, or even for the one in which his teacher lives. Nevertheless, the solution to this problem is not simple. Suppose a child's teacher dies in the year 2000 and that the child lives on to the year 2020. Everyone will agree that the child *will* know more about the years 2000–2020 than the child's teacher knew while the child was in school. The question still remains: Does the child know more *now*, while he is still in school, than his teacher knows *now*, about what the future is likely to be?

---

# 2.6 RELEVANT—TO INQUIRY ABILITY
## Neil Postman and Charles Weingartner

There can be no significant innovation in education that does not have as its center the attitudes of teachers. . . .

The attitudes of the inquiry teacher are reflected in his behavior. When you see such a teacher in action, you observe the following:

*The teacher rarely tells students what he thinks they ought to know.* He believes that telling, when used as a basic teaching strategy, deprives students of the excitement of doing their own finding and of the opportunity for increasing their power as learners.

From *Teaching as a Subversive Activity* by Neil Postman and Charles Weingartner. New York: Delacorte Press, 1969, pp. 33–37, 203, 207. Copyright © 1969 by Neil Postman and Charles Weingartner. Used by permission of the publisher, Delacorte Press.
Author of several books on Language and Education, Neil Postman teaches at New York University.
Charles Weingartner teaches at Queens College, New York.

*His basic mode of discourse with students is questioning.* While he uses both convergent and divergent questions, he regards the latter as the more important tool. He emphatically does not view questions as a means of seducing students into parroting the text or syllabus; rather, he sees questions as instruments to open engaged minds to unsuspected possibilities.

*Generally, he does not accept a single statement as an answer to a question.* In fact, he has a persisting aversion to anyone, any syllabus, any text that offers The Right Answer. Not because answers and solutions are unwelcome—indeed, he is trying to help students be more efficient problem solvers —but because he knows how often The Right Answer serves only to terminate further thought. He knows the power of pluralizing. He does not ask for the reason, but for the reasons. Not for the cause, but the causes. Never the meaning, the meanings. He knows, too, the power of contingent thinking. He is the most "It depends" learner in his class.

*He encourages student-student interaction as opposed to student-teacher interaction. And generally he avoids acting as a mediator or judge of the quality of ideas expressed.* If each person could have with him at all times a full roster of authorities, perhaps it would not be necessary for individuals to make independent judgments. But so long as this is not possible, the individual must learn to depend on himself as a thinker. The inquiry teacher is interested in students' developing their own criteria or standards for judging the quality, precision, and relevance of ideas. He permits such development to occur by minimizing his role as arbiter of what is acceptable and what is not.

*He rarely summarizes the positions taken by students on the learnings that occur.* He recognizes that the act of summary or "closure" tends to have the effect of ending further thought. Because he regards learning as a process, not a terminal event, his "summaries" are apt to be stated as hypotheses, tendencies, and directions. He assumes that no one ever learns once and for all how to write, or how to read, or what were the causes of the Civil War. Rather, he assumes that one is always in the process of acquiring skills, assimilating new information, formulating or refining generalizations. Thus, he is always cautious about defining the limits of learning, about saying, "This is what you have learned during the past 45 minutes," or "This is what you will learn between now and the Christmas holidays," or even (especially), "This is what you will learn in the ninth grade." The only significant terminal behavior he recognizes is death, and he suspects that those who talk of learning as some kind of "terminal point" are either compulsive travelers or have simply not observed children closely enough. Moreover, he recognizes that learning does not occur with the same intensity in any two people, and he regards verbal attempts to disregard this fact as a semantic fiction. If a student has arrived at a particular conclusion, then little is gained by the teacher's restating it. If the student has not arrived at a conclusion, then it is presumptuous and dishonest for the teacher to contend that he has. (Any teacher who tells you precisely what his students learned during any lesson, unit, or semester quite literally does not know what he is talking about.)

*His lessons develop from the responses of students and not from a previously determined "logical" structure.* The only kind of lesson plan, or syllabus, that makes sense to him is one that tries to predict, account for, and deal with the authentic responses of learners to a particular problem: the kinds of questions they will ask, the obstacles they will face, their attitudes, the possible solutions they will offer, etc. Thus, he is rarely frustrated or inconvenienced by "wrong answers," false starts, irrelevant directions. These are the stuff of which his best lessons and opportunities are made. In short, the "content" of his lessons are the responses of his students. Since he is concerned with the processes of thought rather than the end results of thought (The Answer!), he does not feel compelled to "cover ground" (there's the traveler again), or to insure that his students embrace a particular doctrine, or to exclude a student's idea because it is not germane. (Not germane to what? Obviously, it is germane to the student's thinking about the problem.) He is engaged in exploring the *way* students think, not what they should think. . . . That is why he spends more of his time listening to students than talking to or at them.

*Generally, each of his lessons poses a problem for students.* Almost all of his questions, proposed activities, and assignments are aimed at having his students clarify a problem, make observations relevant to the solution of the problem, and make generalizations based on their observations. His goal is to engage students in those activities which produce knowledge: defining, questioning, observing, classifying, generalizing, verifying, applying. As we have said, *all knowledge is a result of these activities.* Whatever we think we "know" about astronomy, sociology, chemistry, biology, linguistics, etc., was discovered or invented by someone who was more or less an expert in using inductive methods of inquiry. Thus, our inquiry, or "inductive," teacher is largely interested in helping his students to become more proficient as users of these methods.

*He measures his success in terms of behavioral changes in students:* the frequency with which they ask questions; the increase in the relevance and cogency of their questions; the frequency and conviction of their challenges to assertions made by other students or teachers or textbooks; the relevance and clarity of the standards on which they base their challenges; their willingness to suspend judgments when they have insufficient data; their willingness to modify or otherwise change their position when data warrant such change; the increase in their skill in observing, classifying, generalizing, etc.; the increase in their tolerance for diverse answers; their ability to apply generalizations, attitudes, and information to novel situations.

These behaviors and attitudes amount to a definition of a different *role* for the teacher from that which he has traditionally assumed. The inquiry environment, like any other school environment, is a series of human encounters, the nature of which is largely determined by the "teacher."

"Teacher" is here placed in quotation marks to call attention to the fact that most of its conventional meanings are inimical to inquiry methods. It is not uncommon, for example, to hear "teachers" make statements such as, "Oh, I taught them that, but they didn't learn it." There is no utterance made in the Teachers' Room more extraordinary than this. From our point of view, it is on the same level as a salesman's remarking, "I sold it to him, but he didn't buy it"—which is to say, it makes no sense. . . .

Perhaps you have noticed that most examinations and, indeed, syllabi and curricula deal almost exclusively with the past. The future hardly exists in school. Can you remember ever asking or being asked in school a question like "If such and such occurs, what do you think *will* happen?"? A question of this type is usually not regarded as "serious" and would rarely play a central role in any "serious" examination. When a future-oriented question is introduced in school, its purpose is usually to "motivate" or to find out how "creative" the students can be. But the point is that the world we live in is changing so rapidly that a future-orientation is essential for everybody. Its development in schools is our best insurance against a generation of "future shock" sufferers. . . .

[We conclude with a statement by Norbert Wiener in *The Human Use of Human Beings:*] "We have modified the environment so radically that we must now modify ourselves in order to exist in this new environment."[1]

---

[1] *EDITOR'S NOTE:* The child-centered versus subject-matter-centered curriculum is a problem which has persisted from the time of John Dewey, and before. The Postman-Weingartner selection emphasized *how* we think rather than *what* we think as the most crucial element in learning. The next selection deals with the same issue; but here the implication is that many so-called inquiry-oriented courses degenerate into Mickey Mouse courses precisely because they give insufficient attention to formally structured subject matter.

For another criticism of the Postman-Weingartner thesis, and for a defense of the view that "question-asking can be just as sterile as question-answering," read Arthur Pearl (University of Oregon), *The Atrocity of Education*, St. Louis, Mo.: New Critics Press, Inc., 1972, pp. 253–263.

---

# 2.7 RELEVANT—TO SOLID SUBJECT MATTER
## Alexander Calandra

Some time ago, I received a call from a colleague who asked if I would be the referee on the grading of an examination question. He was about to give a student a zero for his answer to a physics question, while the student claimed he should receive a perfect score and would if the system were not set up against the student. The instructor and the student agreed to submit this to an impartial arbiter, and I was selected.

I went to my colleague's office and read the examination question: "Show how it is possible to determine the height of a tall building with the aid of a barometer."

The student had answered: "Take the barometer to the top of the building, attach a long rope to it, lower the barometer to the street, and then bring it up, measuring the length of the rope. The length of the rope is the height of the building."

I pointed out that the student really had a strong case for full credit, since he had answered the question completely and correctly. On the other hand, if full credit were given, it could well contribute to a high grade for the student in his physics course. A high grade is supposed to certify competence in physics, but the answer did not confirm this. I suggested that the student have another try at answering the question. I was not surprised that my colleague agreed, but I was surprised that the student did.

I gave the student six minutes to answer the question, with the warning that his answer should show some knowledge of physics. At the end of five minutes, he had not written anything. I asked if he wished to give up, but he said no. He had many answers to this problem; he was just thinking of the best one. I excused myself for interrupting him, and asked him to please go on. In the next minute, he dashed off his answer which read:

"Take the barometer to the top of the building and lean over the edge of the roof. Drop the barometer, timing its fall with a stop-watch. Then, using the formula $S = \frac{1}{2}at^2$, calculate the height of the building."

At this point, I asked my colleague if *he* would give up. He conceded, and I gave the student almost full credit.

In leaving my colleague's office, I recalled that the student had said he had other answers to the problem, so I asked him what they were. "Oh yes,"

Alexander Calandra, "The Teaching of Elementary Science and Mathematics" (*ACCE Reporter*, 1969); reprinted in *American Education: Foundations and Superstructure*, Scranton, Pa.: International Publishers, 1970, pp. 436–437. By permission.
Alexander Calandra is Professor of Physics, Washington University, St. Louis.

said the student. "There are many ways of getting the height of a tall building with the aid of a barometer. For example, you could take the barometer out on a sunny day and measure the height of the barometer, the length of its shadow, and length of the shadow of the building, and by the use of a simple proportion, determine the height of the building."

"Fine," I said. "And the others?"

"Yes." said the student. "There is a very basic measurement method that you will like. In this method, you take the barometer and begin to walk up the stairs. As you climb the stairs, you mark off the length of the barometer along the wall. You then count the number of marks, and this will give you the height of the building in barometer units. A very direct method.

"Of course, if you want a more sophisticated method, you can tie the barometer to the end of a string, swing it as a pendulum, and determine the value of 'g' at the street level and at the top of the building. From the difference between the two values of 'g,' the height of the building can, in principle, be calculated."

Finally he concluded, there are many other ways of solving the problem. "Probably the best," he said, "is to take the barometer to the basement and knock on the superintendent's door. When the superintendent answers, you speak to him as follows: 'Mr. Superintendent, here I have a fine barometer. If you will tell me the height of this building, I will give you this barometer.' "

At this point, I asked the student if he really did not know the conventional answer to this question. He admitted that he did, but said that he was fed up with high school and college instructors trying to teach him how to think, to use the "scientific method," and to explore the deep inner logic of the subject in a pedantic way, as is often done in the new mathematics, rather than teaching him the structure of the subject. With this in mind, he decided to revive scholasticism as an academic lark to challenge the Sputnik-panicked classrooms of America.

# 2.8 RELEVANT TO INTELLECTUAL COMPETENCE AND TO SOCIAL PROBLEMS
## Jerome S. Bruner

[The word "relevance"] has two senses. The first is that what is taught should have some bearing on the grievous problems facing the world, the solutions of which may affect our survival as a species. This is social rele-

Reprinted from *The Relevance of Education* by Jerome S. Bruner, edited by Anita Gil. By permission of W. W. Norton and Co., Inc. Copyright © 1971 by Jerome S. Bruner.

vance. Then there is personal relevance. What is taught should be self-rewarding by some existential criterion of being "real," or "exciting," or "meaningful." The two kinds of relevance are not necessarily the same, alas. . . .

[I firmly believe that students should come face to face with the] great issues of life in our time. But I do not believe that the cure in the classroom is to be endlessly concerned with the immediacy of such issues—sacrificing social relevance to personal excitement. Relevance, in either of its senses, depends upon what you know that permits you to move toward goals you care about. It is this kind of "means-ends" knowledge that brings into a single focus the two kinds of relevance, personal and social. It is then that we bring knowledge and conviction together, and it is this requirement that faces us in the revolution in education through which we are going. . . .

[Unfortunately, during the 1960s] the concept of discovery, originally formulated to highlight the importance of self-direction and intentionality, had become detached from its context and made into an end in itself. Discovery was being treated by some educators as if it were valuable in and of itself, no matter what it was a discovery of or in whose service. The essay attempts to remedy some of the misuse into which the concept had fallen. . . .

Man is not a naked ape but a culture-clothed human being, hopelessly ineffective without the prosthesis provided by culture. The very nature of his characteristics as a species provides a guide to appropriate pedagogy, and the nature of his nervous system and its constraints provides a basis for devising reasonable if not inevitable principles for designing a testable pedagogy. . . . [Accordingly,] the human, species-typical way in which we increase our powers comes through converting external bodies of knowledge embodied in the culture into generative rules for thinking about the world and about ourselves. It is by this means that we are finally able to have convictions that have some consequences for the broader good. Yet I am convinced, as are so many others, that the way in which our ordinary educational activities are carried out will not equip men with effective convictions. I would like to propose, in the light of what I have said about skill and intentionality, and to honor what I believe about the two faces of relevance, that there be a very basic change in pedagogical practice along the following lines.

First, education must no longer strike an exclusive posture of neutrality and objectivity. Knowledge, we know now as never before, is power. This does not mean that there are not canons of truth or that the idea of proof is not a precious one. Rather, let knowledge as it appears in our schooling be put into the context of action and commitment. The lawyer's brief, a parliamentary strategy, or a town planner's subtle balancings are as humanly important a way of knowing as a physicist's theorem. Gathering together the data for the indictment of a society that tolerates, in the United States, the ninth rank in infant mortality when it ranks first in gross national product—

this is not an exercise in radical invective but in the mobilizing of knowledge in the interest of conviction that change is imperative. Let the skills of problem solving be given a chance to develop on problems that have an inherent passion—whether racism, crimes in the street, pollution, war and aggression, or marriage and the family. . . .

There is a very crucial matter about acquiring a skill—be it chess, political savvy, biology, or skiing. The goal must be plain; one must have a sense of where one is trying to get to in any given instance of activity. For the exercise of skill is governed by an intention and feedback on the relation between what one has intended and what one has achieved thus far— "knowledge of results." Without it, the generativeness of skilled operations is lost. What this means in the formal educational setting is far more emphasis on making clear the purpose of every exercise, every lesson plan, every unit, every term, every education. If this is to be achieved, then plainly there will have to be much more participatory democracy in the formulation of lessons, curricula, courses of study, and the rest. For surely the participation of the learner in setting goals is one of the few ways of making clear where the learner is trying to get. . . .

Second, education must concentrate more on the unknown and the speculative, using the known and established as a basis for extrapolation. This will create two problems immediately. One is that the shift in emphasis will shake the traditional role of the teacher as the one who knows, contrasting with the student who does not. The other is that, in any body of men who use their minds at all, one usually gets a sharp division between what Joseph Agassis (1969) calls "knowers" and "seekers." Knowers are valuers of firm declarative statements about the state of things. Seekers regard such statements as invitations to speculation and doubt. The two groups often deplore each other. Just as surely as authority will not easily be given up by teachers, so too will knowers resist the threatening speculations of seekers. Revolution does have difficulties!

With respect to encouraging speculative extrapolation, I would particularly want to concentrate on "subjects" or "disciplines" that have a plainly visible growing edge, particularly the life sciences and the human sciences: human and behavioral biology, politics, economics, sociology, and psychology, organized around problems which have no clearly known solutions. The reward for working one's way through the known is to find a new question on the other side, formulated in a new way. Let it be plain that inquiry of this kind can be made not just through "the social sciences" but equally via the arts, literature, and philosophy, as well as by the syntactical sciences of logic and mathematical analysis.

Third, share the process of education with the learner. There are few things so exciting as sensing where one is trying to go, what one is trying to get hold of, and then making progress toward it. The reward of mastering something is the mastery, not the assurance that some day you will make more money or have more prestige. There must be a system of counseling that assures better than now that the learner knows what he is up to and that he has some hand in choosing the goal. This may be raising the spectre problem of totally individualized instruction. But learning *is* individual, no matter how many pupils there are per teacher. I am only urging that in the organization of curricula, units, and lessons, there be option provided as to how a student sets his goal for learning.

Fourth and finally, I would like to propose that as a transition we divide the curriculum into a Monday-Wednesday-Friday section that continues during the transition to work with what has been best in our school curricula up to this point, and a Tuesday-Thursday curriculum that is as experimental as we care to make it—seminars, political analyses, the development of position papers on school problems, "problem-finding" in the local community, you name it. Let it be as controversial as needs be. We are lacking diversity in experiment and can afford controversy in order to get it. Tuesday and Thursday need be no respecter of conventional teaching qualification. Indeed, it might provide the proper occasion for bringing outsiders into the school and "hooking" them with its challenge. I would also want to bring to the school—other than the conventional media of learning—film, political debate, and the carrying out of plans of action, all to be subject to scrutiny, discussion and criticism. . . .

[We will succeed in making education relevant in so far as we] highlight the role of intention and goal directedness in learning and the acquisition  of knowledge, and the conversion of skill into the management of one's own enterprises. The objective is to produce skill in our citizens, skill in the achieving of goals of personal significance, and of assuring a society in which personal significance can still be possible. . . .

*Educating for the Future.* I suspect that there are three forms of activity that no device is ever going to be able to do as well as our brain with its $5 \times 10^9$ cortical connections, and I would suggest that these three represent what will be special about education for the future.

The first is that we shall probably want to train individuals not for the performance of routine activities that can be done with great skill and precision by devices, but rather to train their individual talents for research and development, which is one of the kinds of activities for which you cannot easily program computers. Here I mean research and development in the sense of problem finding rather than problem solving. If we want to look ahead to what is special about a school, we should ask how to train generations of children to *find* problems, to look for them. I recall that wonderful prescription of the English Platonist, Weldon, to the effect that there are three kinds of things in the world: There are troubles which we do not know quite how to handle; then there are puzzles with their clear conditions and unique solutions, marvelously elegant; and then there are problems—and these we invent by finding an appropriate puzzle form to impose upon a trouble.

What this entails for education is necessarily somewhat obscure although its outlines may be plain. For one thing, it places a certain emphasis on the teaching of interesting puzzle forms: ways of thinking that are particularly useful for converting troubles into problems. These are familiar enough in any given field of knowledge: they are the useful abstractions. What is needed is a sense of how to teach their use in converting chaotic messes into manageable problems. Much of the attraction of the use of discovery in teaching comes, I suspect, from the realization of the need to equip students in this way.

A second special requirement for education in the future is that it provides training in the performance of "unpredictable services." By unpredictable services, I mean performing acts that are contingent on a response made by somebody or something to your prior act. Again, this falls in the category of tasks that we shall do better than automata for many years to come. I include here the role of the teacher, the parent, the assistant, the stimulator, the rehabilitator, the physician in the great sense of that term, the friend, the range of things that increase the richness of individual response to other individuals. I propose this as a critical task, for as the society becomes more interdependent, more geared to technological requirements, it is crucial that it not become alienated internally, flat emotionally, and gray. Those who fret and argue that we are *bound* to go dead personally as we become proficient technically have no more basis for their assertion than traditional romanticism. Recall that the nineteenth century that witnessed the brunt of the Industrial Revolution also produced that most intimate form, the modern novel.

Third, what human beings can produce and no device can is art—in every form: visual art, the art of cooking, the art of love, the art of walking, the art of address, going beyond adaptive necessity to find expression for human flair.

These three—research and development, unpredictable services, and the arts—represent what surely will be the challenge to a society which has our capacity to provide technical routine. I assume we shall teach the technical routines, for that is built into our evolving system. Will we be daring enough to go beyond to the cultivation of the uniquely human?

# C. Relevant–To the Electronic Age

## 2.9 THE LINEAR TEACHER AND THE NON-LINEAR McLUHAN
### Hayden R. Smith

Now hear this:

"We march backwards into the future."
"Man was born with eyelids but no ear lids."
"The classroom—a cell for citters to cit in."
"Step into my parlor said the computer to the specialist."
"The medium is the massage."

The above are typical of the recent writings of Herbert Marshall Mc-Luhan, former Canadian Professor of Literature and "the oracle of the new communications." The serious teacher is immediately turned off by such gibberish—garbage and trash! As one critic exclaimed, "He plays a harmonica, a twelve stringed guitar, cymbals, and a bass drum, all at once—and not very well." Yet, there are many he has turned on, resulting in his being called: "The major intellectual influence of our times." "The most important thinker since Newton, Darwin, Freud, and Pavlov."

Somewhere amidst the satire, the invectives, the adulation, the praises heaped, lies the truth about McLuhan. He does have a message and it does have relevancy for teachers. However, a casual acquaintance with McLuhan reveals little, for his message is often obscured by his style. For this writer,

Hayden R. Smith, "The Linear Teacher and the Non-Linear McLuhan," *Clearing House* 45: 126–128, October 1970. By permission.
    Hayden R. Smith teaches at California State College, San Diego.
    We include Dr. Smith's bibliography, on the assumption that this one article, together with its bibliography, will suffice as a springboard for a discussion of the impact of television on education.
    Although included in Chapter 2, this article may also be viewed as a prelude to Chapter 3 and to Chapter 4.

after struggling through 8 books and some 40 articles, there is but one conclusion—McLuhan *is* the oracle of the new communications!

The Canadian professor has been criticized as a communicator who cannot communicate and as a writer who cannot write. His 6 books and over 150 articles (in some excellent journals) that he has written since 1934 are in direct contradiction to such criticism. A more plausible criticism of McLuhan might be in terms of his writing style. His puns, metaphors, gags, clichés, and wisecracks not only obscure, they often infuriate. What we fail to realize is that McLuhan, as showman, circus performer, and sideshow hawker, is virtually standing truth (as he sees it) on its head to get our attention.

Prior to the 1960's McLuhan's writing style is logical, linear, and comparatively easy to read. Suddenly, in the sixties (*The Gutenberg Galaxy, Understanding Media*), he discovers that the medium (print) is the antithesis of the very message he is sending. Thus his medium disturbs us more than his message, and he is criticized for not delivering his insights in their most practical and lucid form—exactly the opposite of his message. McLuhan's oral writing style (similar to the stream of consciousness writing of James Joyce) is purposive and attempts to create, through print, the fragmented, disorganized, *allatonceness* of today's electronic environment. While you may object to the way he writes, he was forced to adorn his message with puns, aphorisms, and neon lights before anyone would listen. In the short span of three years (1964–67) he has catapulted to world fame and renown.

Why is McLuhan important to teachers? Of course, any figure who is famous, controversial, and about whom so much has been written, should be of interest to teachers. Yet, it is his message, along with the massage, that must be of immediate concern to us all. The message, while simple, is difficult to grasp because of our linear mode of thinking—the Gutenberg complex. All things, to be understandable, must be linear, logical, organized, and sequential. Modern man lives in a reality which is just the opposite of these. McLuhan maintains that "All media, irrespective of content, do something to us. They massage us consciously or unconsciously—they work us over completely!" With the advances in modern electronics, man now has available to him a total instantaneous communication system similar to his own central nervous system. This new electronic environment is *allatonce*, here and now, total, illogical, non-linear, non-fragmented, and often ridiculous and absurd. This is the reality our students live in. The linear postulates of the *Gutenberg Galaxy* and Shakespearean Man are inadequate to meet the needs of our present non-linear reality. The world of print has created a linear cognitive man to the complete neglect of affective man. This sensory deprivation has been most keenly felt by modern youth whose senses are being constantly bombarded and heightened by the electric imagery of T.V., motion pictures, radio, advertising, and photography. Today's youth seek involvement and "happenings"—be it delinquency, sit-ins, riots, pot, L.S.D., Black Power, flower power, and even the Peace Corps. They are rediscovering color and sound in their "way out" aural, oral, tactile, and kinesthetic excursions into affective reality. Students are *allatonce* involved in today's world, a rice paddy in Viet Nam, the slaughter in the D.M.Z., the assassination of a president, the riots in Chicago, and even the man on the moon!

Unfortunately for education, theorists can easily forestall reality, but the classroom teacher is closeted with reality all day long. "They are co-prisoners with electronic-age students in a pencil box cell," says McLuhan. He seems to be asking teachers this large question: How can teachers see to it that the necessary specialist sensibilities, inculcated by whatever the form of medium employed, does not become the dominating factor in the entire field of our awareness? Of this he says, "Education must be the civil defense against media fall-out." . . .

The chief ingredients of education are learners, that which is to be learned, and teachers to facilitate the learning. Of this triumvirate the principal ingredient is the learner, because he determines not only what will be learned but how it will be learned. . . .

This whole complicated system of formal education is in business to motivate, to get through to, and to help students learn that which will be of value to them and society now and tomorrow. The principal business of the school is to communicate and facilitate learning, not to grade, label, or babysit. Of course the teacher communicates, but often the wrong things; how to cheat, how to forge pop's signature on a report card, how to antagonize teachers, how to avoid work, how to elude "fuzz" and "squares."

Teachers are forced to work in a world of modern technological reality. Their students live in the present, the first generation to live in a world in which there was always T.V., jet transportation, and space travel—someday they may live on the moon! They are quite different from their fuddy-duddy teachers who entered the picture just before the electric age was getting up steam.

Unfortunately, this is what is, and not what should be. The old analogy of the wax tablet walking to school is ludicrous. He enters the hallowed halls of learning already brimming over with information. As he grows, along with others of the electric generation, his standards for relevance are determined not by what he receives in the school, but by what he receives outside the school. And so, it would seem, these precious commodities in our classrooms have one foot in Huxley's Brave New World and the other in Queen Victoria's Drawing Room. We fix their eyes upon the galaxy of Gutenberg while their bodies are being transformed by the electronic phantasmagoria. The gap between the ouside world and the classroom, as well as the gap between generations, is no longer a gulf; it is gradually eroding into a chasm.

Learning is something people do for themselves; and people, places, and things can either impede or facilitate the process. The learner comes to the classroom with a vast array of experiences and loosely related facts learned through active, dynamic, sensory involvement and discovery. This is a new kind of learner who calls for a new kind of learning. We try to shape today's students with yesterday's learning theory: schedules, classrooms, memorization, and the like. Conflict is the natural outgrowth when the products of an *allatonce* electronic environment are forced into the mold of a one-thing-at-a-time linear classroom environment. The straight-line theory of development, logical and chronological, and the uniformity it dictates, is out of tune with the needs of the new learner. The total environment now becomes the great teacher, and if we are not "with it," our students are no longer with us. The current educational innovations represent a sharp break between the linear classroom and its world of print: team teaching, flexible scheduling, no bells ring, non-graded schools, oral-aural language training, multi-media, systems, seminars, research, individualized instruction. Slowly but surely, the responsibility for learning is being shifted from the teacher to the student—where it should be!

In the last fifty years many things have happened to all of us, and most of them involve an ignition key, a plug in the wall, or an electric eye to open a supermarket door. The six-year-old of today knows a great deal before he enters that linear cell called the classroom. At a tender age he was patted on the head, planted in front of a glass tube, and told to "shut-up." And there he sat for some 4,000 hours before he met his first teacher. By the time he graduates from high school (he may drop out or be pushed out) he will have clocked some 15,000 hours of cartoons, violence, sex, commercials, and sometimes, something we call "educational." The machine-gun bombardment of messages and massages to assure the "right perception" will follow him from the cradle to the grave.

The walls of our classrooms and the artificial walls of subject separation have been literally blown out by technology and the knowledge explosion. The life of the specialist will become even more lonely as teaching, learning, and knowledge move toward wholeness and convergence. However, technology can create monsters and only an educated citizenry, wise in the ways of the message and massage of the media, can determine whether we are to be masters or slaves of the technology we have created.

Unfortunately, much of McLuhan is, as yet, unpalatable for teachers for they are, of all people, the most linear. Young people are more at home than we with the new language. They lack only the ability to articulate and express their views in our language, and why should they? It is not they who have to communicate to us; we are the ones who must communicate to them!

## Suggested Readings

(1) CARPENTER, EDMUND and MARSHALL McLUHAN. *Explorations in Communication.* Boston: Beacon Press, 1966.
(2) CROSBY, HARRY and GEORGE BOND. *The McLuhan Explosion.* New York: American Book Company, 1968.
(3) McLUHAN, MARSHALL. *The Gutenberg Galaxy.* Toronto, Canada: University of Toronto Press, 1962.

(4) ————. *The Mechanical Bride.* Boston: Beacon Press, 1967.
(5) ————, and QUENTIN FIORE. *The Medium Is The Massage.* New York: Bantam Books, 1967.
(6) ————. *Understanding Media.* New York: McGraw-Hill Book Co., 1964.
(7) ————. *Understanding New Media.* Cooperative Research Project, Title VII, No. 179, U.S. Office of Education, 1960.
(8) STEARN, GERALD. *McLuhan Hot and Cool, A Symposium.* New York: Dial Press, 1967.[1]

---

[1] *EDITOR'S NOTE:* Read also Anthony Quinton, "Salvation through McLuhan," *New York Review of Books* 9: 6–13, November 13, 1967; Raymond B. Rosenthal, editor, *McLuhan: Pro and Con,* New York: Funk & Wagnalls, 1968; Sidney W. Finkelstein, *Sense and Nonsense of McLuhan,* New York: International Publishers, 1968.

In an age when almost every hour of our life depends on electricity, it seems unnecessary to present a lengthy response to the above defense of McLuhan's non-linear "thinking." It may be true that many of those sitting in *front* of boob tubes are able to enjoy the fruits of modern civilization even if they are unable to understand it or contribute to it. But those who make this civilization possible are persons highly skilled in the art of scientific analysis and the ways of linear thinking. Every time we use a telephone, or listen to a radio, or watch a television screen, we should recognize the momentous importance of linear (discursive, step-by-step, analytical) reasoning.

How, for example, are air waves (which carry the sound of our voice) changed into electric impulses (which are then transmitted by wire or by air to distant places), and then, at the other end of the telephone or radio or TV, how are these electric impulses changed back again into sound waves? The answer is that sound waves and electric currents, which represent two different branches of physics,

". . . are understood in terms of similar formal structures. Acoustical engineers have analyzed air-borne sounds in terms of frequency (pitch), amplitude (volume) and phase (timbre or quality). Electrical engineers have analyzed the flow of electric currents in terms of inductance, capacitance, and resistance. The transformation of air-borne sound waves into wire-borne electrical currents depends on precise "translation" of mechanical into electrical phenomena and vice versa. It is only because every detail of these two domains of physics (sound waves and electric currents) has been given precise statement in terms of Fourier analysis that we have our present-day telephone, phonography, radio, and television."—Henry Ehlers, *Logic By Way of Set Theory,* New York: Holt, Rinehart and Winston, Inc., 1968, p. 345.

# CHAPTER
# 3

## Utilize Educational Technology

# A. Operant Conditioning and Programmed Learning

## 3.1 INTRODUCTION

The process called operant conditioning is sometimes demonstrated to students like this: A hungry pigeon is placed in a box or cage, and the demonstrator undertakes to teach it to do a simple trick—for example, to turn around in a clockwise direction. He begins by waiting for the pigeon to make some move that might lead to the clockwise turn—turning its head to the right, for example. When he sees such a move, he *instantly reinforces* the desired move by giving the pigeon a grain of corn. Usually the pigeon will then repeat the move and the demonstrator will reinforce it again. Having established this movement, the demonstrator next withholds the corn until the pigeon chances not only to turn its head to the right, but, let us say, moves its left foot forward also. This combined movement is then reinforced with corn.

Proceeding in this manner, an experienced demonstrator can generally manage in a very short time to teach the pigeon to make a clockwise turn. Using the same method, pigeons have been trained to discriminate among playing cards of different suits, to peck out tunes on a piano keyboard, and many other tricks never before performed in psychological laboratories.

About 1950, B. F. Skinner (and others) began applying this method to human subjects, and they found that "programmed learning sequences" could be structured in book form, and also in teaching machines. Since that time, a period of only twenty years, a whole new education industry has developed.

Some teachers panicked at the thought that schoolmasters were to be replaced by machines—perhaps recalling that in the late 1920s, 2,000,000 theatre musicians were replaced by "talkies." A closer look at teaching machines reveals, however, that machines can replace teachers only in the more mechanical chores of pedagogy. It underscores the fact, also, that in most traditional schools a great proportion of teachers' time was devoted to having students memorize a sequence of mechanically presented data. Insofar as teaching machines can replace, or even reduce, this aspect of teaching, the teacher is now, for the first time, freed for higher levels of teaching than has ever been possible before. Or, as the saying goes, "If a teacher can be replaced, he should be."

A teaching machine is no better than the programs which are fed into that machine. It is an exceedingly difficult task to devise really excellent learning sequences suitable to varied students. The situation in education today is somewhat analogous to that in other mass production industries during their early stages. For example, when shoes were first manufactured, rather than made by hand, the local shoe salesman had to refit and refashion almost every pair of shoes he sold. But today's large shoe stores house thousands of shapes and sizes of shoes; and if a salesman cannot find a good fit he will generally order the right size from the factory rather than to attempt on-the-spot refitting for his customer. In the teaching machine industry, we are still in that stage of development where only a few "shapes and sizes" are available to fit the many dimensions of children's minds. So, "the necessary revolution in education," as its proponents call it, is not going to happen overnight. But a revolution seems to be on the way, even though it may be applicable only to the most mechanical and elementary aspects of the several subject matter areas.

The selections which follow do not deal with the practical day-to-day difficulties which face today's teachers who try to utilize the new media.[1] They deal only with the more theoretical aspects of operant conditioning, and with the competing psychologies implied.

The editor's prejudices on the subject may perhaps be revealed by repeating a statement made by J. P. Eckert, who with J. W. Mauchey, was responsible for the deisgn of ENIAC, the first digital computer: "After seventeen years, I've finally been forced to adopt the definition that thinking is what computers cannot do. This definition is very workable, since it changes from year to year as computer progress is made."[2]

The basic issue seems to be not whether we are to employ teaching machines and other mechanical aids. The issue is whether we are in danger of becoming so obsessed with the new and the experimental and the mechanical, that we lose sight of the larger dimensions of education—dimensions which help students to become critical yet open-minded, alert, and receptive to new factual observations but also responsive to new theoretical schema, adjusted to living in a pluralistic society yet unsatisfied with its present levels of attainment, aware of the constraints and limitations of human nature but also conscious of man's creative abilities.

Nevertheless, we must give serious consideration to the view that the best solution to the problems caused by modern technology is to develop countervailing technologies—in this case, to develop teaching machines and other teaching aids appropriate to the technotronic era.

[1] For a brief treatment of this topic, read Helen Coppen, "The New Media and the Teacher," in *The Teacher and the Needs of Society in Evolution*, edited by Edmund J. King, New York: Pergamon Press, 1970, pp. 159–177.
[2] J. P. Eckert, cited by Donald G. Fink in *Computers and the Human Mind*, New York: Doubleday, 1966, p. 208.

This new approach will certainly make for tremendous changes in the teaching profession. Today, the typical teacher's range of knowledge is probably greater than at any age in the past; but, at the same time, his *share of the total* body of knowledge is far less. As he steps into the classroom, a teacher may say what Neil Armstrong said when he placed his foot on the moon: "This is one small step for man, one giant step for mankind." In today's world, the teacher's task, like the astronaut's, is becoming more and more dependent on the work of others. The ever-increasing use of television, recordings, tapes, programmed learning, plus a multitude of new books and study guides, means that today's teacher is aided by the previous labor of others much more than was the case when the McGuffey Readers were his only teaching aids; or when, like an explorer who built and paddled his own canoe, individual prowess was more obvious than a sense of reliance on others.

The fact that each of us is only one tiny part of a complex and interdependent age does not mean that we should feel helpless or frustrated. Think of a modern physician. Surely in medicine the most important skill is the ability to diagnose a patient's disease. Similarly in education the most important ability is the proper diagnosis of a child's needs. And after diagnosing a child's needs, to be able also to prescribe the appropriate "medicine," that is to help a child find the most suitable learning experience, is a skill which may someday place teachers in as high professional esteem as the medical profession enjoys today.

# 3.2 B. F. SKINNER'S OPERANT CONDITIONING
## John Platt

Until recently, psychology has seemed to be standing still for lack of a general organizing principle. Freud's formulations are greatly discredited by recent experiments. Pearsonian measurements and correlations usually do not show

John Platt, "Beyond Freedom and Dignity: A Revolutionary Manifesto," *The Center Magazine* 5: 34–52.

Reprinted, with permission, from the March/April 1972 issue of *The Center Magazine*, a publication of the Center for the Study of Democratic Institutions in Santa Barbara, California.

John Radar Platt is a research biologist and associate director of the Mental Health Research Institute at the University of Michigan. This excerpt includes only Professor Platt's *exposition* of Skinner's operant conditioning, not his criticisms. The next several selections are, in one respect or another, critical of Professor Skinner's views.

us how to do anything. Personality "traits" and even intelligence tests are under fire. The theories of "drives" could not even explain such compulsive behavior as gambling. The great learning theorists did not show us how to teach faster. The "classical conditioning" methods of the early behaviorists were of little use in schools, or child training, or even animal training. And the schools of loving responsiveness, group therapy, and "peak experiences" have been inspiring but not very scientific.

Into this sea of ineffectiveness, Skinner has brought, over the last thirty-five years, a technique and theory of "operant conditioning" and behavior modification that has transformed every behavioral problem and approach. His method speeds up animal learning by ten to one hundred times, and can be used to improve behavior in psychiatric wards, solve such problems as bed-wetting and stuttering that have resisted psychiatric treatment, cure disruptive or delinquent behavior, and double the learning rate in schools from kindergarten through college. It can be used for self-control of unwanted habits, and even for Yoga-like voluntary control over heartbeat and blood pressure and other autonomic functions that had been supposed to be beyond conscious control.

It is evidently important to understand just how such a powerful method works and what it implies about biology and human nature. . . .

## Contingent Reinforcement

The basis of Skinner's methods of learning and behavior modification is his principle of contingent reinforcement or "operant conditioning," which he stated in 1938. He showed that a three-term formulation is necessary to describe how an animal or human being is induced to change its behavior. (This is why the usual one-term or two-term learning theories are so ineffective, such as learning-by-experience, learning-by-doing, trial-and-error, and stimulus-and-resonse, or, in computer language, input-output. Koestler confused Skinner's method with stimulus-and-response.)

The three necessary terms are stimulus, behavior, and reinforcement. Their relation can be symbolized as follows:

$$\begin{matrix} & B & & & B & & B & & B \\ S & & R, \text{thought of as repeated:} & S & & R \ldots S & & R \ldots S & & R. \end{matrix}$$

The lower line represents the environment's actions on the organism and the upper line represents the organism's actions on the environment. S is the preliminary stimulus situation; B is some behavior the organism may then show or "emit"; and R is then any change or "reinforcement" from the environment which is *immediate* and *contingent* on a particular B. (A particular behavior B emitted by the organism is called an "operant," and when this is induced to be emitted regularly under a given S and R, the process is called "operant conditioning.")

Any R which is followed by an increase in the probability of B is called a positive reinforcer, or $R^+$. Any R which is followed by a decrease is called a negative or aversive reinforcer, or $R^-$. Some critics object to this as being a circular definition of reinforcement, as for example in the phrase, "the enhancement of behavior by positive reinforcement." But the problem is no more difficult than that of the useful Darwinian phrase, "the survival of the fittest." In fact, reinforcers, unlike "fitness," can be fairly reliably predicted or extended to other situations and other species.

The $R^+$ and $R^-$ differ from ordinary "rewards" and "punishments" in being more precisely defined. Ordinary "rewards," such as too much food, may become aversive, while "punishment" to a response-starved child may be positively reinforcing. Skinner also defines an $R^0$, called "time out" (removal of S), which plays a useful role in shaping behavior.

Skinner showed the importance of the immediacy and contingency of R in inducing a changed B. An immediate R—within one second or less—singles out the B which is being reinforced from all the other B's of minutes or hours earlier. And for fast and accurate learning, R must never come except after B has been emitted.

However, R does not have to follow a given B every time. In fact, the fastest method of changing behavior is to give $R^+$ every time after some initial B is emitted, and then withhold it until B fluctuates a little in the desired direction. An $R^+$ then reinforces this new B, and can be again repeated and again withheld, so proceeding on a "reinforcement schedule" step by step to reach the final desired behavior. In the later stages of learning, an intense and repeated B can be maintained by "stretching the ratio" and giving $R^+$ randomly and more and more rarely, as with a slot machine. This is the basic explanation of gambling, on the one hand, and of certain types of patience and perseverance on the other. By stretching the ratio a little at a time, pigeons have been induced to keep pecking for more than ten thousand times for a grain of corn, though wasting away steadily—like the gambler.

The size of the reinforcer is much less important than its immediacy and contingency in shaping behavior. An animal will work harder for a sequence of small bites of food than for a dinner which would be satiating, and a gambler can be hooked by repeated small payoffs. And an animal or child will work at one task just to get to do another task he likes better (Premack principle). Or animals will work where the reinforcer is nothing but a sharpening up or clarification of the stimulus situation—just as humans will work to get a better map or a clarification of their problems.

The role of "secondary reinforcers" is extremely important. A positive reinforcer, $R^+$, can be replaced most of the time by some secondary reinforcer, $R_s^{(+)}$, that has been associated with it. Thus a baby obtaining the primary reinforcer of milk also comes to be reinforced by secondary maternal responses and by adult voices and smiles, so that these come to serve as generalized social reinforcers throughout our lives. . . .

Putting this all together, we find that any simple initial behavior B, such as a body movement, or an eye-blink, or a secretion, or an intestinal contraction, can be increased or decreased in probability or intensity by the correct reinforcement schedule of R's. Or it can be "shaped" step by step into new forms, or compounded with other B's into a complex chain of behaviors. (A chain, $B_1$-$B_2$ . . . $B_N$, is built up by working backward from the last element so that each learned B is used as the reinforcer for the previous B.) A large repertoire of modes of behavior can thus be built up.

By having a reinforcement schedule that depends on S, any of these behaviors can then be "brought under the control" of some new S-situation, or can come to be emitted with finer and finer discriminations between different S's. We learn to respond to the green light, with $R^+$, and ignore the red light, with $R^-$. (And the Terrace technique permits these discriminations to be transferred to another set of discriminations without errors!)

These B's can then be maintained indefinitely in full strength by a weak and intermittent $R^+$ or by a secondary reinforcer, $R_s^{(+)}$. Or a B may finally be "extinguished" and no longer emitted if it ceases to be followed by any $R^+$, or if the reinforcer continues to be given but is no longer contingent on B. In short, Skinner's central discovery is that "immediate reinforcement contingencies—the schedule of R's as related to S and B—are what shape successive behavior in all learning animals."

To change behavior, first change the reinforcing contingencies.

This is far removed from Pavlov's discovery in 1910 of the "conditioned reflex" and "classical conditioning," although this work of over sixty years ago is still confused with Skinner's work by his critics—for instance, as recently as 1971 in the pages of *Science*. Pavlov rang a bell as he presented food to a dog, and then found that the dog would salivate to the bell alone. In this case, the experimenter does both things beforehand, not waiting for the animal's "operant" behavior; and the animal does nothing but "associate" them, so the method is useless for shaping new behavior. (The role of the third term, the $R^+$ of food, in maintaining the bell-induced salivation, remained to be recognized.)

The other leading early behaviorist, J. B. Watson, in 1921, actually used intense bangs to make a baby fear small animals, much as described by Aldous Huxley in his *Brave New World*. (Again, Skinner's critics confuse his work with Watson's pairing, and his behavioral utopia *Walden Two* with the stereotyped behavior methods in *Brave New World*.) But Watson interpreted his shock treatment again as "association" or stimulus response, neglecting the preshock behavior B, which he thus could not enlarge.

Today, by contrast, an animal can be taught by reinforcement methods, not in days but in a few minutes, to control autonomic behaviors like salivation or the blushing of one ear, or even the pulses of individual brain cells. Pigeons can be taught to dance a figure eight for the first time in just a half-hour. Pryor induced a porpoise, not to emit a particular behavior, but continual novelties of behavior. And the Gardners have taught a young chimpanzee to "talk" in deaf-and-dumb sign language with a vocabulary of over a hundred words.

It goes as far beyond Pavlov as the atomic bomb goes beyond dynamite.

## Cybernetic and Evolutionary Parallels

In spite of the time it took to straighten out the effects of reinforcement, the principle is not alien to other ways of formulating the organism-environment relationship. Thus, the parallel between reinforcement and the way we learn from the natural environment is obvious. An animal or baby is rewarded by food after it reaches for food, and so learns reaching more and more accurately. The reinforcement principle is also somewhat parallel to the older "transaction theory" of interpersonal relationship, where A maintains his behavior because of response by B, and vice versa.

There is an even closer parallel to Wiener's theory of cybernetics, which describes the behavior of a goal-directed organism, or an automation such as an automatic gun-director. Such a goal-directed system can "track" a target and hit it accurately because there is an ongoing feedback-loop process of detecting the distance from the target (S), moving toward it (B), and then detecting the error or success (R), which serves in turn as the (S) for the next move (B), and so on. . . .

In *Beyond Freedom and Dignity*, Skinner [shows the] parallel between the reinforcement principle and the Darwinian mechanism of natural selection. New behavior patterns in the individual are like variations or mutations in the species, which are not directed in advance but are selected afterward by the environment, in the one case by reinforcement and in the other case by survival. As he says, "The environment does not push or pull, it *selects*." So over the lifetime of an individual organism, numerous types of complex behavioral responses are built up and evolved by the long sequence of natural and social reinforcement contingencies from birth—just as in the course of organic evolution, numerous species of animals have been evolved by the long sequence of evolutionary survival contingencies.

This is the reason why Skinner's theory and experiments, like Darwin's, are generalizable from pigeons to human beings, in spite of the enormous genetic and neurophysiological differences between such organisms. Learning by reinforcement may go back five million years or more, so it is primitive, even though not quite so primitive as the survival mechanism. . . .

## Against Punishment

The reinforcement experiments have led to conclusions and applications . . . [concerning] punishment or aversive reinforcement, R⁻. Skinner discusses the consequences of punishment and the alternatives to punishment more systematically in *Beyond Freedom and Dignity* than in his previous books. It is true that punishment can stop unwanted behavior almost immediately. This of course reinforces the parent or punisher, leading him to do it again and again. But the experiments show that punishment is ineffective unless applied immediately every time (quite opposite to the situation with $R^+$ reinforcers), and the punished behavior always comes back, along with additional behavior such as attempts to escape or to evade punishment or to retaliate. Skinner says this is why windows are broken in schools and not in drugstores.

There are also general behavioral effects. The punished animal or child cowers and loses his confidence and creativity, or else he becomes defiant; and in the human case he acquires long-lasting anxiety and guilt feelings. It might be supposed that "not being punished" for being "good" would be equivalent to being "rewarded," but the behavioral effects are very different. (Changing from $R^-$ to Not-$R^-$ may be equivalent to changing from no reward to $R^+$ in mathematics or economics, but it is not the same in behavior. This profound discovery has not been appreciated by many critics.)

The most effective fast way to stop unwanted behavior without these severe additional effects is by $R°$, or "time out." The machine simply stops working for the pigeon, which starts pecking madly in every direction to turn it back on so it can work for its corn; or the child is put in a bare room for exactly five minutes. The effect is to encourage return to the creative environment and exploration for positive reward, rather than to discourage it, as $R^-$ does. [$R°$ is basic to the thinking of those who advocate the Open Classroom, a topic to be discussed in Chapter 4].

But the best long-run way to eliminate unwanted behavior is by completely eliminating the $R^+$ reinforcements that maintain it, so that it becomes extinguished, and working at the same time to displace it by providing $R^+$ reinforcements for wanted behavior which is incompatible with it. . . .

Skinner regards the principle of operant conditioning as a law of nature, like the law of gravity, by which nature and other people have been pulling and shaping each of us, badly or well, from the moment of our birth. . . . [In his later years, especially in *Walden II* and in *Beyond Freedom and Dignity*, Skinner has moved from psychology *per se* into the realm of philosophy and social science, and has considered what might happen if a society were] designed to achieve its ends through positive reinforcements in all our interactions and to see what it might do to us as individuals and to our collective life. . . . Skinner believes that if his psychological discoveries were applied to a whole generation, we might see a transformation in our constructive creativity and in the pleasure of life. . . .

[Since the next three selections of this anthology are critical of Skinner —critical, not of his operant conditioning within restricted areas, but critical of his comprehensive social determinism—we here pass over John Platt's criticisms. We conclude with Platt's statement that, in spite of such criticism,]

Skinnerian methods are loose in the world and cannot be put back. They offer us the brightest hopes of any methods we now have for the rapid restructuring of many of our obsolete and dangerous social institutions and for building, not merely a Skinnerian society, but any new society for the world ahead.[1]

---

[1] *EDITOR'S NOTE*: Elsewhere, after summarizing the fabulous achievements of the past century in travel, in communication, in the computer and electronic industries, in the multiplication of electron-volt energy, in biogenetics, and in other areas, Platt concludes:

There have been many revolutions in our time, but I think that in the long run this psychological revolution . . . will be the most important of all for the success and happiness of man on this planet.—John Radar Platt, *The Next Step to Man*, New York: Wiley, 1966, p. 168.

---

# 3.3 PROGRAMMED INSTRUCTION AND TEACHING MACHINES: STRENGTHS AND LIMITATIONS
## Jerome Kagan

---

The teaching machine is defined as "a carefully prepared program for a specific segment of knowledge housed in some apparatus that presents the programmed material and indicates to the student when a response is right and when it is wrong." Unlike most educational innovations, the teaching machine is based on a theory of how children learn. In addition, the machines are more readily available than good teachers. Thus many parents and educators believe that proper use of a sufficient number of teaching machines will solve the awesome problems of contemporary education. The machine clearly has a useful role, but it is not a panacea.

There are three basic psychological assumptions behind the use of teaching machines, each of which requires examination. First, the use of the

Jerome Kagan, *Understanding Children: Behavior, Motives, and Thought*, New York: Harcourt Brace Jovanovich, Inc., 1971, pp. 120–125. Copyright © 1971, by Harcourt Brace Jovanovich, Inc., and reprinted with their permission. Footnote references here omitted. See also pages 108–119, 130–147.
Jerome Kagan is Professor of Psychology, Harvard University.

teaching machine is based on the notion that responses are learned more effectively if there is minimal delay between the child's offering of an answer and his subsequent knowledge of its accuracy. However, some recent experiments and reflection on the psychological nature of children lead us to question the universal application of this principle. The notion that learning is impeded by a long delay between the making of a response and delivery of a reward is based on results from learning experiments with animals. If a hungry rat presses a bar or runs a complex maze for food, and the food appears thirty seconds after the action rather than immediately, the animal is not likely to learn how to press the bar or run the maze. Thus many people assume that if a child makes a response and does not get the correct answer quickly (the answer is his reward), he will be unlikely to learn anything. But such a conclusion neglects the fact that human beings are thinking creatures who brood about what they are doing as well as what they have done. Since people can and do fill the time between making a response and receiving the correct answer by thinking about their behavior, the importance of an immediate answer is minimized.

In one study, a group of undergraduate students was given a multiple-choice test and informed of the answer to each question immediately; another group of students received each answer after a ten-second delay. All the students were then given a retention test to measure what they had learned and were tested again five days later. There were no differences in score on the first retention test between those who received each answer immediately and those who were told the answer after ten seconds. However, on the test given five days later, the students who received delayed answers performed much better than those who received immediate answers. (Sassenrath and Yonge, 1969.) It is likely that the students were mentally rehearsing each problem and answer during the ten-second delay, and this extra time for synthesis and rehearsal aided their learning.

Another study tested students on their knowledge of statistics. One group of students received their test scores immediately—as the tests were turned in; each student was then instructed to find the correct responses to his mistakes. A second group learned their test scores twenty-four hours later. When the test was administered again a week later, the students who had had to wait twenty-four hours to learn of their performance on the first test obtained higher scores than those who had been informed immediately. (Daniel, 1968.)

Since some students brood about their performance on tests, delay of an answer can on occasion facilitate learning. Suppose a child is being taught to associate a color word with an animal word. The teacher says "bird," and if the child responds with a color word, the teacher says "good." If the child does not say a color word, the teacher says nothing. If the teacher imposed a delay before saying the reward "good" after the child stated a color word, the child would have time to consider the two words and the relation necessary to solve the problem. In order for material in short-term memory to be transferred to long-term memory, there must be time for this synthesis, time for the implicit rehearsal of information. Since imposing a delay in the delivery of an answer gives the child a chance to rehearse and synthesize information, it can have a beneficial effect on learning. Thus the first principle guiding the use of teaching machines *is not true all the time.*

A second assumption behind the use of the teaching machine is that the systematic structuring of a large unit of knowledge is superior to a random presentation of that knowledge. To some extent this principle is true, for a teacher's lecture on a topic cannot possibly simulate the orderliness of a carefully thought-out program. But as with the principle of delay, there are exceptions. For example, students majoring in education were given two programmed-instruction units while sitting at a typewriter terminal linked to a computer system. One group of students was assigned programs that were ordered and logical; another group was assigned programs that were completely disorganized. The two units to be learned consisted of a modern mathematics program on the transformation of numbers in the base-10 system to equivalent values in a nondecimal system and a program on the anatomy of the ear. The unit on numbers lent itself to organization and was therefore expected to benefit from logical programming. The unit on the anatomy of the ear consisted of a set of unrelated anatomical facts to be memorized and was assumed to derive relatively little benefit from a structured program.

As expected, there were no differences in ease of learning for test performance on the anatomy unit between the group of students given the structured material and the group given the disorganized program. It did not make any difference for rote memory whether the units were programmed or not. However, on the mathematics unit the students with the logical program made *more errors* than the group with the disordered program. The first group of students made more errors as the ordered program progressed because the material became more difficult. The group given the disorganized program made significantly more errors than the first group during the early stages of the unit, but by the last part of the program they became more confident and made fewer errors. The scrambled program was also better for bright students than for average students, for it was more challenging than the ordered program and led to greater student involvement. (Wodtke *et al.*, 1968.)

Thus, assuming a student is motivated, he is more likely to learn when he tries to impose a structure on new material than when the structure is given to him ready-made. The careful structuring of information ignores the effect of increased problem difficulty on expectancy of failure and the motivational value of challenge. Programs make new material maximally easy to understand, on the assumption that the student *wants* to learn the material as easily as possible. Some children do not want the task made too easy; they thrive on challenge. The fun is in getting to the top of the mountain, not in being there. As a result, some children find programmed materials boring, or even condescending, and they do poorer than if the material had been presented in a less systematic manner. Thus the second principle guiding the use of teaching machines *has occasional limitations, especially for brighter students.*

The third assumption behind the use of the teaching machine is that the child learns best when adults stay out of his way, when he is able to have a solitary dialogue with the material to be learned. In the discussion of motives in the first part of this book it was suggested that just the opposite is true, for the young child is often more highly motivated to learn when he feels he will obtain the responses of a teacher.

In one experiment on this issue, a group of fourth-grade students worked with a teacher on a programmed sequence on the geography of Japan. A second group of pupils worked with a teacher aide and the materials. A third group worked alone with the program, and a fourth group was given no instruction at all. The students exposed to the teacher with the program performed much better than those exposed to the program alone. The assumption that adults should not be involved in the child's learning is clearly not supported by this experiment. (Ryan, 1968.)

In another study, a group of high school boys worked alone on a programmed unit on number concepts, recording their answers in a booklet. A second group watched the teacher and other students interact with the program in the fashion of traditional recitation. The teacher wrote each problem on the blackboard and the students came forward to recite. A third group was made up of those students from the second group who answered the teacher's questions aloud. A fourth group watched and listened while the teacher recited each question of the program to herself and then answered it herself, as if she were describing her own thoughts. A fifth group was given no training at all. In a test given to all students at the end of the experiment, the first four groups performed better than the fifth group. But none of the four experimental groups performed better than any other. Watching the teacher was as effective as doing the program alone. (Craig, 1968.) Thus the third assumption behind the use of teaching machines also *has its exceptions.*

We must conclude therefore that the three basic principles behind the use of the teaching machine—delay of reward, structured programming, and elimination of the adult—are not always true. When these principles do not hold, the failure can usually be explained by taking into account the motives and expectancies of the child. The child's view of the machine is a critical factor in the success of any program. What does the act of sitting at a machine represent to him? His view will depend on whether he believes that completion of seven units by Friday afternoon will bring the teacher's praise and recognition, avoidance of punishment, or internal satisfaction. The child's feeling of freedom to use the machine is also critical. Does he have a choice of using a machine or a textbook, or must he use one or the other? The machine will be viewed more positively by the child who feels that he has a choice.

As in most issues, there is no absolute statement that can be made about the value of teaching machines. The machine has gained popularity because it enables educators to do something effective at a time when it is not clear what should be done. Action always reduces apprehension in a time of crisis, and it is easier to change the material than to alter the child's behavior or his relationship to the teacher. But in the long run it may be more advantageous to improve the child's motivation to learn. The teaching machine should neither be rejected out of hand nor be embraced as a cure to the problem of pupil apathy. The machine's novelty should be exploited fully; its emphasis on rational analysis of a segment of knowledge should be heeded. But inflexible reliance on the machine for all children and for all types of learning is probably unwise.

# 3.4 LEARN WITH *BOOK*
## R. J. Heathorn

A new aid to rapid—almost magical—learning has made its appearance. Indications are that if it catches on all the electronic gadgets will be so much junk.

The new device is known as Built-in Orderly Organized Knowledge. The makers generally call it by its initials, BOOK.

Many advantages are claimed over the old-style learning and teaching aids on which most people are brought up nowadays. It has no wires, no electric circuit to break down. No connection is needed to an electricity power point. It is made entirely without mechanical parts to go wrong or need replacement.

Anyone can use BOOK, even children, and it fits comfortably into the hands. It can be conveniently used sitting in an armchair by the fire.

How does this revolutionary, unbelievably easy invention work? Basically, BOOK consists only of a large number of paper sheets. These may run to hundreds where BOOK covers a lengthy program of information. Each

R. J. Heathorn, "Learn with BOOK," *Phi Delta Kappan*, 44: 153, December 1962. This article appeared originally in *Punch*, the British humor magazine, and is here used by permission of *Punch*. © *Punch*, London.

sheet bears a number in sequence, so that the sheets cannot be used in the wrong order.

To make it even easier for the user to keep the sheets in the proper order, they are held firmly in place by a special locking device called a "binding."

Each sheet of paper presents the user with an information sequence in the form of symbols, which he absorbs optically for automatic registration on the brain. When one sheet has been assimilated, a flick of the finger turns it over and further information is found on the other side.

By using both sides of each sheet in this way a great economy is effected, thus reducing both the size and cost of BOOK. No buttons need to be pressed to move from one sheet to another, to open or close BOOK, or to start it working.

BOOK may be taken up at any time and used by merely opening it. Instantly it is ready for use. Nothing has to be connected up or switched on. The user may turn at will to any sheet, going backward or forward as he pleases. A sheet is provided near the beginning as a location finder for any required information sequence.

A small accessory, available at trifling extra cost, is the BOOKmark. This enables the user to pick up his program where he left off on the previous learning session. BOOKmark is versatile and may be used in any BOOK.

The initial cost varies with the size and subject matter. Already a vast range of BOOKS is available, covering every conceivable subject and adjusted to different levels of aptitude. One BOOK, small enough to be held in the hands, may contain an entire learning schedule.

Once purchased, BOOK requires no further upkeep cost; no batteries or wires are needed, since the motive power, thanks to an ingenious device patented by the makers, is supplied by the brain of the user.

BOOKS may be stored on handy shelves and for ease of reference the program schedule is normally indicated on the back of the binding.

Altogether the Built-in Orderly Organized Knowledge seems to have great advantages with no drawbacks. We predict a big future for it.

# 3.5 BEHAVIOR MODIFICATION
## Harvey Wheeler

One of the functions of politics has always been to modify behavior. Plato stated this as his leading goal in writing *The Republic*. Our educational practices are devoted to behavior modification. Each time we draft a new law we have in mind the modification of behavior to conform with the provisions of the law. The aim of modifying behavior is not new, but recently the techniques for achieving it have developed a high degree of sophistication. The most familiar example comes from the behavioral drugs, tranquilizers, energizers and so on. Moreover, we are told that the world's leading nations are engaging in large, highly classified research projects in behavioral drugs: drugs that can be sprayed over population centers to render the residents docile or disoriented and easy for an invading army to manipulate.

Such drugs may be used for other purposes: to quell a riot or to calm angry commuters caught in traffic jams and subway failures. Many fear that if they can be used for this, they can also be used for more general, repressive purposes. A modern Hitler, for example, might use behavioral drugs.

Electronics combined with brain research presents another technique of behavior control. Electrodes implanted in the brain can stimulate pleasure centers so effectively that the subjects come to abandon all their needs and normal functions to press the pleasure button over and over again. Already these stimuli can be activated by remote, wireless control. Perhaps some day it will no longer be necessary to actually implant electrodes in the brain in order to achieve similar results.

Molecular biologists seem to be on the verge of understanding the way in which the DNA-RNA replication process works. When they do, the prospect of genetic engineering will become a reality. Many good things can be done: genetic surgery can correct congenital defects in the foetus or the newly born. But beyond this, it may be possible to alter man's instinctual equipment. Suppose we think that the human being as we know him is too war-like. Perhaps we can adjust him genetically so as to produce a more pacific creature. Should we do so? If we do, what might be the unintended consequences? What kinds of controls should be adopted to regulate this new technology?

Harvey Wheeler: "Social and Philosophical Implications of Behavior Modification," *Center Report*, Vol. 5, No. 1, pp. 3–5. Reprinted, with permission, from the February 1972 issue of *The Center Magazine*, a publication of the Center for the Study of Democratic Institutions in Santa Barbara, California.

Harvey Wheeler is a Senior Fellow at the Center for the Study of Democratic Institutions.

This brings us to a fourth type of behavior modification, one somewhat more traditional in technique, but one, so we are told, that is already available to us. This is the technique of "operant conditioning" developed by B. F. Skinner of Harvard. Skinner claims that this new psychological approach is not only effective but that it renders all our traditional ideas of political theory, jurisprudence and ethics, obsolete. Here he joins with certain philosophers who claim the old mind-body dualism lacks foundation: there is not a "ghost in the machine" (to use Gilbert Ryle's formula); there is not an inner psyche or an autonomous, decision-making mind. Hence, Skinner argues, free will, dignity, and many other noble or god-like attributes, are not inherent in man. Moreover, Skinner contends, once we abandon such notions we will be able to apply operant conditioning to structure a new kind of social and political environment that will regulate human behavior more effectively and more rationally than anything previously possible. The technique is available, claims Skinner; it should be used to improve the human condition. But what is this so-called improvement? How do we know we would be better off?

Operant conditioning differs from traditional behavioralism in two ways. First, it does not regard both pleasure and pain stimuli as being equally effective, nor does it regard them as representing linear variables along a single scale reaching from pleasure on one end to pain on the other. On the contrary, it makes a qualitative distinction between the two, calling pleasures positive reinforcements and pains negative reinforcements. Moreover, it claims that it is not feelings we respond to but reinforcements themselves, directly. Positive reinforcements (rewards for doing something) are said to be more effective behavior modifiers than are negative reinforcements (punishments for doing something other than what is desired). It is easy to see how this would be the case. A reward may be direct, as in paying a worker to produce; a punishment may be indirect, as in arresting a drunken driver. In the latter case one may learn only what is to be avoided, getting arrested, not what is to be performed. Of course, when the lesson to be taught is avoidance (aversion, rather than performance), it would appear that the tables are turned. If we wish to teach someone not to touch a hot stove, to reward him each time he does something else is not likely to be as directly effective as a controlled aversive demonstration that hot stoves may burn. This raises questions about the efficacy of operant conditioning in therapeutic situations wherein the problem is often to teach some variant of the lesson that hot stoves burn.

A second distinguishing feature of operant conditioning is that the conditioner does not impose his own notion of positive and negative reinforcement on the subject. His idea of a reward may not be accurate. Accordingly, he must discover what rewards are from the subject. The way he does this is to observe what stimuli best reinforce desired behavioral patterns. These stimuli are, by definition, positive reinforcers: meat is not a positive reinforcer for a cow but it is for a dog, and so on. Carried to extremes this might seem to involve operant conditioning in circularity, the familiar sadist-masochist (or each to his own pleasure) trap. There is a way out of this but it raises a new problem.

The way out is to say that, in general, we can observe what is a healthy positive reinforcer (one that does not bring deferred aversive results) by observing its long term effects on the subject. If these effects are good (simply in terms of survival) the reinforcer that produces it is a proper positive reinforcer; if bad, it is an improper positive reinforcer. Hence, for those who respond positively to improper positive reinforcers, as in the case of drug addicts, the task of therapy, or of operant conditioning, in general, is to rearrange the subject's response pattern to conform with more generally observed norms. The case may seem clear with regard to drug addicts (even here there is a serious argument) but in other cases, such as whether "work" is better for people than "play," the situation is not so clear. It is in these latter areas that professor Skinner has met his most vigorous opposition.

He answers this by resorting to a proposition about cultural evolution: cultures that reinforce behavior properly will survive, those that do not will die. This is not satisfactory either for it might lead to the conclusion that our contemporary primitives, such as the Australian bushmen, have a good reinforcement system for they have survived as a culture longer than most other cultures. It might even lead to the conclusion that a spectacular culture such as that of Athens, was inferior to the culture of less glorious but victorious Spartans. Skinner's Darwinian retreat into cultural survival does not seem to help unless one is able to make qualitative distinctions between different cultures. But this involves making value judgments. However, values have doubtful status in the lexicon of operant conditioning: values are forms of verbal behavior and not qualitatively different from other forms of behavior whose adoption has been produced by environmental reinforcement. Hence we reach another level of circularity.

It is hard to see how this impasse can be resolved within the assumptions of operant conditioning. Professor Skinner seems at times to want to resolve it by referring to something like a traditional conventional wisdom, arguing in effect that people in general would be better off if certain behavioral patterns were adopted by all. And yet, in order to demonstrate the validity of the particular patterns he espouses he seems to be forced to fall back on some version of natural law; the implicit natural law of the social Darwinists. However, natural law is anathema to him on other grounds. Not only is it merely verbal behavior, what is worse, it is aversive. The apparent result is that his fundamental position turns out to be rootless.

On the other hand, if it is not rootless then we have a right to ask him to explain exactly what his fundamental position is and whence comes its validity. If he does not satisfy us on this score we are justified in citing his own doctrine back at him. Why, we may ask, should anyone accept the Skinner behavioral goals over those of anyone else? Operant conditioning teaches us that we are all creatures of environmental forces. This applies to our goals (our verbal behavior) as well as our actions. Hence, Professor Skinner and the system of verbal behavior we know as operant conditioning is also a product of the particular schedule of reinforcements he himself experienced. As such, the goals associated with Skinner's operant conditioning have no greater validity than do the different goals of those who have experienced a quite different schedule of reinforcements. The behavioralism that produces a Skinner is no better than that which produces an anti-Skinner. There is no way to resolve this argument within the terms of behavioralism.

Finally, we may raise a somewhat more subtle question. Even assuming the above difficulties can be resolved, what about the positive role that notions such as freedom and dignity may have played? Professor Skinner argues they are bad because they stand in the way of full-fledged adoption of operant conditioning principles in human affairs. He argues further that they are wrong because a behavioralist point of view reveals them to be myths. Suppose we agree that such concepts, formerly deemed ennobling, are in fact myths. May it not be the case, even from a behavioralist point of view, that such ennobling myths are necessary positive reinforcers for a humane and decent society? If this is the case, the role of behavioralism would be to induce a firm belief in the intrinsic validity of verbal behavior it claims is no more valid than an archaic code of chivalry.[1]

---

[1] *EDITOR'S NOTE*: With respect to verbal behavior, the views of Noam Chomsky and other specialists in linguistics deserve to be heard. Chomsky maintains that it is language which makes man unique, and gives his life a different dimension than that of other animals. More specifically, Chomsky insists that every language is "open-ended," that is to say, the input of any language in terms of words and phrases is finite and limited, whereas the output in terms of new combinations of words and phrases is unlimited. Like the nursery rhyme which begins with "This is the house that Jack built," sentences can be made more and more complex. For example: "John wished . . . that he could play . . . ball . . . with his brother . . . in the field . . . by the brook . . . on the farm . . . of his uncle . . . where they visited . . . last summer . . . on Sundays . . . and swam . . . and picked berries . . ." And so on and on.

To illustrate Chomsky's thesis, suppose our input consisted of exactly six words: *door, mouth* (nouns), *open, close* (verbs), *and, or* (connectives). These six words may be restructured in many ways: *open door, close mouth, open mouth or door, open and close mouth*, etc. When we consider that even the most primitive languages contain thousands of nouns, hundreds of verbs and scores of connectives, we see that the number of meaningful combinations is so vast as to be called infinite. This is not to deny that some aspects of human life are mechanically or behavioristically determined. But it is to insist that, because of their unique ability to recombine words and ideas into new and creative patterns, men—all men—are able to transcend their environment, perhaps not in the *geosphere* nor in the *biosphere*, but certainly in the *noosphere*—the realm of thought and language, the realm of ideas and ideals. There is a sense in which we are out of space and time and causality: We are out of space and time every time we *think* about them. We are exempt from causality every time we discover a causal law, since we could never make such discoveries unless thinking is based on the free weighing of evidence, and is not altogether the result of biological and psychological antecedents. For more on this point, read T. E. Jessop, *The Freedom of the Individual in Society*, Toronto: Ryerson Press, 1948, pp. 45–47.

---

# 3.6 TOWARD GOAL-ORIENTED PSYCHOLOGY
## Floyd W. Matson

Humanistic psychology tries to tell it not like it is, but like it ought to be. It seeks to bring psychology back to its source, to the *psyche,* where it all began and where it finally culminates. But there is more to it than that. Humanistic psychology is not just the study of "human being"; it is a commitment to human becoming.

It was a humanistic philosopher, Kurt Riezler, who said that "science begins with respect for the subject matter." Unfortunately that is not the view of all scientists, whether in the hard sciences of nature or in the softer sciences of man and mind. It is almost, as it seems to me, a defining characteristic of behaviorist psychology that it begins with *dis*respect for the subject matter, and therefore leads straight-away to what Norbert Wiener (a pretty hard scientist himself) called the "inhuman use of human beings." At any rate, I know of no greater disrespect for the human subject than to treat him as an object—unless it is to demean that object further by fragmenting it into drives, traits, reflexes, and other mechanical hardware. But that is the procedure of behaviorism, if not of all experimental psychology; it is a procedure openly admitted, indeed triumphantly proclaimed, in the name of Science and Truth, of Objectivity and Rigor, and of all else that is holy in these precincts. And it leads in a straight line out of the ivory tower into the brave new world of Walden Two. . . .

There have been, as I believe, three distinct conceptual revolutions in

Floyd W. Matson, "Humanist Theory: The Third Revolution in Psychology." This article first appeared in *The Humanist* 31: 7–11, March/April 1971 and is reprinted by permission. The article appeared in a slightly revised form in *Existential Humanist Psychology,* edited by Thomas C. Greening, Monterey, Calif.: Brooks/Cole Pub. Co., 1971.

Floyd Matson, Professor of American Studies at the University of Hawaii, Honolulu, is author of *The Broken Image* (1964). The Doubleday paperback edition of this book (1966) would make an excellent supplement.

psychology during the course of the present century. The first, that of behaviorism, struck with the force of a revelation around 1913 and shook the foundations of academic psychology for a generation. Behaviorism arose in reaction to the excessive preoccupation of 19th-century psychology with consciousness, and with introspection as a way of getting at the data of conscious mental activity. The behaviorists reacted with a vengeance. They threw out not only consciousness, but all the resources of the mind. The mind, to them, was the ghost in the machine, and they did not believe in ghosts. The founding father of the movement, John B. Watson, declared in an early proclamation, a kind of behaviorist manifesto, that the behaviorist began "by sweeping aside all medieval conceptions. He dropped from his scientific vocabulary all subjective terms such as sensation, perception, image, desire, purpose, and even thinking and emotion as they were subjectively defined" (*Behaviorism* [1924], University of Chicago Press, Chicago, 1958, pp. 5-6).

Overt behavior, that which could be seen and measured, was all that counted. And all that was needed to explain it was the simple and classical formula of stimulus-response—with one added refinement, that of the conditioned reflex. It was this concept of conditioning, borrowed from the Russian laboratories of Pavlov and Bechterev, that gave the real revolutionary impetus to Watson's behaviorist movement. Conditioning was power; it was control. This was no merely objective psychology, for all its scientific claims; it was an applied psychology—and what it was applied to, or rather against, was man. "The interest of the behaviorist," said Watson, "is more than the interest of a spectator; he wants to control man's reactions as physical scientists want to control and manipulate other natural phenomena" (Ibid., p. 11). Just as man was simply "an assembled organic machine ready to run," so the behaviorist was no pure scientist but an engineer unable to keep from tinkering with the machinery. Pointing out that such sciences as chemistry and biology were gaining control over their subject matter, Watson inquired, "Can psychology ever get control? Can I make someone who is not afraid of snakes, afraid of them, and how?" The answer was clear: And how!

"In short," said Watson, "the cry of the behaviorist is, 'Give me the baby and my world to bring it up in and I'll make it crawl and walk; I'll make it climb and use its hands in constructing buildings of stone or wood; I'll make it a thief, a gunman, or a dope fiend.' The possibility of shaping in any direction is almost endless" (*The Ways of Behaviorism,* Harper, New York, 1926, p. 35).

That should be enough to suggest the general character (and authoritarian personality) of behaviorist psychology, the first of the three psychological revolutions that have taken place in our century. The second revolution was, of course, that of Freud. It is noteworthy that psychoanalysis and behaviorism made their appearance at roughly the same time, give or take a decade, and that both of them emerged in reaction against the accent on consciousness in traditional psychology. Apart from these coincidences, however, there was little in common between these two movements, and there was a great deal that put them at opposite poles.

Whereas behaviorism placed all its stress upon the external environment (that is, upon stimuli from the outer world) as the controlling factor in behavior, psychoanalysis placed its emphasis upon the internal environment (upon stimuli from within, in the form of drives and instincts). For Freud, man was very much a creature of instinct—and in particular of two primary instincts, those of life and death (*Eros* and *Thanatos*). These two instincts were in conflict not only with each other but with the world, with culture. Society was based, said Freud, on renunciation of the instincts via the mechanism of repression. But the instincts did not give up without a struggle. In fact, they never gave up; they could not be vanquished, only temporarily blocked. Life, then, was a constant alternation between frustration and aggression. Neither for the individual person nor for the culture was there a permanent solution or "happy ending"; there were only compromises, expedients, working adjustments. The price of civilization, indeed, was mass neurosis—the result of the necessary suppression of the natural instincts of man. But if that seems bad, the alternative was worse; whenever the repressive forces are for a moment relaxed, declared Freud, "we see man as a savage beast to whom the thought of sparing his own kind is alien" (*Civilization and Its Discontents,* Hogarth, London, 1930, p. 86. . . .)

The main point I want to make immediately about the psychoanalytic movement, in its Freudian form, is that it presents a picture of man as very much the "victim-spectator," as Gordon Allport has put it, of blind forces working through him. For all its differences with behaviorism, Freudian theory agrees in the fundamental image of man as a stimulus-response machine, although the stimuli that work their will upon the human being come from within rather than from without. Freud's determinism was not environmental, like Watson's, but psychogenetic; nevertheless, it was a determinism, and it left little room for spontaneity, creativity, rationality, or responsibility. The declared faith in conscious reason that underlay Freudian therapy (rather more than Freudian theory) did not prevent his insistently minimizing the role of reason as an actual or potential determinant of personality and conduct —nor, on the other hand, from maximizing the thrust of irrational forces that press their claims both from "below" (the id) and from "above" (the superego). In Freud's topographical map of the mind, the ego, itself only partially conscious, never achieves full autonomy but functions as a kind of buffer state between the rival powers of instinct and introjected culture, between animal nature and social nurture.

I have been deliberately hard on Freud in these remarks in order to emphasize those aspects of his theory and therapy that, by virtue of their pessimism and determinism, have called out over the years the critical and creative response that (for want of a better term) we may call "humanistic psychology." This new psychology, the third revolution, represents a reaction against *both* behaviorism and orthodox psychoanalysis; it is for that reason that humanistic psychology has been called the "third force." But perhaps the first thing to say about it is that, unlike the two movements of thought that precede and oppose it, humanistic psychology is not a single body of theory but a collection or convergence of a number of lines and schools of thought. If it owes nothing to behaviorism, it does owe much to psychoanalysis, although less perhaps to Freud himself than to the considerable number of Freudian heretics and deviationists, beginning with his own associates of the original Vienna Circle and culminating in the so-called neo-Freudians (anti-Freudians, really) of the second generation.

For despite the many differences among them, those who broke away one by one from the side of Freud shared a number of crucial insights and commitments. Adler, Jung, Rank, Stekel, Ferenczi—all these early associates found themselves unable to accept Freud's theory of instinctual determinism (specifically, his libido theory) and his tendency to find the source of all difficulty and motivation in the remote past. These deviationists began to place equal or greater emphasis upon the present (that is, upon the here and now, the "presence" of the patient) and also upon the future (that is, upon the pull of aspiration and purpose, the goal or life-plan of the individual). What this implied was a greater reliance upon the consciousness of the person in analysis or therapy: a new respect for his powers of will and of reason, his capacity to choose and to understand.

In Adler's work, this emphasis took the form of virtually converting the psychoanalytic therapy session into a dialogue or conversation on the conscious level—which of course enraged Freud, who thought that Adler had betrayed the basic postulate of unconscious motivation. In Jung's work, the new approach took the form of emphasizing what he called the "prospective factor," the pull of purpose as opposed to the push of instinct (and in particular the push of erotic instinct); it also took the form, in Jung's later years, of increasing stress upon understanding the other, whether neurotic patient or normal individual, in his unique identity. This involved a kind of intuitive and sympathetic understanding, which Jung distinguished from scientific knowledge and which led him finally to advocate abandoning the textbooks altogether in any venture into helping or healing. In the case of Otto Rank, another of the heretics of the original Freudian circle, the deviation took the form of an emphasis upon the existential will of the person, that is, upon his capacity for self-direction and self-control.

The common denominator in these various lines of theory and therapy was, I believe, *respect for the person,* recognition of the other not as a case, or an object, or a field of forces, or a bundle of instincts, but as himself. In terms of theory, it meant respect for his powers of creativity and responsibility; in terms of therapy, it meant respect for his values, his intentions, and, above all, his peculiar identity.

This recognition of *man-in-person*, as opposed to *man-in-general*, goes to the heart of the difference between humanistic psychology, in any of its forms or schools, and scientific psychologies such as behaviorism. Not only in psychoanalysis, but in other fields as well, increasing numbers of students have found themselves drawn to the unsettling conclusion that the definitive features of a human being cannot be made out at all from a "psychological distance," but can be brought into focus only by understanding (literally, by "standing under") the unique perspective of the individual himself. [This is particularly important in teacher-student relationships.]

This emphasis upon the human person, upon the individual in his wholeness and uniqueness, is a central feature of the "psychology of humanism." But there is an important corollary without which this personalistic emphasis would be inadequate and distorted. That corollary is the recognition, to use a phrase of Rank, that "the self needs the other." This recognition is variously expressed: For the neo-Freudians, it points to the importance of relationship in the growth of personality; for the existentialists, it leads to emphasis on the themes of dialogue, encounter, meeting, intersubjectivity, and so on.

While this recognition is broadly shared by humanistic psychotherapists, analysts, personality theorists, perceptual psychologists and others, perhaps the most impressive and systematic development of the idea has been provided by existential thinkers, both in psychology and philosophy. There is a striking similarity in the formulation of this self-other relationship by various existentialists. Martin Buber's philosophy of dialogue, centering around the I-Thou relation, is probably the most influential and possibly the most profound. Among other fruitful effects, it has given rise to a "psychology of meeting" that finds its paradigm in the therapeutic encounter. The significance of Buber's general concept has been well described by Will Herberg:

> The term I-Thou points to a relation of person to person, of subject to subject, a relation of reciprocity involving "meeting" or "encounter," while the term I-It points to a relation of person to thing, of subject to object, involving some form of utilization, domination, or control, even if it is only so-called "objective" knowing. The I-Thou relation, which Buber usually designated as "relation" par excellence, is one in which one can enter only with the whole of his being, as a genuine person. (*The Writings of Martin Buber*, Meridian Books, New York, 1956, p. 14)

It follows that the relationship of therapy in its ideal development represents an authentic encounter "on the sharp edge of existence" between two human beings, one seeking and the other helping. This mutual recognition, which is never immediate but only a possibility to be achieved, cuts through the conventional defenses and postures of both partners to permit each to reach out as a person to the other as a person. What is demanded of the doctor in particular, says Buber, is that he "himself step forth out of his protected professional superiority into the elementary situation between one who asks and one who is asked" (Maurice Friedman, *Martin Buber: The Life of Dialogue,* Harper Torchbooks, New York, 1960, p. 190).

Apart from its uses by existential psychologists and psychoanalysts—such as Ludwig Binswanger, Viktor Frankl, Rollo May, and others—Buber's immensely fertile concept of I-Thou "meeting" finds parallels and reverberations in the work of other existential philosophers, especially those commonly referred to as the religious existentialists or existential theologians. For Gabriel Marcel, who came independently to the formula of I-and-Thou, the sense of genuine encounter is conveyed by the term "intersubjectivity," implying an authentic communication on the order of communion. "The fact is," writes Marcel, "that we can understand ourselves by starting from the other, or from others, and only by starting from them; . . . it is only in this perspective that a legitimate love of self can be conceived" (*The Mystery of Being,* Gateway, Chicago, 1960, Volume II, p. 9). This insight, quite similar to Fromm's concept of productive love and self-realization, implies a reciprocity of knowing in which what "I am" as well as what "Thou art" is made known only through the mutual experience of what "We are." Each communicant recognizes himself in the other.

In Paul Tillich's "therapeutic theology," this general appreciation of the enlightening role of engagement or meeting is applied directly to psychotherapy, which is regarded as the "community of healing." In common with other existentialists, Tillich believes that the personal troubles represented by neurosis stem fundamentally from failures in relationships with others, thereby resulting in self-alienation from any genuine contact with the world. The central therapeutic problem thus becomes one of "acceptance" or, more precisely, of successive stages of acceptance culminating in acceptance of oneself and of the world of others.

In this new kind of therapeutic encounter—and here is another humanistic tenet—there are no silent partners. The existential therapist (which is to say, the humanistic therapist) is no longer the blank screen or "mute catalyzer" that he was in Freud's day, but rather is a participant with the whole of his being. He participates not only for the purpose of helping, but even more basically for the purpose of knowing or understanding. "You must participate in a self," according to Tillich, "in order to know what it is. By participation you change it" (*The Courage to Be,* Yale University Press, New Haven, 1959, p. 124). The inference is that the kind of knowledge essential to psychology and psychotherapy is to be gained not by detached observation but by participant-observation (to use Harry Stack Sullivan's phrase). It may be possible, through detachment, to gain knowledge that is "useful"; but only through participation is it possible to gain the knowledge that is *helpful.*

In any adequate account of the sources and forces that have nourished the movement of humanistic psychology (which this brief sketch does not pretend to be), much more would have to be said in acknowledgment of the contributions of individual theorists and therapists. Fortunately, there are a number of comprehensive surveys available; among them, James Bugental's *Challenges of Humanistic Psychology*, Anthony Sutich and Miles Vich's *Readings in Humanistic Psychology*, and my own *The Broken Image* (especially Chapters 6 and 7). But even the present essay cannot avoid mention of at least a few of the movers and shakers behind the third revolution, notably: Abraham Maslow, who more than any other deserves to be recognized as the "spiritual father" of the humanistic movement in psychology; Gordon Allport, the great American personalist and heir to the mantle of William James; Rollo May, who introduced the existential approach to American psychology and has developed it creatively; Carl Rogers, whose therapeutic mandate of "unconditional regard" for the client resembles Tillich's philosophy of ultimate concern; Erich Fromm, the most influential of the neo-Freudians, who has long since moved from psychoanalysis to the higher ground of social philosophy and cultural criticism; Henry A. Murray, inspired teacher and exemplar of humanism; Charlotte Buhler, who has made us all aware of how important personal goal-values and the whole course of human life are to psychological understanding. . . .

In conclusion . . . I'd like to propose one line of commitment, and of protest, that we might well undertake as humanistic psychologists. That course is, following Jefferson, to swear undying opposition to all forms of tyranny over the mind of man. I propose that we commit ourselves to the defense of psychological liberty. For I believe that quite possibly the greatest threat to freedom in the world today (and tomorrow) is the threat to freedom of the mind—which is, at bottom, the power to choose.

That freedom is threatened now on all sides. It is threatened by what Herbert Marcuse has called the "one-dimensional society," which seeks to reduce the categories of thought and discourse to a kind of consensual endorsement of the directives of an aggressive and acquisitive culture. It is threatened by the technology of mass society, mass culture and mass communication, which manufactures (*pace* Marshall McLuhan) a marshmallow world of plastic pleasures in which the bland lead the bland endlessly into the sea of tranquility. . . .

Freedom of the mind is also threatened by the biological revolution and its psychological corollaries—not only by the familiar cuckoo's nest of lobotomies and shock treatments, over which no one can fly, but by the imminent breakthroughs in "genetic surgery" and kindred interventions that promise to make feasible the rewiring and reprogramming of the brain mechanism.

Perhaps most critically of all, our psychological liberty is threatened by failure of nerve: by our inability to live up to and live out the democratic dogma, which rests upon faith in the capacity of the ordinary human being to lead his own life, to go his own way and to grow his own way, to be himself and to know himself and to become more himself. This failure of nerve is rampant in the field of education; it is a kind of occupational disease of social work, where the aided person becomes a client who is treated as a patient who is diagnosed as incurable. And it is a pervasive feature of the landscape of academic psychology and behavioral science. . . .[1]

---

[1] *EDITOR'S NOTE*: Compare the following statement by the late Abraham Maslow:

[Existentialism] deals radically with that human predicament presented by the gap between human aspirations and human limitations (between what the human being *is*, and what he would *like* to be, and what he *could* be). This is not so far off from the identity problem as it may sound . . . the quest for identity [emphasized by Allport, Rogers, Goldstein, Fromm, Wheelis, Erikson, Horney, May, et al.] . . . On the whole, most philosophies and religions, Eastern as well as Western, have dichotomized [this twofold nature of man], teaching that the way to become "higher" is to renounce and master "the lower." The existentialists however, teach that *both* are simultaneously defining characteristics of human nature. Neither can be repudiated; they can only be integrated. But we already know something of these integrating techniques—of insight, of intellect in the broader sense, of love, of creativeness, of humor and tragedy, of play, of art. I suspect we will focus our studies on these integrative techniques more than we have in the past. . . .

[Existentialism] also implies another truth and another problem that calls urgently for attention. Practically every serious description of the "authentic person" extant implies that such a person, by virtue of what he has become, assumes a new relation to his society and, indeed, to society in general. He not only transcends himself in various ways; he also transcends his culture. He resists enculturation. He becomes more detached from his culture and from his society. He becomes a little more a member of his species and a little less a member of his local group. My feeling is that most sociologists and anthropologists will take this hard. I therefore confidently expect controversy in this area. . . .

I think it fair to say that no theory of psychology will ever be complete that does not centrally incorporate the concept that man has his future within him, dynamically active at this present moment. In this sense, the future can be treated as ahistorical in Kurt Lewin's sense. Also we must realize that *only* the future is *in principle* unknown and unknowable, which means that all habits, defenses, and coping mechanisms are doubtful and ambiguous because they are based on past experience. Only the flexibly creative person can really manage the future, *only* the one who can face novelty with confidence and without fear. I am convinced that much of what we now call psychology is the study of the tricks we use to avoid the anxiety of absolute novelty by making believe the future will be like the past. . . .

I do not think we need take too seriously the European existentials' harping on dread, on anguish, on despair, and the like, for which their only remedy seems to be to keep a stiff upper lip. This high-I.Q. whimpering on a cosmic scale occurs whenever an external source of values fails to work. They should have learned from the psychotherapists that the loss of illusions and the discovery of identity, though painful at first, can be ultimately exhilarating and strengthening.—Abraham H. Maslow, in *Existential Psychology*, edited by Rollo May, pp. 52–60. Copyright © 1961, 1969 by Random House, Inc. Reprinted by permission of the publisher.

# 3.7 FREEDOM—A PREREQUISITE OF BOTH MORAL AND SCIENTIFIC LAWS
## Cecil J. Schneer and Archibald MacLeish

## SCHNEER

[Science] differs from the arts in one major way. It is self-corrective. All the ideas of science, the good, the bad, the wild and the mild, are sooner or later subject to test. An authoritarian scientist can impose his discipline and his

This selection consists of two short excerpts. The first is abridged from pp. 374–377 in *The Search for Order* by Cecil J. Schneer, New York: Harper & Row, 1960. Copyright © 1960 by Cecil J. Schneer.

The second excerpt is from Archibald MacLeish, "To Make Men Free," *Atlantic* 188: 27–30, November 1951; reprinted in Archibald MacLeish, *Freedom is the Right to Choose*, Boston: Houghton, Mifflin Co., 1952. By permission of the author.

It is common to refer to "science and the humanities" as if they were altogether different from one another. To counteract this fallacious view, we here very deliberately join into a single article statements by a geologist and a poet.

Note that the first statement by Professor Schneer (geologist, University of New Hampshire) makes the free, unpredictable mind of man the very essence of science: Viewed as a *method*, or as a way of thinking, science is not to be defined in terms of indisputable generalizations, or determined laws, but rather in terms of freedom and creativity. Similarly, the second statement by Archibald MacLeish (formerly Boylston Professor of Rhetoric and Oratory at Harvard, Pulitzer Prize winner in poetry, Librarian of Congress, pioneer executive for UNESCO) makes the free-thinking, self-reliant individual the basis of democracy and of civilization.

This excerpt was prepared initally as a response to two books, *The Greening of America* by Charles Reich (Random House, 1970) and *Beyond Freedom and Dignity* by B. F. Skinner (Knopf, 1971); to the excellent review of them by Donald R. J. Hermann in 70 *Michigan Law Review*, pp. 415–433, December 1971; and to the problem whether dissenting youth are "cop-outs" or "prophetic voices," discussed by Kenneth Keniston in *Youth and Dissent: The Rise of a New Opposition* (Harcourt Brace Jovanovich, 1971. Especially pp. 38–39, 68–71, 295–297, and 376–400).

At opposite poles on most points, these two contemporary utopians are alike in one important respect: Both Reich and Skinner overemphasize the fact that (by reason of its universal generalizations and its dependable laws) science is deterministic. Neither Reich nor Skinner pay sufficient heed to the innovative, creative, unpredictable side of science —science viewed as a growing body of knowledge, as a key factor in man's changing attitudes towards man and society, as is seen in the philosophical revolutions brought about by the Copernican or the Darwinian theories.

We are all too prone to view science as a *product*, and to think of democracy only as an *achievement*—forgetting that, in its deeper meaning, science is a *process*, and democracy is a *method*. The success of science, like that of democracy, depends on men and women who are open-minded and receptive to reason. Anyone receptive to reason is unlikely to embrace those brethren of certainty: the absolute principle, the unchanging formula, the rigid dogma, the fixed idea. The enquiring mind will continue to ideas on an entire generation—but there will be another generation and other experiments. Nature lies open to all. The Copernican theory smoldered underground for fifty years before the flames of Bruno's pyre broke out. Cuvier demolished the arguments of Lamarck and St. Hilaire but Darwin and evolution won out nevertheless. This is the meaning of science and this is its purpose—to negate the book-burnings, to destroy the Inquisition, to establish the fundamental dignity of man. . . .

We wish to exploit science, to milk it of the plastics and the hydrogen bombs. Like Gregory setting astronomers to work on reform of the calendar, we have a clear idea in mind of the results we wish. But the tools we must employ to satisfy our material wants are men, and exceptional men. Gregory got his calendar reform, but his successors inherited the Copernican theory as well. There is a kind of second-rate thinker who will guarantee to produce only the results required—who will not stray like Newton into forbidden paths of Unitarian theology, whose thoughts have never pushed beyond the limits of orthodoxy. These are the thinkers of a static society. They will never account for a doctrine of evolution, a theory of relativity, a concept of universal law. They are safe and they are competent, but they are dull. They form the legion of the slide rule, the white-coated multiude. Their productivity fills the skies with jets and the home with gadgets. They are the new scholastics, their dogma a jelly of conformity, oozing from the universities and the laboratories, flowing into the societies and the technical journals, drowning out question and answer alike. These men will never give us security. These men are the most dangerous of all. They are the illusion but not the stuff of which civilization is made. It is the free mind, the free thought that determines the future.

In the sixteenth century the Spanish Empire circled the globe. The armored troops of Spain, the gold of the Indies, the fleets of floating castles bristling with cannon, the hardened cutthroats that in Peru alone slaughtered 30 million people, that captured the Aztec Empire, the silks, the gems, the slaves—all [this] vanished in a generation, swept away by the power of the free mind in Holland and England. This is the ultimate weapon, this is the intercontinental ballistic missile with hydrogen warhead.

The idea of the power of the mind, of the force of truth, is the most difficult of all. We see it demonstrated again and again, but with our hands on the gag in the mouths of our enemies we seldom believe it. The full power, clerical and secular, of the authority of the seventeenth century could not

---

inquire; the democratic citizen will continue to work toward the realization of liberty, equality, and fraternity.

To phrase the matter differently: The democratic citizen will maintain a patient faith that reasonable solutions to new and difficult problems are possible; he will show charity toward his fellow humans whose viewpoints, though different from his own, are offered with sincerity; and he will persist in hoping that persistent inquiry and open discussion will, sooner or later, bring about acceptable solutions to the personal and social problems which beset men in a time of rapid change.

suppress Galileo, and the exercise of that power only served to advertise the pernicious doctrine. The full power of the modern totalitarian state could not establish the inheritance of acquired characteristics.

All this means essentially that science is intimately connected with the values which our society and our world respect. There is a basic contradiction between tyranny and science. The contradiction is in this: that the fruits of science essential to the continuation of any kind of civilization rest on the activities of the free mind, freely thinking, freely creating. The free mind can be destroyed, individually as in the case of Bruno, collectively as in the case of modern Germany, but it thereupon ceases to create. Technology is limited to the exploitation of the science already won. As it presses beyond these limits it treads on the stuff of creativity and merges into science. The men, the societies which embark upon creative thinking pass into regions where the censor and policeman cannot follow. This is the dilemma of the tyrant. If he calls back the march of thought, if he reigns in the free mind with his laws of history, he must renounce all hope of the laws of nature. The paradox is in the relationship of the fruit to the tree. The press, the radio, the weapons, the abundant food, the *technology* are indispensable to the modern state. But behind them and before them, inseparably intertwined with them, is the free mind. The penalty for checking it is not only the loss of freedom, it is the loss of civilization.

## MacLEISH

Freedom, in American usage, means the freedom of the individual human being to think for himself and to come to the truth by the light of his own mind and conscience. It is the freedom defined by the American Constitution. Congress is forbidden to make any law abridging the freedom of speech. There is to be no establishment of religious authority or supervision. There is to be no meddling, in other words, by state or by church with a man's thoughts or what he chooses to say about them. When it comes to thoughts, when it comes to ideas, when it comes to opinions and their expression, a man is free. His freedom is guaranteed by the fundamental law of the Republic. The opinions of others are not to be imposed upon him, no matter whose opinions they may be—the opinions of a church or the opinions of the governments or the opinions of his fellow citizens—even the opinions of a majority of his fellow citizens.

A man's freedom to believe, that is to say, does not depend on *what* he believes. It does not depend on his being "right" as others see the right, no matter how numerous they may be or how well entrenched or how powerful. Right and wrong as others judge the right and wrong are irrelevant to the American conception of freedom to think and believe and say. That, of course, is the nub of the whole matter, and the essential distinction between freedom as we mean it and freedom as it is meant in certain other quarters of the earth.

In the American conception of freedom, the man and his conscience come first and the established opinions, the accepted verities, the official views come after. . . .

The American Proposition is the proposition, advanced at the beginning of the Republic and enacted into law when the Constitution was adopted, that a man's freedom to be a man, and to find and speak the truth that is in him, is more important than the protection of any accepted belief, any official verity, against criticism, against challenge, against dissent. More important not only to that man but to all men, to the society which all men compose, to the nation, to the world, to life itself. It is a proposition, in other words, which rests upon an act of faith, the most courageous of all earthly acts of faith—an act of faith in man and in the God whom man, in the freedom of his conscience and his thought, can find.

When it was first enacted into law the American Proposition was new. It is still new: the one wholly new and revolutionary idea the modern world has produced, for all its triumphs in science and technique—an idea so new and so revolutionary in its literal and explicit meaning that half the patriotic societies which celebrate their attachment to the American Revolution have yet to understand it or accept it. But it is new and revolutionary, not solely because it proclaims human liberty, nor solely because it founds its conception of human liberty on the freedom of the individual human mind, defending that freedom in the most explicit and peremptory terms against the tyranny of organized opinion. It is new and revolutionary because of the act of faith which it expresses.

Our reliance in this country is on the inquiring, individual human mind. Our strength is founded there: our resilience, our ability to face an ever-changing future and to master it. We are not frozen into the backward-facing impotence of those societies, fixed in the rigidness of an official dogma, to which the future is the mirror of the past. We are free to make the future for ourselves. And we are free because it is the man who counts in this country: always and at every moment and in any situation, the man. Not the Truth but the man: not the truth as the state sees the truth or as the church sees the truth or as the majority sees the truth or as the mob sees the truth, but the truth as the man sees it, as the man finds it, for himself as man. Our faith is in the infinite variety of human beings and in the God who made them various and of many minds; in their singularity, their uniqueness, the creativeness of the differences between them. Our faith, in simple, sober truth, is in the human Being, the human spirit, the hungers and the longings that lead it toward its images of truth, its perceptions of the beauty of the world.

Those who launched the great human adventure which this Republic is, dared to put their trust in the individual man, the man alone, the man thinking for himself. They dared to believe in a *people*, which is a nation of individual men constituting among themselves a society; for a people is not what the totalitarians call "the masses"; a people is an agreement of many alone to make together a world in which each one of them can live as himself. The founders of the American Republic believed in a people. They not only provided no censors for the thoughts of those who were to come after them: they prohibited censors. They not only provided no moral or intellectual or religious authority to govern the beliefs of their successors: they rejected forever the establishment of any such authority. They trusted men.

It is in that trust that the Republic can still be defended. Indeed it is only in that trust that it can be defended as the kind of country it is.

# B. Performance Contracts and Accountability

## 3.8 INTRODUCTION

The following selections will deal briefly with performance contracting, and then move into the broader area of accountability.

The first selection is by Leon M. Lessinger who, in 1969, while Associate United States Commissioner of Education, helped initiate the first performance contract by authorizing twenty thousand dollars to the Texarkana contract. Texarkana paid eighty dollars for each student who increased one grade level in reading or math within eighty hours of instruction, or proportionally for each fraction thereof. For the next two or three years performance contracting was headline news in American education, and a variety of contracts were initiated across the country.[1]

But in 1972 a Rand Corporation study for HEW (summarized in *Science News*, Vol. 100, No. 25) found that public school programs run by private business firms (with one exception—Gary, Indiana) produced no overall gains over normal school programs. Early in 1972 the United States Office of Economic Opportunity, and its director, Philip V. Sanchez, decided that performance contracting was not a useful tool for improving learning in the schools.[2]

However, 1972 is an election year, and the future of performance contracting cannot be judged at this time:

Clearly, the final verdict on performance contracting is far from in. Some contracts have shattered complacency, inspired creativity, improved learning, and turned the spotlight of public attention on the quality of classroom instruction. But others have inspired greed and chicanery, created poor environments for children, and fomented unhealthy dissension.

Performance contracting has as its kernel a powerful idea: Someone other than children must bear the responsibility for whether children learn successfully. Who bears that responsibility, and to what measure, are questions loaded with dynamite. Surround these questions with money, risk, publicity, new

[1] Law firms make a specialty of performance contracts. Read Reed Martin, "Performance Contracting: Making It Legal," *Nation's Schools* 87: 62–64, January 1971.
[2] For details, read *Phi Delta Kappan* 53: 451–452, March 1972.

teaching strategies, new people, new rhetoric, systems analysis, contingency management, and more, and it is no wonder that this recent, and thus far minuscule, phenomenon has raised such a ruckus in public education."[3]

Even if performance contracting should disappear entirely, the movement initiated by Lessinger and others would have permanent significance; for it represents the first major step in the direction of "accountability" with which most of the articles in this section will deal.

As for accountability, the following statement by John W. Porter should serve as an overview:

[Accountability] is compelling American educators to ask this question:
Are there institutions other than the school that might be or could be used to assist some of the children of some of the people in accomplishing some of the tasks? . . .
"Perhaps we have always had accountability—we always checked out what went into education—facilities, materials, attendance, hot lunches—but too inconsistently did we "do something" new about what came forth; what pupils learned; what skills were obtained. In fact, we went out of our way to find excuses for those children who did not learn—broken homes, language barriers, ethnic or national background, malnutrition. That is, we placed too much responsibility for success upon the student and his parents. But, if the student didn't perform, we began passing him up the educational ladder anyway. What is envisioned now is a strengthening of the role of the teacher, so that he or she is not placed in such a situation. The future, as accountability becomes firmly entrenched, will allow for very few excuses. We educators will be responsible for failure, and the exciting, fantastic goal before us is to have *achievement* realized by nearly the total school population; and I am convinced the educational community . . . will respond to this challenge.[4]

[3] James A. Mecklenburger and John A. Wilson, "Performance Contracting: Learning C.O.D. Can the Schools Buy Success?" *Saturday Review* 54: 62–65, 76–79, September 18, 1971.
[4] John W. Porter (Superintendent of Public Instruction, State of Michigan), "Accountability in Education," in the NSSE Anthology *Accountability in Education*, edited by Leon M. Lessinger and Ralph W. Tyler, Worthington, Ohio: Charles A. Jones Publishing Company, 1971, pp. 42–52.

# 3.9 FIVE BENEFITS OF PERFORMANCE CONTRACTS
## Leon M. Lessinger

[Certainly, performance contracts] are not a magic solution to all of our problems. When used casually, they may solve nothing at all; and if used wrongly, they could even do harm. For example, a performance contract is appropriate only when the results we desire are measurable. If nobody can reliably measure "maturity," or "good style" in composition, we have no business applying performance contracts to programs that are intended, somewhat vaguely perhaps, to teach these qualities. But the obvious fact that many valuable results of education are loosely defined or ill-suited to quantitative measurement should not deter us from dealing with other results that we *can* specify and assess rather precisely. . . . There is plenty of work to be done on the basic skills, and if performance contracts help us do it, they will have won honor enough. Through performance contracts, a school board can introduce a more sophisticated technology of instruction. Undoubtedly this technology will rely in part on various media in addition to the blackboard and textbook. In some cases these new media will take over routine jobs that now distract the teacher from helping individual students with special problems and overburden him with the less challenging parts of his work. If the new media are successful, they will transform people who are now serving much of the time as instructors into what they want to be: teachers. Nothing in schools is more mechanical and dehumanizing than the dreary, endlessly repetitive routine of instructing too many children in the most basic skills. The technology that we develop ought not to *compete* with teachers: it ought to *free* them to do other things that now are sadly, and necessarily, neglected. In itself, the new technology is not good or bad. Its value depends on the way we use it and, as we have said, on the results it can produce.

So, too, with performance contracting. Properly used, it can facilitate the trial and evaluation of new programs. Many good instructional programs have not been given the opportunity to demonstrate their potential because of the lack of an effective delivery system at the local level. Instead of insisting that we install these programs directly in our regular school curriculum, the educational engineer would propose that we try them first in a separately managed center with its own accounting procedures and operating practices. In this case, the risk is small, and the delivery is relatively simple.

Leon M. Lessinger, *Every Kid a Winner: Accountability in Education*, Chicago: Science Research Associates, 1970, excerpts from pp. 68–71. By permission. Footnotes here omitted.
Leon M. Lessinger is Gallaway Professor of Education at Georgia State University.

Second, performance contracting for instructional services can introduce greater resources and versatility into our public schools. Right now, new programs are being offered to the public outside the school system: the process of fragmentation has begun. Several large corporations are establishing franchise learning centers across the country. One firm has at least forty centers operational, and at least ten other firms are entering the business. In these centers, a kind of performance contract to improve student achievement in certain areas is signed between the parents and the franchisee. The dollars that parents pay are over and above the property taxes they pay for the operation of the public schools. As these franchised centers expand, it is conceivable that parents in some areas will begin to withhold support from the public schools by defeating bond issues and even by insisting that taxes be reduced. In contrast, the process of educational engineering would allow the school system to utilize the services of various firms so as to renew themselves through the turnkey feature. Thus performance contracting can serve as a means for fostering structural reforms within a school system, thus allowing it to continue operations and become competitive with private schools and franchised learning centers without endangering the system.

Third, performance contracting allows a school system to experiment in an orderly, responsible manner with low costs and low political risks . . . so that schools could estimate the costs both of initial adoption and of continued operation. In this sense, educational engineering allows board members to make rational, informed choices when choosing new techniques to be used in the regular curriculum.

Fourth, according to various court decisions, school systems are required to implement desegregation programs. Often the minority-group children have lower scores, sometimes drastically lower scores, on system-wide reading tests or other measures of educational achievement: and one of the worries of the favored community is that, upon integration, the presence of many students with low scores will hinder the progress of their own children. . . . Performance contracting can help [solve this problem, and thus] help communities to desegregate smoothly.

Finally, performance contracting, as part of a competitive process, can call forth a high quality both of proposals and of work. . . . Competition encourages diversity, thoroughness, and practicality. . . .

Dwight W. Allen has said that "when educators look at technology as a resource for developing new alternatives and individualizing instruction, rather than as a dangerous, mechanistic intruder, then the existing wealth of technological developments will have its desired effect upon the world of education."

# 3.10 ACCOUNTABILITY, VOUCHERS, PERFORMANCE CONTRACTING
## Albert Shanker

I think the first thing that needs to be said about accountability from the point of view of the teacher is that the concept is very much feared. It is feared because accountability in its recent thrust to prominence has had at least three separate meanings.

The first meaning is associated with the schools where the parents say, "You, the teachers, are paid to teach. Our children have been going to school year after year and they are falling further and further behind. We demand that you be accountable to us. If the children don't learn we demand the right to remove you.". . .

The second meaning derives from the great desire to control educational expenditures. How is the school accounting for the dollars that we are spending for education? How do we know we are getting our money's worth?

The third meaning of accountability deals with the development of professional standards. For example, there is a body of agreement in other fields, such as medicine and law, as to what constitutes competence and incompetence. . . .

Teachers are also deeply concerned about the concept of innovation, which is so frequently associated with accountability. They have learned through years of experience—and rather bitter experience—that educational innovation in the American public schools has nothing to do with the improvement of education.

It is, instead, a kind of public relations device whereby the reigning political power—whether it's a school board, or the principal or school superintendent trying to convince the community that he or she is a bright, shiny individual doing all sorts of new and creative things—brings out all kinds of ideas which force teachers and children and others to march in different directions. A year later, that lot is dropped as a new set of innovations is produced like rabbits from a hat. These innovations, rather than being honest attempts at educational improvement, are really public relations efforts. . . .

Teachers are also disturbed by the frequent association of accountability with something called "teacher motivation," a doctrine which holds that many

Albert Shanker, "Accountability: Possible Effects on Instructional Programs," in *Accountability in Education,* edited by Leon M. Lessinger and Ralph W. Tyler, one of a ten-book series in *Contemporary Educational Issues* under the auspices of the National Society for the Study of Education, Worthington, Ohio: Charles A. Jones Publishing Company, 1971, pp. 66–74. By permission.

Albert Shanker is President, United Federation of Teachers, New York City.

teachers fail to reach the children because they don't really want to. These teachers are accused of just being job holders—not really trying and not really wanting to do anything productive. Hence the calls for an individual system of punishments and rewards, geared to the children's progress.

This view of accountability poses a great threat, because, to be honest, most teachers *aren't* doing the best they can. And for a very simple reason: they don't know any other way of doing things. They are the victims, if you like, of a system that has seen eight thousand new teachers move into New York, for example, every year for the past twenty years. These new teachers, drawn from many different colleges and universities, are a remarkably diverse group: Catholics and Protestants, Jews and nonbelievers, blacks and whites, liberals and conservatives. Yet, after four weeks of teaching in New York City it is almost impossible to distinguish the newcomers from those they replaced. Which leads to a rather obvious conclusion: With the exception of the few outstanding figures who somehow operate on an individual basis, the overwhelming majority of teachers do what the school as a system compels them to do.

In these circumstances, it obviously makes little sense to talk in terms of individual rewards and punishments when the individual has no freedom to change his ways. It is exactly for this reason that [some] writers . . . are rejected by teachers. They are rejected because of the arrogance of the writing. Essentially, these New Left critics are behaving like a star of the Metropolitan Opera who criticizes his audience for being unable to sing as well as he does. Many of these books are written by self-proclaimed star performers for no other purpose than to say, "Look at all those lowly characters out there who are not as artistic as I am!" That, of course, is not very helpful to the ordinary practitioner. . . .

[Faced with such problems,] how does one get teachers to accept this odd notion of accountability? To begin with, the first two conceptions of accountability that I mentioned must be firmly opposed. I think it is quite clear that teachers are going to reject the notion that they are just hired hands. Secondly, they are not overly concerned with arguments about budgets. Teachers will react negatively to statements that they must change their ways either because few or many dollars are being spent.

The third concept of accountability as being the development, with other groups, of common objectives is, I believe, acceptable to teachers, because strictly speaking it is not for teachers alone to determine what the objectives of education are. Nor are teachers as intractable on the subject as might be supposed, for they have already moved in this direction. In June, 1969, the United Federation of Teachers in New York City became, I believe, the first organization in the country with a contract clause stating that the Federation and the Board of Education would work together to develop objective standards of professional accountability, in cooperation with parent groups, community boards, universities, and other interested parties. . . .

[Closely related to accountability are] three currently popular ideas. These ideas—vouchers, performance contracting, and school decentralization[1] —all seem to possess either basic flaws in the reasoning that promotes them, or in the manner in which they are being promoted. Hitherto, I have been talking about accountability mainly in connection with its impact on, and concerns for, one segment of the educational community—teachers. But the three ideas that I've just mentioned should be of concern to all of us, because they can be serious obstatcles to the development of a true accountability system.

First, vouchers—which are being proposed as a national answer to providing accountability by offering a choice to the consumer—the student or his parents. It might be more accurate to say "the semblance of choice," because no one seems to have considered the implications of a nationwide voucher system. So let us consider them, and to make things a little simpler we won't talk about the whole country, just New York City, much simpler.

Let's suppose that just 50 percent of the students decided they would go to private or parochial schools in the future. That's a small matter of 600,000 youngsters. Their decision would set off a chain of events, resembling nothing more than a child's game of "Ring Around the Rosie." With the public schools half-empty, half the teachers would be fired. Neighboring schools would be consolidated for efficiency and economy. Surplus buildings would be closed. The private institutions, besieged by 600,000 youngsters waving vouchers, would urgently need buildings, teachers, textbooks, and materials. And the only readily available source of buildings, of 30,000 needed teachers, would be those closed public schols and surplus teachers who are out looking for jobs. We have come full circle: The same children, in the same schools, with the same teachers. The great innovative voucher program has accomplished only one thing—it has removed responsibility from the government, because the schools are now private, not public.

Those who would drastically limit the scope of a voucher program in order to avoid these problems must necessarily turn the program into one available only to the elite few—a program hardly worthy of national debate and national support.

So much for vouchers. On performance contracting I want to start with the statement that, in a field as complex as education, there can be no guarantee of performance. The position is similar to that in other complex fields: a doctor or a lawyer cannot guarantee performance. If they did, they'd run the risk of being jailed as quacks. Perhaps those who purport to guarantee performance in education should also be jailed for quackery.

The second problem with performance contracting . . . [is that it] moves

---

[1] EDITOR'S NOTE: Although very important in contemporary education, the issue of school decentralization is so much in ferment that this anthology does not include a section on it; and since pros and cons are not here presented, we have omitted Albert Shanker's comments on this topic. But it is a topic worthy of study.

us away from real accountability, away from analysis of what a competent practitioner should be doing, to consideration of a specific end product—away from the process which the competent practitioner engages in to the *product,* which depends on many factors not within the control of teachers or schools. . . .

[Third,] I am opposed to the manner in which the technology of performance contracting is being promoted. Performance contractors are behaving and talking as if a technological answer to all problems is already available. It isn't, and these companies should admit that they are trying to develop such a technology and need the children in today's schools to do it, that it is only a try, and not a cure for today's ills. Anything less than such frankness smacks of deception.

My fourth objection concerns the special motivational devices featured in most performance contracting programs. Radios, baseball bats, and green stamps are among the goodies being used. I'm not all that "holier than thou" about such things. I tell my son that if his report improves, he can have a new bike. We all use this approach, and there's no question that such rewards play an important role in our family life and our society. So we can't say that rewards must never be used, but we must ask some serious questions—because no one else seems to be doing so.

What happens to the student after he leaves the motivated, reward-oriented climate of the performance contract classroom and returns to a regular class? Does he refuse to learn? Does he fail to learn? Does the use of motivation in one room—which is not available to teachers elsewhere—create learning in one place and destroy it in another? And what happens next year, when the motivational goodies are withdrawn? I don't know the answer to these questions, and I suspect that no one else does, either. And because we don't know the answers, it is incumbent upon anyone who uses this type of reward system to build an analysis of it into the research design for his program.

Finally on performance contracting, I suggest a case of false packaging. I've already touched on the impossibility of guaranteeing a specified result, or level of performance. We are, of course, confronted with suggestions that this can and will be done. But what we are actually presented with is a *non-*guarantee. That is, it's not the student's performance that *is* guaranteed, but the contractor's payment that is *not* guaranteed.

We have even been oversold on the idea that the contractor doesn't get paid if the student fails. That just isn't true in the overwhelming majority of contracts. In fact, the contractor receives a succession of payments: when he signs, when he moves the hardware in, again at the halfway point, leaving only a fairly limited amount which he does not get if the children fail to succeed. In addition, many contracts absolve the company from responsibility for youngsters who fail to show up for the program a certain number of times— usually fairly small. So it is that we have in the Bronx a program with a tremendous amount of absenteeism, and the company . . . gets paid a good amount whether or not there are results; it gets paid for truants and dropouts. . . .

[In conclusion, our] public schools, with all their faults, are worth keeping, and their improvement will come not from gimmicks but from the same type of slow, painful, unrestricted, free, scientific inquiry that brought other areas of human concern into the modern world.[2]

---

[2] *EDITOR'S NOTE:* The chief difficulty with accountability consists in answering the question "Accountable for *what?*" Should a teacher be held accountable for the *attitudes* he engenders in students as well as for the *information* he extracts from them? If so, how should we grade a teacher, some of whose students receive an A in his course in Shakespeare, but who end up hating Shakespeare? Should we look upon *creativity* as an educational value? If so, consider the results of tests by Getzels and Jackson at the University of Chicago, and by Paul Torrance and others at the University of Minnesota. Their studies indicate that if an I.Q. test is used to select top level talent, about 70 percent of the persons who have the highest 20 percent of the scores on a creative ability test battery will be missed. Stated otherwise, if the typical I.Q. test is used as a measuring stick, then more cases with high creativity scores will be missed than are identified.

William Bender puts the problem this way:

The student who ranks first in his class may be genuinely brilliant, or he may be a compulsive worker or the instrument of domineering parents' ambitions, or a self-centered careerist who has shrewdly calculated his teachers' prejudices and expectations and discovered how to regurgitate efficiently what they want. Or he may have focused narrowly on grade-setting as compensation for his inadequacies in other areas, because he lacks other interests or talents or lacks passion and warmth or normal healthy instincts or is afraid of life. The top high school student is often, frankly, a pretty dull and bloodless or peculiar fellow. The adolescent with wide-ranging curiosity and stubborn independence, with a vivid imagination and desire to explore fascinating bypaths, to follow his own interests, to contemplate, to read the unrequired books, the boy filled with sheer love of life and exuberance, may well seem to his teachers troublesome, undisciplined, a rebel, may not conform to their stereotype, and may not get the top grades and the highest rank in class. He may not even score at the highest level in the standard multiple choice admission tests, which may well reward the glib, facile mind at the expense of the questioning, independent, or slower but more powerful, more subtle, and more interesting and original mind. . . . We need a new definition of excellence. . . . We must find ways to identify such characteristics as motivation, creativity, imagination, and emotional maturity.—William Bender [formerly Dean of Admissions at Harvard], cited by Ronald C. Doll and Robert S. Fleming, eds., in *Children Under Pressure*, Columbus, Ohio: Charles E. Merrill Books, Inc., 1966, p. 57.

# 3.11 EVALUATION OF SOCRATES AS A TEACHER

### A. PERSONAL QUALIFICATIONS

*Rating*
(*high to low*)

| | 1 | 2 | 3 | 4 | 5 | Comments |
|---|---|---|---|---|---|---|
| 1. Personal appearance | ☐ | ☐ | ☐ | ☐ | ☒ | Dresses in an old sheet draped about his body |
| 2. Self-confidence | ☐ | ☐ | ☐ | ☐ | ☒ | Not sure of himself—always asking questions |
| 3. Use of English | ☐ | ☐ | ☐ | ☒ | ☐ | Speaks with a heavy Greek accent |
| 4. Adaptability | ☐ | ☐ | ☐ | ☐ | ☒ | Prone to suicide by poison when under duress |

### B. CLASS MANAGEMENT

| | 1 | 2 | 3 | 4 | 5 | |
|---|---|---|---|---|---|---|
| 1. Organization | ☐ | ☐ | ☐ | ☐ | ☒ | Does not keep a seating chart |
| 2. Room appearance | ☐ | ☐ | ☐ | ☒ | ☐ | Does not have eye-catching bulletin boards |
| 3. Utilization of supplies | ☒ | ☐ | ☐ | ☐ | ☐ | Does not use supplies |

### C. TEACHER–PUPIL RELATIONSHIPS

| | 1 | 2 | 3 | 4 | 5 | |
|---|---|---|---|---|---|---|
| 1. Tact and consideration | ☐ | ☐ | ☐ | ☐ | ☒ | Places student in embarrassing situation by asking questions |
| 2. Attitude of class | ☐ | ☒ | ☐ | ☐ | ☐ | Class is friendly |

### D. TECHNIQUES OF TEACHING

| | 1 | 2 | 3 | 4 | 5 | |
|---|---|---|---|---|---|---|
| 1. Daily preparation | ☐ | ☐ | ☐ | ☐ | ☒ | Does not keep daily lesson plans |
| . Attention to course of study | ☐ | ☐ | ☒ | ☐ | ☐ | Quite flexible—allows students to wander to different topics |
| . Knowledge of subject matter | ☐ | ☐ | ☐ | ☐ | ☒ | Does not know material—has to question pupils to gain knowledge |

* *Source:* This chart is by John Gauss (El Cajon, Calif.), *Phi Delta Kappan* 43: outside back cover, January 1962. By permission.

E. PROFESSIONAL ATTITUDE

*Rating*

(*high to low*)

*Comments*

| | 1 | 2 | 3 | 4 | 5 | |
|---|---|---|---|---|---|---|
| 1. Professional ethics | ☐ | ☐ | ☐ | ☐ | ☒ | Does not belong to profes sional association or PTA |
| 2. In-service training | ☐ | ☐ | ☐ | ☐ | ☒ | Complete failure here—ha not even bothered to attend college |
| 3. Parent relationships | ☐ | ☐ | ☐ | ☐ | ☒ | Needs to improve in thi area—parents are trying to get rid of him |

RECOMMENDATION: Does not have a place in Education. Should not be rehired.

# 3.12 A CRITIQUE OF ACCOUNTABILITY
## Martin Levit,
## Robert J. Nash, and Russell M. Agne

### LEVIT

[Accountability] seems to be an attempt to refine and extend the already widespread programs of unreflective habit formation. There are many reasons to believe that social and schooling programs that consistently reward success which is defined in terms of unequivocal responses to items or events within unquestioned contexts do not develop habits of inquiry. What will be the effect of the accountabilists' thrust on the ability of students to have second

This selection consists of two short excerpts from two lengthy papers. The first is by Martin Levit (University of Missouri, Kansas City) from a paper, "The Ideology of Accountability in Schooling," in *Philosophers Speak on Accountability in Education,* Copyright 1973 by the Interstate Printers and Publishers. The paper was first read at a conference on Accountability held at Lehigh University on March 9, 1972. Reprinted by permission.

The second excerpt is from Robert J. Nash and Russell M. Agne (University of Vermont), "The Ethos of Accountability—A Critique," *Teachers College Record* 73: 357–370, February 1972. By permission. Footnote references from both articles here omitted.

thoughts about things? What do such programs do to the drive to go on learning—unlearning and relearning—when such extrinsic rewards are absent? Do
these measures promote a self-centered, instrumental conception of learning—
the view that "learning is O.K. if it pays off for me." Do the measures increase
our inability to escape bondage to the "programs," that is, the institutionalized reward systems of our society?

From all present indications, it seems clear that we may never know the
answers to such questions if we rely on accountabilists to respond after inquiry. Accountabilists often identify themselves with the scientific enterprise.
But unlike a scientific program, the accountability program is not concerned
with controlling or modifying its procedures and principles by searching for
diverse, and in principle, "all" consequences of the interactions or treatments
that are proposed. The scientific style uses principles and procedures if and
because they promote the ability to inquiry, to refine and expand knowledge.
This is not a simple activity. It requires wide and integrated knowledge, and
it requires understanding of logic and scientific method. Internally, it requires
a host of values implicated in continuing inquiry, and it needs a large array
of supportive social conditions. It would be self-destructive for scientific programs to develop efficient procedures for closing minds, though this might
well be done by technocrats guided by this aim rather than by scientific
criteria. . . .

Accountabilists keep their eyes fixed on only a limited set of cues and
they use efficiency—the ability to predict certain things or to get certain things
done—as *the* criterion of success. If scientists placed such trust in predictability or efficiency in limited domains, we might still have the geocentric theory
of the universe, for it could be used to predict the course of the planets just
about as well as could the heliocentric theory. Accountability is not a scientific
movement. It is a technocratic and efficiency-oriented, one.

## NASH AND AGNE

Proponents of accountability fail to realize that every educational program
has at least *three* kinds of ends or purposes. The proximate ends include the
learning of basic skills, and Lessinger deals with accountability preponder-
antly on this level. But there are two other kinds of purposes which are the
*sine qua non* of the educational endeavor, and they obdurately resist being
specified in the rigorous language of educational engineering. The intermediate ends include those educational objectives toward which the basic skills
ought to be directed, and for which the basic skills should be applied. These
are the ends which initially may have attracted people into teaching and they
are best expressed in the emotive language of "appreciation," "understanding," "enthusiasm," "discrimination," "judgment," and "enjoyment." These
ends continue to thwart precise behavioral classification, but they are no less
important because they do so. And, finally, there are long-range ends which
galvanize the first two levels and bestow ultimate meaning on the total edu-

cational experience. These are the sociopolitical ends which guide all educational activity serving as a constant reminder that the ultimate objective of any learning experience is to help the private person communicate with, evaluate, and reform the public world. . . .

When the systems engineer describes the school in the nomenclature of "inputs," "outputs," "entropy," "suprasystem," "subsystem," and "deathstate," (the imagery of organizational management and physics) he illustrates an all-encompassing faith in the basic tenets of the technocratic ethos. In his controlled euphoria over predictability, accuracy, reliability, integration, and organizational tautness, he expresses a commitment to the ideals of efficiency engineering for the effective organization of men and machines.

The fallacy of the systems model resides in the assumption that a physicsmanagement prototype can be used to explain adequately the polymorphous intricacy of an institution like the school. A corollary fallacy is that people can be considered as simple, mechanomorphic units within a structure of interactions as unique and as diverse as the educational experience.

Perhaps the major misuse of the systems model is the implicit faith that a systems approach will guarantee predictability, objectivity, and efficiency in the educational enterprise. Lessinger has written that the new educational engineer will be a "manager" who will function to construct a management system and support group. Together, they will develop programs, design requests for proposals based on *objective* and *predictable* performance specifications, assist in evaluating proposals, and provide *efficient* management services to performance contractors. Herein lies the ultimate *reductio ad absurdum*. Simply stated, educators have failed to understand that in an enterprise like education, where human beings are always ontologically prior to the system they constitute, the technocratic values of predictability, objectivity, and efficiency are either undesirable or unattainable. . . .

Raymond E. Callahan has traced the history of "the cult of efficiency" and the tragic misapplication of business and industrial values to education during the last fifty years. He concludes his study with the admonition that in the future the quest for efficiency in education must always be secondary to the pursuit of quality learning experiences—even if these are inefficiently administered and costly. The scientist has learned what the educational engineer has not—that a concern with efficiency (maximizing output while minimizing input) is a technocratic value which has produced effective guillotines, bombs, and assembly lines, but has never created an audacious experimental insight, or major scientific breakthrough. Efficiency is a normative term which tends to impede rather than facilitate the creative endeavor.

Much of the current literature on accountability is filled with the metaphor of the school as a malfunctioning machine that systems engineers can repair with massive infusions of predictability, objectivity, and efficiency. What is so often ignored in these proposals is the root question which must guide the total educational experience: what kind of human beings do we want our students to become? If we reconstruct the profession of education in the image of technocracy, then we are going to produce a society of technocrats. If we convert the school to a systems model, then we run the risk of unconsciously establishing as our primary educational objective the maintenance of an inert, airtight system, devoid of the unpredictable sparkle which dynamic human beings must provide if an organization is to be self-renewing. . . .

But what if the existing system is in need of sweeping reform? What if accountability is stretched to include the educator's responsibility to analyze, discredit, disassemble, and reconstruct his profession so that it is more directly responsive to the cries of human beings who suffer from the iniquitous defects of the social order? Where in the present efflux of literature exhorting us to adopt accountability techniques is there a voice, like Paulo Freire's, which goads educators to be accountable to the oppressed peoples of the world? Where are we being urged to apply Freire's concept of "praxis," which directs us to help our students to reflect upon the social, political, and economic contradictions in the culture and to take systematic political action against the oppressive power blocs? Who among the spokesmen for accountability would ask us to be accountable for helping students to come to the deepest possible understanding of themselves and their relationship to society? Where is the accountability advocate who speaks out against a concept of education which has been dessicated into programmatic forms and paralyzed by a dead-end preoccupation with careerism?

What is evident in much of the apologia for educational accountability is a shocking blindness to the political structure upon which the theory and practice of American education are based. The school and the society cohere in a sociopolitical unit. Whether educators know it or not, education is a ruthlessly political process. Frequently when eductors are cautioned to act as "professionals," they are being reminded that their principal and exclusive function must continue to be to integrate the younger generation into the unquestioned logic of the present sociopolitical system. The more effortlessly this can be accomplished, the better. But to restrict the function of education to the mechanical fitting of young people to the economic demands of a social system is to use the schools to maintain social realities as they are. . . .

Ten years ago Jules Henry, an anthropologist, charged the schools with fueling the free enterprise drives of achievement, competition, profit, mobility, performance, skills competency, and expansiveness. He warned that unless the schools stopped serving the narrow interests of the economic system, and began to stress the values of love, kindness, quietness, honesty, simplicity, compassion, cooperation, critical judgment, and autonomy, then the United States would become a "culture of death." Today Bertram M. Gross, an expert on urban affairs, has described the American society in terms which make Henry's "culture of death" a prophetic reality. Gross claims that the United States can best be epitomized as follows:

A managed society ruled by a faceless and widely dispersed complex of warfare-welfare-industrial-communications-police bureaucracies caught up in devoting a new style empire based on a technocratic ideology, a culture of alienation, multiple scapegoats and competing control networks.

What is so often ignored in the literature on accountability is the realization that educators are as responsible for learning outcomes which are moral and political as they are for outcomes which are skills-centered. It makes little sense to speak of accountability to our students solely because we are teaching them to read, write, and compute, if, as an unintended outcome, we are also preparing them to fit—painlessly and interchangeably—into Gross' nightmarish vision of American society. To the extent that we produce citizens who are one-dimensional in their thinking, compulsively rigid in their value orientations, and excessively competitive in their interpersonal relationships, we have produced human selves who are fractured, and for this we are accountable.

# 3.13 MEASURING MAN
## Joseph Uemura

Measuring man means knowing a Rembrandt, a Shakespeare, a Mozart, or a Spinoza, when we see one. It also means knowing how the rest of mankind might rank in the same human order. Now, anyone willingly or knowingly speaking out on such a subject, is, at least, outrageously audacious. Luckily, I only wish to clean the Augean stables of Zeus of a refuse that seems to be driving men of reason from academe.

I will present my remarks in three sections: (1) The Myths of the Great Measurers; (2) The Mistake of the Great Conditioners; and (3) Toward Taking the Measure of Man.

### I. The Myths of the Great Measurers

First, the most obvious myth of the Great Measurers is, "What I cannot measure does not exist." For instance, in intelligence testing. Since the beginning days of Stanford-Binet, the point that has been perfectly clear is that intelli-

Excerpts from an address at the Minnesota Intercollegiate Faculty Conference, University of Minnesota, Minneapolis, May 7–9, 1971. By permission of Professor Uemura.
Joseph Uemura is Professor of Philosophy, Hamline University.

gence tests test what intelligence tests test. The problem has always been whether or not they really tested intelligence. Honest, sanguine psychologists have always said that the answer to that question is not clear, that at best it is only one kind of intelligence, that it is weighted toward the verbal, that it might well be culture-bound and *petit bourgeois*. However, the vast majority of psychologists, playing upon public demand for the simple answer, have perpetrated the myth, and have taken the money and the power and have run!

We have measured mind by Iowa Basic Skills, SAT, at one end, and GRE and Ph.D. at the other. Beyond that, we know that mind does not exist! It probably serves us right that Frost, Hemingway, Scott Fitzgerald deliberately chose to ignore that kind of mind in favor of their own.

The second myth of the Great Measurers is: "What I cannot account for or understand does not exist." We have perpetrated this myth in a wholesale way in academe. Greek is so hard to understand that you notice, on most campuses, it no longer exists. We, then, add insult to injury by saying that because it did not survive, it could not have been very good. We coin terms like "primitive" and erase entire millenia of human experience. We label whole ages "Dark" to justify ignoring their existence. We cannot account for it, we do not understand it, so it does not exist, and surely it does not matter. So, when students say things and do things we cannot account for or understand, our myth comes to our rescue. We know that what we cannot understand does not exist and we simply do not pay attention to them, we ignore them, or flunk them out of our world for their audacity.

The third, perhaps the most pernicious of all of the myths of the Great Measurers is: "What I cannot control does not exist." The most obvious of these is the "political pragmatist" who thinks that if he cannot control it, surely it must not exist. But B. F. Skinner is no different and he's a full professor on tenure at Harvard. When confronted with the problem of freedom, says Skinner, "I must deny it or my entire science is absurd." So, in his *Walden Two*, the keeper of the utopia, Mr. Frazier, suggests that everyone is happy, even if they are not free. They are completely determined to be happy. The conditioning mechanisms are complete. The denial of human freedom is necessary because what Frazier cannot control cannot possibly exist. The Great Measurer has won.

The determinists, however, of the past century are all on his side. The economic determinists, like Karl Marx, surely cannot disagree with this, for individual choice is at the mercy of material conditions. The historical determinists, like Oswald Spengler, are quite sure that the organism of history controls and individual human conscience has no effect on the "ineluctable march of events." The sociological and psychological determinists are no different from the political totalitarians. The premises are the same, the only difference is who is in charge.

So, in teaching, students who cannot be controlled must be "disappeared," expelled, flunked out, or counselled into leaving; thus, "ceasing to exist." Faculty who cannot be controlled are denied tenure, promotion, raises, and soon "no longer exist." In either event, each is denied membership in academia and ceases to be of "academic consequence"—even if he succeeds, publishes first, or does better than the rest of us.

## II. The Mistake of the Great Conditioners

The trouble with myths is that they *are* partly true. The myths of the Great Measurers are, also, partly true, and even true to a great degree. And when you are right most of the time, a little arrogance takes care of the times when you are not.

Let me, for economy's sake, say that the Great Measurers quite usually regard teaching as "conditioning," a branch of "scientific classroom experimentation" practiced upon those who are "willing subjects for experimentation," the young. The Great Measurers are the Great Conditioners.

Now, in their judgment, traditional and classical ways of teaching are "prescientific, mystical, superstitious, and ineffective." "Scientific" teaching, rather, sets "positive conditions for the behavioral reinforcement of certain desired experiences." The classroom, therefore, is a laboratory in which desired experiences are reinforced so that every basic human need can be properly satisfied. Teaching is not that hit-and-miss use of worn-out and boring technique, whose results are impossible to verify, or positively identify, with no systematic or scientific analysis of results, no strict control of behavioral responses.

Now, I would like to point out a few things to those who hold this position. First, I think it is clear that teaching conceived as conditioning is, indeed, possible. In fact, it is also probable that most human beings will respond, and in the predicted way, to such a scheme of conditioning. Ivan Pavlov is at least half right. However, I would argue that while such conditioning is possible, it simply is not crucial in genuine education.

The second thing I would say to the Great Conditioners is that no one denies that in certain situations positive behavioral conditioning is even necessary. It would seem clear that given the animal nature of human beings, it is quite necessary that learning by conditioning is bound to take place. Human beings, indeed, are to a certain extent creatures of habit and natural satisfactions. Natural desires must be gratified. Hobbes, Marx, Freud, Darwin are at least partially correct. Men, for instance, need their fears and insecurities minimally removed, or, as Hobbes put it, their lives would indeed be "nasty, poor, brutish, and short." But, is that all that education is up to: removing fears and insecurities? Will we, now, insist that education is over? A moment's reflection should convince us that such a victory is less than worth winning; that when teaching has been reduced to policing, it is a sad day, indeed.

The mistake of the Great Conditioners is patently clear from one of the best-buried, yet most crucial stories we have about Ivan Pavlov, patron saint of the Great Conditioners. Konrad Lorenz, an unimpeachable source, relates the following:

A very strange story was told to me by Howard Lidell, a famous neurological specialist who was Pavlov's student in St. Petersburg. Lidell had conditioned a dog to salivate when a metronome accelerated. He asked himself, "What will happen if I release my dog from his harness?"

Lidell went ahead and unleashed the dog. What do you think the dog did? Though the metronome hadn't accelerated, he leaped toward the mechanism, pushed it with his nose, wagged his tail, and, while salivating furiously, asked the metronome to accelerate! What had previously been conditioned was quite simply the reaction of a beggar. The dog had formed the hypothesis that the metronome was the cause of his food. The great Pavlov was so furious that he forbade Lidell to divulge his experiment! Think of the complexity of what had happened and the simplism of the explanation. The conditioned reflex does exist, but it is not the only element of behavior.[1]

Even the dog made an hypothesis. Human students do even more than that, especially if they have decent teachers.

Yes, we can condition human beings to be satisfied and happy. We can, in a word, bring them up to zero. My question is, are we going to be satisfied with that kind of education? It is perfectly obvious to me that conditioning cannot really account for hypothesis-making. And it takes a strange, hollow, and small man to be happy with that kind of teaching.

### III. Taking the Measure of Man

If the above remarks are true, then some very important things follow in our consideration of the question of measuring educational "outcomes." Let me mention three:

First, pursuant to Lidell's point, we must admit that we cannot restrict our attention to simple stimulus and response. Lidell's point is that even dogs make hypotheses that S–R cannot take into account. I suggest that the best men I know have always *chosen* their stimuli. Any potential stimulus does not *become* a stimulus unless and until it is chosen by the man—the hypothesis-maker, the spinner of tales, the contemplator of beauty, the actor of Hamlet, the inventor of steam engines, or the stonemason. And, if Pavlov and the behaviorists are embarrassed by Lidell's hypothesis-making dog, it should be clear that the "rat-model" for man is only appropriate as a slur on human nature.

Facts, clearly, do *not* speak for themselves. Theories, explanations, hypotheses are the crucial matter in knowing *how* they must be read, and also whether they can be considered "facts" at all. The fact of a stimulus only comes into being as a result of a man's choice, and the Great Conditioners, by their own admission, cannot explain such a state of affairs.

Second, the question of positive evidence—behavior, if you like—is extremely problematic and, surely, admits of no simple reading. Empirical evi-

[1] Konrad Lorenz, "A Talk with Konrad Lorenz," *New York Times Magazine*, July 5, 1970, p. 29.

dence, any elementary logician knows, can be read in distinctly different, even contradictory, ways with complete adequacy and fairness to the facts. The point is that empirical evidence is *not* what is conclusive. Rather, *explanatory theories* which account for such evidence *are*.

The upshot of this question of evidence, Karl Popper has pointed out clearly, is that positive evidence or behavioral evidence is restricted in its function to denying or falsifying certain theories and hypotheses. Strictly speaking, inductive evidence can support and reinforce a theory, but it can never fully establish it; on the other hand, inductive evidence can falsify a theory beyond doubt.

We must be extremely careful in reading behavioral evidence in human activity. And where it comes precisely to just what human beings *know*, or to what they *think*, when they behave in given ways, we have a problem of immense dimensions. Simplistic readings are prone to trivialize the thoughts of even the dullest mind, let alone a potential Rembrandt or Shakespeare. I wish to caution us in our propensities toward trivial, simplistic, and unimaginative interpretations of the so-called "best of positive evidence."

Third, the question of negative evidence needs to be taken into account. I submit that very often the *lack* of evidence, the *lack* of any response whatsoever, is more meaningful than its *presence*. Particularly is this so where human beings are concerned. In strictly physical matters, for instance, the lack of positive evidence is regarded, quite properly, as sufficient to disprove certain hypotheses. The Michelson-Morley experiment, you recall, reasonably concluded that the ether-theory was untenable because they found *no* evidence. The same, I suggest, must be said for matters involving human experience. The point is: A man can know enough *not* to act. In fact, men are often mightily distinguished by what they *refuse* to do.

So, the question of knowing what a great man is thinking from what he *refuses* to do, I suggest, is a legitimate question. And the tendency for behaviorists and positivists to read things reductively, i.e., no behavior, no thinking, is plainly mistaken.

## IV. Conclusion

The question, then, is: How do *you* know that your students know anything, are learning anything, or are making any kind of academic progress? As the judge, measurer, and measuring rod, how do you go about it?

Let me suggest that the well-known and prosaic means of "measuring man" still seem to be the best—as imprecise and as intuitive and mystical as they might seem to the "hairy-eared worshippers of science." I still think that measuring a man's knowledge, his progress, and his ability, is known best by asking him the right questions, by listening carefully to his answers, by having him write extensively what he really thinks, by talking with him to see if he really means what he says. There is still no substitute for reading, writing, talking, and listening. The lecture hall, the library, the seminar room, the carrel, and the "sym-posium" ("the party"), are still the best places for finding out what goes on in the heads of both "measurer" and "measuree."

Of course, those "hairy-eared worshippers of science" will still dub those things "outdated," "crude," "prescientific," and "imprecise." But I simply suggest that the most civilized men I have ever known, from Socrates to the present, have gotten to know what I know with fantastic precision, better even than I cared to allow them. I only follow their lead.

Everything depends, I will admit, upon the quality of the mind who is taking the measure. It does take a good mind to detect a good mind and take the proper measure of it. Alas, if we are sow's ears, silk purses shall never be made. If worse comes to the worst, we shall simply perpetuate the Myths of the Great Measurers, and continue to make the Mistake of the Great Conditioners; and Lidell's poor puppy-dog will still be in need of human vindication!

# CHAPTER
# 4

# Humanize the Learning Process

# A. Close Down the Schools?

## 4.1 INTRODUCTION: HUMANISM FOR A POST-INDUSTRIAL ERA

The word "humanism" refers to any system of beliefs and values whose primary emphasis is on man's natural abilities. On the societal level, humanism stresses man's—every man's—natural ability to think and to reason, to speak up and to debate, to compromise and to conciliate, and thus to resolve conflicting interests to form a humane community. Humanism is opposed to systems whose chief emphasis is on the subrational urgencies of blood, soil, and race, or on the superrational absolutes of revelation and mystic intuition.

On the personal level, humanism emphasizes man's ability to rise above his surrounding circumstances, to transcend the limitations which hold other species of animals to a constant level, and to attain to heights of excellence which distinguish, not only men from animals, but civilized men from barbarians.

But humanism recognizes man's limitations as well as his potentialities. It is wonderful that men are able "to dream the impossible dream," but it is even more wonderful that men realize that they are men, not angels, and that the realization—even the partial realization—of any dream requires the cultivation of habits of self-discipline and self-direction. In an age of mass production and of automation, we are prone to think of the twelve or fourteen years in school as analogous to twelve or fourteen stages along a mass-production assembly line. Such assembly lines may produce good automobiles or washing machines, but they can never produce men of excellence. The simple truth of the matter is that men of excellence cannot be *produced*, they must *produce* themselves. John Stuart Mill summarized the humanist point of view when in his essay *On Liberty* he wrote: "He who lets the world or his own portion of it, choose his plan of life for him has no need of any other faculty than the apelike one of imitation. He who chooses his plan for himself employs all his faculties. He must use observation to see, reasoning and judgment to foresee, activity to gather materials for decision, and when he has decided, firmness and self-control to hold to his deliberate decision."

Humanism is built, not on a fixed creed or on a system of regimented ideas, but on the sure knowledge that frontiers are never stationary, that the thrust of events is steadily forward, that there are no privileged ideas around which magic circles can be drawn to protect them from competition. Obstacles exist to be overcome, humanists believe, and therefore they are overcome. New frontiers await discovery, humanists believe, and therefore new frontiers are discovered. When Daniel Boone's frontier is gone, Thomas Edison's frontier appears. The wider the sphere of man's knowledge, the greater its contact with the unknown; and if men will only remain confident of their own great powers, the process knows no limit.

Humanists are not cop-outs. Like St. Paul, they are dedicated to "fight the good fight" and, in spite of the breath-taking social transformations that are occurring on all sides, they never abandon hope of making some sense out of this confusing, changing world. Most Americans are deeply humanistic, and would agree with Zbigniew Brzezinski when he speaks of ". . . unprecedented opportunities for innovation and experimentation." And he continues:

> In summarizing the social transformation wrought by technology, Daniel Bell listed five key areas of change: " (1) By producing more goods at less cost, technology has been the chief engine of raising the living standards of the world. . . . (2) Technology has created a new class, hitherto unknown in society, of the engineer and the technician. . . . (3) Technology has created a new definition of rationality, a new mode of thought, which emphasizes functional relations and the quantitative. . . . (4) The revolutions in transportation and communications, as a consequence of technology, have created new economic interdependencies and new social interactions. . . . (5) Esthetic perceptions, particularly of space and time, have been radically altered." . . . To these should be added the new sense of self-awareness induced by society's increasing ability to see itself in the mirror provided by television, buttressed by increased reliance on statistical analysis, and intensified by a systematic preoccupation with managing not only the present but the future. . . .
>
> There is something awesome and baffling about a society that can simultaneously change man's relationship to the universe by placing a man on the moon, wage and finance a thirty-billion-dollar-per-annum foreign war despised by a significant portion of its people, maintain the most powerful and far-flung military forces in history, and confront in the streets and abet in the courts a revolution in its internal racial relations, doing all this in the context of the explosion of higher learning in its rapidly expanding and turbulent universities, of rotting urban centers, of fumbling political institutions, and of dynamically growing frontier industries that are transforming the way its citizens live and communicate with one another. Any one of the above aspects would suffice to transform the values and self-image of a society, and a few might be enough to overthrow its system. All together, they create a situation that defies analogy to other societies and highlights the singular character of the contemporary American experience.[1]

But there are other humanists who are not cop-outs, but who view the future with great apprehension, and who have serious misgivings about the

[1] From *Between Two Ages: America's Role in the Technotronic Era* by Zbigniew Brzezinski (Columbia University), excerpts from pp. 203–204, 195. Copyright © 1970 by Zbigniew Brzezinski. Reprinted by permission of The Viking Press.

thoughtless optimism which seems to characterize the present leadership of our society. They note that the word *America* no longer calls to mind unlimited opportunity for freedom and for self-realization. Instead, *America* calls to mind student unrest, black revolt, work which has lost all joy and meaning, leisure dominated by professionals rather than by participants—a nation that seems to allow a creeping degradation of both the human mind and the physical environment. The romantics may still wave the flag, see the country as one of manifest destiny, and view the quest for power and affluence as unending. But the more realistic (which their critics call "more radical") students of the present situation believe that it is no longer possible to conduct business as usual.

Most of all they deplore the waste of human and of natural resources. They recall the sixteenth-century when Spain controlled most of Europe and the two Americas, when it possessed what seemed to be unbounded wealth, and when Spain's future seemed to be nothing less than universal domination and power. Yet within less than a century Spain fell into oblivion, having squandered her wealth as she tried to overextend her power. And then these humanists look at twentieth-century America, where they see an ever-increasing pollution of air, defiling of landscapes, contamination of rivers and harbors, despoiling of soils and forests, and—worst of all—the demoralization of man himself, as he spends his substance on useless wars. Since 1945, the United States has spent one thousand billion dollars ($1,000,000,000,000) on its military budget. Surely Spain was never so wasteful.

In summary: Everyone agrees that our technological and natural resources are vast, powerful, and adequate for our own generation. But not everyone agrees that we are using them wisely. Their proper use is surely the most crucial issue of our age.

In this chapter we shall study the views of those who advocate the de-schooling of society, and who recommend a loosening of the bureaucratic grip of our educational establishment. We will appreciate the critics' viewpoint best if we consider, not only what the critics advocate (for their positive suggestions are generally quite vague and speculative), but also what they fear. And what they fear most is this: that the military-industrial establishment, which President Eisenhower warned about, seems to be changing into a military-industrial-educational establishment.[2]

Like Everett Reimer and Paulo Freire, Ivan Illich reflects what for Latin Americans is a very realistic view: Countries south of the border (and countries in other parts of the world also), impoverished as they are, cannot hope to duplicate the expensive system of education found in the United States.

[2] In *The Sociology of Religion* (New York: Prentice-Hall, 1966, pp. 82–104), Thomas O'Dea discusses "five dilemmas of institutionalized religion." Perhaps the critics of our establishment would become somewhat more charitable towards the present social order if they would study and ponder some of the problems and dilemmas which confront any organization or social institution.

As we follow them in their search for alternatives, we find ourselves discarding—or at least questioning—some almost universally held assumptions and deeply entrenched prejudices. To do this is worthwhile. For it is only by challenging accepted beliefs that we are able to think freely and creatively about any problem.

If the selections in this chapter "Humanize the Learning Process" have any common theme, it is this: we must not confuse "schooling" with "education," and we must not unthinkingly suppose that traditional patterns of schooling are *necessarily* the patterns best fitted to the modern age. On the other hand, we are not justified in supposing that traditional patterns are *necessarily* unsuited to the modern age. If we abandon the extreme positions, then we may perhaps agree with the following summary statement by Paul N. Ylvisaker, Dean of the Harvard Graduate School of Education:

> The greatest need in American education today is what it has always been, only more so: a sense of the importance of education and a readiness to do something positive about it.
>
> [What are some of the positive things we should be doing?]
>
> We can start releasing the nation's self-educational energies by making better use of the media. We can go further by building new learning environments and offering enough of a variety of learning experiences to do justice to the diversity of American learners. We can do still more by pulling down the walls that insulate the guilds from consumers of learning and from each other. And by breaking through the medieval encrustations that divert educational effort into a sterile concern with certificates and away from more legitimate goals of learning.
>
> Whatever the route, it is the direction and the commitment to press on that's important. Toward a community in which learning is endemic, spontaneous, and as much as possible self-directed. Where learning is taken for granted and not neglected. And where being taken for granted means that it is assumed that learning is the most lasting and revered endeavor the community can engage in—a means of fulfillment and a noble end in itself.[3]

[3] Paul N. Ylvisaker, "Beyond '72: Strategies for Schools," *Saturday Review* 55: 33–34, November 11, 1972.

# 4.2 THE FUTURE OF EDUCATION
## Marshall McLuhan and George Leonard

The time is coming, if it is not already here, when children can learn far more, far faster in the outside world than within schoolhouse walls. "Why should I go back to school and interrupt my education?" the high-school dropout asks. His question is impudent but to the point. The modern urban environment is packed with energy and information—diverse, insistent, compelling. Four-year-olds, as school innovators are fond of saying, may spend their playtimes discussing the speed, range and flight characteristics of jet aircraft, only to return to a classroom and "string some more of those old beads." The 16-year-old who drops out of school may be risking his financial future, but he is not necessarily lacking in intelligence. One of the unexpected statistics of recent years comes from Dr. Louis Bright, Associate U.S. Commissioner of Education for Research. His studies show that, in large cities where figures are available, dropouts have higher average I.Q. scores than high-school graduates.

This danger signal is only one of many now flashing in school systems throughout the world. The signals say that something is out of phase, that most present-day schools may be lavishing vast and increasing amounts of time and energy preparing students for a world that no longer exists. Though this is a time of educational experiments, the real reforms that might be expected have as yet touched only a small proportion of our schools. In an age when even such staid institutions as banks and insurance companies have been altered almost beyond recognition, today's typical classroom—in physical layout, method and content of instruction—still resembles the classroom of 30 or more years ago.

Resistance to change is understandable and perhaps unavoidable in an endeavor as complex as education, dealing as it does with human lives. But the status quo may not endure much longer. The demands, the very nature of this age of new technology and pervasive electric circuitry, barely perceived because so close at hand, will shape education's future. By the time this year's babies have become 1989's graduates (if college "graduation" then exists), schooling as we know it may be only a memory.

Marshall McLuhan and George Leonard, "The Future of Education," *Look* 31: 23f., February 21, 1967. Copyright Marshall McLuhan and used by his permission.

This article has been reprinted in its entirety in *Radical School Reform*, edited by Ronald and Beatrice Gross, New York: Simon & Schuster, 1969, pp. 106–115.

Marshall McLuhan is Director of the Center for Culture and Technology at the University of Toronto and author of the widely read *Understanding Media* (1964) and *The Medium Is the Massage* (1967).

George Leonard is Vice-President of the Esalen Institute of California, and the author of *Education and Ecstasy* (1969).

Mass education is a child of a mechanical age. It grew up along with the production line. It reached maturity just at that historical moment when Western civilization had attained its final extreme of fragmentation and specialization, and had mastered the linear technique of stamping out products in the mass.

It was this civilization's genius to manipulate matter, energy and human life by breaking every useful process down into its functional parts, then producing any required number of each. Just as shaped pieces of metal became components of a locomotive, human specialists become components of the great social machine.

In this setting, education's task was fairly simple: decide what the social machine needs, then turn out people who match those needs. The school's function was not so much to encourage people to keep exploring, learning and, therefore, changing throughout life as to slow and control those very processes of personal growth and change. Providing useful career or job skills was only a small part of this educational matching game. All students, perhaps more so in the humanities than the sciences and technologies, were furnished standard "bodies of knowledge," vocabularies, concepts and ways of viewing the world. Scholarly or trade journals generally held a close check on standard perceptions in each special field.

Specialization and standardization produced close resemblance and, therefore, hot competition between individuals. Normally, the only way a person could differentiate himself from the fellow specialists next to him was by doing the same thing better and faster. Competition, as a matter of fact, became the chief motive force in mass education, as in society, with grades and tests of all sorts gathering about them a power and glory all out of proportion to their quite limited function as learning aids.

Then, too, just as the old mechanical production line pressed physical materials into preset and unvarying molds, so mass education tended to treat students as objects to be shaped or manipulated. "Instruction" generally meant pressing information onto passive students. Lectures, the most common mode of instruction in mass education, called for very little student involvement. This mode, one of the least effective ever devised by man, served well enough in an age that demanded only a specified fragment of each human being's whole abilities. There was, however, no warranty on the human products of mass education.

That age has passed. More swiftly than we can realize, we are moving into an era dazzlingly different. Fragmentation, specialization and sameness will be replaced by wholeness, diversity and, above all, a deep involvement.

Already, mechanized production lines are yielding to electronically controlled, computerized devices that are quite capable of producing any number of varying things out of the same material. Even today, most U.S. automobiles are, in a sense, custom produced. Figuring all possible combinations of styles, options and colors available on a certain new family sports car, for example, a computer expert came up with 25 *million* different versions of it for a buyer. And that is only a beginning. When automated electronic production reaches full potential, it will be just about as cheap to turn out a million differing objects as a million exact duplicates. The only limits on production and consumption will be the human imagination.

Similarly, the new modes of instantaneous, long-distance human communication—radio, telephone, television—are linking the world's people in a vast net of electric circuitry that creates a new depth and breadth of impersonal involvement in events and breaks down the old, traditional boundaries that made specialization possible.

The very technology that now cries out for a new mode of education creates means for getting it. But new educational devices, though important, are not as central to tomorrow's schooling as are new roles for student and teacher. Citizens of the future will find much less need for sameness of function or vision. To the contrary, they will be rewarded for diversity and originality. Therefore, any real or imagined need for standardized classroom presentation may rapidly fade; the very first casualty of the present-day school system may well be the whole business of teacher-led instruction as we now know it.

Tomorrow's educator will be able to set about the exciting task of creating a new kind of learning environment. Students will rove freely through this place of learning, be it contained in a room, a building, a cluster of buildings or (as we shall see later) an even larger schoolhouse. There will be no distinction between work and play in the new school, for the student will be totally involved. Responsibility for the effectiveness of learning will be shifted from student to teacher.

As it is now, the teacher has a ready-made audience. He is assured of a full house and a long run. Those students who don't like the show get flunking grades. If students are free to move anywhere they please, however, there is an entirely new situation, and the quality of the experience called education will change drastically. The educator then will naturally have a high stake in generating interest and involvement for his students.

To be involved means to be drawn in, to interact. To go on interacting, the student must *get somewhere*. In other words, the student and the learning environment (a person, a group of people, a book, a programmed course, an electronic learning console or whatever) must respond to each other in a pleasing and purposeful interplay. When a situation of involvement is set up, the student finds it hard to drag himself away.

The notion that free-roving students would loose chaos on a school comes only from thinking of education in the present mode—as *teaching* rather than *learning*—and from thinking of learning as something that goes on mostly in classrooms. A good example of education by free interaction with a responsive environment already exists, right before our eyes. Watch a child learn to talk or, for an even more striking case, watch a five-year-old learn a new language. If the child moves to a foreign country and is allowed to play intensely and freely with neighborhood children—*with no language "instruction" whatever*—he will learn the new tongue, accent free, in two or three months. If instruction is attempted, however, the child is in trouble.

Imagine, if you will, what would happen if we set the five-year-old down in a classroom, allowed him to leave his seat only at prescribed times, presented only a few new words at a sitting, made him learn each group before going on to the next, drilled him on pronunciation, corrected his "mistakes," taught him grammar, gave him homework assignments, tested him and—worst of all—convinced him that the whole thing was work rather than play. In such a case, the child might learn the new language as slowly and painfully as do teen-agers or adults. Should an adult try to learn a language by intense play and interaction, he would probably do much better than he would in a classroom, but still fall short of a young child's performance. Why? The adult has already learned the lessons that the old schooling teaches so well: inhibition, self-consciousness, categorization, rigidity and the deep conviction that learning is hard and painful work.

Indeed, the old education gives us a sure-fire prescription for creating dislike of any type of human activity, no matter how appealing it might seem. To stop children from reading comic books (which might be ill-advised), you would only have to assign and test them on their content every week.

Learning a new language is a giant feat, compared to which mastering most of the present school curriculum should prove relatively simple. Long before 1989, all sorts of equipment will be available for producing responsive environments in all the subject matter now commonly taught, and more. Programmed instruction, for example, creates high involvement, since it draws the student along in a sort of dialogue, letting him respond at frequent intervals. Programming at its best lets the student learn commonly agreed-upon cultural techniques and knowledge—reading, spelling, arithmetic, geography and the like—in his own time, at his own pace. But present-day programming may soon seem crude in light of current developments. Computers will be able to understand students' written or spoken responses. (Already, they understand typed responses.) When these computers are hooked into learning consoles, the interplay between student and learning program can become even more intense.

When computers are properly used, in fact, they are almost certain to increase individual diversity. A worldwide network of computers will make all of mankind's factual knowledge available to students everywhere in a matter of minutes or seconds. . . .

We are only beginning to realize what a tiny slice of human possibilities we now educate. In fragmenting all of existence, Western civilization hit upon one aspect, the literate and rational, to develop at the expense of the rest. Along with this went a lopsided development of one of the senses, the visual. Such personal and sensory specialization was useful in a mechanical age, but is fast becoming outmoded. Education will be more concerned with training the senses and perceptions than with stuffing brains. And this will be at no loss for the "intellect." Studies show a high correlation between sensory, bodily development—now largely neglected—and intelligence.

Already, school experimenters are teaching written composition with tape recorders (just as students play with these marvelous devices) in an attempt to retain the auditory sense, to recapture the neglected rhythms of speech. Already, experimental institutes are working out new ways to educate peoples' neglected capacities to relate, to feel, to sense, to create. Future schooling may well move into many unexplored domains of human existence. People will learn much in 1989 that today does not even have a commonly accepted name.

Can we view this future, the hard and fast of it? Never, for it will always come around a corner we never noticed, take us by surprise. But studying the future helps us toward understanding the present. And the present offers us glimpses, just glimpses: seven-year-olds (the slowest of them) sitting at electronic consoles finishing off, at their own pace, all they'll ever need in the basic skills of reading, writing and the like, eight-year-olds playing games that teach what we might call math or logic in terms of, say, music and the sense of touch; nine-year-olds joining together in large plastic tents to build environments that give one the *experience* of living in the Stone Age or in a spaceship or in an even more exotic place—say, 19th-century America; ten-year-olds interacting with five-year-olds, showing them the basics (now unknown) of human relations or of the relationships between physical movements and mental states.

In all of this, the school—that is, an institution of learning confined to a building or buildings—can continue to hold a central position only if it changes fast enough to keep pace with the seemingly inevitable changes in the outside world. The school experience can well become so rich and compelling that there will be no dropouts, only determined drop-ins. Even so, the walls between school and world will continue to blur.

Already it is becoming clear that the main "work" of the future will be education, that people will not so much earn a living as learn a living. Close to 30 million people in the U.S. are now pursuing some form of adult education, and the number shoots skyward. Industry and the military, as well as the arts and sciences, are beginning to consider education their main business. . . .

Someday, all of us will spend our lives in our own school, the world. And education—in the sense of learning to love, to grow, to change—can become not the woeful preparation for some job that makes us less than we could be but the very essence, the joyful whole of existence itself.

# 4.3 DESCHOOLING SOCIETY
## Ivan Illich

School has become the world religion of a modernized proletariat, and makes futile promises of salvation to the poor of the technological age. The nation-state has adopted it, drafting all citizens into a graded curriculum leading to sequential diplomas not unlike the initiation rituals and hieratic promotions of former times. The modern state has assumed the duty of enforcing the judgment of its educators through well-meant truant officers and job requirements, much as did the Spanish kings who enforced the judgments of their theologians through the conquistadors and the Inquisition.

Two centuries ago the United States led the world in a movement to disestablish the monopoly of a single church. Now we need the constitutional disestablishment of the monopoly of the school, and thereby of a system which legally combines prejudice with discrimination. The first article of a bill of rights for a modern, humanist society would correspond to the First Amendment to the U.S. Constitution: "The State shall make no law with

Abridged from pp. 4, 10–11, 75–79 in *Deschooling Society* by Ivan Illich. Copyright © 1970, 1971 by Ivan Illich. By permission of Harper & Row, Publishers, Inc.

Ivan Illich is Director, Centro Intercultural de Documentacion, Cuernavaca, Mexico, and author of *Celebration of Awareness* (1970).

Compare the following statement by Everett Reimer:

Different schools do different things of course, but increasingly schools in all nations, of all kinds, at all levels, combine four distinct social functions: custodial care, social-role selection, indoctrination, and education as usually defined in terms of the development of skills and knowledge. It is the combination of these functions that makes schooling so expensive. It is conflict among these functions that makes schools educationally inefficient. It is also the combination of these functions that tends to make school a total institution, has made it an international institution, and makes it such an effective instrument of social control. . . .

"As late as the turn of the century, schools were still a minor institution and all who were not suited for them and by them had other educational options. Fifty years ago, no country in the world had 10% of its teen-age population in school. Schools have grown so fast partly because they happened to be doing what was important to a technological era when this era began. Their monopoly of education has been achieved as one aspect of the monopoly of technology. The main reason we need alternatives to schools is that they close the door to humanity's escape from this monopoly. They insure that those who inherit influence in a world dominated by technology will be those who profit by this domination. . . . Not only the leaders but their followers are shaped by the school game to play the game of competitive consumption—first to meet and then to surpass the standards of others. Whether the rules are fair or the game worth playing is beside the point.—Everett Reimer, *School is Dead: Alternatives in Education*, New York: Doubleday, 1971, pp. 29–33. By permission.

respect to the establishment of education." There shall be no ritual obligatory for all. . . .

Supreme Court Justice William O. Douglas observed that "the only way to establish an institution is to finance it." The corollary is also true. Only by channeling dollars away from the institutions which now treat health, education, and welfare can the further impoverishment resulting from their disabling side effects be stopped. . . .

A good educational system should have three purposes: it should provide all who want to learn with access to available resources at any time in their lives; empower all who want to share what they know to find those who want to learn it from them; and, finally, furnish all who want to present an issue to the public with the opportunity to make their challenge known. Such a system would require the application of constitutional guarantees to education. Learners should not be forced to submit to an obligatory curriculum, or to discrimination based on whether they possess a certificate or a diploma. Nor should the public be forced to support, through a regressive taxation, a huge professional apparatus of educators and buildings which in fact restricts the public's chances for learning to the services the profession is willing to put on the market. It should use modern technology to make free speech, free assembly, and a free press truly universal and, therefore, fully educational.

Schools are designed on the assumption that there is a secret to everything in life; that the quality of life depends on knowing that secret; that secrets can be known only in orderly successions; and that only teachers can properly reveal these secrets. An individual with a schooled mind conceives of the world as a pyramid of classified packages accessible only to those who carry the proper tags. New educational institutions would break apart this pyramid. Their purpose must be to facilitate access for the learner; to allow him to look into the windows of the control room or the parliament, if he cannot get in by the door. Moreover, such new institutions should be channels to which the learner would have access without credentials or pedigree—public spaces in which peers and elders outside his immediate horizon would become available.

I believe that no more than four—possibly even three—distinct "channels" or learning exchanges could contain all the resources needed for real learning. The child grows up in a world of things, surrounded by people who serve as models for skills and values. He finds peers who challenge him to argue, to compete, to cooperate, and to understand; and if the child is lucky, he is exposed to confrontation or criticism by an experienced elder who really cares. Things, models, peers, and elders are four resources each of which requires a different type of arrangement to ensure that everybody has ample access to it. . . .

Educational resources are usually labeled according to educators' curricular goals. I propose to do the contrary, to label four different approaches which enable the student to gain access to any educational resource which may help him to define and achieve his own goals:

1. Reference Services to Educational Objects—which facilitate access to things or processes used for formal learning. Some of these things can be reserved for this purpose, stored in libraries, rental agencies, laboratories, and showrooms like museums and theaters; others can be in daily use in factories, airports, or on farms, but made available to students as apprentices or on off-hours.

2. Skill Exchanges—which permit persons to list their skills, the conditions under which they are willing to serve as models for others who want to learn these skills, and the addresses at which they can be reached.

3. Peer-Matching—a communications network which permits persons to describe the learning activity in which they wish to engage, in the hope of finding a partner for the inquiry.

4. Reference Services to Educators-at-Large—who can be listed in a directory giving the addresses and self-descriptions of professionals, para-professionals, and free-lancers, along with conditions of access to their services. Such educators . . . could be chosen by polling or consulting their former clients.

# 4.4 FAREWELL TO SCHOOLS?—YES!
## John Holt

[Let us begin by noting how the Bazilian educator, Paulo Freire, taught reading without schooling. The northeastern part of Brazil is one of the great poverty areas of the world. Most of the people are tenant farmers or share-croppers. They own nothing. They must pay even for the water they get from the landlord's well. They live in the most wretched poverty, in isolated villages virtually without print. They have none of the books, newspapers, signs, or TV advertising that surround almost all children in modern society. Some years ago a Brazilian educator, Paulo Freire, and colleagues trained by him, were able to teach large numbers of wholly illiterate adults in these

From the book *Freedom and Beyond* by John Holt. Copyright © 1972 by John Holt. Published by E. P. Dutton & Co., Inc. and used with their permission. Excerpts are from pp. 238–239, 217–220, 223–225, 228, 125–127, 188–189, 235.

John Holt is author of *How Children Fail* (1964), *How Children Learn* (1967), *The Underachieving Child* (1969), and *What Do We Do On Monday?* (1971).

villages to write and read in a few months, and at a cost of $25 per person. Most of our schools spend $200 or more per pupil per year to teach literacy. At the end of six, seven, ten years and $1,500 or more worth of work, not only do many of our children not read as well as these Brazilian peasants, but also many of them have become so demoralized that they think they are incapable of learning anything.

When Freire and his co-workers came into a new village their first step was to try to get the villagers to come together in a meeting, to discuss their lives, interests, needs, problems, and concerns. Many people were afraid (like many people in the United States) that if they spoke out in public they would get in some kind of trouble. Many more felt that since nothing they said could make any difference in their lives, what was the use of saying anything? Why even think? Better live out your short and wretched life in a kind of numbed resignation. Freire describes the culture in which such people live (the culture of poverty is in a sense worldwide) as the Culture of Silence. Words are not used because they would be wasted. His first step in trying to teach these villagers he called "the awakening of consciousness."

When the meetings first began, the villagers talked diffidently, ashamedly, as even many middle-class Americans talk when they have to speak in public. How could anyone be interested in their thoughts? But as they talked, they gained courage, put more of themselves into their words, spoke with passion and conviction. In this talk certain words began to appear, key words, what Freire calls "generative" words—they generate ideas, and they generate syllables out of which other words can be made. Freire would write these words down and show the villagers how to write them, and by writing them, take hold of them, own them, possess them, have them for their own use. Once they reached this point, the rest was relatively easy. From this beginning they were able to help these villagers become functionally literate in evening classes after a hard day's work, over a period of roughly eight weeks.

Some might say, "But after all, Freire *had* to have schools to do his teaching in." The answer is that in three critical respects his "schools" were altogether different from the schools we know and have, and that I and others, in our talk of deschooling, want to get away from. In the first place, they were not compulsory. In the second, they neither required nor gave any credentials. In the third, they did not lock the student into a prescribed sequence of learning determined in advance.

Clearly our national reading problem is not a necessary problem. Reading is easy. It can't be said too often. Reading is easy. And yet large numbers of children seem not to be able to do it. What has gone wrong? . . .

[There is abundant evidence showing that, when free from fear, and when motivated to learn,] almost all the children that schools call non-readers can in fact read. . . .

[There is also abundant evidence showing that today's system of schooling has led many children to believe] that reading is terribly difficult, that they are too stupid to learn it, that they cannot reach out and take hold of it and make it their own, but must sit passively while someone who "has" reading pours it into them, or perhaps injects it into them, like a doctor giving a shot. Once people look at learning this way, as something someone else will do *to* them, there is no chance of their learning anything. A man once told me that his child was having trouble learning to read even though she desperately wanted to learn. I said, "That word 'desperately' is the key to the trouble. We don't learn difficult things desperately. When we learned to speak, we did not 'desperately' want to learn it, we hardly knew we were learning it, it was part of everything else we did." What this desperate child desperately wanted was not to learn to read but, as Dennison once so well put it, *to have learned to read.* In other words, she wanted to escape from the stigma and shame of being a nonreader. But it is that very shame that more than anything else prevents her from learning to read.

Maybe we need to say "Illiteracy Is OK." Maybe we need signs and buttons saying ILLITERATE POWER. For to make not knowing something a disgrace is to make it certain that many people will never learn it. This gives us a clue why forbidding reading, making reading illegal would be so much more likely to produce readers. If we seriously tried to forbid reading, we might say things like: "If I catch you reading, I'm going to punish you—yell at you, send you to your room, spank you, no supper, can't play outside, etc." But the hidden message would be loud and clear—"Reading is fascinating, there's all kinds of exciting, secret, and forbidden stuff in there, you'll really like it. And you smart little devil, you, I know you, if I turn my back on you for just ten seconds, you'll be in there reading away, in spite of my having told you not to, so I'm going to have to watch you like a hawk." Thus the child would get the idea that reading was both fascinating and easy, and that people who were in a position to know judged him more than competent to master it. Master it he would.

All this is fanciful, of course. But there is something useful we might do. We could just cool it for a while. We could try to learn what experience ought by now to have made plain, that learning to write and read is much simpler than many things children learn for themselves, something that any-one with a good reason for learning it can master it in a matter of months or even weeks. Above all, we could try to revive or to keep alive in children the sense that learning to read is not external to them, somehow lying outside them, but is instead within them, a natural extension of their own powers.

People have asked, "If schools didn't teach reading, how else would anyone learn it? What kinds of arrangements might we make, other than schools or schoollike places, to help people learn to read? What might be both better and cheaper?" Paul Goodman once suggested that we pay a small extra salary to many kinds of workers and craftsmen, such as garage mechanics, in return for which they would agree to let some kids hang around while they were working, and answer any questions they might ask about what they were doing. This gave me the idea of what we might call "reading guides." They would be volunteers. A reading guide would not have to do his guiding all the time, only as much of the time as he wanted, fitting it in along with the rest of his life. College or high school students, or even younger children, if they could read, could be reading guides; or housewives; or older or retired people; or librarians; or parking lot attendants; or anyone else who in his daily life might come into contact with children or other non-readers. The guides would wear some kind of identifying armband, hat, button, etc. so that people wanting information could easily spot them. The understanding would be that when a guide was wearing his sign anyone who wanted could ask him either one of two kinds of questions. He could show him a written word and ask, "What does this say?" and the guide would tell him. Or he could say to the guide, "How do you write such and such a word," and the guide would write it for him. Nothing else; that's all a guide would have to do.

It should cost almost nothing to get such a program going. We might have to spend a little money for the identifying signs, but even this is not necessary; people could make their own. We might have to spend a little money to get the word out about the program, to get people to volunteer as guides, to let other people know what the guides were for. What about testing the guides? No need for it. There is no reason why a guide should be able to read or write every word he might be asked. If he is asked a word he doesn't know, he can say, "I don't know that one, you'll have to ask another guide." A school, a church, a group of parents, or students themselves could start such a program. Indeed, the work could be started without an organized program. Anyone who reads these words, likes the idea, and wants to make himself a reading guide can make his own sign and become one, even if no one else does. Others may later follow his example.

In many cities people, usually young people, have set up what they call "switchboards"—phone numbers that people can call to get various kinds of help or information. Following this example, we might have a reading guide switchboard. The number would be listed in the phone book, and perhaps shown in other places. A caller could call the number, and as before, ask the switchboard either one of two kinds of questions. He could spell the word, and ask the switchboard what the word said, or he could say the word, and ask the switchboard how to spell it. Older people might be glad to take such calls, or invalids, or people otherwise shut in. It would give them a little contact with the world, and a true sense of being useful. Parents in low-income neighborhoods might also take turns doing this. . . .

[Why must education occur] only in classrooms? Why not paint some of these things on the walls of buildings, or on the sidewalks? Why not post in the windows of stores pictures of things, with the name printed underneath— CAT, RAT, HAT, BAT—or a series of phonically regular sentences, like those we can find in Leonard Bloomfield's book, *Let's Read*. Why not put signs—labels—on many of the things children see in the streets—STREET LIGHT, LAMPPOST, FIRE HYDRANT, CURB, STREET, DOOR, WINDOW, BRICK WALL, and so on? In short, let the whole community take the responsibility and initiative in educating its young, instead of turning the job over to a few specialists of doubtful competence that in many cases the community doesn't trust anyway.

Many poor and minority group people are demanding better reading programs in their schools. They might be wiser to try to get more branch libraries in their districts, or better yet, neighborhood storefront libraries or traveling bookmobiles, with newspapers, periodicals, and paperbacks—the kind of reading material that we know kids like to read. What's the point of having kids learn to read if after they've learned there's nothing *to* read. How many adults would read if every time they wanted a book they had to go two or three miles into a completely different part of their city? Access to reading matter, not reading methods, is the name of the game. . . .

[As played today, the rules of the schooling game are so designed as to *prevent* the poor and the disadvantaged from moving up into the higher strata of society.] When we define education as schooling, and put public educational resources into schools, the children who benefit most are the children who can stay in school the longest. These are, necessarily and in all but a few cases, the children of the well-to-do. Tax-supported schools, and even more so tax-exempted colleges and universities, simply create a situation in which the poor have to pay a large share of the cost of schooling the children of the rich. In poor countries, the children of the well-to-do have hundreds of times as much public money, tax money, invested in their schooling as the average child. In the United States the disproportion is not so great; holders of college and graduate degrees, almost all of them from the middle class, have had roughly ten times as much public money invested in their schooling as the average low-income child. Now the richer child will naturally have more of Daddy's money invested in his schooling than the poor child. But that he should also have much more tax money invested in it, money raised in considerable part from poor people, is most unjust. It is also an injustice that we cannot remedy unless and until we give educational resources to learners instead of to schools, and beyond that let these learners decide whether they want to do their learning in school or in some other place and way. For the rich, for obvious reasons, will always be able to outlast the poor in school. And schools, even if their intentions are good, and in spite of anything poor people may do to get control of them, are by their very nature, structure, style, and purpose bound to be middle-class institutions favoring middle-class kids. . . .

[Another consequence] of our defining education as schooling . . . [is this: People] come to believe, even after they have left school, that learning must mean schooling, something that must be done and can only be done in a school. They think that if they want to learn something they have to go to some place called a school and there get some person called a teacher to teach it to them. Many times people have said to me that they felt their brains were getting rusty, that they hadn't learned anything in a long time, and that they needed to go to some school or university and sign up for a course, as if there were no way to learn on their own. . . .

[Moreover, as] we put more and more of our educational resources into schools, we have less and less left over for those institutions that are truly open and educative and in which more and more people might learn for themselves. One example would be the public libraries. In any community, compare the local public library, which serves everybody, with the local public high schools, which serve only a four-year age span. In most places the schools are probably twenty to fifty times as large as the library and spend twenty to fifty times as much money. It is this kind of imbalance that we ought to change. Whatever money we put into institutions should go to those that are truly open, which anyone can use, without preconditions, and for his own purposes. Such institutions are what Illich, Reimer, and others call networks, and the public library is only one very special and perhaps rather conventional example of these. . . .

In a schooled society you have to go to school to learn something. But even there you cannot learn just what you want to learn. You can only learn what they want to teach, and in the order and manner in which they want to teach it to you. Most of what they teach is strictly placed and locked in what Ivan Illich calls a graded curriculum, a sort of ladder of learning. This ladder is very hard to get on and off. As a rule, a learner may not take a step on that ladder unless he has taken many steps before it (all in school) and unless he is willing to take (again in school) many steps after it. Suppose you find that a school is teaching something you want to learn, and you go there, money in hand, and say, "I want to come here for a year (month, week, day) and learn that." They will tell you, "No, you can't do that, you have to learn or prove that you have already learned (in school, of course) many other things *first*, and you will also have to learn many other things *besides*. Where are your prerequisites? How do we know you are good enough to learn here? What previous schooling have you had (not "What have you done, what do you know?") ? Where are your transcripts, your diplomas? Are you a candidate for a degree? Which one?" And so on . . .

Suppose you are a student at a school and want to learn something they are not teaching. One day you find that some other school is teaching it. You say, "I want to go to this other school and learn this thing they are teaching. Will you give me credit for it?" In almost all cases, their answer will be No. The other school probably wouldn't let you learn the thing they are teaching anyway. They would say, "If you want to learn something here, you have to be one of *our* students and learn all the other things *we* are teaching." Learning, in short, comes in packages—four-year packages, sometimes twelve-year packages. You may have a choice of packages, but you always have to buy a whole package, or get nothing. A strange procedure. Obviously it has more to do with merchandising than with learning.

This we want to change. Conversely, by a deschooled society we don't mean a society without any arrangements and resources for learning. Ivan Illich, in *Deschooling Society*, Everett Reimer, in *School Is Dead*, and I in this book, among others, have suggested what some of these resources and arrangements might be, and others will add many other ideas to the list. We don't even mean a society without any schools. Some things—languages, music, dance—may be better learned in a school than in any other way, or may even require a school. If some people like schools and learn well there, let them by all means go to schools. If some people think they cannot learn anything unless they pay a teacher to teach it to them, let them by all means find and pay their own teachers. But in a deschooled society nobody would be compelled to go to school, neither by the law nor by the threat of joblessness, poverty, discrimination, and exclusion from society—all of which are in force today. No one would be punished or disadvantaged for not liking schools, not finding them good places to learn, and not learning there, or for wanting and trying to learn in other ways. No one, whether for lack of money, previous schooling, or any other reason, could be denied access to the opportunity and resources to learn or try to learn whatever he wants to learn. No one could have his right to learn made to depend on his first being able to pass some sort of test. Thus, it is fair and sensible to say that anyone who wants to drive a car must first pass a driving test, to show that he can in fact drive it. But it would not be at all fair or sensible to say that he must pass a test before he can even try *to learn to drive*. In sum, a deschooled society would be a society in which everyone shall have the widest and freest possible choice to learn whatever he wants to learn, whether in school or in some altogether different way. This is very far from being a society in which poor kids would have no chance to learn things. On the contrary, poor kids, like poor people, and indeed all people, would have many more chances to learn things and many more ways of learning them than they have today. It would be a society in which there were many paths to learning and advancement, instead of one school path as we have now—a path far too narrow for everyone, and one too easily and too often blocked off from the poor. . . .

[We conclude this selection, as we began it, with the viewpoint of the great Brazilian educator, Paulo Freire (*Pedagogy of the Oppressed*, 1966)]. The idea that inspired and informed all of his work, and made it work, is that education for the poor and powerless cannot be effective unless it seems *to them* to offer a real chance of increasing their power to change and better the general conditions of their lives. True education doesn't quiet things down; it stirs them up. It awakens consciousness. It destroys myths. It *empowers* people, as George Dennison [in *The Lives of Children* (1969)] so well put it, to think and do for themselves. The Brazilian dictatorship understood this very well and drove Freire out of the country. They did not want the poor empowered, and so they could not have them educated. The lesson for us is that unless we want the poor empowered, we *cannot* have them educated. Education as pacifier has always failed, is failing, and is bound to fail.

# 4.5 FAREWELL TO SCHOOLS?—NO!
## Philip W. Jackson, Amitai Etzioni and John Ohlinger

## JACKSON

Schools have long been the favorite targets of critics, both from the outside and from within. And, given the importance of education and the variety of interpretations to be put upon it, such a condition would be surprising if it were otherwise. But, though historically commonplace, attacks upon our schools do vary from time to time in both their magnitude and their substance. At present the volume is unusually high and we find ourselves in the midst of a particularly intensive barrage of catcalls, complaints, diagnoses, and freely proffered remedies for our educational ills. Moreover, in recent months, . . . the critic's voice is becoming harsher and his ideas more radical. His tools seem to be changing from hammers and saws to battering rams and bulldozers—from instruments of construction to ones of destruction. Moreover, as these new land-clearance engineers rumble toward the schools, an increasingly large crowd of onlookers seems to be on hand to cheer them along and to enjoy the sport.

Excerpts from *Farewell to Schools???*, edited by Daniel U. Levine (University of Missouri, Kansas City) and Robert J. Havighurst (formerly at the University of Chicago). This is one of ten booklets on *Contemporary Educational Issues* sponsored by the National Society for the Study of Education (NSSE), Kenneth J. Rehage, general editor, Worthington, Ohio: Charles A. Jones Publishing Co., 1971. Excerpts from pp. 59–64, 95–97, 66–70. By permission. Footnote references here omitted.

Philip W. Jackson is professor of education and of human development, and Director, the Laboratory Schools, University of Chicago. Amitai Etzioni is professor of sociology, Columbia University, and Director, Center for Policy Research. John Ohlinger is associate professor of adult education, Ohio State University, Columbus. All three men have authored many books and articles. For further criticism, read Sidney Hook, "Illich's Deschooled Utopia," *Encounter*, January 1972; reprinted in *Current*, April 1972.

Why such radical action is necessary is, of course, the most important question to be asked. The only acceptable answer to that question (aside from acknowledging that some people derive perverse pleasure from the act of destruction for its own sake) is to claim that our schools today are so hopelessly bad that nothing can be done to salvage them. This being so, it follows that no matter what takes their place, the resultant arrangement is bound to be an improvement over what we now have.

Some form of this contention, with various elaborations and qualifications, is advanced by almost all the radical critics of our schools. As Goodman puts it, "Only a small fraction, the 'academically talented'—about 15 percent according to James Conant—thrive in schools without being bored or harmed by them." Reimer takes Goodman's assertion one step further by claiming that, "The school system also fails in part to educate most of its nominally successful students, stultifying, rather than nurturing, their lifetime capacity and desire for learning." Illich is quoted in a national magazine as saying, "Preventive concentration camps for predelinquents would be a logical improvement over the school system." Other critics, though less extreme, echo similar sentiments. . . .

If we turn to the search for facts, a disenchantment with the radical critics is quick in coming. For even under the most liberal definition of proof, there is precious little to substantiate the basic premise on which the de-schooling argument rests. That is, there is no solid evidence to support the blanket assertion that schools in our society are failing to educate our children, much less that they are actually doing them harm. This is not to say that there are not students—too many, we know—for whom such a charge is true. We hardly need proof, for example, to convince us that life in many of our inner-city high schools is miserable indeed. We are also painfully aware that a sizable number of our middle-class adolescents are being turned off by their school experience. But to move from such knowledge, lamentable as it is, to a general indictment of our entire school system is to take a giant step indeed, totally unwarranted by the evidence at hand.

Not only is there no basis for concluding that public school pupils across the land are gnashing their teeth in despair and rattling their tin cups against the bars of the classroom in protest against the injustices they are suffering but the few scraps of evidence that do exist point to quite the opposite conclusion. From the middle 1930's to the present day, almost every systematic study of educational attitudes that has been undertaken has revealed the vast majority of students, from the middle grades onward, to be surprisingly content with their school experience. Apparently, almost four out of five students, if asked directly, would confess a liking for school, with all its faults.

Such evidence must of course be taken with a grain of salt, for it can always be argued that the majority of students are content with school simply because they have little else with which to compare it (save summer vacation). Nonetheless, even if accepted with great reservation, it is difficult to reconcile the few facts that do exist with the iconoclastic condemnations of the deschoolers.

In addition to basing their arguments on scant evidence concerning the state of our schools today, the proponents of deschooling seem curiously lacking in historical perspective. Though educational progress, like human progress in general, has clearly had its ups and downs throughout history and leaves no reason to believe that future improvement is inevitable, it does seem true that schools in our country, and probably in the entire Western world, are superior in many respects to those that existed a century or two ago. They serve a larger segment of our citizenry, they follow curricula that are more varied and better suited to the future needs of our students than was true in the past, and they are staffed by teachers who, on the whole, are better educated and more humane in their dealings with children than were their predecessors a few generations back. Gone are the hickory stick, the rapped knuckles, and the dunce's cap, together with the heavy reliance on rote memory, the rigidity of the recitation method, and the bolted-down desk. Some of the educational practices that have taken their place leave much to be desired, it is true, but with all of our present educational shortcomings, it is difficult to avoid the terribly smug conclusion that our schools are better today than they have ever been before.

Such smugness should not be accompanied by complacency, however, for whatever progress has been made has required hard work, and there is much yet to be done. Moreover, we have no guarantee that things will not get worse rather than better. Nonetheless, the overall impression of progress, unstable though it may be, does not sit well with the assertion that our present system is one great failure. Faced with such a charge, one is tempted to say to the critic, "If you think our schools are bad now, you should have seen them in your grandfather's day!"

Much as it might dampen the critics' flame, a calm look at what goes on in our classrooms reveals them to be neither Dickensian nor Orwellian horrors. They are neither prisons, presided over by modern-day Fagins who take delight in twisting ears and otherwise torturing children, nor are they gigantic Skinner boxes, designed to produce well-conditioned automatons who will uncritically serve the state. Anyone who believes in the truth of such fictions should take a few days off to visit his local schools. Should he find the fiction to be matched by reality, he would indeed have reason to seek change by whatever means are available. But anyone who, with or without such personal experience, proceeds to argue that such is the state of all or even most of our schools, must either be misinformed or irresponsible. . . .

The chief difficulty with many advocates of the incidental-learning position is their failure to distinguish between learning and education. For most of us, incidental learning of one sort or another is indeed occurring all the time. As I glance up from my desk at this very moment, for example, I have just "learned" that my neighbor is about to mow his lawn! But education obviously involves much more than the accumulation of such fortuitous bits of information. It involves learning that is prescribed and planned and guided. Humans can indeed educate themselves, but experience seems to show that the process occurs more effectively with outside help. It was with this realization that the idea of a teacher was born. When our forebearers began to come to grips with the fact that not all adults could spend their time at such a pursuit, the notion of a school was in the offing.

Doubtlessly, there *are* children who, freed from the formal demands of schools and with a minimum of adult guidance, would set about the laborious task of educating themselves. But whether all or most children, if pressed to do so, would turn out to be such self-motivated learners is indeed doubtful. Moreover, there is at least some reason to believe that those who would suffer most from the absence of classroom constraints and teacher guidance would be those children who already exhibit signs of educational impoverishment. Thus, left largely to their own devices, our out-of-school learners would likely behave in ways that would result in exaggerating the cleavages that already separate social class groups within our society.

Finally, even if educators or their critics wanted to set children free to learn on their own without the confines of a school and all the restrictions it implies, there is ample reason to believe that parents and other adults in our society would not stand for it. Like it or not, our schools presently perform a custodial function as well as an educational one. Parents, particularly those of young children, simply do not want their offspring to be unsupervised during much of the day. We could, of course, substitute compulsory day-care centers or neighborhood clubs for compulsory schools, but, when we consider such alternatives, they begin to look not all that different from what used to go on in the empty schoolhouse down the block.

In summary, the arguments of the deschoolers suffer from two serious flaws. They begin with a false picture of how bad things are in our schools today, and they end with a highly romanticized notion of what might be substituted for our present educational system.

Meanwhile, back in the classroom, there is a lot of work to be done. Our inner-city schools, particularly high schools, *are* disaster areas; too many of our students, particularly our adolescents, *are* being turned off by their school experience; the bureaucratic structure of our schools, particularly our larger ones, *is* more abrasive than it needs to be; our graded system *is* too rigid and requires loosening up; our teacher certification laws *are* shamefully archaic and prevent many good people from taking their place in the classroom; our schools *do* need to be linked more imaginatively to the communities they serve.

These *are* serious problems, badly in need of solution. The crucial question is whether their solution requires the abandonment or the overthrow of the entire system. To answer that question, we must consider what is *right* about our schools as well as what is wrong with them. In balance, at least as seen from the inside, the pros clearly outweigh the cons. . . .

## ETZIONI

[Those who advocate deschooling society seem to] believe that the child, by nature, is eager to learn. If his nature is allowed to unfold, free from the distorting effects of the school, he will take to education like a sunflower to sunshine. Illich thus argues that "we can depend on self-motivated learning instead of employing teachers to bribe or compel the student to find time and the will to learn." . . .

The main suggestion endorsed by all four authors [Goodman, Reimer, Illich and Bereiter], albeit in varying degrees, is that the amount and scope of schooling must be drastically reduced in order to "free" education from its institutional cage. By and large, school is not to be replaced by anything. Education is to occur chiefly by itself, by the child's participation in *on-going* activities and his selection of which set of resources he will apply to himself. This position has two attributes: first, it suggests that by merely doing away with institutions (a position taken elsewhere vis-à-vis sexual taboos and authority), we not only eliminate the existing system but also provide a viable foundation for the new world. Second, it frees the analyst from having to think out what new system will have to be erected—the child knows best where he should be and what he needs. Practically all the specific suggestions made here are based on this double assumption: the child wishes to learn and he needs less, not more, institutional support. Goodman's notion of incidental learning, Bereiter's and Illich's notion of providing the child with educational resources, and the shared view of the teacher as a child's "source person," all assume that the child is able *and* motivated to learn and that his choices are the educated and educating ones.

The evidence in favor of those cheerful assumptions is slim and very difficult to evaluate. A review of the data and the methodological difficulties involved is a task we cannot undertake here. However, two points can be made, drawing not on empirical data but on the logic of the arguments involved. First, educational institutions are clearly part of the societal web. The child, even if he "naturally" would have been education-eager, obviously does not enter school unaffected by his family, his neighborhood, the mass media, etc. Obviously he was exposed to these influences *before* he was of school age, and they also continue to affect him while he is at school. By and large, these forces are similar to the *old* school system—they tend to make the child passive, dependent, alienated.

The question hence must be raised: What child do the optimists talk about—the postrevolutionary child, born to a liberated home and community in a society in which all means of production are collectivized, the media are educational, etc.? Or is he the one who is actually entering our schools now? Can he be truly freed simply by releasing him from school? Must we not try to help children—at least until the revolution comes—to overcome the distortions they bring to school from their nonliberated backgrounds? And are not these distortions deep and severe enough to require a teacher and a school which can motivate, plan, and guide, rather than relying on the child of a distorted society to supervise his own rehabilitation? Are not children like those workers who have not yet acquired class awareness—in need of resourceful, active, effective leadership and a master educational plan? They will never awake from their TV-induced, parent-supported slumber if they follow Goodman's prescription:

> The goal of elementary education should be a very modest one: it is for a small child, under his own steam, not on a leash, to be able to poke interestedly into whatever goes on and to be able, by observation, questions, and practical imitation, to get something out of it on his own terms.

One answer, of which Illich is a particularly keen proponent, is that education is the realm in which the revolution would be generated. By redoing the child, we set into motion a major force which could redo society. But I find it difficult to see how one can assume that the forces which sustain the existing economic and political stratification and the structures of mass media will allow the educational resources to be used against them. And I am not aware of any evidence that education can be used as a lever to lift the world. I am inclined to hold that education can change along with other institutions, both helping to change them and being helped to change by their change. But education cannot be the prime transformer.

And, if we are to educate children, let us not kid them and ourselves about the scope, depth, and extent of the project involved. Transforming a society is not an ego trip or a love-in. It is not merely a question of changing one's lifestyle but of unlocking millions caught in the psychic, economic, and political tangle of the existing society. Whoever wishes to participate in this enterprise will have to have much of the self-discipline, the commitment to society above self and immediate peers, and the long-run perspective so unpopular among the education rebels.

Thus, for the time being, to eradicate educational institutions is to turn children over to other nonfree institutions, for example, from the authoritarian family to the exploitative labor market. To provide children with educational resources and teachers who respond rather than guide is to assume that children are already liberated, while in fact they must yet be set free. And to assume that there will be an easy transformation of the modern society to a good society is to underestimate greatly the tenacity of modernity and hence the magnitude of the educational and revolutionary mission.

**OHLINGER**

[Whether or not we agree with his radical proposals, we should be grateful to Illich for warning us that there are trends abreast in contemporary education which] could mean the advent of a "brave new world" dominated by well-intentioned administrators or programmed instruction.

At least five times in his new book [*Deschooling Society*, 1971, Illich] points to the horrible alternative that faces us:

If we do not challenge the assumption that valuable knowledge is a commodity which under certain circumstances may be forced into the consumer, society will be increasingly dominated by sinister pseudoschools and totalitarian managers of information.

The other possible direction for deschooling is the one Illich is proposing toward self-directed learning in a society where meaningful choices will be possible for the first time. His pure model is obviously only intended as a series of rough suggestive guidelines. . . .

The choice is ours. We educators can play a part in the revolutionary leadership that will help to nurture the power of the individual to really choose *what, when, why, how,* and *if* he will learn or *not*; or we can become the lackeys of the "therapeutic Big Brother." If we choose the humanistic path, we must have faith—"faith in the educability of man"—and we must recognize that such faith, as it is fulfilled, will lead inevitably to other types of revolutionary change in political, economic, and other controlling power configurations.

# 4.6 RECENT MOVEMENTS IN EDUCATIONAL REFORM
## Michael B. Katz

There are two distinguishable major strands in contemporary educational radicalism. One concentrates on the compulsory and bureaucratic structure of education, which it seeks to alter through the creation of alternatives to

Michael B. Katz, "The Present Movement in Educational Reform," *Harvard Educational Review* 41, August 1971, 351–357. Copyright © 1971 by President and Fellows of Harvard University. Adapted from M. B. Katz, *Class, Bureaucracy, and Schools: The Illusion of Educational Change*, New York: Praeger, 1971. Footnote references here omitted.

Michael B. Katz is with the Ontario Institute for Studies in Education and the University of Toronto.

public schooling or through the redistribution of educational power to local communities within cities. . . . Another focuses on the spirit-breaking quality of current administrative and pedagogical practices and stresses the liberation of both teacher and student. Just as advocates of the former care more for community involvement than for administrative efficiency, the latter put happiness and warm human relations above classroom subjects, skills, and order. . . . [This group, during] the last several years has provided a beautiful, moving, and right-hearted body of pedagogical literature. The most effective of the radicals to me are experienced, deeply committed teachers who sensitively distill the history of their involvement with schools: I think of Sylvia Ashton-Warner, George Dennison, and A. S. Neill as examples. They are romantic about human potentiality and about education, and they are vulnerable as well to the logic-chopping ax of the academic critic. But that is irrelevant, for they are great teachers. And it is their presence, which manages to survive print, rather than any specific suggestion of method, that gives their writing its lucidity and inspiration. . . .

The problem that educational radicalism as a critique now faces is how to maintain its urgency and driving forces, for it is becoming popular, and its leading tenets, sometimes in distorted form, are expressed by a wide variety of people. At the mercy of lesser people, educational radicalism, like progressivism in an earlier era, rigidifies into a new orthodoxy that is nearly as dry and gutless as the old. Its history, I fear, will fall into the pattern cut earlier in the century by progressive educational thought, which, as a moment in intellectual history, combined an emphasis on community with a desire to liberate the child. In practice, though, progressivism often added only a set of new wrinkles to an already overdeveloped educational bureaucracy. Rather than liberate the child from scholasticism, repression, and drill, the discovery of individual differences, as an instance, fueled the development of massive psychological testing and the creation of the guidance bureaucracy stretching from school counselors to university departments. Similarly, the professor of educational administration remains a more permanent artifact of the progressive era than Dewey's laboratory school. It was administrative values —the addition of supervisory positions, the war on inefficiency, the introduction of ability grouping—rather than the promotion of social reform through the democratic liberation of human intelligence, that most often defined the progressive spirit in practice.

Contemporary educational radicalism . . . may already be recapitulating the progressive experience. . . .

[Throughout the entire history of American education, troubles have arisen whenever] schools were asked to do the impossible. As we have seen, the purpose of the school people has been more the development of attitudes than of intellect, and this continues to be the case. It is true, and this point must be stressed, of radical reformers as well as of advocates of law and order. The latter want the schools to stop crime and check immorality by teaching obedience to authority, respect for the law, and conformity to conventional standards. The former want the schools to reform society by creating a new sense of community through turning out warm, loving, noncompetitive people.

The human qualities that radical reformers seek in and through the schools are very beautiful ones; if achieved, they would give us a worthier and lovelier society. But it is no more realistic to charge the schools with the creation of such qualities than it is to expect them to fulfill traditional moralistic aims. Whatever values one attaches to the counter-culture, whatever interpretation one gives to social conflict and crime, it is clear that the powers of schooling have been vastly overrated. Despite substantial financing and a captive audience, the schools have not been able to attain the goals set for them, with remarkably little change, for the last century and a quarter. They have been unable to do so because those goals have been impossible to fulfill. They require fundamental social reform, not the sort of tinkering that educational change has represented. If, by some miracle, the radical reformers were to capture the schools, and only the schools, for the next century, they would have no more success than educational reformers of the past.

The moral should be clear. Educational reformers should begin to distinguish between what formal schooling can and cannot do. They must separate the teaching of skills from the teaching of attitudes, and concentrate on the former. In actual fact, it is of course impossible to separate the two; attitudes adhere in any form of practice. But there is a vast difference between leaving the formation of attitudes untended and making them the object of education. . . .

My point is that educational theory should define strictly educational tasks and that schools should concentrate on those. Any such definition must include, at one end of the spectrum, fundamental skills; at the other, it must exclude the conscious attempt to formulate social attitudes. I am not arguing for what has been traditional in much educational practice; mental gymnastics for their own sake or the forced study of useless discipline is indefensible. So is the rigid, authoritarian atmosphere of most schools. Schools should be made open, humane places for the simple reason that children have every right to be happy and to be treated with dignity and respect.

Second, my reading of the history of educational reform leads to the position that the reformulation of educational purposes cannot be accomplished within current educational structures. . . . It is difficult to see the functional relationships between large size, economies of scale, bureaucratic organization, and so on, on the one hand, and learning to read, write, and do math, on the other. Unless the effectiveness of electronic computers proves revolutionary at these tasks (which I doubt), it is hard to see why the business of learning these things cannot be managed more simply, directly, and informally by skilled teachers working with small groups of children wherever they can find some space. The public can provide the equipment and materials and pay the salaries and rent, as now, but the activities do not have to be carried on within what we now call a school. The setting can be warm, colorful, comfortable, and humane without being expensive. Perhaps in some instances children need special facilities and special teachers, as in art, music, or history; perhaps even at an early age they should have access to laboratories for science. These facilities should be very good indeed. Children could go to them as they need and want to. It is not my intention to offer a detailed plan here. Rather, I wish to emphasize what seems to me a very common-sensical position. Let us examine each of the activities children will undertake as they grow up and ask how it might best be handled, best in the sense of economy, of humaneness, of making the setting a happy one. In the process, we should avoid large institutions, bureaucratic organization, and complexity whenever anything else will serve as well.

# 4.7 CONCLUDING EDITORIAL ESSAY:
# FIVE FUNCTIONS OF A MODERN SCHOOL

In these remarks we shall briefly describe five functions which schools perform today.

*Schools are Quasi-Homes.* For several generations parents have been placing their offspring in the trustful custodial care of schools and colleges, in the fond hope that teachers would not be mere baby-sitters, but would provide their children with improved minds and unsullied characters. By the year 1970 *in loco parentis* is dying if not dead, and it is time to redefine the kind of quasi-home a school really is. Today our schools assume many of the roles that in former times were performed by parents, and everyone expects teachers to play a role that is supportive, loving, guiding, sharing, and personally concerned. However, the "curse of bigness" has made the educational establishment increasingly impersonal, so that more and more students manifest disenchantment, alienation, and disgust. Those who view schools as quasi-homes ask: What can educators do to develop and sustain attitudes of social commitment and of individual responsibility?

Lawrence Cremin has put this problem in historical perspective:

Compulsory school attendance marked a new era in the history of American education. The crippled, the blind, the deaf, the sick, the slow-witted, and the needy arrived in growing numbers. Thousands of recalcitrants and incorrigibles who in former times might have dropped out of school now became public charges for a minimum period. And as the school-leaving age moved progressively upward, every problem was aggravated as youngsters became bigger, stronger, and more resourceful. The dreams of democratic idealists may have resided in compulsory-attendance laws, but so did the makings of the blackboard jungle.

Had there never been a progressive movement, had there been no social settlements, municipal reform associations, country life commissions, or immigrant aid societies, no William James, Stanley Hall, Edward Thorndike, or John Dewey, the mere fact of compulsory attendance would have changed the American school. . . .[1]

In summary, if the statement that "Schools are Quasi-Homes" means that the *only* purpose of schools—or even the *main* purpose—is to "keep kids off the streets," then those who advocate the deschooling of society have a strong argument.

*Schools are Tribal Rites.* If we view our educational institutions as anthropologists view a strange culture, the American tribe seems generally agreed that one of the important rites of passage into privileged positions in the adult world is the rite of passage through school. All cultures have symbols of status, and in ours, a high school diploma and a college degree have become major status symbols.

But when a ritual loses meaning, it should be abandoned. Recall how in pre-Lutheran Germany and England the Latin phrase "Hoc est Corpus Filii" ("This is the body of the Son"—used in the Mass) gradually came to mean "hocus pocus filicus," then "hocus pocus," then "hoax." If schooling is pure ritual, and completely lacking in significant meaning, then it, too, has become a meaningless hoax.

This certainly is not true of most of our schools. But it is true of some of them, and it seems to be especially true of schools for Blacks, Puerto Ricans, Chicanos, Indians, and of schools in depressed areas. Insofar as "ritual" has replaced "meaningful education," we should be thankful for books such as Paul Goodman's *Growing Up Absurd* (1956) and *Compulsory Miseducation* (1962); John Holt's *How Children Fail* (1966); Jonathan Kozol's *Death at an Early Age* (1968); and Daniel Fader and Elton B. McNeill's *Hooked on Books* (1968).

On the other hand, we should realize that such criticisms are not applicable to all schools or to all students.

*Schools are Transmission Belts.* A primary role of the school is to preserve man's heritage. The story of man's experiences through 35,000 years of time is told in our museums, libraries and textbooks, and most

[1] Lawrence A. Cremin, *The Transformation of the School: Progressivism in American Education 1876–1957*, New York: Alfred A. Knopf, Inc., 1961, pp. 127–128. By permission. Read also Carleton Washburne, "An Eighty-Year Perspective on Education," *Phi Delta Kappan,* 45: 145–150, December 1963.

classrooms are designed to help students relive these experiences and to understand what their ancestors have seen and done. With a proper mixture of appreciation and candor, teachers help students become familiar with the glory and with the horror of man's past: what man has accomplished and where he has bungled, how he has soared to angelic heights of beauty and creativity, and how he has plunged into depths of ugliness and degradation.

In comparing man with other animals, G. N. Lewis has written:

> The use of tools is but one symptom of what might be called externalization. The bee stores honey for posterity, the bird teaches its young to fly, but what are these compared with the enormous hordes of material and spiritual wealth that man accumulates from generation to generation! His habits of instruction, his stores of oral and written lore, his schools, his universities, his libraries— all these external accumulations represent the greater part of that adaptation to environment which in the human species has nearly taken the place of instinct.
>
> The enormous power which this habit of hoarding has given him, perhaps leads man to overestimate his own talents. If we should define intelligence as ability to meet successfully situations of an entirely new character, it is generally conceded that modern man is no more intelligent than his Cro-Magnon ancestors, whose total material wealth was represented by a few beads and implements of stone and ivory, and whose lore fell equally short of the accumulated knowledge of today. . . .
>
> Our present era, which is sometimes called the age of science and invention, might perhaps be more appropriately designated as the age of publicity and conservation. In former days, inventions and discoveries often died with their discoverers, but now there are fewer of these "mute inglorious Miltons." Every discovery, every trifling invention, every new trick of salesmanship is at once broadcast from any part of the world and garnered into our large granaries of knowledge.[2]

Man is a time-binding animal, and in the modern world our educational system is the one institution specifically designed to preserve this legacy from the past and to hold it in trust for the future.

*Education is Exploration.* Schools should contain scholars, whose ideal (on a college and university level) has been expressed as follows:

> Men of scholarship recognize the impermanency of truth, the shifting perceptions of beauty and the contextual character of justice and they attempt to make this recognition known and appreciated by all members of the college community. The physics of Newton is not the physics of Einstein; the paintings of Raphael are not the paintings of Picasso; and the justice of the preindustrial age is not the justice of the postindustrial era. The colleges must preserve the critical marketplace of ideas, where error can be challenged in the glare of rational argument rather than in the heat of violent conflict. When John Stuart

[2] G. N. Lewis, *The Anatomy of Science*, Yale University Press, 1926, pages 205–207.

Mill contended that all mankind has no right to silence one dissenter and that people should be convinced, not coerced, he was providing not only the rationale for a free society, but also an eloquent statement upon which stands the case for the college as critic.[3]

"The trouble with the world," Paul Valery once wrote, "is that the future is not what it used to be." And since the future and the present—and our views about the past, the present and the future—are forever changing, criticism is not only desirable—it is absolutely necessary. And the more rapidly that changes occur, the more imperative it is that criticisms be heard and evaluated.

Those who think of education as blanket, unthinking approval of the past find it difficult to understand youth's desire—or man's necessity—to explore. Because many schools have overemphasized the old and have neglected the new, many of today's students would now reverse this unfortunate dichotomy, and ask: Why not forget the old, and consider *only* the new? Why not all Beatles, no Beethoven? All Carmichael, no Comte? All Fanon, no Weber? All Warhol, no Rubens? Conservative teachers tend to overemphasize the old, radical students tend to overemphasize the new, but a balanced curriculum should provide a place for both old and new.

Because society is changing—and changing drastically—students increasingly raise the question of "relevance." Do their courses and programs really prepare them to meet the confusing challenges of the coming age? Why war? Whither population growth? Why imperialism? Why famine amidst plenty? When ecological balance? The knowledge revolution has outdistanced the schools' ability to digest it, and our students are insisting that teachers not only assimilate this new knowledge, but also present it to them in meaningful patterns.

*Schools as Places for Self-Discovery.* "Relevance" means, among other things, that schools should be places of conscience as well as places of knowledge. They should help youth in their search for meaning in life, and should help them find ways to cope with the self-destructive potentials of modern society. Lacking such educational help, can we wonder that some students elect the alternatives of opting out of society either by apathetic alienation or by departure into the other worlds of psychodelia or primitive communalism?

As a very minimum, students could learn how people in the past, and in cultures different than our own, answer questions about proper conduct. What is the good life? How should people relate to one another? What may we expect to be the guiding values of the future? In striving to find answers

[3] From "The Nine Lives of the College" in *Unfinished Rebellions*, by DeVere Pentony, Robert Smith and Richard Axen, San Francisco: Jossey-Bass, Inc., Publishers, 1971, pp. 3–20. By permission.
This concluding editorial essay borrows heavily from this excellent book.

to such problems, no question is too profane, no idea is too dangerous, no answer is to be suppressed. Too often our classroom walls have contained an enforced orthodoxy; but these walls can no longer withstand the volleys of penetrating questions from today's eager youth.

Our *conclusion*, then, is this: *the educational establishment fulfills many functions*—functions so varied and complex that some contradict others. To quote again from Pentony, Smith, and Axen, the school is:

> Instrument of change, yet vehicle for preservation. A quasi-home, yet a semi-factory. A critic, yet a defender. An explorer, yet a conserver. An arena for romance, yet a place for serious study. A portal to opportunity, yet a gate of selectivity and quality control. A way for freedom and originality, yet a channel for deceptivity and conformity.

Schools can be destroyed by those who force it to choose one value at the expense of all others, or by those who fail to appreciate the complexity of its goals and the elegance of its mission. For, in spite of their many inadequacies, schools and colleges remain today what they have been since the twelfth and thirteenth centuries—nurturing places for the collective conscience of mankind.

# B. Open Up the Classrooms?

## 4.8 THE CONCEPT OF OPEN EDUCATION
### Ewald B. Nyquist

We are at a crossroads in American education, and it seems to me that the concept of open education as practiced in many of the British Infant and Junior Schools offers unique opportunities for humanizing and individualizing learning, making it relevant, meaningful, and personally satisfying. School must be a place to prepare young people to take their place in society—not a place where they are isolated from the main currents of life. This can be done by making education at every age level person-centered, idea-centered, experience-centered, problem-oriented, and interdisciplinary, with the community and its other institutions a part of the process. This is in contrast to the prevalent educational experience with its information-gathering, fact-centered, course-centered, subject-centered, grade-getting, and bell-interrupted activity. . . .

Open education is an approach to teaching which discards the familiar elementary classroom organization and the traditional stylized roles of teacher and pupils for a much freer, more informal, highly individualized, child-centered learning experience. Respect for and trust in the child are perhaps the most basic principles. It is assumed that all children are motivated to learn and will learn if the emphasis is on learning and not on teaching; on thinking, and not on memorizing; on freedom and responsibility, rather than on conformity and following directions.

Open education is based on the concept of childhood as something to be cherished—a vital part of life itself to be lived richly each day. In an open classroom children learn more effectively, because the environment is free, supportive, and nonthreatening.

Open education recognizes that children are different, that they learn in different ways, at different times, and from each other. There is little uni-

Ewald B. Nyquist, "The Concept of Open Education," *The Science Teacher* 38: 25–28, September 1971. Reprinted in *Education Digest* 37: 9–12, November 1971. Excerpt used by permission of *The Science Teacher* and the author.

Ewald B. Nyquist is Commissioner of Education and President of the University of the State of New York.

formity in an open education classroom. Children move about freely, talk with each other, make choices, work alone or in small groups, and peruse materials which they feel are relevant to them. There is an absence of mere busywork, mindless drill, and conforming activity. It is a happy learning environment for children.

## Characteristics

In the classroom designed for open education, you see many inviting nooks and corners for math, science, reading, writing, cooking, art, and dramatics —not rows of children's desks with the teacher up front. Corridors are used along with classrooms for carpentry, art work, small and large group activities, and displays of children's work. Doors are open and children go in and out freely. Teachers also move in and out of rooms and corridors, "pinching" ideas from each other, sharing exciting happenings, and helping each other.

The purpose of open education is to provide a kind of schooling which permits children to learn at their own pace and in their own way. The teacher serves as a facilitator of learning, furnishing an invitingly arranged environment, materials, motivation, guidance, and assistance. She works with individuals and small groups, helping them to set goals and achieve them, raising questions, intervening when necessary, observing, and assessing the children's progress. Their growth is evaluated on an individual basis in order to diagnose their strengths and weaknesses and to better plan their programs. . . .

Simply stated, the goals of open education are:
1. Happy children who feel successful and confident.
2. Self-disciplined children who have wholesome attitudes toward life and learning.
3. Independent thinkers who are self-propelled and continuing learners.
4. Readers who are increasingly fluent and who enjoy reading.
5. Children who write because they want to record and convey thoughts.
6. Competent students who are able to cope with fundamental math, science, and social science concepts because these are necessary to answer important questions and to solve problems.

Open education puts learning where it belongs—squarely within the youngster. It is partly a matter of motivation.

## Historical Perspectives

Open education is not new. Its tenets were central to the progressive movement in American education, and vestiges of their implementation are still to be found in many schools and individual classrooms throughout this country. But actually, progressive education never really got off the ground . . . [because the] important role of the teacher as organizer of the learning environment; manager of time, space, and materials; and guide in the learning experience was neglected or misinterpreted.[1]

Public education in this country faces the fact that even good traditional practices and theories have failed too many of our students. Educators talk glibly about "meeting the needs of the individual," and yet schools continue to foster competition, pass and fail children, and teach whole classes of children as though everyone were alike. . . .

To be practical, we must realize that education must prepare children for work that may not even exist today and whose nature 30 or 40 years hence cannot even be imagined. This can only be done by teaching children how to learn. For many youngsters we are doing a poor job of motivating them to work on their own, dig for information, and test out ideas. The child must be the principal agent in his own learning in order that he be a continuing learner.

It is for these reasons that I have supported open education as an approach which offers us hope. It is not the only way, of course, but it is a promising way.

## Implications

Implementation of open education presents dangers and difficulties as well as tremendous opportunities. If our characteristic enthusiasm for whatever is "new," our predilection for attractive, mass-produced packages, and our craving for guaranteed success lead us to see open education as a mechanism for immediate educational improvement, we will fail to understand the opportunities being presented; and open education, like progressive education, can degenerate into sloppy permissiveness, wistful romanticism, and shallow imitation. . . .

We must make haste slowly. It is not necessary that the whole school or the whole day be immediately converted to open education. Rather, the schools should change a little at a time so that children and teachers can grow with the change. It takes a great deal of learning on the part of everyone involved—administrators, teachers, parents, and children—before open education can become a successful venture.

[1] EDITOR'S NOTE: For a brief statement concerning the persisting values of Progressive Education, read William Van Til, "Is Progressive Education Obsolete?" *Saturday Review* 45: 56–57, 82–84, February 17, 1972. For a lengthy treatment, read *New Look at Progressive Education*, Washington, D.C.: Association of Supervision and Curriculum Development (N.E.A.), 1972, pp. 1–392 (bibliography). See also C. C. Ritchie, "Eight-Year Study: Can We Afford to Ignore It?" *Educational Leadership* 28: 484–486, February 1971 (The entire issue, pp. 455–572, is devoted to "The Open Classroom"); Walter Feinberg, "Progressive Education and Social Planning," *Teachers College Record* 73: 485–505, May 1972 (bibliography); Clarence P. Karier, "Liberalism and the Quest for Orderly Change," *History of Education Quarterly* 12: 57–80, Spring 1970.

# 4.9 THE PUPIL-CENTERED SCHOOL
## John Holt and Paulo Freire

**HOLT**

The intelligent person, young or old, meeting a new situation or problem, opens himself up to it; he tries to take in with mind and senses everything he can about it; he thinks about *it*, instead of about himself or what it might cause to happen to him; he grapples with it boldly, imaginatively, resourcefully, and if not confidently at least hopefully; if he fails to master it, he looks without shame or fear at his mistakes and learns what he can from them. This is intelligence. Clearly its roots lie in a certain feeling about life, and one's self with respect to life. Just as clearly, unintelligence is not what most psychologists seem to suppose, the same thing as intelligence only less of it. It is an entirely different style of behavior, arising out of an entirely different set of attitudes. . . .

Nobody starts off stupid. You have only to watch babies and infants, and think seriously about what all of them learn and do, to see that, except for the most grossly retarded, they show a style of life, and a desire and ability to learn that in an older person we might well call genius. Hardly an adult in a thousand, or ten thousand, could in any three years of his life learn as much, grow as much in his understanding of the world around him, as every infant learns and grows in his first three years. But what happens, as we get older, to this extraordinary capacity for learning and intellectual growth?

What happens is that it is destroyed, and more than by any other one thing, by the process that we misname education—a process that goes on in most homes and schools. We adults destroy most of the intellectual and creative capacity of children by the things we do to them or make them do. We destroy this capacity above all by making them afraid, afraid of not doing what other people want, of not pleasing, of making mistakes, of failing, of being *wrong*. Thus we make them afraid to gamble, afraid to experiment, afraid to try the difficult and the unknown. Even when we do not create chil-

This selection consists of excerpts from the writings of two contemporary writers who oppose the regimentation which goes on in so many classrooms.

The first excerpt is from John Holt, *How Children Fail*, New York, Pitman Publishing Corporation, 1964, pp. 165–168, 178–179; and from John Holt, *How Children Learn*, New York: Pitman Publishing Corporation, 1967, pp. vii–viii. Reprinted by permission.

The second excerpt is from Paulo Freire, *Pedagogy of the Oppressed*, translated from the Portuguese by Myra B. Ramos, New York: Herder and Herder, 1970. Excerpts from pp. 134–136, 58–73. By permission. Footnote references here omitted.

Paulo Freire is a Brazilian educator. Although his remarks are intended mainly for Brazilian adults, they apply (to some extent, at least) to minority groups in the United States, and to children as well as to adults.

dren's fears, when they come to us with fears ready-made and built-in, we use these fears as handles to manipulate them and get them to do what we want. Instead of trying to whittle down their fears, we build them up, often to monstrous size. For we like children who are a little afraid of us, docile, deferential children, though not, of course, if they are so obviously afraid that they threaten our image of ourselves as kind, lovable people whom there is no reason to fear. We find ideal the kind of "good" children who are just enough afraid of us to do everything we want, without making us feel that fear of us is what is making them do it.

We destroy the disinterested (I do *not* mean *un*interested) love of learning in children, which is so strong when they are small, by encouraging and compelling them to work for petty and contemptible rewards—gold stars, or papers marked 100 and tacked to the wall, or *A*'s on report cards, or honor rolls, or dean's lists, or Phi Beta Kappa keys—in short, for the ignoble satisfaction of feeling that they are better than someone else. We encourage them to feel that the end and aim of all they do in school is nothing more than to get a good mark on a test, or to impress someone with what they seem to know. We kill, not only their curiosity, but their feeling that it is a good and admirable thing to be curious, so that by the age of ten most of them will not ask questions, and will show a good deal of scorn for the few who do. . . .

It is not subject matter that makes some learning more valuable than others, but the spirit in which the work is done. If a child is doing the kind of learning that most children do in school, when they learn at all—swallowing words, to spit back at the teacher on demand—he is wasting his time, or rather, we are wasting it for him. This learning will not be permanent, or relevant, or useful. But a child who is learning naturally, following his curiosity where it leads him, adding to his mental model of reality whatever he needs and can find a place for, and rejecting without fear or guilt what he does not need, is growing—in knowledge, in the love of learning, and in the ability to learn. He is on his way to becoming the kind of person we need in our society, and that our "best" schools and colleges are *not* turning out, the kind of person who, in Whitney Griswold's words, seeks and finds meaning, truth, and enjoyment in everything he does. All his life he will go on learning. Every experience will make his mental model of reality more complete and more true to life, and thus make him more able to deal realistically, imaginatively, and constructively with whatever new experience life throws his way.

We cannot have real learning in school if we think it is our duty and our right to tell children what they must learn. We cannot know, at any moment, what particular bit of knowledge or understanding a child needs most, will most strengthen and best fit his model of reality. Only he can do this. He may not do it very well, but he can do it a hundred times better than we can. The most we can do is try to help, by letting him know roughly what is available and where he can look for it. Choosing what he wants to learn and what he does not is something he must do for himself. . . .

We like to say that we send children to school to teach them to think. What we do, all too often, is to teach them to think badly, to give up a natural and powerful way of thinking in favor of a method that does not work well for them and that we rarely use ourselves.

What are the results? Only a few children in school ever become good at learning in the way we try to make them learn. Most of them get humiliated, frightened, and discouraged. They use their minds, not to learn, but to get out of doing the things we tell them to do—to make them learn. In the short run, these strategies seem to work. They make it possible for many children to get through their schooling even though they learn very little. But in the long run these strategies are self-limiting and self-defeating, and destroy both character and intelligence. The children who use such strategies are prevented by them from growing into more than limited versions of the human beings they might have become. This is the real failure that takes place in school; hardly any children escape.

When we better understand the ways, conditions, and spirit in which children do their best learning, and are able to make school into a place where they can use and improve the style of thinking and learning natural to them, we may be able to prevent much of this failure. School may then become a place in which *all* children grow, not just in size, not even in knowledge, but in curiosity, courage, confidence, independence, resourcefulness, resilience, patience, competence, and understanding. To find how best to do this will take us a long time. We may find, in fifty or a hundred years, that all of what we think of as our most up-to-date notions about schools, teaching, and learning, are either completely inadequate or outright mistaken. But we will make a big step forward if, by understanding children better, we can undo some of the harm we are now doing.[1]

---

[1] *EDITOR'S NOTE*: Like John Holt in the United States, A. S. Neill in England is in the vanguard of those seeking radical reform in the classroom. A. S. Neill is the author of *Summerhill* (1962, pp. 4–5, 12, 28) from which the following is taken:

The function of the child is to live his own life—not the life that his anxious parents think he should live, nor a life according to the purpose of the educator who thinks he knows what is best. All this interference and guidance on the part of adults only produces a generation of robots. . . .

My view is that a child is innately wise and realistic. If left to himself without adult suggestion of any kind, he will develop as far as he is capable of developing. Logically, Summerhill is a place in which people who have the innate ability and wish to be scholars will be scholars; while those who are only fit to sweep the streets will sweep the streets. But we have not produced a street cleaner so far. Nor do I write this snobbishly, for I would rather see a school produce a happy street cleaner than a neurotic scholar.

What is Summerhill like? Well, for one thing, lessons are optional. Children can go to them or stay away from them—for years if they want to. There is a timetable—but only for the teachers. . . .

## FREIRE

### Education as a Means of Social Control

Every act of conquest implies a conqueror and someone or something which is conquered. The conqueror imposes his objectives on the vanquished, and makes of them his possession. He imposes his own contours on the vanquished . . . . [and] reduces men to the status of things . . . . [To achieve this end,] the oppressors develop a series of methods precluding any presentation of the world as a problem and showing it rather as a fixed entity, as something given—something to which men, as mere spectators, must adapt.

It is necessary for the oppressors to approach the people in order, via subjugation, to keep them passive. This approximation, however, does not involve *being with* the people, or require true communication. It is accomplished by the oppressors' depositing myths indispensable to the preservation of the status quo: for example, the myth that the oppressive order is a "free society"; the myth that all men are free to work where they wish, that if they don't like their boss they can leave him and look for another job; the myth that this order respects human rights and is therefore worthy of esteem; the myth that anyone who is industrious can become an entrepreneur—worse yet, the myth that the street vendor is as much an entrepreneur as the owner of a large factory; . . . the myth of the heroism of the oppressor classes as defenders of "Western Christian civilization" against "materialist barbarism;" . . . the myth that the dominant elites, "recognizing their duties," promote the advancement of the people, so that the people, in a gesture of gratitude, should accept the words of the elites and be conformed to them; the myth that rebellion is a sin against God; the myth of private property as fundamental to personal human development (so long as oppressors are the only true human beings); the myth of the industriousness of the oppressors and the laziness and dishonesty of the oppressed, as well as the myth of the natural inferiority of the latter and the superiority of the former. . . .

[The *methods* of teaching, as well as the *content* of education, reflect the conqueror's mentality.] Narration (with the teacher as narrator) leads the students to memorize mechanically the narrated content. Worse yet, it turns them into "containers," into "receptacles" to be "filled" by the teacher. The more completely he fills the receptacles, the better a teacher he is. The more meekly the receptacles permit themselves to be filled, the better students they are.

Education thus becomes an act of depositing, in which the students are the depositories and the teacher is the depositor. Instead of communicating,

---

In all countries, capitalist, socialist or communist, elaborate schools are built to educate the young. But all the wonderful labs and workshops do nothing to help John or Peter or Ivan surmount the emotional damage and the social evils bred by the pressure on him from his parents, his schoolteachers, and the pressure of the coercive quality of our civilization. . . .

the teacher issues communiqués and makes deposits which the students patiently receive, memorize, and repeat. This is the "banking" concept of education, in which the scope of action allowed to the students extends only as far as receiving, filing, and storing the deposits. . . . ["Banking education" manifests] the following attitudes and practices, which mirror oppressive society as a whole:

(a) the teacher teaches and the students are taught;
(b) the teacher knows everything and the students know nothing;
(c) the teacher thinks and the students are thought about;
(d) the teacher talks and the students listen—meekly;
(e) the teacher disciplines and the students are disciplined;
(f) the teacher chooses and enforces his choice, and the students comply. . . .

[In contrast, liberating] education consists in acts of cognition, not transferrals of information. . . . Through dialogue, the teacher-of-the-students and the students-of-the-teacher cease to exist and a new term emerges: teacher-student with students-teachers. The teacher is no longer merely the-one-who-teaches, but one who is himself taught in dialogue with the students, who in turn while being taught also teach. They become jointly responsible for a process in which all grow.

# 4.10 A SCHOOL WITHOUT WALLS
## John Bremer and Michael von Moschzisker

[In August, 1968, the] Philadelphia Board of Education, in cooperation with the cultural, scientific and business institutions along and around the Benjamin Franklin Parkway, initiated a four-year educational program for students

John Bremer and Michael von Moschzisker, *The School Without Walls: Philadelphia's Parkway Program*. Copyright © 1971 by Holt, Rinehart and Winston, Inc. Excerpts from pages 7, 291–294, 277–280. Adapted and reprinted by permission of Holt, Rinehart and Winston, Inc.
John Bremer is Director of the Parkway Program.
Michael von Moschzisker, Philadelphia journalist, has been a teacher and a publicist for the program.
Compare the following:
    Late in the 1960s, pedagogical planners dreaming about "educational parks" for 10,000 students and a wonderland of technology to serve them discovered a funny thing. Behind them a grass roots movement was going in the opposite direction. The rise of the free school, the community school, the school-within-a-school—whatever the individual intent or style—was a reaction to the increasing anonymity and

of high school age. The Parkway Program, as it is called, has starting points which differ from those of conventional high school education in at least two basic respects. In the first place, the Parkway Program does not have a schoolhouse, a building of its own—it is a school without walls; in the second place, the institutions and organizations along and near the Parkway constitute a learning laboratory of unlimited resource.

The adoption of these two starting points opens the way for a complete reformulation of what education means for the present-day urban student. . . .

The unique and specific importance of the Parkway institutions lies in the unparalleled wealth of material and human resources which they bring to a very small area of the city. Within a few short blocks there can be found some of the best museums and collections in the world, and the research work that is conducted along the Parkway is of civic, national and even international importance. To have easy and continuous access to the fine collections of paintings, sculpture, scientific instruments and books available along the Parkway would enhance any educational program. Beyond this, however, business, industrial and communications organizations—again of national and international reputation—have expressed interest in providing opportunities for students to study intensively with them, and to pursue work-study programs. . . .

If learning is not confined within the spatial limits of schools and classrooms, then it is not confined within the conventional temporal limits either. The concepts of class period, school day, school week and school year all need serious modification and possible abandonment. The Parkway Program has abandoned them, for the most part, and it provides a year-round, full-

---

assembly-line treatment that had become the staple of public education, particularly in the cities. Before long, schoolmen who had recently boasted about large enrollments, sprawling school plants, and computerized efficiency were ascribing everything from student unrest to high truancy rates and low reading scores to the impersonal and highly institutionalized style of their operations.

To counter the effects of size, more than fifty city and suburban school systems have introduced alternate programs within the past two years—particularly at the high school level. A number of these, in Philadelphia, Chicago, Hartford and Providence, are "schools without walls" that use the resources of the urban areas as the learning ground for a relatively small group of students. Other projects—in St. Paul, Minnesota; Great Neck and New Rochelle, New York; and Newton, Massachusetts —stress independent work and small-group intimacy in an unstructured setting. While a number of these mini-schools are designed for bright, middle-class students disenchanted with the rigid routines of high school, others are aimed at salvaging poor and minority group youngsters about to drop out of schools where they have never known success. All are attempts to personalize the process of a high school education and to make it meaningful.—Diane Divoky, "New York's Mini-Schools: Small Miracles, Big Troubles," *Saturday Review* 54: 60–67, December 18, 1971.

For some of the difficulties attending "schools without walls" read "The Sudden Rise and Decline of New Jersey Street Academies" by James Baines and William M. Young, *Phi Delta Kappan* 53: 240–242, December 1971.

time learning opportunity for anyone in the Program. The schedule of each student is determined by his learning requirements and not by the clock hours of administrative and organizational convenience. . . .

The usual view of teachers is that, first, you must control students and then, second, you teach them. They need to realize, however, that when you control a student, you cannot ever help him learn. You may force him to repeat what he hears or reads, and thereby pass examinations. You may succeed in modifying his outward behavior—although not necessarily its significance; you may corrupt him by bribery; you may even make him obedient. But help him learn? Never. Learning is something he must do for himself.

This is why the factory model must go. So long as the student is regarded as something to be kept under control, as raw material to be processed, he will not learn. He cannot learn, he can only be taught. His role is essentially passive, not active. He has no contribution to make to his own education. The greatest harm is done by the fact that in no way are students ever given a clear, human, and responsible role in the organization of the school. They are not really a part of the educational system at all. They are just the material upon which it feeds. The students know it, and they respond negatively to their position of indignity. This is what must be changed. . . .

Our schools imagine that students learn best in a special building separated from the larger community. This has created a refuge in which students and teachers do not need to explore but only to accept. Within this separated refuge, students are expected to learn in so-called homogeneous groups known as classes, and within these classes students are isolated, separated from each other by the seating arrangement and by the competition for approval. It is seldom that they are allowed to cooperate in a systematic, friendly manner. Finally, within these "boxes," the school houses and the classrooms, life is self-reflecting, with no relation to anything outside of itself, and so it becomes a fantasy, it becomes unreal. The students' learning is evaluated within the "boxes," and it is never tested against the realities of life. It is a common feeling (particularly on the part of students) that what is learned in school is learned only for the purposes of the school. This is the well-known irrelevance of education. . . .

It is the boundary conditions that are all wrong. It is the division between inside and outside, between insiders and outsiders . . . [To combat this false view,] the year around Parkway Program sets up new boundaries, and provides a new framework in which the energy of all of us can be used in learning, and not in maintaining an obsolete, inefficient system. There is no school house, there is no separate building; school is not a place but an activity, a process. We are, indeed, a school without walls. Where do the students learn? In the city. Where in the city? Anywhere and everywhere. If students are to learn about television, they cannot do this apart from the studios and locations in which television is produced. So we use television studios and we use radio stations, and we use the museums, social service organizations, and we use the business community. The Philadelphia City government departments assist us—the Police Department, and the District Attorney's office to name only two. Parents help us. . . .

Most educational programs treat learning like a journey to some distant destination and students are graded in terms of how far they get along the road. If you go all the way you get an A. The Parkway Program is set up differently. It views the educational problem as being one of finding a starting point for learning. Many students in ordinary schools never get started, but if they ever were to get started their journeys would far exceed the expectations of their teachers. We have great faith in our students, and they do not disappoint us, even though we have a credit or no-credit system. The only grade given is pass.

Every student and faculty member belongs to what we call a tutorial group consisting of about fifteen students, a faculty member, and a university intern. The group has three functions. First, to act as a support group in which counseling can take place. Second, it is the group in which the basic skills of language and mathematics are dealt with. Third, it is the unit in which the program and the students' performance are evaluated, and evaluation is seen as part of the educational process and not something separated from it.

Within the four years of the Parkway Program every student always has a choice available to him. Similarly, no student is ever assigned to the program, they always volunteer and if we have more applicants than places, as seems the usual situation (we had nearly 10,000 in June 1969), we publicly draw names from a hat. Every student in the city in grades nine through twelve is eligible without regard to his academic or behavioral record. In addition, we allocate equal numbers of places to the eight school districts within the City of Philadelphia, so that our student body, like our faculty, is properly integrated. We also have many students from ten or more suburban systems mostly on an exchange basis, and the demand for our program among suburban students is getting to be as great as that among city students.

Our students have to learn to be responsible for their own education, to make choices and to face the consequences of those choices. It is difficult, and many people at the beginning thought that it would not work, but it is working and the demand is so great that we shall expand rapidly. It is our intention to set up a series of units of about 150 students, ten faculty members, and ten university interns, in various parts of the city, because this unit enables the students to have a human relationship with each other and with the faculty. The educational community should really be small enough so that everyone can know everyone else. It is also true that above that number the group can no longer control itself. Although our community unit should not exceed 150, there is no reason why we could not set up 100 such units in Philadelphia. In the first place, we do not require large capital expenditure and school buildings, and in the second place, our operating costs are approximately the same as those in an ordinary school. What could be more practical?[1]

---

[1] EDITOR'S NOTE:

Many of the movements for reform in the educational system in the last 20 years have been in response to a number of crises—the deficit in personnel and facilities following World War II; the inadequacy of training in science and mathematics brought to prominence by the Sputnik scare; and, more recently, the awareness that the system is failing a major segment of the population—an awareness brought about through the official recognition of poverty and the growing militancy of ethnic minorities. The current emphasis on improving education for the poor, or disadvantaged, should not obscure the fact that the current system is failing large numbers of students from all kinds of backgrounds.—Mario D. Fantini and Milton A. Young, *Designing Education for Tomorrow's Cities*, New York: Holt, Rinehart and Winston, Inc., 1970, p. 13.

---

# 4.11 SO YOU WANT TO CHANGE TO AN OPEN CLASSROOM!
## Herbert R. Kohl and Roland S. Barth

---

## KOHL

[In answer to the question, "How long does it take to work out more open ways of teaching?" let me describe] what I went through the first time I taught. For me the first six months were a disaster. I wanted my class to be

This selection consists of two portions. The first is from Herbert R. Kohl, *The Open Classroom*. Reprinted with permission from *The New York Review of Books*. Copyright © 1969 Herbert Kohl.

After teaching for several years in Harlem schools, Herbert R. Kohl became director of an experimental school in Berkeley.

The second portion of this selection is excerpted from Roland S. Barth, "So You Want to Change to an Open Classroom," *Phi Delta Kappan* 53: 97–99, October 1971. By permission.

Roland S. Barth is principal of the Angier (Public) School, Newton, Mass.

For a further discussion of these assumptions see *Open Education and the American School* by Roland S. Barth, published by Agathon Press, Inc., 150 Fifth Avenue, New York, N.Y. 10011. For a fuller description of "The Open School," see Roland S. Barth and Charles H. Rathbone, annotated bibliographies: "The Open School: A Way of open and my students to do what was interesting to them. Yet the demands the system made upon me were overwhelming. Worse, however, was my inability to develop an environment in which my students could discover things that interested them. It took me at least a year to feel comfortable in a school environment and know young people well enough to present them with options for learning which might prove meaningful to them.

But six months were not enough—after six months of chaos I experienced at least six months of groping and getting to understand students as people and not merely as pupils. It took at least a year for me to be at ease in my classroom and to stop worrying about what was supposed to happen and start reacting directly to what was actually happening. Nothing developed magically; freedom and openness are not formulas for success, and it is very difficult indeed to explore the diverse possibilities of life in schools. To have a free classroom is to present an environment where many people can discover themselves, and there is no simple set of rules to prescribe how this can be created.

It is almost certain that open classrooms will not develop within our school systems without the teachers and pupils experiencing fear, depression, and panic. There will always be the fear that one is wrong in letting people choose their own lives instead of legislating their roles in society. There will be depression, for one can never know in the short range if one is succeeding in opening possibilities to people or merely deceiving and seducing them. And there will be panic because we all fear chaos—fear that things have gotten so far out of hand in our lives that if we face the truth we will no longer be able to tolerate life.

Our schools are crazy. They do not serve the interests of adults, and they do not serve the interests of young people. They teach "objective" knowledge and its corollary, obedience to authority. They teach avoidance of conflict and obeisance to tradition in the guise of history. They teach equality and democracy while castrating students and controlling teachers. Most of all they teach people to be silent about what they think and feel, and worst of all, they teach people to pretend that they are saying what they think and feel. To try to break away from stupid schooling is no easy matter for teacher or student. It is a lonely and long fight to escape from believing that one needs to do what people say one should do and that one ought to be the person one is expected to be. Yet to make such an escape is a step toward beginning again and becoming the teachers we never knew we could be.

Thinking About Children, Learning and Knowledge," *The Center Forum*, Vol. 3, No. 7, July 1969, a publication of the Center for Urban Education, New York City; and "A Bibliography of Open Education, Early Childhood Education Study," jointly published by the Advisory Council for Open Education and the Education Development Center, Newton, Mass., 1971. See also Bruce R. Joyce, *Alternative Models of Elementary Education*, Waltham, Mass.: Blaisdell, 1969; John Holt, *Freedom and Beyond*, New York: Dutton, 1972, pp. 77–88.

234 / Humanize the Learning Process

## BARTH

I would like to suggest that before you jump on the open classroom surfboard, a precarious vehicle appropriate neither for all people nor for all situations, you pause long enough to consider the following statements and to examine your own reactions to them. Your reactions may reveal salient attitudes about children, learning, and knowledge. I have found that successful open educators in both England and America tend to take similar positions on these statements. Where do you stand?

## ASSUMPTIONS ABOUT LEARNING
## AND KNOWLEDGE

*INSTRUCTIONS*: Make a mark somewhere along each line which best represents your own feelings about each statement.

*Example*: School serves the wishes and needs of adults better than it does the wishes and needs of children.

---

| strongly agree | agree | no strong feeling | disagree | strongly disagree |

## I. Assumptions About Children's Learning

*Motivation*

*Assumption 1*: Children are innately curious and will explore their environment without adult intervention.

---

| strongly agree | agree | no strong feeling | disagree | strongly disagree |

*Assumption 2*: Exploratory behavior is self-perpetuating.

---

| strongly agree | agree | no strong feeling | disagree | strongly disagree |

*Conditions for Learning*

*Assumption 3*: The child will display natural exploratory behavior if he is not threatened.

---

| strongly agree | agree | no strong feeling | disagree | strongly disagree |

*Assumption 4*:   Confidence in self is highly related to capacity for learning and for making important choices affecting one's learning.

---

| strongly agree | agree | no strong feeling | disagree | strongly disagree |

*Assumption 5*:   Active exploration in a rich environment, offering a wide array of manipulative materials, will facilitate children's learning.

---

| strongly agree | agree | no strong feeling | disagree | strongly disagree |

*Assumption 6*:   Play is not distinguished from work as the predominant mode of learning in early childhood.

---

| strongly agree | agree | no strong feeling | disagree | strongly disagree |

*Assumption 7*:   Children have both the competence and the right to make significant decisions concerning their own learning.

---

| strongly agree | agree | no strong feeling | disagree | strongly disagree |

*Assumption 8*:   Children will be likely to learn if they are given considerable choice in the selection of the materials they wish to work with and in the choice of questions they wish to pursue with respect to those materials.

---

| strongly agree | agree | no strong feeling | disagree | strongly disagree |

*Assumption 9*:   Given the opportunity, children will choose to engage in activities which will be of high interest to them.

---

| strongly agree | agree | no strong feeling | disagree | strongly disagree |

*Assumption 10*:   If a child is fully involved in and is having fun with an activity, learning is taking place.

---

| strongly agree | agree | no strong feeling | disagree | strongly disagree |

*Social Learning*

*Assumption 11*: When two or more children are interested in exploring the same problem or the same materials, they will often choose to collaborate in some way.

---

strongly agree    agree    no strong feeling    disagree    strongly disagree

*Assumption 12*: When a child learns something which is important to him, he will wish to share it with others.

---

strongly agree    agree    no strong feeling    disagree    strongly disagree

*Intellectual Development*

*Assumption 13*: Concept formation proceeds very slowly.

---

strongly agree    agree    no strong feeling    disagree    strongly disagree

*Assumption 14*: Children learn and develop intellectually not only at their own rate but in their own style.

---

strongly agree    agree    no strong feeling    disagree    strongly disagree

*Assumption 15*: Children pass through similar stages of intellectual development, each in his own way and at his own rate and in his own time.

---

strongly agree    agree    no strong feeling    disagree    strongly disagree

*Assumption 16*: Intellectual growth and development take place through a sequence of concrete experiences followed by abstractions.

---

strongly agree    agree    no strong feeling    disagree    strongly disagree

*Assumption 17*: Verbal abstractions should follow direct experience with objects and ideas, not precede them or substitute for them.

---

strongly agree    agree    no strong feeling    disagree    strongly disagree

*Assumption 18:*   The preferred source of verification for a child's solution to a problem comes through the materials he is working with.

---

    strongly      agree      no strong      disagree      strongly
      agree              feeling                      disagree

*Assumption 19:*   Errors are necessarily a part of the learning process; they are to be expected and even desired, for they contain information essential for further learning.

---

    strongly      agree      no strong      disagree      strongly
      agree              feeling                      disagree

*Assumption 20:*   Those qualities of a person's learning which can be carefully measured are not necessarily the most important.

---

    strongly      agree      no strong      disagree      strongly
      agree              feeling                      disagree

*Assumption 21:*   Objective measures of performance may have a negative effect upon learning.

---

    strongly      agree      no strong      disagree      strongly
      agree              feeling                      disagree

*Assumption 22:*   Learning is best assessed intuitively, by direct observation.

---

    strongly      agree      no strong      disagree      strongly
      agree              feeling                      disagree

*Assumption 23:*   The best way of evaluating the effect of the school experience on the child is to observe him over a long period of time.

---

    strongly      agree      no strong      disagree      strongly
      agree              feeling                      disagree

*Assumption 24:*   The best measure of a child's work is his work.

---

    strongly      agree      no strong      disagree      strongly
      agree              feeling                      disagree

## II. Assumptions About Knowledge

*Assumption 25*:    The quality of being is more important than the quality of knowing; knowledge is a means of education, not its end. The final test of an education is what a man *is*, not what he *knows*.

| strongly agree | agree | no strong feeling | disagree | strongly disagree |
|---|---|---|---|---|

*Assumption 26*:    Knowledge is a function of one's personal integration of experience and therefore does not fall into neatly separate categories or "disciplines."

| strongly agree | agree | no strong feeling | disagree | strongly disagree |
|---|---|---|---|---|

*Assumption 27*:    The structure of knowledge is personal and idiosyncratic. It is a function of the synthesis of each individual's experience with the world.

| strongly agree | agree | no strong feeling | disagree | strongly disagree |
|---|---|---|---|---|

*Assumption 28*:    Little or no knowledge exists which it is essential for everyone to acquire.

| strongly agree | agree | no strong feeling | disagree | strongly disagree |
|---|---|---|---|---|

*Assumption 29*:    It is possible, even likely, that an individual may learn and possess knowledge of a phenomenon and yet be unable to display it publicly. Knowledge resides with the knower, not in its public expression.

| strongly agree | agree | no strong feeling | disagree | strongly disagree |
|---|---|---|---|---|

Most open educators, British and American, "strongly agree" with most of these statements. I think it is possible to learn a great deal both about open education and about oneself by taking a position with respect to these different statements. While it would be folly to argue that strong agreement assures success in developing an open classroom, or, on the other hand, that strong disagreement predicts failure the assumptions are, I believe, closely related to open education practices. Consequently, I feel that for those sympathetic to the assumptions, success at a difficult job will be more likely. For the educator to attempt to adopt practices which depend for their success upon general adherence to these beliefs without actually adhering to them is, at the very least, dangerous.

At the same time, we must be careful not to assume that an "official" British or U.S. government-inspected type of open classroom or set of beliefs exists which is the standard for all others. Indeed, what is exciting about British open classrooms is the *diversity* in thinking and behavior for children and adults—from person to person, class to class, and school to school. The important point here is that the likelihood of successfully developing an open classroom increases as those concerned agree with the basic assumptions underlying open education practices. It is impossible to "role play" such a fundamentally distinct teaching responsibility.

For some people, then, drawing attention to these assumptions may terminate interest in open education. All to the good; a well-organized, consistent, teacher-directed classroom probably has a far less harmful influence upon children than a well-intentioned but sloppy, permissive, and chaotic attempt at an open classroom in which teacher and child must live with contradiction and conflict. For other people, awareness of these assumptions may stimulate confidence and competence in their attempts to change what happens to children in school.

In the final analysis, the success of a widespread movement toward open education in this country rests not upon agreement with any philosophical position but with satisfactory answers to several important questions: For what kinds of people—teachers, administrators, parents, children—is the open classroom appropriate and valuable? What happens to children in open classrooms? Can teachers be *trained* for open classrooms? How can the resistance from children, teachers, administrators, and parents—inevitable among those not committed to open education's assumptions and practices— be surmounted? And finally, should participation in an open classroom be *required* of teachers, children, parents, and administrators?

# 4.12 GLORIOUS IDEALS—
# AND HARSH REALITIES
## Amitai Etzioni

**Definition of the Problem**

I cannot summarize Silberman's definition of the problem more effectively than Christopher Lehmann-Haupt who wrote:

> Mr. Silberman has sailed up the shallow creek of American education, surveyed the landscape and pronounced it joyless, mindless, barren. The natives, he says, are pinched and crabbed, and stand before their children mumbling empty incantations; the children stare back silently, hollow-eyed, and pick their scabs. (*New York Times*, October 8, 1970). . . .

Typically, Silberman does not seek a revolution and is careful to disassociate himself from the more radical writers such as John Holt, Paul Goodman, and Edgar Z. Friedenberg. At the same time, he asks for *more* than piecemeal, limited reform. He believes that the total educational system of America must be transformed through the accumulation of sweeping, peaceful, and encompassing changes. In the course of these, the nation will be redone, since the ills of education are diagnosed as reflecting and reinforcing those of a society in deep crisis. . . .

The main features of informal schools . . . are the replacement of the teacher as directing a passively seated class of children, by several "interest areas" in which children *do*, at their own pace, a variety of things *they* are interested in, for varying time intervals, with the help of teachers and teacher-aides. Self-directed, self-disciplined, the children enjoy rather than work at their tasks. The teachers' main duty is to provide a stimulating, encouraging environment. This informalization of the schools entails more than reorganization. Teachers must be re-educated to be able to fulfill their roles in the new

Amitai Etzioni, "Review of *Crisis in the Classroom* by Charles E. Silberman" in *Harvard Educational Review* 41: 87–98, February 1971. Copyright © 1971 by President and Fellows of Harvard College. Footnotes here omitted.

Amitai Etzioni, Chairman of the Department of Sociology at Columbia University since 1968, is author of *Modern Organizations* (1964), *The Active Society* (1968), *Readings on Modern Organizations* (1969) and other books and articles.

Charles E. Silberman, *Fortune* editor and author of *Crisis in Black and White* (1964), wrote *Crisis in the Classroom* (Random House, 1970, paperback, 1971) as a summary of a study sponsored ($300,000) by the Carnegie Corporation. The study involved extensive interviews, travel and much staff work, and is recommended as a supplement to this chapter. For a review of five other books, which, like Silberman's, are overwhelmingly favorable to open education, and for a good overview of the meaning of "open education," read Mary Jo Bane, "Essay Review: Open Education," *Harvard Educational Review* 42: 273–281, May 1972.

classroom. The substance of the curriculum must be adapted to be more meaningful, open to the child's interests, and "balanced" to include the affective next to the cognitive, and esthetics and ethics next to acquiring information and skills.

Informal schools were recommended by the Plowden Report of Great Britain and are being introduced there. "Open classroom" is a similar, albeit more radical, concept endorsed by a variety of American writers on education and practiced in a few places in this country. The progressive movement harbored a similar idea. Silberman stresses the differences between the idea he endorses, the informalizing schools, and the open or progressive mode of education. In the informal school, he says, the teacher does have a guiding role. Spontaneity, it is recognized, is not all that is needed; encouragement to growth is also to be provided. . . .

## Specificity

Critical to the whole idea of the informal classroom is the role of the teacher. If he overly exerts his influence by making children learn his ways, his lines, the informal school will be little more than the old system in a new disguise. However, if he is too passive, allowing anarchy and indulgence to prevail, the new school may be rather like some of the least structured progressive schools. Silberman speaks about the "right balance" between allowing the child's interests to guide the educational process and allowing the teacher to guide the child toward the knowledge, skill, and development of self-discipline. However, he gives the reader no set of indicators by which he can discern if such a balance exists in a classroom under observation. Even in these general terms, he leaves the range quite open, stating at one point about the system he approves, ". . . the teachers and administrators with whom I talked and whose informal classrooms I observed were more than simply 'here'; they were very much in charge" (p. 210). Discussing Piaget's contribution to what educational practice ought to be, Silberman says that "the child is the principal agent in his own education and mental development" (p. 215). . . .

While Silberman generally stays on a level of generality, which in a sense protects the ideas he promotes, at one key juncture his vagueness casts doubt on the validity of the whole conception. This concerns his evidence. . . . [and his] lack of clarity concerning schools which have been successfully informalized. Silberman recommends informal schools on the basis of "it has been done, successfully, in Britain" [and in a few cases in the United States].[1] That is, there *are* viable prototypes. The evidence of success of these

---

[1] *EDITOR'S NOTE*: The British innovations are summed up in the two-volume Plowdon Report, *Children and Their Primary Schools* (London, 1967). Vito Perrone chose the following extracts from that report to suggest its general character:
The best preparation for being a happy and useful man or woman is to live fully as a child.

schools is, by necessity, limited and incomplete since the approach is fairly new and full evaluation is very difficult. But the very fact that schools can be organized in this way, and that they graduate students who are at least not very poorly educated, is itself of great significance. One must then ask—*which* schools have been informalized in Britain? Are these infant schools (age 5 to 7) *or* schools in general, including secondary ones? It is a very different proposition to state that the first grade should be quite similar to the Kindergarten and to limit the informalization largely to the first two school years, than to state that "schools" should be full of learn-through-play, do-your-own-thing and so on. At one point Silberman makes quite clear that the British experience is much more extensive in infant schools than in higher grades of primary schools. Infant schools provide much of the "it works" data and they are frequently cited as the source of his first-hand observations. However, in contrast to the factual materials presented, his discussion tends to imply that at least all grades of the primary school should be informalized and, to a somewhat lesser extent, also those of the secondary schools. To put it more sharply —where the evidence is relatively solid, for the "infant age,"—the recommendations offer little that is new either for educational thought *or* practice; where the recommendation requires far-reaching changes, it has little grounding in empirical reality.

Furthermore, the data gives an unclear picture as to the value of these schools for pupils from a working class or lower middle class background. It is also unclear whether there are special factors in Britain which are not transferable to American schools; for example, the role of the principal seems to be quite different in the two school systems. Finally, as long as attendance is required, children are evaluated (graded), and many parents demand "achievements," it is unclear if informalized schools will really be fundamentally different from the existing ones—an assumption which runs throughout Silberman's book.

---

The distinction between work and play is false, possibly throughout life, certainly in the primary school . . . play is the principal means of learning in early childhood. It is the way through which children reconcile their inner lives with external reality.
Good teaching practice insists that knowledge does not fall into neatly separate compartments and that work and play are not opposite but complementary.
. . . informal education is ideally suited to the needs and nature of young children and to their development as human beings.—Vito Perrone, *Open Education: Promise and Problems*, Bloomington, Indiana: Phi Delta Kappan Educational Foundation, 1972, p. 11. By permission.

This Perrone booklet is one of a half dozen short Phi Delta Kappan booklets (all 1972) dealing with "crucial issues in American education." They are recommended as supplements to this anthology.

For a brief summary of about twenty experimental programs in the United States, read Jack V. Edling, "Individualized Instruction: The Way It Is—1970," *Audio-Visual Media* 15: 13–16, February 1970. See also "Does School + Joy = Learning?" *Newsweek* 77: 60–68, May 3, 1971; Charles E. Silberman, "Remaking of American Education" in *Current Issues in Higher Education* 26: 227–233, 1971.

## Human Nature, Institutionalization, and Piaget

Any educational theory is predicated on certain implicit or explicit assumptions about human nature. To what extent is man open to instruction or is he biologically pre-determined? And, is man straining toward the light of reason or must he be coaxed to look at it? The prevailing view of man's nature in the social sciences and in the educational establishment downgrades biological factors (often viewed as racist) and tends to assume that man is very educable. Silberman subscribes to this highly optimistic position.

Among the optimists, there are those who see man taking to education as naturally as a duck to water; this propensity approximates the unfolding of an instinct, which can be helped or hindered by the educational institutions, but which cannot be fundamentally shaped by them. Piaget's theory, which Silberman embraces, is interpreted as a major support of this view.

This great confidence in human nature is coupled with a great suspicion of institutions. Schools, at least as they are presently constituted, are viewed as hindering or distorting this natural development. The more extreme proponents favor doing away with schools as institutions. The more moderate counsellors, like Silberman, favor, in effect, curbing their scope, reducing their institutionalization, and restructuring the remaining elements in such a way that the child is helped in his growth rather than being directed. The informalizers stress the second element (of help), while the liberators concentrate on the first (reducing the scope). Silberman's program is rich in both, although he talks as if it is chiefly a matter of moving from control to assistance.

My view of human nature is less optimistic. Recent evidence suggests that physiological factors (such as nourishment) and social background factors (such as those recorded by the Coleman report and studies by compensatory educators) are quite powerful. As a result, we see that pre-school and extra-school forces can damage many children to the point where their "pre-programmed" sequence of capacities, as Piaget followers see them, are so severely disturbed that they will not unfold and can be tapped by the *educator only through very great efforts and costs.* For me, the normative conclusion derived from this evidence is *not* to reduce our educational efforts for the disadvantaged, but to start earlier, to move more broadly, to be more persistent, and to invest many more resources in such efforts. But, it also means that school organization and curriculum often cannot be based on an optimistic assumption about the unfolding natural powers of the child. Educators must recognize that the natural sequence is often derailed and that only large guided efforts *on their side* can put the child back on this high actualization track. . . .

The critical question becomes then—how much, how detailed, how encompassing a guiding hand is needed? Silberman does not hold the radical position, which in effect eliminates such guidance; he does see a role for a teacher. But, he philosophically leans towards a teacher who is child-centered, not in the sense of responding to the child's underlying capacities, but to his *expressed* needs. Informalization aims to give prime emphasis to the child's *interests*, which may or may not correspond with his natural capacities, and to construct the educational process around his wishes.

In my opinion, the majority of the children in *our* society need more of a guiding hand, a more institutionalized school than the highly informal school that the theorists advocate. A school system is needed which exercises less control than the present but provides more guidance than the one Silberman advocates. The exact mix cannot be spelled out within the limits of a review essay. Nor should it be based on idle speculation; different mixes should be tried and evaluated. It may well be established that children who come from privileged homes, often inconsistent or ultra permissive, may have to learn to function within a *somewhat* more structured environment. No society could function if all its members acted as selfishly as those who seek to maximize their freedoms, disregarding the costs such maximization imposes on others. Children from lower middle-class homes may have to be guided in learning to cope with more freedom than they are accustomed to, so that they will not backlash in frustration when they are given more of it. (Possibly here the first grades would be more formal than the later ones, within the primary school, to reduce the discontinuity in the transition from the authoritarian home to the informal school.) A still different approach may have to be designed for those whose natural potential capacities have been suppressed by the conditions which prevail in disadvantaged communities. The concept of the same school structure for all never had any broad reality in a society where children come from such divergent starting points. Children may now go to what looks like the same school but actually there are great differences among schools in the way the same rules and organizational principles are applied, and these differences are correlated with class background. Nor has the notion of one school for all, on the face of it a great equality, any normative validity. "Informality for all" is no more realistic than assuming you can teach all fifth graders the same math just because the Piaget scheme suggests that they all ought to be "ready" for it.

Most important of all, the school is unavoidably a funnel which leads from infancy at home to the adult occupational structure in the greater society. Hence, just as earlier grades are and ought to be much more like home, the later grades ought to be more like the society in which the students will live. This ought to be a better society than the present one; hence the higher grades may be geared not only to the present, but also to a brighter future, although not to a utopia. Otherwise, one burdens the educational system with more pressures than it can possibly sustain; this in turn could backfire both against the schools and their graduates. Therefore, an adequate theory of education requires a conception of the society from which the child comes and which he will enter as an adult—and an understanding of the amount of leverage the school can be reasonably expected to have on either of these aspects of society. To reiterate, I see the backgrounds of the majority of children as highly suppressive to their natural capacities and hence, the school organization, first of all, must serve a corrective function for these. It is not only the disadvantaged who are in need of decompressive education, but also those from the silent majority and from ultra permissive or inconsistent homes. It is precisely in this area that the school's greatest potential leverage lies, especially if it works in connection with other social institutions, ranging in scope from labor exchanges to housing authorities. . . .

Silberman correctly stresses that our schools are organized as if everyone will graduate either to work on an assembly line or in a civil service. They are best suited to preparing indifferent cogs for an industrial-bureaucratic machinery, that is, at best, to be part of yesterday's world. Schools must, hence, be reorganized, not just in the substance of their teaching but in the very educational environment and experience they provide, to prepare their students for the different societies of 1980 and even for the year 2000 and beyond. But, despite the hip talk about rapid societal change, as far as I can foresee, our society will continue to have major instrumental and technical needs. True, we will be able to work less, and less efficiently, and still be affluent. And we can realistically help prepare students for a world with more "work" and less "labor" (to use Hannah Arendt's terms) and a world in which more energy and time are devoted to personal and interpersonal growth, and less to productivity—all educational purposes for which informal schooling is suited. However, we must also recognize that the transition from one societal pattern to another will not be abrupt, even if there will be a radical revolution, and a revolution does not seem imminent. Hence, schools must help prepare the child for a better society but unfortunately it is premature to prepare him for the good society. To cease to educate children for discipline or to put a ceiling on their spontaneity, to build up their intolerance for periods of labor, and their acceptance of rules and authority—is to prevent the educational system from helping to bring about that change for which the society is *ripe*. Our efforts to prepare students for a society that may exist at a later time or for a society which cannot exist *reduces* the impact of the educational system, as an agent of societal change. Its graduates will be too utopia-minded to join with other groups working for societal change, and this in turn will lead the graduates to withdraw into apathy, romantic revolutionary infantile acts, or to reject their education in favor of the world around them, as it is. The well-known principle of physical education applies here: one helps the pupil to evolve goals which require that he stretch his muscles, but not to run one mile in three minutes. One helps the pupil to raise his sights, as his actualized capacities (as distinct from his potential ones) grow. Such a posture would spell, 'for the organization of schools, moving from a relatively informal organization in the early years (subject to great variations according to varying decompressive needs) to a *relatively* less informal, more uniform, more specialized schooling as we move closer to graduation.

It may seem ungrateful to a book which raises many provocative issues to conclude by saying that the best we can hope to do is to outgrow it rapidly —both as a policy guide for educational reforms and as a form of policy research. But this recommendation seems appropriate not only for this work but for many which recently provided a stimulating but also "soft" basis for new policy making in education and societal guidance in general.[1]

---

[1] *EDITOR'S NOTE*: Reviewing another book advocating open education and greater student autonomy, Ned O'Gorham writes (*Saturday Review* 54: 27–28, 81, October 23, 1971):

[I believe we teachers] exist so that young children can learn within a serious, joyous, mannerly, and reverent atmosphere those civilizing graces they must have to survive in a racist world. . . .

Perhaps the gurus, ranging from Ivan Illich . . . to camp followers of misread Montessori and Freud, ought to detach themselves from the comforting notion that chucking the past and liberating children from schools, parents, sexual morality, good manners, classrooms, elitist education, clean hands, all hierarchies, and deference to the wishes of parents and the commands of tradition is going to solve the problems of the child—his schools, his family, or the world. I hope too that soon the slovenly, pious notions that nothing is worth a damn unless it is relevant and meaningful (those words by now have an obscene ring to them), and no school or family is stable and healthy unless in a state of constant riot and "democratic process," will no longer direct so much of contemporary educational and "moral" reform. . . .

If everyone will be taught only what is relevant, what becomes of ancient history, music, astronomy, Latin, Greek, French, El Greco, Mozart, Aristotle, Plato, Shakespeare, and Vergil? What of the struggle for knowledge, of the disciplines that teach a child to write well, enjoy a good novel, rejoice in poetry, and simply to sit and listen while someone *wiser* than himself teaches? No one has dared answer this question yet. It is a risky thing to mention the agonies and rigors of growth in a world so thrilled by the notion of freedom and experimentation. . . . In a brutal cacophony for change, the liberated educator has let the structures fall down. Tradition, discipline, morality, and religion (and there is some good yet in the old things) come crashing down upon the children in an ugliness of half-truths and irresponsible demands by stricken adults. We must build now a philosophy and a theology, a science and an esthetic of childhood that would try to see a child as holy, wise, fragile, pure—and never as free as when he rejoices in that holiness, wisdom, fragility, and purity.

# CHAPTER
# 5

Emphasize
Values

# A. State Aid to Parochial Schools

## 5.1 INTRODUCTION

When our nation was founded, values—moral and spiritual values—were almost universally equated with religious belief. So we begin these remarks with a few highlights from American history.

During the colonial period of American history, when European nationality groups were becoming firmly entrenched into various forms of nationalist church-states, the American colonies were pioneering in new directions. Briefly, the American movement toward a pluralistic society progressed through three stages:

*Religious Establishment.* This meant that a state (or colony) gave financial support to one and only one church, and that the state enforced by law the public worship and doctrines of the established church, with punishment for nonadherents.

*Multiple Establishment.* This took two forms. The earlier form granted freedom of worship to dissenting groups, but maintained tax support for the established church. As time went on, the relatively isolated colonial communities came to be populated, not only by Calvinists but by Lutherans, Mennonites, Quakers, Anglicans, and other diverse groups. Under multiple establishment, each local township was required to support a minister and a school, but the religious affiliation was to be determined by the majority within each local community. Under multiple establishment (or local option), everyone still paid a general tax for religion (and for education—which was considered an integral part of religion) but the way had been opened for all religious groups to participate equally in the privilege of the establishment.

*Disestablishment.* As America continued to welcome immigrants from all racial, nationality, and religious groups, its common schools could no longer be built around narrow denominational lines. Emphasis shifted to the three R's, with the fourth R, religion, steadily reduced in emphasis.

The movement from (1) establishment, to (2) multiple establishment, to (3) disestablishment (separation of church and state) has been well stated by Butts and Cremin:

In a society where religious freedom is allowed but where education must be religious, a common public school system for all children is well nigh impossible. In the eighteenth century prior to the Revolution the people cherished religious freedom and a diversity of religious education more than they cherished a common school system. To maintain religious freedom and at the same time achieve a common school system the people would have to decide to exclude religion from the common school and to nourish religion in their homes and churches. . . .

More and more people came to believe that freedom of religion requires the assumption that there are different religious roads to the good life and that genuine religious freedom requires that the state guarantee equal rights of conscience to all religious claimants with no distinctions. . . . The test of good citizenship is morality, not religious belief. Thus, when the colonists decided to renounce their connection with Britain and become Americans, they also decided that their differing religious beliefs could not be allowed to stand in the way of the common ties of good citizenship. They therefore moved to separate the state from all churches as well as from any one church so that all Americans could become equally good citizens in the eyes of the civil law and of the state.[1]

The reason why disestablishment was chosen in preference to other alternatives has been well stated by Zechariah Chaffee, Jr.:

We have made our choice and chosen the dream of Roger Williams. It was not a choice between a good dream and a bad dream, but between a good dream which on the whole works and a good dream which occasionally turned into a nightmare of the . . . hanging of Mary Dyer on Boston Common. Sometimes nostalgia for what we have given up creeps over us. Men sometimes lament, for instance, that our public schools are godless. Suppose we admit frankly that this is a loss to the public schools, that one very important part of our nature has to be wholly neglected in the place where we receive much of the shaping of our characters and minds. It is a price to pay, but we must look at all which we have bought thereby. We cannot reject a portion of the bargain and insist on keeping the rest. If the noble ideal of the Puritan had persisted, there would be no godless schools in Massachusetts and there would be nobody in her churches except Congregationalists. Through the choice which all of the United States has made, it becomes possible for men of many different faiths to live and work together for many noble ends without allowing their divisions in spiritual matters to become, as in the old days, unbridgeable chasms running through every aspect of human lives.[2]

Or, as Justice Robert H. Jackson put it, the purpose of the First Amendment was

. . . not only to keep the states' hands out of religion, but to keep religion's hands off the state, and, above all, to keep bitter religious controversy out of

[1] R. Freeman Butts and Lawrence A. Cremin, *A History of Education in American Culture*, New York: Holt, Rinehart and Winston, Inc. 1953, pp. 98–99, 152, 153.
[2] Zechariah Chaffee, Jr., *The Blessings of Liberty*, pp. 255–256. Copyright © 1956 by Zechariah Chaffee, Jr. Reprinted by permission of J. B. Lippincott Co.

public life by denying to every denomination any advantage from getting control of public policy or the public purse. . . .

This policy of our Federal Constitution has never been wholly pleasing to most religious groups. They all are quick to invoke its protections; they all are irked when they feel its restraints. . . .

But we cannot have it both ways. Religious teaching cannot be a private affair when the state seeks to impose regulations which infringe on it indirectly, and a public affair when it comes to taxing citizens of one faith to aid another, or those of no faith to aid all. If these principles seem harsh in prohibiting aid to Catholic education, it must not be forgotten that it is the same Constitution that alone assures Catholics the right to maintain these schools at all when predominant local sentiment would forbid them. *Pierce v. Society of Sisters*, 268 U.S. 510. Nor should I think that those who have done so well without this aid would want to see this separation between Church and State broken down. If the state may aid these religious schools, it may therefore regulate them.[3]

In an era of ecumenism and interdenominational friendliness, it is well to remind ourselves how extremely intolerant religious sects were from the Reformation until the beginning of the twentieth century. For example, in the late nineteenth century era, when the White Anglo-Saxon Protestant (WASP) majority dominated American culture, a child could legally be expelled from school if he followed the instructions of his priest to cut public school classes in order to attend Mass on a Holy Day.[4]

It is a moot question whether the Protestants who looked upon themselves as "the saving remnant" or as "God's chosen few" were more tolerant, or less so, than their Catholic fellow-citizens who, while admitting that it was *politically expedient* to tolerate other religious views, also insisted that in religion "error has no rights." The views of Leo XIII (Pope, 1878–1903) have been summarized as follows:

It may be that under certain circumstances, such as the exceptional good will of the political powers, the Church deems it preferable to acquiesce to a factual separation of Church and State, but in no case will she ever admit that Church and State should be kept separate. Their separation remains an evil even while, for reasons of expediency, it is being tolerated. The same remark applies to the school problem.[5]

[3] *Everson v. Board of Education*, 330 U.S. 1 (1946). This is part of a dissenting opinion in a 5–4 decision which gave constitutional sanction for the public transportation of children to parochial schools.
[4] *Ferriter v. Tyler*, 48 Vt. 444 (1876). For other cases of this kind read P. A. Freund, A. E. Sutherland, M. D. Howe and E. J. Brown, *Constitutional Law*, Boston: Little Brown & Co., 1961, Volume II, p. 1694.
[5] Etienne Gilson, ed., *The Church Speaks to the Modern World: The Social Teachings of Leo XIII*, New York: Doubleday & Co., Inc. (Image D7), 1954, p. 17.

This nineteenth-century view persists in the following definition:

*Freedom of Worship.* The inalienable right of all men to worship God according to the teaching of the Catholic Church. No state can justifiably prevent the exercise of this right; and indeed it has a duty to foster this true worship, since God's supremacy calls for man's acknowledgement in worship; and Christ established one form and content of public worship in establishing one only Church, to which all are commanded to submit. But to avoid greater evil or to achieve a higher good, public authority can tolerate false religions, so long as they do not teach open immorality. The practice that should distinguish Catholics in this matter today was tersely summarized by Cardinal Gibbons in the words, "Full liberty must be granted to all men to worship God according to the dictates of their conscience."[6]

Perhaps dogmatism was the prevailing religious attitude precisely because the theological beliefs of the various sects differed so radically from one another. Within the Christian tradition alone, notes I. N. Thut,

. . . a multiplicity of God-theories has appeared. There is, for example, the Quaker theory, which looks upon God as a kind, loving father, who walks so closely with each of his children that no man or institution should be permitted to come between them. Then there are the well-known Congregationalist and Unitarian theories which disagree so sharply on the question of whether God has three forms or one. Similarly, the Mormon theory and the Shaker theory lead to decidedly opposite views on the matter of procreation. Some sects picture God as a fearful Being likely to punish violently anyone who dares approach Him without proper credentials. Others look upon Him as a somewhat vague, formless spirit that may be felt in one's heart but may not be known directly.[7]

The public school, well named "the common school," reflected the changes in the direction of religious tolerance, and helped bring about the broadening base of citizenship in our country from Puritan to Protestant, to Christian, to Christian and Jew, to adherents of all religions, and, finally, to all men. The United States Supreme Court, and the several state courts, also reflected the changing attitudes of the American people. In 1844, Mr. Justice Story, for a unanimous Court, could assume that this is "a Christian country" and refer to "Judaism, or Deism, or any other form of infidelity." *Vidal v. Girard's Ex'rs.,* 43 U.S. (2 How.) 127, 198 (1844). A century later the Court declared only that "we are a religious people," *Zorach v. Clauson,* 343 U.S. 306, 313 (1952), and just a few years ago it unanimously struck down a requirement "of belief in the existence of God," *Torcaso v. Watkins,* 367 U.S. 488, 495 (1961), as a condition to eligibility for public office. . . . More

[6] *A Catholic Dictionary,* Donald Attwater, ed., New York: Crowell-Collier and Macmillan, Inc., 2d rev. ed., 1949, pp. 201–202.
[7] I. N. Thut, "Shall the Public Schools Teach Religion?" *Teacher Education Quarterly* (Connecticut State Department of Education), Winter 1951, Vol. 7, pp. 75–79.

and more, the law has come to respect the human spirit and the dignity and worth of man.[8]

*The Meaning of Religious Pluralism.* When we say that the United States is a pluralistic society, we mean that it contains a variety of societies, organizations and religious sects, some of whose beliefs are hostile to those of other groups. To maintain law and order in such a society, the Courts have consistently interpreted the United States Constitution to mean that the state must refrain from either positive or negative intervention into the religious beliefs of its citizens. The only exceptions are cases in which religious beliefs upset the peace and order of society. Thus in *Davis v. Beason*, 133 U.S. 333 (1890), the Court classified bigamy and polygamy as crimes, not as religious rights. In *Zucht v. King*, 260 U.S. 174 (1922), the Court declared that school

---

[8] These and other cases are from a lengthy article on religious freedom by Arner Brodie and Harold P. Southerland, 1966 *Wisconsin Law Review*, pp. 214–330.

In *Torcaso v. Watkins*, 367 U.S. 499 (1961), the U.S. Supreme Court held that a state could not make declaration of belief in God a condition for appointment as a notary public. Such a condition on any public benefit would put state power "on the side of one particular sort of believers. . . ." This is a forbidden establishment, since

. . . neither a State nor the Federal Government can constitutionally force a person "to profess a belief or disbelief in any religion." Neither can constitutionally pose laws nor impose requirements which aid all religions as against non-believers, and neither can aid those religions based on a belief in the existence of God as against those religions founded on different beliefs. (Among religions in this country which do not teach what would generally be considered a belief in the existence of God are Buddhism, Taoism, Ethical Culture, Secular Humanism, and others.)

In *United States v. Seegar*, 360 U.S. 163 (1965), the Court dealt with exemption clauses for conscientious objectors to military service, and interpreted the congressional requirement of "belief in relation to a Supreme Being" to mean a belief that is sincere and meaningful [and that] occupies a place in the life of its possessor parallel to that filled by the orthodox belief in God of one who clearly qualifies for the exemption. Where such beliefs have parallel positions in the lives of their respective holders we cannot say that one is "in a relation to a Supreme Being" and the other is not.

Paul W. Burton has summarized the prevailing attitude in these words:

Most persons in this country live by some philosophy of the cosmos, whether it be Catholicism, Trinitarian Protestantism, Unitarianism, Judaism, Humanism, Buddhism, agnosticism or atheism. In the eyes of the Constitution, all of these philosophies are entitled to equal respect from the civil authority. This does not mean that an equal value has been placed upon each one of them, but simply that the individual is to be completely free to make his own choice and to express his views in public places as well as private. To say that this evidences an attitude of Godlessness on the part of our constitutional system or establishes a religion of secularism is to completely misunderstand the theory of our constitution.

—Paul W. Burton, "Education, Religion and the Bill of Rights Today," in Leo O. Garber (ed.), *Current Legal Concepts in Education*, Philadelphia: University of Pennsylvania Press, 1966, pp. 91–92.

officials have a constitutional right and responsibility to require vaccination as a means of protecting public health.

However, the Court has consistently refused to act as an arbiter as to whether a religious belief is true or false. In *Watson v. Jones*, 13 Wallace, 679 (1872), which dealt with a dispute between two Louisville Presbyterian church factions, the Court held that the freedom and independence of churches would be in grave danger if *the Court* undertook to define religious heresy or orthodoxy or to decide which of two factions was the "true faith." A somewhat similar opinion is found in *Kedroff v. Saint Nicholas Cathedral*, 344 U.S. 94 (1952). Again, although laws against the fraudulent use of the mail are constitutional, the Court in *United States v. Ballard*, 322 U.S. 78 (1944), ruled that secular authorities may not use such laws to determine the truth of religious claims and beliefs—in this case, the "I am" movement; for, no matter how "preposterous" or "incredible" these claims may be, religious beliefs are not subject to findings of "truth" by fact-finding bodies.

Wherever possible, the Court has sought to accommodate secular laws to religious traditions. In *McGowan v. Maryland* and three other similar cases, 366 U.S. 420 (1961), the Court upheld the constitutionality of "Sunday Closing Laws" on the grounds that such laws were "preeminently secular" and could thus be upheld as general welfare regulations. "To say that the States cannot prescribe Sunday as a day of rest for these purposes [that is, as a day of relaxation for all citizens] solely because centuries ago such laws had their genesis in religion would give a constitutional interpretation of hostility to the public welfare rather than one of mere separation of church and state."

Because religious organizations promote their own special beliefs and values, there are some who argue that any form of state aid to any religious group represents a threat to our free democratic processes. Thus Laurant B. Frantz declares:

> I would define the freedom of speech as the exclusion of governmental force from the process by which public opinion is formed on public issues. Any governmental action which makes it more difficult or hazardous to take one side of a public issue than to take the other is an abridgment, whether or not this was its avowed purpose. "Public issues" for this purpose, are not limited to those on which governmental action may be taken, but include philosophy, religion, ethics, esthetics, social sciences, etc.—all these, in other words, on which an enlightened public opinion may be deemed desirable. . . .
>
> Governmental action which tends to regulate the content of public debate, either directly, or by singling out ideological groups or tendencies for special treatment, is permissible only if it . . . has no unnecessary deterrent effect on unprotected speech.[9]

[9] Laurant B. Frantz, "The First Amendment in the Balance," 71 *Yale Law Journal*, 1424–1450 at 1449, July 1962. Frantz' quotation raises this question: Does aid to parochial schools "make it more difficult or hazardous to take one side of a public issue than to take the other" with respect to such controversial problems as "naturalism," "scepticism," "birth control," "divorce"?

Others believe that the teaching "about" religion in the public schools is inadequate and distorted because it tends to overemphasize reason to the detriment of wholehearted religious commitment and faith. Such persons firmly defend open discussion and freedom of dissent in *politics*, and maintain the need for critical thinking in *science*; but they nevertheless feel that such freedom and openmindedness have little or no place in *religion*. For such persons, the characteristic constituents of religious education consist of divine revelations or of moral commitments. These, some educators believe, should be taught as authoritative truths, not as questionable hypotheses subject to rational inquiry or to empirical verification.

*Commitment versus Objectivity.* Let us briefly contrast the two opposing views. Our discussion will be in the context of Christianity, and would necessarily be much more extended if it included non-Christian religions or various forms of naturalism.

Kierkegaard and others argue that objectivity is unchristian. A Christian must commit all his heart, soul, mind, and strength to the love of God (*Mark* 12:30) and can never be uncommitted or "objective" concerning the existence, commands, and promises of God. The conclusion of a religious belief is not so much a conclusion as a resolution. Hence, for most religious existentialists, faith is not a form of knowledge. It is a direction of the will—a feeling of passionate concern, unswerving dedication, whole-hearted commitment. There are depths of feeling and heights of aspiration that reach beyond the powers of reason.

The rationalist admits that there are moments when we must let ourselves go, in love, in poetic rapture, in mystic communion. But we must be sure that the light that leads us is not darkness, and we can be reasonably sure of this only if we follow St. Paul's injunction to prove (probe) all things. The chief troubles in the world today are not caused by lack of faith, but by too much unreasoning faith in areas where reason should be free to bring order out of chaos. The truly religious person is as a little child (*Mark* 10:15; *Luke* 18:17) who finds delight in wonder, curiosity, expectancy, and who is continually surprised and reverent before the Mystery around him. A child does not look upon his beliefs as ultimate or final, but is ever eager to search for new possibilities. Thus we should approach religion in the spirit of Isaiah's "Come now, let us reason together, sayeth Jehovah" (*Isa.* 1:18). The reasonable man is always willing to weigh and measure his own commitments against alternative commitments; for in this manner his own commitments gain in breadth and depth of meaning; and in this way the spirit of truth is both counsellor and comforter (*John* 14:16).

A few sentences from Pascal's *Thoughts* nicely summarize the two opposing points of view:

> Man is visibly made to think; this is his whole dignity and his whole merit.
> Reason commands us much more imperiously than a master; for if we disobey the one we are unfortunate, but if we disobey the other we are fools.
> [But]

It is the heart which feels God, and not the reason. For that is what faith is, God touching the heart, not the reason.

There is nothing so conformable to reason as the disavowal of reason in those things which belong to faith. And nothing so contrary to reason as the disavowal of reason in the things that do not belong to faith. There are two excesses equally dangerous: to exclude reason, and to admit reason alone.

*Conclusion.* Let us now return to the original problem: State Aid to Parochial Schools. This anthology is based on the belief that in our society the individual is the basic source of values. To affirm the primacy of the individual means that no one may be condemned to second-hand citizenship because he is a mystic rather than a positivist, because he is a fideist rather than a rationalist, because he is a supernaturalist rather than a naturalist, because he is a Catholic or a Jew rather than a WASP, or because his basic beliefs and attitudes have been shaped by Oriental, African or Amerindian cultural and religious backgrounds, rather than by European.

But this anthology is also based on the belief that widespread discussion and deliberation are the surest way to bring about fair and equitable solutions to disputed issues. This is the principle of "minority rights and majority rule," which, in the words of John H. Hallowell, means this:

> It is the *reasoned* judgment of the majority that obligates our compliance with its decisions, not the *will* of the majority as such. To the extent, therefore, that the rule of the majority becomes more an expression of will and less an expression of reasoned judgment, to that degree it becomes less democratic and more tyrannical.[10]

In our pluralistic society, law and order require that men and women of extremely diverse beliefs and outlooks live and work peacefully together.

---

[10] John H. Hallowell, "The Meaning of Majority Rule," *Commonweal* 56: 167–169, May 23, 1962. See also Henry Steele Commager (ed.), *Living Ideas in America,* New York: Harper & Row, Inc., 1951, Chapter 5, "Democracy: Majority Rule *and* Minority Rights."

It is very difficult to be reasonable, and especially so in times of rapid change. There is no doubt but that we are living in a period of extremely rapid change in many areas, including changes in basic values. Such changes are more likely to come about in a peaceful manner if there is no rigid orthodoxy, no favored beliefs, no fixed method, no unchanging rules, which might tend to restrict or to  prevent the modification of old values to fit new situations:

> The optimum conditions for the realization of revolution are those in which the forces of change exist in an atmosphere of constitutional benevolence that allows them to make enormous progress without the necessity of provoking an actual civil war. In other words, the more that change is possible through legal means, the better the chance of [peaceful, and therefore, lasting] revolution.

—Jean François Revel, *Without Marx or Jesus,* New York: Doubleday, 1971, p. 185.

In contrasting it with earlier systems of government, Edmund Cahn writes that the American Constitutional system represents a change

Ours is a system whose laws are applicable to all men, and this system requires that all men be treated equitably.

But "equity" does not require that citizens be alike. Furthermore, "equity" is a multi-dimensional word. What is equitable from the standpoint of freedom and civil liberty (the problem discussed in this Introduction) is not necessarily equitable from a taxpayer's point of view.

And so we come to our central problem: Since parochial schools teach not merely religion, but mathematics, science, and other secular subjects as well, should not some financial assistance be allowed to those who, because of their special religious commitments, wish to place their children in private schools? The next selection summarizes the reasoning of our courts on this vital issue.

|  | As to Objective | As to Content | As to Sanction |
|---|---|---|---|
| From: | perpetuity | immutability | appeal to heaven |
| To: | efficacy | adaptation | appeal to the courts. |

—Edmund Cahn, *Confronting Injustice*, Boston: Little, Brown & Company, 1962, p. 68. See also pp. 168–175, 216f.

Professor Cahn contrasts "Constitutional law" with "Natural law" theories of morality. However, the doctrine of Natural Law is not necessarily a doctrine of rigid and unchanging legal or moral laws. On this point, read R. M. Hutchins, "Second Edition: The Natural Law," *The Center Magazine* 4: November/December 1971; John Cogley (ed.), *Natural Law and Modern Society*, Cleveland: The World Publishing Company, 1963, especially pp. 199–276; Albert Dondeyne, *Faith and the World*, Pittsburgh: Duquesne University Press, 1963, p. 232 especially; F. C. Carney, "Outline of a Natural Law Procedure for Christian Ethics," *The Journal of Religion* 47: 26–38, January 1967; Margaret MacDonald, "Natural Rights," *Proceedings of the Aristotelian Society* 67: 225–250, 1946–1947; reprinted in May Brodbeck (ed.), *Readings in the Philosophy of the Social Sciences*, New York: Crowell-Collier and Macmillan, Inc., 1968; Carl J. Friedrich, "Man the Measure: Personal Knowledge and the Quest for Natural Law," in *Intellect and Hope*, T. A. Langford and W. H. Poteat (ed.), Durham, N.C.: Duke University Press, 1968, pp. 91–110; and especially Robert N. Bellah, "Civil Religion in America," *Daedalus* 96: 1–21, Winter 1967; reprinted in *Religion in America*, William G. McLoughlin and Robert N. Bellah, (eds.), Boston: Beacon (BP306), 1968, pp. 3–23.

Like the common law, *Crucial Issues in American Education* begins with specific cases; since the so-called overarching principles, or the "natural laws," which help to decide the outcome of such cases, are not clearly known. But we are more likely to discover such principles, or laws, if we begin with concrete issues and later generalize, than if we begin with what (in a prescientific, predemocratic age) were presumed to be eternal or natural laws, and then make artificial and often misleading deductions from these. On this point read Carl J. Friedrich, *Rational Decision*, New York: Atherton Press, 1964, pp. 69f, 122f. It is for this reason that this chapter on values comes at the end, rather than the beginning, of this anthology.

# 5.2 THE PROSPECTS FOR PUBLIC AID TO PAROCHIAL SCHOOLS
## Paul G. Haskell

The function of this article is to describe the holdings of the several decisions involving the use of public funds in support of church schools, to analyze critically the reasoning of these decisions, and to consider whether there are constitutionally permissible alternatives for public funding of elementary and secondary church schools.

*Everson v. Board of Education* [1947] was the first case in which the United States Supreme Court dealt directly with the constitutionality of the use of state funds in support of church schools under the "establishment of religion" clause of the First Amendment. . . . [The Court began its 5–4 decision by declaring:]

> No tax in any amount, large or small, can be levied to support any religious activities or institutions, whatever they may be called, or whatever form they may adopt to teach or practice religion. . . .

The Court nevertheless concluded that:

> . . . we cannot say that the First Amendment prohibits New Jersey from spending tax-raised funds to pay the bus fares of parochial school pupils as a part of a general program under which it pays the fares of pupils attending public and other schools. . . .

The Court likened the provision of transportation to the furnishing of the services of the police and fire departments, connections for sewage dis-

Paul G. Haskell, "The Prospects for Public Aid to Parochial Schools," 56 *Minnesota Law Review* 158–188, December 1971. By permission. Footnote references here omitted.
Paul G. Haskell is Professor of Law, Case Western Reserve University.
Read also Neil J. King, "Rebuilding the 'Fallen House'–State Tuition Grants for Elementary and Secondary Education," 84: *Harvard Law Review* 1057–1089, March 1971; John R. Coyne, Jr., "Slates and Hamsters," *National Review* 23: 309–311, March 23, 1971; and (for the other side of the issue) various publications by *Americans United* [for separation of Church and State], 8120 Fenton Street, Silver Springs, Md. 20910.
Consider also the following statement by the late Judge Learned Hand:
The First Amendment protects one against action by the government . . . but it gives no one the right to insist that in the pursuit of their own interests others must conform their conduct to his own religious necessities. . . . We must accommodate our idiosyncrasies, religious as well as secular, to the compromises necessary in communal life; and we can hope for no reward for the sacrifices this may require beyond our satisfactions from within, or our expectations of a better world.—Judge Learned Hand, *Otten v. Baltimore & O.R.R.*, 205 F.2d 58, 61 (2d Cir. 1953).

posal, and highways and sidewalks to the parochial schools. The payment of bus fares was characterized as a safety measure and in no sense a subsidization with public funds of religious instruction. . . .

Twenty-one years after *Everson* the Court dealt with state financial assistance to church schools in the form of furnishing secular textbooks. In *Board of Education v. Allen* [(1968) . . . the] Court stated that just as the establishment clause did not prevent New Jersey from paying the bus fares of parochial school pupils as part of a general program of paying fares of school students, it did not prevent New York from making secular textbooks available to parochial school students as part of a general program of furnishing textbooks to school students. . . .

The appellant school boards attempted to distinguish *Everson* from this case by contending that buses have nothing to do with teaching but books do, and that the function of the church school is to weave religion into the teaching of what are normally secular subjects. The Court responded by noting the dual secular and religious functions of the church schools and the state requirements that they comply with secular educational standards. The Court also pointed out that the case was decided by summary judgment entered on the pleadings, and that there was nothing in the record to support the contention that the secular books would be used to teach religion or that secular and religious instruction were intertwined in the parochial schools. . . .

Two years later the Supreme Court decided [in *Walz v. Tax Commission* (1970)] that the exemption from the property tax granted to church property used for worship was not violative of the establishment clause. . . . The Court stated its guiding principle to be

> that we will not tolerate either governmentally established religion or governmental interference with religion. Short of those expressly proscribed governmental acts there is room for play in the joints productive of a benevolent neutrality which will permit religious exercise to exist without sponsorship and without interference.

The Court noted . . . that certain types of institutions that foster moral and mental improvement should not be inhibited in their activities by property taxation. Such institutions include nonprofit hospitals, libraries, schools and houses of religious worship, among others. Churches were not singled out for special tax treatment; rather they were considered to come within the classification of organizations entitled to tax exemption because they shared certain charitable characteristics.

The Court went on to state that "[d]etermining that the legislative purpose of tax exemption is not aimed at establishing, sponsoring, or supporting religion does not end the inquiry, however. We must also be sure that the end result—the effect—is not an excessive government entanglement with religion." The Court pointed out that both taxation and exemption from taxation involve some degree of entanglement, but taxation would involve a greater degree of entanglement because of the problems of valuation, liens, foreclosures and the accompanying confrontations of state and church arising from the legal processes. Although exemption is a type of economic benefit, it produces minimal involvement or entanglement and tends to separate the church and the state and insulate each from the other.

The Court concluded by pointing out that exemption of churches from various forms of taxation for two centuries indicated that the establishment clause was never intended to prohibit such exemption. The Court also noted that two centuries of exemption has not produced anything remotely resembling an establishment, but rather has operated to guarantee the free exercise of all religions. . . .

[Early in the 1970s the Court dealt with three cases calling for more direct financial aid to parochial schools.] In 1969 Rhode Island enacted legislation providing a 15% supplement to the salaries of teachers of secular subjects in nonpublic elementary schools. The supplement was paid directly to the teacher. As supplemented, the salary could not exceed the maximum paid to teachers in the public schools. It was required that the recipient be certified in the same manner as public school teachers and teach in a non-public school at which the average per pupil expenditure on secular education was less than the average in the public schools. The legislation also required that the teacher must teach only those subjects that are offered in the public schools, use only teaching materials used in the public schools, and agree that he will not teach a course in religion while he is receiving the salary supplement. The schools also were required to submit financial information in connection with some of the above requirements.

In 1968 Pennsylvania enacted legislation which authorized the "purchase" of certain "secular educational services" from nonpublic schools. The state would reimburse nonpublic schools directly for their actual expenditures for teachers' salaries, textbooks and instructional materials in connection with courses offered in the public schools in mathematics, modern foreign languages, physical science and physical education. Textbooks and instructional materials were required to be approved by the state educational authority. Any school seeking reimbursement was required to maintain prescribed accounting procedures identifying the separate costs of the secular educational service for which reimbursement was requested, which accounts were subject to state audit. . . .

[In a consolidated opinion {*DiAnso v. Robinson*, (Rhode Island, 1969) and *Lemon v. Kurtzman* (Pennsylvania, 1971)} the U.S. Supreme] Court stated the criteria for determining whether the state aid to the church schools in these cases violated the establishment clause. The statute must have a secular purpose, and its principal or primary effect must be one that neither advances nor inhibits religion (required by *Allen*, 1968); and the statute must not foster an excessive governmental entanglement with religion (required by *Walz*, 1970). The Court concluded that the legislative purpose in each case was secular. As to the effect of the state aid, the Court noted that while elementary and secondary church schools have a significant religious mission, the legislation attempted to guarantee that the aid would be restricted to secular purposes. State funding of religious instruction would be constitutionally impermissible. The Court, however, deemed it unnecessary to resolve the issue of whether the primary effect of the legislation would be to advance religion, since it concluded that the "cumulative impact of the entire relationship arising under the statutes in each State involves excessive entanglement between government and religion." . . .

A comprehensive, discriminating, and continuing state surveillance will inevitably be required to ensure that these restrictions are obeyed. . . . Unlike a book, a teacher cannot be inspected once so as to determine the extent and intent of his or her personal beliefs and subjective acceptance of the limitations imposed by the First Amendment. These prophylactic contacts will involve excessive and enduring entanglement between state and church. . . .

[In *Lemon* the] Court also noted that the funds were paid directly to the parochial school; in *Everson* the bus fare reimbursement went to the parent, in *Allen* the books were lent to the student, and in Rhode Island the supplement went directly to the teacher. The Court saw in this form of continuing direct subsidy added dangers of government control and surveillance.

A different but significant form of entanglement was also seen by the Court to follow from the Rhode Island and Pennsylvania legislation, namely, the divisive political potential of these programs. The issue of the size of annual appropriations for church schools would potentially divide the electorate along religious lines since most of the aid benefits one denomination. Political division along religious lines was one of the evils against which the First Amendment was intended to protect. The Court also noted that governmental programs have an expanding propensity, and the likelihood of greater state involvement in and contribution to church schools over time is indicated by the serious financial needs of such schools and the considerable political support for public aid. This was in contrast to the absence of any substantial state involvement with religion resulting from 200 years of tax exemption for churches as discussed in *Walz*. . . .

On the same day that the Supreme Court decided the *Lemon* case, it also decided *Tilton v. Richardson* [1971] which involved the constitutionality under the religion clauses of the First Amendment of certain provisions of the Higher Education Facilities Act of 1963 authorizing federal grants and loans to colleges and universities for the construction of a wide variety of facilities. The act did not prohibit aid to church-related colleges and universities as such, but did exclude aid for "any facility used or to be used for sectarian instruction or as a place for religious worship, or . . . any facility which . . . is used or to be used primarily in connection with any part of the program of a school or department of divinity. . . ."

[In the 5–4 *Tilton* decision, the] establishment issue was analyzed in terms of the principles expressed in several previous cases: Does the act reflect a secular legislative purpose? Is the primary effect of the act to advance or inhibit religion? Does the administration of the act foster an excessive government entanglement with religion? The legislative purpose was expressed in the preamble to the act, stating that it is important to assist colleges and universities to accommodate the rapidly growing number of young people seeking higher education. This was summarily accepted as a legitimate secular purpose. On the question of whether the legislation advanced religion, it was noted that bus transportation and textbooks for parochial school children and tax exemption for church property assist religion and have been upheld as constitutional; the crucial question is not whether benefit accrues but rather whether the *primary* effect of the legislation is to advance religion. The grants . . . were for buildings serving secular educational purposes. There was no evidence that religious education seeped into the use of these secular educational facilities. The primary effect of the grants was not to advance religion. . . .

Concerning the issue of excessive entanglement between church and state resulting from this legislation, the Court discussed the differences in the educational purposes of the parochial elementary and secondary school and the church-related institution of higher learning and the differences in the nature of the aid in this case from the aid in the *Lemon* case. Religious indoctrination is a significant function of the parochial school, whereas it is not a substantial purpose of these four colleges and universities although they are governed by Roman Catholic organizations. There are non-Catholics on the faculty and in the student body, and the academic atmosphere of these institutions appeared to be intellectually free. Thus there is little likelihood that religion will permeate secular education, and consequently the need for governmental surveillance is limited and the danger of excessive entanglement is reduced. The act subsidizes facilities dedicated to secular educational purposes, which require less governmental surveillance to assure religious neutrality than surveillance of teachers who are themselves not religiously neutral. In addition, the grants under the act occur only once, and as a consequence there are no continuing financial relationships and periodic analyses of expenditures as required under the Rhode Island and Pennsylvania legislation. . . .

It should be noted that Chief Justice Burger's opinion emphasized that the Court was deciding the establishment issue only with respect to church-related institutions of higher learning with the primarily secular educational purposes of these Connecticut schools. The conclusion might well be different with respect to aid to church-related colleges whose educational purposes were more religious in nature. . . .

In the *Lemon* and *Tilton* cases, the Supreme Court clearly enunciated the three criteria which were to be employed in the determination of the constitutionality under the establishment clause of public aid to church schools: (1) The statute must have a secular legislative purpose; (2) the principal or primary effect of the statute must be one that neither advances nor inhibits religion; and (3) the statute must not foster an excessive government entanglement with religion. If any of the three criteria is not complied with, the legislation is unconstitutional as a law "respecting the establishment of religion."[1]

## Conclusion

In its recent decision involving the constitutionality of Rhode Island and Pennsylvania legislation providing support for parochial schools, the Supreme Court has cast serious doubt upon the power of the state or federal government to aid such schools in any substantial way. A strong argument can be made, however, for the constitutionality of a "shared time" arrangement. Possibly the Court will uphold some form of voucher or tuition reimbursement system under a "child benefit" theory, or allow some form of tax deduction or tax credit to the parents of church school children, but it is difficult to understand why the Court would uphold such indirect unrestricted subsidies when the direct unrestricted subsidy to the parochial school would be unconstitutional.

[1] *EDITOR'S NOTE*: In a concurring opinion in *Schempp* (1968), Justice Brennan noted that the types of involvement the drafters of the Constitution meant to avoid were those which (a) serve essentially religious activities of religious institutions, (b) employ the organs of government for religious purposes, or (c) use religious means where secular means would suffice.

In discussing "American Catholic Education Since Vatican II" (an article written especially for a previous edition of *Crucial Issues in Education*, 1969, pp. 136–145), John W. Donohue, S.J. (Fordham University) observes that

as Catholic colleges become academically more sophisticated they also become more secularized, just as Protestant colleges did some generations ago. . . . Since they are schools, they are fully committed to secular values and share all the specifically educational problems of American higher education. In addition, they encounter special issues of their own, which may be summed up in three questions asked with varying degrees of seriousness. Is there a definable sense in which an institution can be truly Catholic and truly a university? If so, what precisely makes such a university *Catholic*? Even if it is possible to have a Catholic university, is it desirable? Might not Catholics simply conduct good secular institutions that are no more Catholic than Harvard is Congregational?

"Questions of this sort are posed more insistently after the Second Vatican Council. . . . [from which there seem to emerge] four nuclear ideas that are already shaping Catholic school theory and practice. These are the themes of (1) the endorsement of the process of secularization; (2) the importance of the role and responsibility of the laity both in the Church and in the whole of human society; (3) freedom as the root of personal worth and dignity; and (4) community as a focal value flowing from the human family's oneness and common destiny—demanding expression in friendship and cooperation across all lines and at all levels, including not least the international.

# 5.3 MYTHS, MONEY, AND CATHOLIC SCHOOLS
## Louis R. Gary and K. C. Cole

By now it has become an accepted fact of public life that the nation's Catholic schools are in trouble. The reasons are all too familiar. Costs are going up, enrollments are going down, and Catholic schools are closing their doors at the rate of one a day. Indeed, enrollments in the U.S. Catholic elementary and secondary schools have dropped 18 per cent in the last three years—and conservative estimates predict they will drop another 42 per cent by 1980.

Political leaders, most notably President Nixon and New York's Governor Rockefeller, repeatedly have promised to save the Catholic schools with some type of public aid. To be sure, the substantial Catholic vote plays a part in their thinking. But political leaders, reinforced by church leaders, also fear that, if the Catholic school system is allowed to collapse, the four million pupils now in Catholic schools throughout the country will be dumped into public schools, which already have more than enough problems of their own.

Unfortunately, public debate about the future of Catholic schools is filled more often with myths and rhetoric than with facts and analysis. The debate, therefore, is confused, the public is misled, and the proposed solutions are ill-chosen. An examination of the real reasons for the enrollment decline—and of the real possibilities of getting large amounts of new public money—leads to the conclusion that the best solution for Catholic schools is to regroup, consolidate, and cut their losses.

The major myth in the debate centers on tuition. The three major aid alternatives considered by the President, Governor Rockefeller, and others are (1) tax credits for families that pay tuition to Catholic schools, (2) direct grants to parents to cover the cost of tuition, and (3) vouchers that schools redeem for cash. All are based on the false premise that enrollments are falling because Catholic parents cannot afford to pay tuition charges to

Louis R. Gary and K. C. Cole, "The Politics of Aid [to Catholic Schools]—and a Proposal for Reform" *Saturday Review* 55: 31–33, July 22, 1972. © 1972 by Saturday Review and used by permission. This article is one of three under the heading *Myths, Money, and Catholic Schools*. Most of the nation's 11,000 Catholic schools are struggling to stay alive, and many have already closed down. A personal account of how much the schools have changed—and a provocative proposal to change them even more."

Louis R. Gary, former chairman of Cardinal Spellman's Committee on Educational Research and consultant to President Nixon's Commission on School Finance, wrote "Collapse of Nonpublic Education: Rumor or Reality?" for New York State's Fleishmann Commission.

K. C. Cole, editor of the Fleishmann Commission Report, is an associate editor of *Saturday Review*.

Catholic schools. The assumption is that, if somehow the government can give aid to Catholic schools, tuition will stop rising; if tuition stops rising, enrollments will stop falling. Although this reasoning may be valid for a small proportion of individual families, it is not true as a whole.

In the past, tuition in most Catholic schools has been so low that it has not played a major part in the enrollment decline. Two years ago average yearly tuition in U.S. Catholic elementary schools was only $42. Last year it had jumped to $120—but enrollments have been dropping for a decade.

If enrollments were dropping primarily in inner cities, then it could correctly be inferred that even modest tuition presented an unbearable family burden. But enrollment is dropping even faster in affluent suburbs. The very families that can pay tuition most easily are the ones that are choosing to send their children to free public schools. Further, fully one-third of the Catholic elementary schools that closed in the past five years in New York State, for example, charged no tuition at all.

The real reason why enrollment is dropping is that Catholic parents—for many reasons—simply are choosing not to send their children to Catholic schools. Even in 1962, the high point of Catholic school enrollment, only half of the nation's Catholic school-age population was attending Catholic schools. Today only 33 per cent of that population is enrolled in Catholic schools. Moreover, the schools are just beginning to reflect the recent drop in Catholic birth rates. Infant baptisms of U.S. Catholics fell from 36 per 1,000 in 1955 to 23 per 1,000 in 1970. The Pill is in the Catholic community, and the potential pool of Catholic school children is decreasing rapidly.

Increasingly, Catholic families moving to the suburbs are choosing public schools, which often have attractive physical facilities, gyms, learning labs, and other niceties that Catholic schools can't afford. Academically, however, Catholic schools are as good as public schools—if not better. Catholic schools also are caught in ideological conflicts in the church itself. Liberal parents believe that teaching in Catholic schools can be too restrictive; conservative parents are dissatisfied with the new permissiveness and lack of fidelity to Roman Catholic dogma.

Many Catholic schools are losing their distinctiveness. The growing substitution of lay teachers for nuns and brothers in Catholic classrooms leaves the schools with a less religious flavor; it also leaves the Catholic schools less distinct from public schools.

Along with falling enrollments, the decline in numbers of teaching brothers and nuns is the most serious economic problem for Catholic schools. In dollar terms, the presence of the religious-order teacher represents a great subsidy to the school. On a national average, religious-order teachers receive cash stipends and room and board worth $2,550 for teaching in Catholic schools, compared with the average salary of $5,597 paid to laymen.

The problem is that this kind of sacrifice is coming to an end. Fewer young people are entering religious orders. In 1950, 93 per cent of the teachers in Catholic schools across the country were brothers or nuns; today fewer than half are brothers or nuns.

Lay teachers are becoming more expensive. Traditionally, lay teachers in Catholic schools have been paid far less than teachers in public schools. But as the number of lay teachers has increased, so has their bargaining power. They still earn less than their public school counterparts, but in many cities they have joined unions, and by 1980 they probably will be paid as much as public school teachers.

Catholic schools depend on two main sources of income to cover these rising costs: general church revenue and tuition. General church revenue comes from Sunday collections and fund-raising events to which all Catholics (not just those with children in Catholic schools) contribute. Today more than 55 per cent of general revenue is channeled into parish schools, leaving little for all other parish services, which also have rising costs. Meanwhile, the level of contributions is falling off and failing to keep up with inflation. Overall, Catholic families contribute less than 2 per cent of their incomes to their parish church, and the rich contribute a far smaller proportion of their income than do the poor.

The other source of income—tuition—also is not likely to produce new money. To be sure, some private Catholic high schools—those with an excess of upper-middle-class applicants—could increase tuition without causing an enrollment decline. But as there is no mechanism in the church to redistribute money between rich schools and poor schools, or rich parishes and poor parishes, this would not help the elementary schools, which make up three-fourths of the nation's 11,000 Catholic schools.

Across the country Catholic schools are predominantly middle-class institutions. If the schools increased tuition to cover their costs, tuition would be so high that it would price out many middle-income (and large) families. Thus, while the cost of tuition generally has not caused enrollment decreases in the past, if it is increased, it might precipitate a mass exodus from Catholic schools in the future. The poor certainly would be driven out, and Catholic schools play an important role in many cities, where the enrollment often includes a large percentage of non-Catholic black pupils. Obviously, Catholic schools in the cities cannot raise tuition if they are to provide alternatives to the public schools for the poor. Conversely, tuition should be raised in wealthier parishes, based on the family's ability to pay.

The past rhetoric of Catholic leaders, however, will make such a strategy extremely difficult, if not impossible. For years church leaders—in order to get aid—have tried to convince politicians that Catholics couldn't contribute more to their schools. They were, of course, telling their people the same thing. Now, if massive aid does not come from the government, the clergy will have so convinced the people that they *cannot* afford to sustain their schools that the people—even those who can afford it—will never believe that they *can*.

But not even substantial amounts of new income from tuition, contributions, or the government are going to help the Catholic schools until church leaders stop concentrating their efforts on keeping schools open that will close in a few years anyway. Instead of continuing to preserve buildings, church leaders should begin to preserve the option of Catholic education itself.

This means they must close inefficient schools and consolidate the system. The fact is, enrollment will drop 42 per cent this decade, whether or not new income is found. The difference between the current policy of over-extension and a policy of planned consolidation will determine whether the Catholic school system will decline to half its present size or will collapse completely.

Church leaders have not planned well for the future. Until recently they continued to hire new teachers; they closed only a few schools; they continued to build new schools in the suburbs. Each year, as enrollment falls, they have been paying higher and higher costs to educate fewer and fewer pupils. If the church leadership persists in trying to keep the school system operating at its present level, Catholic schools will run an annual operating deficit of $2.2 billion by 1975; pupil/teacher ratios in Catholic elementary schools will fall from 30/1 today to 12/1 by 1980. Every move to slow that ratio by consolidation could save Catholic schools millions of dollars.

One reason why church leaders have not consolidated the schools is that they are depending on promises of public aid to keep the system going. But political leaders who promise the aid don't know whether they can deliver it and conform to the Constitution—and they probably can't. In return, Catholic leaders say that public aid will stop the decline in enrollments—which it won't. . . .

In recent cases involving public aid to nonpublic schools, the U.S. Supreme Court has argued that the very precautions the government would have to take to ensure that the aid would be used for nonreligious purposes would entail the kind of church-state entanglement that the Constitution prohibits. If no conditions are attached to the aid, on the other hand, the government would be acting irresponsibly by providing aid for potentially religious purposes. If conditions are attached, then the government would become excessively enmeshed in church affairs. Certainly, the imposition of any condition that Catholic schools must consolidate to be eligible for government aid would constitute such entanglement in the eyes of the High Court.

Many Catholic bishops, however, would welcome a government order to consolidate. They have agreed privately that consolidation is necessary but are reluctant to initiate such a move themselves. Many parishioners simply would ignore any church order to close their beloved—and inefficient—schools. After all, church leadership has been insisting all along that school closings signal the collapse of the system rather than its salvation. Now they're sunk in their own propaganda.

At times, they have tried to close inefficient schools in a systematic way.

They have announced, for example, that they will close a certain school in three years. The few times they have announced this, however, the schools have closed the following September. The reason was panic. Panic on the part of Catholic parents who wanted a stable environment for their children, panic on the part of teachers who wanted a stable job.

It will be difficult for church leaders to abandon their rhetoric. For years the threat of massive school closings has been their trump card in the political game they have played for government dollars, and the politicians have bought this argument. President Nixon has referred to the "tragedy" that one Catholic school closes each day. In fact, the consolidation program needed to keep the Catholic school system alive would involve closing two or three schools a day.

The final myth is that, no matter how much it might cost to aid the Catholic schools, it would cost much more if most of the pupils now in those schools were transferred into the public school system. The fact is, however, that projected enrollment declines in most public elementary schools would make room for most transfers at a cost that makes this a viable public policy option. In New York State alone it would cost the taxpayers $415 million more in public aid through 1980 to keep Catholic schools operating at their current level than it would to absorb Catholic transfers into public schools.

Unfortunately, the policies of both the church and the politicians have been based on sincere misconceptions. They will be difficult to abandon. But the time has come to rapidly reorder public thinking on the future of Catholic schools. If the courts do rule that substantial public aid to nonpublic schools is unconstitutional—and they probably will—then the country must prepare for not only a 50 percent drop in Catholic school enrollment but a substantial phasing out of the system that now holds several million Catholic pupils. The public schools could absorb such an influx over the decade with adequate planning and preparation. But the myths and rhetoric that now dominate the Catholic school debate will lead only to collapse, dislocation, and severe overcrowding in the public schools.

To prevent this collapse, the Catholic leadership must begin immediate, massive consolidation of Catholic schools. At the same time political leaders must tell Catholics how much public aid they can expect over the decade. The remaining aid alternatives should be tested in the courts. Only then can church leaders be freed from their current state of uncertainty. Only then can Catholics confront the present-day value of their schools and decide how much they would be prepared to sacrifice to preserve them if large amounts of public funds are not forthcoming.

# B. Recycling Values in an Age of Ecology

## 5.4 INTRODUCTION: VALUES FOR A POST-INDUSTRIAL ERA

According to an old Moslem legend, the people greatly honored a prophet named Hadji, and eagerly awaited his message to them. When the prophet arrived, he began his sermon with a question, "O true believers, do you know what I am going to say to you?" The congregation answered, "No," and Hadji replied, "Then truly there is no use in my speaking to you."

Some time later Hadji came again to address the congregation, and once more he began his message with the question, "O true believers, do you know what I am going to say to you?" The congregation responded in one voice, "We know! We know!" Then the prophet left the pulpit, saying, "Truly, since you know, why should I take the trouble of telling you?"

Then for the third and last time the prophet came to preach, and the people made extensive preparations for the occasion. When Hadji faced the congregation he again asked the same question, "O true believers, do you know what I am going to say to you?" From the congregation came shouts and cries, "Some of us know and some of us do not know." Then the prophet replied, "It is well in the sight of Allah, O true believers, that some of you know what I am going to say to you and some of you do not. Truly, therefore, let those who know tell those who do not know."

What is the lesson of this ancient fable? According to Carl Sandburg,[1] it is this: How wonderful it might be if we could sift out those who know from those who don't know. But there is no way to do this. Hence we must rely on free communication, on uncensored education, on open debate and public discussion, on the maintenance of an equilibrium between all the great forces and interests in our society. Truth is best found, not by submission, but by the exercise of independent judgment. Indeed, it is only by the exercise of such thought and freedom that man gains his true dignity and his fullest self-realization.

---

For a more adequate treatment of the title of this introduction, read Kurt Baier and Nicholas Rescher (eds.), *Values and the Future: The Impact of Technological Change on American Values,* New York: Free Press, 1969.

[1] Carl Sandburg, *Remembrance Rock,* New York: Harcourt Brace Jovanovich, 1948, pp. 885–886.

In civilized societies, men learn to discuss issues, to meet their opponents face to face, to examine competing hypotheses, to restudy their traditions, to picture a type of life more ideal than that to which they are accustomed. Out of such discussion gradually emerges a body of common opinion. Roman philosophers referred to it as "natural law." Anglo-Saxon jurists called it "common law." Contemporary educators speak of it in terms such as "consensus," "pragmatic agreement," or "judicial precedent." In thus clarifying their agreements and differences, men cease to be children: They learn to modify customs and traditions, and thus develop reason and humanity, the basic virtues of civilization. Paraphrasing Edwin Markham's poem "Outwitted," Horace Kallen has expressed the social side of democracy and science thus:

. . . other ways of thought and life draw circles which shut the differences out, as heretics, rebels, and things to flout, but democracy and science are the methods that win, for the circle they draw brings the differences in.[2]

A free society, like any other society, is held together by its traditions. But if the citizens of a free society are to cooperate with other citizens in striving for a widening social and moral outlook, then students in a free society should be encouraged to be free from a blind and unyielding acceptance of traditions. The earth does not become fruitful until torn up by the plow, nor can the mind of a student develop until challenged by new and unfamiliar points of view. A student should learn not only to answer questions, but also to question answers. Hence, writes William K. Frankena:

In the interests of freedom of conscience, thought, and worship, the public schools, being organs of the state, cannot teach religion. Like the state itself, they must be neutral with respect to the various churches and religions; they must be neutral even as between religion and antireligious philosophies of life. They can and should teach informative courses *about* religion—its history, beliefs, institutions, influences, etc.—but they may not seek to inculcate or propagate any particular kind of ultimate creed, religious or naturalistic. What J. S. Mill says about universities applies to public education as a whole:

. . . it is not the teacher's business to impose his own judgment, but to inform and discipline that of his students. . . . The proper business of a University is . . . not to tell us from authority what we ought to believe, and make us accept the belief as a duty, but to give us information and training, and help us to form our own belief in a manner worthy of intelligent beings. . . .[3]

---

[2] Horace M. Kallen, *Democracy's True Religion*, Boston: The Beacon Press, 1951, p. 10.
[3] The conclusion of W. K. Frankena in "Public Education and the Good Life," *Harvard Educational Review* 31: 413–426, Fall 1966. See also Cheong Lum, George Kagehiro, and Edwin Larm, "Some Thoughts on Moral and Spiritual Values in the Secular Public School," *Progressive Education* 30: 166–171, 192, April 1953.

With respect to open-mindedness and freedom of inquiry, democracy and science have much in common. Morris R. Cohen explains why the continual reevaluation of traditional beliefs is characteristic of modern science:

In former ages values were generally equated with church dogmas and with unchanging beliefs. Even today, there are Scholastics and Marxists who firmly believe that their Church and its God (or their Proletarian State and its inexorable triumph through the workings of Marxian dialectic) is the one and only repository of dependable values. For such persons, to "teach" values is not to "teach about" them. No. It is to "teach" them—by consent, if possible, but by indoctrination, if need be.

Reacting against such views, others insist that schools should never indoctrinate. And, since ours is a pluralistic society, and since the schools *can* teach students *how* to think (even if they cannot, with respect to values, teach them *what* to think), the proper approach to values in democratic education is to explain the *methods* whereby reasonable people arrive at

---

Man's ability to question that which he has from childhood been taught or accustomed to accept is very limited indeed unless it is socially cultivated and trained. It is a very rare individual who can perceive things for himself and trust his own experience or reason so as to question the currently prevailing views. For the typical Mohammedan child growing up in Central Arabia, there is no effective doubt possible as to whether Allah is the true God, and Mohammed his prophet. It is only when his community ceases to be homogeneous, when he comes into contact with those who do not believe in Mohammed, that doubt can take root and begin to flourish. Thus travellers, merchant adventurers, cosmopolitan cities, and the mixing of peoples having diverse traditions, play a predominant role as leaven in the intellectual life of mankind.

As the state of doubt is intensely disagreeable, communities try to get rid of it in diverse ways, through ridicule, forcible suppression, and the like. The method of science seeks to conquer doubt by cultivating it and encouraging it to grow until it finds its natural limits and can go no further. Sober reflection soon shows that though very few propositions are in themselves absolutely unquestionable, the possibility of systematic truth cannot be impugned. . . . Any contention that the whole body of scientific or demonstrative knowledge is false will be found to be in the long run humanly untenable, i.e., incapable of being held consistently with other propositions that claim to be true. Science can be challenged only by some other system which is factually more inclusive and, through the demand for proof, logically more coherent. But such a system would simply be science improved. Science must always be ready to abandon any one of its conclusions, but when such overthrow is based on evidence, the logical consistency of the whole system is only strengthened.

Progress in science is thus possible because no single proposition in it is so certain that it can block the search for one better founded. . . .

—Morris R. Cohen, *Reason and Nature: An Essay on the Meaning of Scientific Method,* New York: Harcourt Brace Jovanovich, Inc., 1930, pp. 83–86. By permission. See also M. R. Cohen, *The Faith of a Liberal,* New York: Holt, Rinehart and Winston, Inc., 1946, pp. 337–361; and Alan Wood, *Bertrand Russell, the Passionate Sceptic,* London: George Allen & Unwin, Ltd., 1957.

For expressions of the same viewpoint by two Catholic writers, read Gustav Weigel, S.J., "American Catholic Intellectualism," *Review of Politics* 19: 275–307, July 1957; and Julian Pleasants, "Catholics and Science," *Commonweal* 58: 509–514, August 28, 1953.

valid value judgments. Jerrold R. Coombs has summarized this viewpoint as follows:

> "What exactly are the legitimate objectives of value analysis in the class-room?" We have attempted to answer this question by examining the logic of value judgment and justification. In so doing we have argued the following points.
>
> 1. It is possible to describe our use of value language and the rules governing our reasoning about matters of value without thereby making any value judgments.
> 2. Value judgments are neither judgments of fact nor mere expressions of attitude.
> 3. Standards of rational value judgment can be specified but they apply to the process of value decision making not to the product of such a decision. These standards include:
>    a. The purported facts supporting the judgment must be true or well confirmed.
>    b. The facts must be genuinely relevant, i.e., they must actually have valence for the person making the judgment.
>    c. Other things being equal, the greater the range of relevant facts taken into account in making the judgment, the more adequate the judgment is likely to be.
>    d. The value principle implied by the judgment must be acceptable to the person making the judgment.
> 4. Since standards of rational value judgment can be specified the following objectives of value analysis in the classroom are defensible.
>    a. Helping students make the most rational, defensible value judgments they can make.
>    b. Helping students acquire the capabilities necessary to make rational value decisions and the disposition to do so.
> 5. There are no logical grounds for deciding that value criteria ought never to be taught nor for deciding that resolution of conflict about value matters is an illegitimate objective of value analysis.[4]

There is much to be said for this approach. It may be the only safe way to avoid indoctrination when dealing with students from a variety of competing value systems. But the approach has one major fault, which may be

---

[4] Jerrold R. Coombs (University of British Columbia), "Objectives of Value Analysis," in *Value Education: Rationale, Strategies, and Procedures*, 41st (1971) Yearbook, National Council for the Social Studies, Washington, D.C.: N.E.A., 1971, p. 27. Reprinted by permission of the National Council for the Social Studies and the author.

Somewhat similar approaches are to be found in Sidney B. Simon, Leland W. Howe and Howard Kirschenbaum, *Value Clarification: A Handbook of Practical Strategies for Teachers and Students*, New York: Hart, 1972; and in Louis E. Raths, Merrill Harmin and Sidney B. Simon, *Values and Teaching*, Columbus, Ohio: Merrill, 1966.

See also Barry I. Chazan and Jonas F. Soltis (eds.), *Moral Education*, New York: Teacher's College Press, 1973.

illustrated by the following story: A farmer who had never been further from home than his small rural village once boarded a train to New York so he could see New York City. On his return home he reported about the many interesting things he had seen—but it turned out that he had never been outside of Grand Central Station.

Grand Central Station is a very good starting point for anyone who wishes to see New York. But seeing Grand Central Station is not the same as seeing New York. Similarly, the method of logical analysis (exemplified in the quotation by Coombs) is a very good way to help students *approach* the study of how to study values. But an approach to the study of how to study values is not the same as a forthright examination of the values men and women actually hold.

The next selection (by Frankena) should make it abundantly clear that the approach to values by way of the method of logical analysis is only one of three major competing approaches (not counting Scholasticism or Marxism) which dominate twentieth century Western thought. If this anthology is to do justice to *all* of the many competing viewpoints which go to make up our pluralistic society, and if this chapter is to adhere to the stated purposes of this anthology as set forth in the Preface, then it cannot equate the many and varied values of our complex society with the particular values of any one philosophical school.

To accept a single viewpoint as the *only* legitimate one would be to return to the middle ages when fixed dogma and inflexible beliefs were thought to be the necessary basis for social unity. It is obvious that in modern times religion is often the cause of disunity. Jew and Gentile, Catholic and Protestant, Hindu and Moslem, theist and atheist—such divisions are pronounced that no one *religion* seems capable of forming a center for the many diverse beliefs of the modern age.

Does the absence of *religious* unity mean that we must therefore accept some philosophical school, such as logical empiricism, as the basis of unity? We think not. We believe that ours is a meeting-of-minds society grounded upon the conviction that opposing interests and conflicting viewpoints can and will be accommodated. Where this confrontation between opposing parties occurs, not with unequal weapons of force nor with concealed strategisms of trickery and deceit, but with man-to-man confrontations on the level of personality, intelligence and freedom, we have confidence that one-sided half-truths will gradually be replaced by more universal truths and that partisan interests will be persuaded to embrace values which can be shared by all men.

Accordingly, the selections which follow will present a broad panorama of beliefs and values—including the belief that a method of attaining values is more important than any other value. For, as the Moslem legend suggests, and as the quotation by Emerson in our Preface stated, it is out of the conflict of opposing beliefs and values that mature minds develop, and it is only mature minds that grow into responsible democratic citizens.

This is a much more ambitious and straightforward approach to value education than that of those who would have students merely study how we should approach the study of values. Were a student to ask such a teacher if he might study values the dialogue would be like that of the mother and daughter in the old song:

Mother dear, may I go swimming? Oh, yes, my darling daughter.
Just hang your clothes on a hickory limb—but don't go near the water!

In contrast, our approach is to ask the student to plunge in—to experience in any and every way he can those values which seem important to his fellow humans. Some of them will be the traditional ones, values found, for example, in the Vedas, in the Bible, in the Sayings of Confucius, in the Eightfold Path to Enlightenment of The Buddha, and in numerous other ancient traditions and treatises. Others will be new, such as those built around "the three P's" of our generation: over-Population, excessive Pollution, and lack of Peace. Our approach joins method with content; for, as in any other study, method without content is empty and meaningless, while a rigid content, which pays no respect to the methods by which the content (i.e., the values) are accepted, is blind. We leave unanswered and undiscussed the question, "At what age, or at what level in school, should problems of value be brought into the curriculum?" But, so far as this anthology is concerned, every chapter has been centered on differences of values.

# 5.5 EDUCATIONAL VALUES AND GOALS: THREE COMPETING CONTEMPORARY PHILOSOPHIES
## William K. Frankena

[This essay is concerned with the aims of education. I shall begin by examining] the three main movements in recent philosophy to see what habits or dispositions they would advocate [for the children in our schools]. The

Excerpt from William K. Frankena, "Educational Values and Goals: Some Dispositions to be Fostered." Reprinted from *The Monist* 52: 1–10, 1968, La Salle, Illinois, with the permission of the author and publisher. Reprinted in *Theories of Value and Problems of Education*, Philip G. Smith (ed.), Urbana, Ill., University of Illinois Press, 1970, pp. 110–118. Footnote references here omitted.

three movements I refer to are (1) Deweyan experimentalism, instrumentalism, or pragmatism, (2) analytical philosophy, and (3) existentialism (*cum* phenomenology). These, apart from Thomism and Marxism, are the main currents in western philosophy today. Let us consider first Deweyanism, the philosophical movement most familiar to American educators. What is characteristic here, so far as education is concerned, is its emphasis on what Sidney Hook calls, "the centrality of method," the method of reflective thinking, scientific intelligence, or experimental inquiry. The concept of the method, with its five stages, is well known. It is thought of as *the* method of thinking, and the main task of education is regarded as that of fostering the habit of thinking in this way in all areas of thought and action. Get the power of thinking thus, Dewey virtually said, and all other things will be added unto you. What interests me now is the fact that this habit of thought is conceived of as involving a whole family of dispositions: curiosity, sensitivity to problems, observational perceptiveness, regard for empirical fact and verification, imaginative skill at thinking up hypotheses, persistence, flexibility, open-mindedness, acceptance of responsibility for consequences, and the like. Being associated with thinking, these dispositions have a strongly intellectual cast, though Deweyans reject the distinction between intellectual and moral dispositions and think of them as at least quasimoral—and sometimes stress this practical aspect of them so much as to be charged with *anti*-intellectualism. They are dispositions whose matrix is the practice of empirical science. If we assume that this practice is one of the things human beings must be good at, then we may take this family of dispositions as among those to be fostered, even if we do not conceive of them exactly as Dewey did.

Analytical philosophy comes in various styles and must not be identified with either the logical positivism and therapeutic logico-analysis of yesteryear or the ordinary language philosophy of today. In one style or another it has become more or less dominant in British and American philosophy, and is beginning to be influential in the philosophy of education. Now, analytical philosophers of all sorts have tended to adjure the actual making or propounding of ethical, normative, or value judgments, and to be chary about laying down aims or principles for education and about making educational recommendations. They tend to limit philosophy to conceptual and linguistic analysis and methodological clarification. This attitude has been relaxing lately, but, in any case, there is a set of dispositions which are held dear by all analytical philosophers, no matter how purist: clarity, consistency, rigor of thought, concern for semantic meaningfulness, methodological awareness,

---

William K. Frankena, Professor of Philosophy at the University of Michigan, is author of *Three Historical Philosophies of Education: Aristotle, Kant, Dewey* (1965).

A more recent and more elaborate statement on this topic by Professor Frankena may be found in Howard Kiefer and Milton K. Munitz, editors, *Contemporary Philosophic Thought, Volume 3: Perspectives in Education, Religion and the Arts,* Albany: State University of New York Press, 1970, pp. 17–42.

consciousness of assumptions, and so on. These dispositions have been nicely characterized as "logical values" or "values in speaking [and thinking]" by J. N. Findlay. Typically, analytical philosophers think, with some justice, that these values have been neglected both in theory and practice by Deweyans and existentialists, as well as by speculative philosophers, Hegelian, Whiteheadian, etc.—and especially by nonanalytical philosophers of education. Whether they are right or wrong in this, it does seem clear that their values should be among our goals of education at all levels. The title of a recent book proclaims that clarity is not enough, and perhaps it is not, but it is nevertheless something desirable, and even imperative, both in our thinking about education and in our thinking about other things.

Existentialism is characteristically opposed both to analytical philosophy (though there are now some attempts at a rapprochement between these two movements) and to pragmatic empiricism. It is suspicious, among other things, of the "objectivity" so much prized, in different ways, by these other two movements. . . . [and] presents us with a third family of dispositions to be fostered: authenticity, decision, commitment, autonomy, individuality, fidelity, responsibility, etc. These are definitely moral (or, at any rate, "practical") dispositions as compared with the more intellectual, logical, or scientific ones stressed by Deweyan and analytical philosophers; but they are moral or practical dispositions that relate to the *manner* of life rather than to its *content*— not to *what* we do so much as. to *how* we do it. To quote a recent writer: "Existential morality is notorious for its lack of content. But it does not cease for that reason to be morality. Everything is in the manner, as its sponsors would, and do, say."

As one of these sponsors does say:

Value lies not so much in what we do as in how we exist and maintain ourselves in time . . . words like *authentic, genuine, real,* and *really* . . . express those more basic "existential values," as we may call them, which underlie all the valuable things that we do or say. Since they characterize our ways of existing in the world, they are universal in scope, and apply to every phase and region of our care. There is nothing that we say, or think, or do that may not be done either authentically . . . or unauthentically. . . . They are not "values" at all, in the traditional sense of this term, for they cannot be understood apart. . . . They are patterns of our lived existence in the world.

I do not wish to suggest that an "existential" manner or posture is enough, and certainly not that we should be in a state of "anxiety" all the time, but it does seem plausible to maintain that there is a place in education for the development of such "existential" virtues along with others supplementing or even modifying them. There is at least *some* point in "the underground man's" remark in Dostoevsky's *Notes,* "perhaps, after all there is more 'life' in me than in you."

Thus we see that even though representatives of all three of our philo-

sophical movements are typically reluctant to "talk about the aims of education," each movement itself enshrines or espouses certain dispositions that
may well be included among the aims of education by those of us who do not
mind such talk. The three philosophies are in general opposed to one another,
and one cannot simply combine them, but the dispositions they value may
be combined and included in our list of those to be cultivated in education,
though perhaps not without some pulling and hauling. This is the main point
I wish to make. I should like, however, to subjoin a few further points.

(1) Of course, we can espouse the Deweyan list of dispositions, even if
we do not conceive them exactly as he does, only if we assume that empirical
inquiry of a scientific kind is a good thing—sufficient, necessary, or at least
helpful to the good or the moral life. This, however, is an assumption that
would be denied only by certain extreme kinds of rationalism, irrationalism,
and otherworldliness. In the same way, an adoption of the analytical philosopher's list of dispositions as among those to be cultivated involves assigning
at least a considerable value to clarity, rigor, etc., an assignment which only
an extreme irrationalist could refuse to make, though, of course, those who
do make it will not all have the same conception of clarity or rigor. As for
the existential virtues—it looks as if they can and must be accepted in some
form by almost anyone who takes morality or religion seriously, that is, by
anyone whose approach is not purely aesthetic, conventional, legalistic, or
spectatorial.

(2) It seems to me that existentialism and its sisters and its cousins and
its aunts do not put sufficient store on rationality, meaning by this roughly
the set of dispositions prized by the Deweyans and the analytical philosophers
taken together. Indeed, they tend to suspect and impugn it. Yet, even if we
confine ourselves to the *how* of our approach to life and let the *what* take
care of itself, it seems at least irrational to nelect the virtues of logic and
science. To quote Israel Scheffler, "We are . . . faced by important challenges
from within and without . . . whatever we do, we ought, I believe, to keep
uppermost the ideal of rationality, and its emphasis on the critical, questioning, responsible, free mind."

(3) Even so, the existentialists . . . are perhaps right in feeling that the
values of rationality must at least be supplemented by those of commitment
and engagement, as S. T. Kimball and J. E. McClellan have argued, along
with many others who think that our western culture is in danger of being
overcome by its "committed" opponents. (In this perspective it is a bit iron-
ical that our "uncommitted" are precisely those who are most attracted by
existentialism.)

(4) Of course, if we try to combine rationality and commitment—the
first without the second being empty and the second without the first blind—
we must find some teachable kind of union of open-mindedness and belief,
of objectivity and decision. This is one of the crucial problems of our culture,
as has often been pointed out.

(5) In my opinion, none of the three families of dispositions includes enough emphasis on sheer (not "mere") knowledge, the intellectual virtue so esteemed by Aristotelians—not just knowing *how* (which was given a big boost by Gilbert Ryle) but knowing *that*, the kind of knowledge contained in the findings of history, science, and other cognitive studies (including knowing *why*). One reads, for example, that a college education must have as its goals "intellectual initiative and mature self-reliance," a statement which roughly synthesizes Dewey and existentialism, but there is enough "formalism" in me to make me convinced that education ought to promote not only certain "qualities of mind [and character]," but also certain "forms of knowledge," even if the knowledge must sometimes be second-hand and not acquired "by doing." To parody Bertrand Russell, the good life, moral and otherwise, is a life inspired by certain qualities of mind and character and guided by knowledge, . . . knowledge that is important both for the guidance of action and for the content of the good life. I therefore feel some agreement with Maritain when he writes that contemporary education has too much substituted "training-value for knowledge-value . . . mental gymnastics for truth, and being in fine fettle, for wisdom." As Jerome Bruner puts it: "Surely, knowledge of the natural world, knowledge of the human condition, knowledge of the nature and dynamics of society, knowledge of the past so that it may be used in experiencing the present and aspiring to the future—all of these . . . are essential to an educated man. To these may be added another: knowledge of the products of our artistic heritage. . . ." John Stuart Mill was, no doubt, right in attacking education that is "all *cram*" and does not provide "exercises to form the thinking faculty itself," but he went too far in adding, ". . . the end of education is not to *teach*, but to fit the mind for learning from its own consciousness and observations. . . . Let all *cram* be ruthlessly discarded." For Mill himself goes on to insist that each person must be "made to feel that . . . in the line of his peculiar duty, and in the line of the duties common to all men, it is his business to *know*." It seems to me to follow that there is place in education for some "teaching" and even some "cram." I grant it may be that, if we seek first to form the thinking faculty itself (i.e., certain qualities of mind), then all other things will eventually be added unto us, including knowledge. But must we wait until after school is over for them to be added? *Can* we?

A recent cartoon about education has a father saying to his child sitting in a high chair with his food before him, "Think. Assimilate. Evaluate. Grow." It seems to me that this is to the point as a spoof of a certain conception of education, since the word "Grow" does not add anything, and that a more sensible view would say, "Think. Assimilate. Evaluate. Know."

(6) There are, of course, certain other sorts of dispositions that must be added to the three families indicated above as goals of education. There are, first, moral dispositions relating to *what* we do and not merely to *how* we do it, e.g., benevolence and justice (i.e., knowing *what* to do and being dis-

posed to do it), second, the dispositions involved in aesthetic appreciation, creation, and judgment (not just "knowledge of the products of our artistic heritage"), and third, the dispositions required by the democratic way of life, so far as these are not already covered.

(7) In what I have said thus far, I have had *public* education primarily in mind. *Private* education, formal and informal, may add still another group of dispositions, namely, those involved in religious faith, hope, love, and worship. However, some care is needed, perhaps even some reconstruction, if one proposes to combine a Deweyan emphasis on scientific intelligence or an analytical philosopher's emphasis on clarity and rigor with anything like a traditional theistic faith. If one proposes to foster such a faith, one must at least give up trying to cultivate also a disposition to rely on logic and science *alone* as a basis of belief and action. If one wishes to insist on the necessity of the latter disposition, one must reconstruct the traditional conception of religion and God—as Dewey did in *A Common Faith.* Of course, if one means by religion merely some kind of basic commitment or other, or any kind of ultimate belief about the world whatsoever, or a vague "duty and reverence" (as Whitehead does), or simply whatever an individual does with his solitude (Whitehead again), then all education is and must be religious (as Whitehead says), even an atheistic or militantly antireligious one. Then "the Galilean" has indeed conquered, but then he has also become very, very pale—so pale as to be indistinguishable from or to his opponents. For, even if one has a "religious" belief in this wide sense, one may still also believe that

> . . . beyond the extreme sea-wall, and
> between the remote sea-gates,
> Waste water washes, and tall ships founder,
> and deep death waits. . . .

as Swinburne did. I say this because of what one finds in some discussions of the place of religion in public schools, where, from the premise that every ultimate belief is a religion, the conclusions are drawn, first, that religion both is and should be taught in public schools, and, second, that therefore theism (or Catholicism, Protestantism, and Judaism) may and should be taught there. As for private schools and colleges—whether they should in fact foster religious dispositions in a narrower theistic sense is too large a question to treat here.

# 5.6 DEMOCRACY'S SUPREME VALUE—
# A METHOD OF PEACEFUL SOCIAL CHANGE
## Neil H. Jacoby

It is widely believed that . . . changes in our social institutions are occurring too slowly . . . to accommodate [to the newer] goals, beliefs and expectations of the public. Hence the potentiality of a revolution—of a sudden drastic restructuring of our social institutions—is rising. Indeed, extremist groups

Neil H. Jacoby, "What Is A Sócial Problem?" Reprinted, with permission, from the July/August 1971 issue of *The Center Magazine*, a publication of the Center for the Study of Democratic Institutions in Santa Barbara, California.

Neil H. Jacoby is Professor of Business Administration, Graduate School, University of California, Los Angeles, and an associate at the Center for the Study of Democratic Institutions, Santa Barbara, California.

This anthology rests on the faith that the United States' constitutional system provides a framework within which revolutionary changes can occur without serious bloodshed. It is a faith well stated by Chief Justice Charles Evans Hughes on March 4, 1939:

> The most significant fact in connection with this anniversary is that after 150 years, notwithstanding expansion of territory, enormous increase in population and profound economic changes, despite direct attack and subversive influences, there is every indication that the vastly preponderant sentiment of the American people is that our form of government shall be preserved. . . .
>
> If we owe to the wisdom and restraint of the [Founding Constitutional] fathers a system of government which has thus far stood the test [of nearly two centuries of revolutionary change] we all recognize that it is only by wisdom and restraint in our own day that we can make that system last. If today we find ground for confidence that our institutions which have made for liberty and strength will be maintained, it will not be due to abundance of physical resources or to productive capacity, but because these are at the command of a people who still cherish the principles which underlie our system and because of the general appreciation of what is essentially sound in our governmental structure. . . .
>
> [In] the great enterprise of making democracy workable we are all partners: one member of our body politic cannot say to another—"I have no need of thee." We work in successful cooperation by being true . . . to the spirit which pervades our institutions—exalting the processes of reason, seeking through the very limitations of power the promotion of the wise use of power, and finding the ultimate security of life, liberty, and the pursuit of happiness, and the promise of continued stability and rational progress, in the good sense of the American people.*

*Address by Chief Justice Charles Evans Hughes at a joint session of the Executive, Legislative, and Judicial Branches of our government, commemorating the 150th birthday of our nation. Cited in Merlo J. Pusey, *Charles Evans Hughes*, New York: Macmillan, 1951 (two volumes), Vol. 2, pp. 783–784.

like the Weathermen and the Black Panthers, along with such mentors as Professor Herbert Marcuse, are actively fomenting revolution. They deliberately reject the course of working peacefully within the social system to shape its development along desired lines. . . .

A basic premise of our inquiry is that peaceful evolution is nearly always to be preferred to violent revolution as a path of social reform. Although revolution may in some circumstances be necessary, man's history shows that it is an extremely wasteful mode of social change. Revolution destroys physical and social capital and leaves in its wake a large reservoir of wrongs and inequities that require generations to liquidate. Evolutionary social change can avoid these setbacks. It can steadily augment social justice and material well-being. It can yield progress without hiatus. . . .

A social problem . . . may be defined as a gap between society's expectations of social conditions and the present social realities. Social expectations are the set of demands and priorities held by the people of a society at a given time. Social realities mean the set of laws, regulations, customs, and organizations, along with the pertinent economic, political, and social processes that prevail at a given time.

Social problems are created by public awareness of, or belief in, the existence of an expectation-reality gap. They are basically psychological phenomena—ideas held in the minds of people—about the disparity between what should be, and what is, in our society. Social problems are not definable solely in physical or biological terms, such as so many calories of food intake per day, or so many square feet of housing per capita. They must be defined in terms of the extent of the expectation-reality gap.

One may illustrate the independence of a social problem from any particular social condition by considering the example of poverty. Poverty is now perceived by Americans to be an important social problem in the United States, because in 1970 eleven per cent of the population had incomes under the official poverty level (about $3,500 per year for a family of four), whereas Americans generally believe that no one should live under the poverty line. Poverty was not perceived to be an important social problem in 1947, although twenty-seven per cent of the population then lived under the poverty line by 1970 standards. Despite an astonishing gain in the real incomes of those in the lowest brackets, public expectations outraced realities. Hence the expectation-reality gap with respect to poverty is wider today than it was in 1947. The problem of poverty has become more serious at the same time that the incidence of poverty has been cut sixty per cent and continues to decline.

Once the concept is grasped that a social problem is a gap between public expectations of social conditions and social realities, it becomes clear that our society, and especially its political leaders, must pay as much attention to the forces that determine public expectations as to those that shape social realities. They should seek to keep the gap at a tolerable size and thereby avoid violent or disruptive social behavior.

The expectation-reality gap is, of course, a dynamic system that changes through time. Public expectations change as a consequence of the expanding size and concentration of the human population, of rising affluence, or of technological advances. Thus, the high priority now assigned to the problem of environmental pollution reflects an elevation in the social expectations of clean air and water and other environmental amenities by a richer and more crowded population. Public expectations are also shaped by the flow of information, words, and pictures that they receive from the mass media of communication—newspapers, magazines, radio, and television. . . .

[As an example, consider] the 1968 Report of the National Advisory Commission on Racial Disorders, commonly known as the Kerner Report. Although this weighty document contained much wisdom, what stood out when it was issued was the inflammatory headlined statement that "this nation is moving toward two societies, black and white, separate and unequal." The vast majority of people who read this headline, but who did not read the whole report, concluded that the Kerner Commission found that racial inequality and separation in America was rising in all dimensions. The implications of the statement were extremely disruptive. By implying that the Establishment was failing to improve racial relations, and that the racial gap was widening, the Kerner Report added fuel to the fiery demands of militant groups for revolutionary changes. Seeds of bitterness were sown in the minds of the uninformed. Racial tensions were exacerbated at home. The nation was denigrated abroad.

Yet the truth is that our democratic political institutions and our market economy, despite imperfections, have been making steady progress in narrowing the economic, educational, political, and social inequalities between the races ever since World War II. The median income of nonwhite families rose from fifty-five per cent of that of white families in 1950 to sixty-three per cent in 1968; and, according to figures cited by Daniel Moynihan, the incomes of black young married couples had become equal to those of white young married couples in 1970. The proportionate reduction in poverty since 1959 has been almost as great among blacks as among whites. Whereas in 1947 black adult Americans completed thirty-four per cent fewer years of schooling than the entire population, by 1969 this difference had narrowed to nineteen per cent; and, for persons in the age bracket from twenty-five to twenty-nine years, it had nearly vanished. The differences between the life expectancies at birth of the two races diminished significantly during the postwar era. The steadily rising proportion of black citizens that are registered and vote in elections and of blacks in public office shows a narrowing of the political gap. Blacks themselves overwhelmingly believe that conditions are improving for their race in this country, as sociologist Gary T. Marx reported in his book *Protest and Prejudice*. All these facts demonstrate impressive postwar progress of the American Negro toward economic and political equality, although many will understandably say "too little and too late." The correct conclusion to be drawn, however, is to keep public policy on the present course and to try to accelerate its pace.

## Four Fallacies

The gravity of the nation's social problems is also enlarged by the teachings and writings of the liberal left. Much liberal left social thought is based upon illusory concepts of the nature of man and society, well described by Professor Harold Demsetz as the "Nirvana," "other grass is greener," "free lunch," and "people could be different" fallacies (*Journal of Law and Economics,* April 1960).

The "Nirvana" approach to social policy presents a choice between a theoretical ideal never approached in man's history and existing conditions. The vast distance between the two naturally creates a social "crisis." The true choice, however, lies between existing conditions and others that are feasible in the sense of being capable of attainment. Because the expectation-reality gap in the latter case is usually small, the "crisis" is reduced to a manageable problem.

The "other grass is greener" illusion credits an alternative social condition, usually in some foreign country, with great virtues said to be lacking in American society. Thus atmospheric pollution is said to be the product of capitalistic enterprise, and its cure is to adopt state socialism. This idea is repeated by social critics who have not taken the trouble to ascertain that pollution levels in socialist countries have risen, along with their G.N.P.'s, even faster than in capitalist countries.

The "free lunch" fallacy is that there are costless remedies for social ills. Since unemployment is an evil, say the critics, abolish it and reduce the unemployment ratio to zero. They choose to ignore the heavy social costs of such a policy in the form of restrictions on individual freedom, lowered productivity, and price inflation. Every decision that produces public benefits imposes costs, and the problem is to weigh both and determine the balance.

The "people could be different" fallacy is that the Good Society can be attained by radical changes in the moral and ethical behavior of people. Thus the "new communist man," imbued with a totally altruistic concern for the public welfare, was seen by the older Marxists as the condition for the ultimate transformation of socialism into true communism. Unfortunately, he has not yet appeared in sufficient numbers to make this possible; and he shows no sign of doing so. While moderate changes in men's values and behavior can occur over time (indeed, changes are essential if our society is to improve, sharp mutations in human nature are a fantasy. In reforming our society, we are wise to take human nature as a datum, and to design structures and processes for imperfect men and women rather than for saints and philosophers. . . .

Our society is a dynamic system in which public values and expectations and social institutions and processes change through time. The central aims of public policy should be to maintain an optimal expectation-reality gap and to achieve an optimal rate of change in both social expectations and social realities. . . .

The general strategy for approaching the optimum gap between expectations and realities will include the following elements: (1) accelerate desired institutional changes in the economic, political, and social systems to an optimum rate; (2) publicize the changes that are occurring in the society to reduce poverty, racial discrimination, crime, or to improve health, housing, and other conditions; (3) instruct the public in the political and economic processes of change and their time dimensions so that there will emerge a general appreciation of what is realistically possible; (4) develop through research more frequent and reliable indicators of social conditions and of the state of public expectations, and of their rates of change through time, as guides to social policymakers. Social scientists should also try to measure the sustainable rates of change in social institutions.[1]

---

[1] *EDITOR'S NOTE*: Compare the following statement by John Gardner:

[Many recent critics of our schools and of other democratic institutions] have fallen victim to an old and naive doctrine—that man is naturally good, humane, decent, just, and honorable, but that corrupt and wicked institutions have transformed the noble savage into a civilized monster. Destroy the corrupt institutions, they say, and man's native goodness will flower. There isn't anything in history or anthropology to confirm the thesis but it survives down the generations.

Those who would destroy the system also fail to understand that periods of chaos are followed by periods of iron rule. Those who seek to bring societies down always dream that after the blood bath *they* will be calling the tune; and perhaps that makes the blood bath seem a small price to pay. But after the chaos, no one knows what kind of dictator will emerge. The proposal to destroy the system dissolves under examination.

—John W. Gardner, *The Recovery of Confidence*, New York: Norton, 1970 (hardcover and paperback); slightly revised in Gary T. Marx, ed., *Racial Conflict: Tension and Change in American Society*, Boston: Little, Brown and Co., Inc., 1971, pp. 212–218.

For another realistic or nonutopian approach to social change, read George F. Kennan, "Rebels Without a Cause," *New York Times*, January 21, 1968; reprinted in George F. Kennan, *Democracy and the Student Left*, Boston: Atlantic Monthly Press, 1968, pp. 3–20.

# 5.7 REASON AND HUMANITY: TWO PERSISTING ENLIGHTENMENT VALUES
## David Fellman and Carl Becker

### FELLMAN

In many ways, democratic government asks much of people. Since it relies upon persuasion and reason, it asks them to do some thinking, and particularly, to think a great deal about difficult public questions. Every educator knows how very painful thinking really is, both for himself and his students. It can hardly be denied that many people have found a considerable measure of satisfaction in dictatorship because it releases them from the irksome obligation of thinking. Furthermore, democracy asks us to be tolerant even of those with whom we may be in sharpest disagreement. Since intolerance of dissident opinions is certainly as "natural" as tolerance, and in fact seems to require much less of an exertion of will, this too is asking a good deal of us. Democracy is incorrigibly skeptical and tends therefore to be unsatisfying for those who demand the security of a full set of the correct answers to all the questions which perplex the human race. Democracy is not so much concerned with correct answers as it is with a methodology for reaching essentially tentative decisions in a workaday world.

We have to recognize that the price we must pay for living in a free speech society is very great, though of course we are persuaded that the price is not too great. . . . Far more wonderful than our oversized automobiles, our television and air-conditioning, our jet planes and our hydrogen bombs, is the free human mind. Good government, the cultivation of the arts, the progress of the sciences and technology, all require an atmosphere of freedom of thought and of freedom to put thought into words. The price may seem to be a steep one, but what is purchased is the greatest bargain in all history.

This selection consists of two short excerpts. The first is from David Fellman, *The Limits of Freedom,* New Brunswick, N.J.: Rutgers University Press, 1949, pp. 122–123. The second is from Carl Becker, *New Liberties for Old,* New Haven: Yale University Press, pp. 149–150.

David Fellman is Professor of Law, University of Wisconsin.

Carl Becker (1873–1945) was for many years Professor of History at Cornell.

In *Children of Light and Children of Darkness* (1944) Reinhold Niebuhr wrote: "Man's capacity for justice makes democracy possible, but man's inclination to injustice makes democracy necessary." By "man's capacity for justice" we mean the "reason and humanity" possessed by most men—the virtues extolled by Professors Fellman and Becker in this selection. By "man's inclination to injustice" we mean what Lord Acton meant when he wrote: "Power tends to corrupt and absolute power corrupts absolutely."

When our nation was founded, democracy was viewed as an improvement over

## BECKER

To have faith in the dignity and worth of the individual man as an end in himself, to believe that it is better to be governed by persuasion than by coercion, to believe that fraternal good will is more worthy than a selfish and contentious spirit, to believe that in the long run all values are inseparable from the love of truth and the disinterested search for it, to believe that knowledge and the power it confers should be used to promote the welfare and happiness of all men rather than to serve the interests of those individuals and classes whom fortune and intelligence endow with temporary advantage —these are the values which are affirmed by the traditional democratic ideology. But they are older and more universal than democracy and do not depend upon it. They have a life of their own apart from any particular social system or type of civilization. They are the values which, since the time of Buddha and Confucius, Solomon and Zoroaster, Plato and Aristotle, Socrates and Jesus, men have commonly employed to measure the advance or

---

European political systems because it substituted what Jefferson called a "natural aristocracy" (i.e., an aristocracy of talent) for an aristocracy of birth or class. But during the past century there has arisen in America a new aristocracy, one originally based mainly on talent and wealth, but one which many believe (because of income and inheritance tax loopholes) is gradually becoming an aristocracy of blood. If it is, the words of John Stuart Mill stand as a warning:

> The moment a man, or a class of men, find themselves with power in their hands, the man's individual interest, or the class's separate interest, acquires an entirely new degree of importance in their eyes. Finding themselves worshipped by others, they become worshippers of themselves, and think of themselves entitled to be counted at a hundred times the value of other people; while the facility they acquire of doing as they like without regard to the consequences insensibly weakens the habits which make men look forward even to such consequences as affect themselves. This is the meaning of the universal tradition, grounded on universal experience, of man's being corrupted by power. [*Representative Government* (1860) Chapter VI].

To avoid such corruption, and to insure its own continued existence, democracy must harken to another famous adage: "Eternal vigilance is the price of liberty," about which Howard Mumford Jones has written:

> Intellectual liberty has always been a battle and a march. Persecution is the first law of society because it is always easier to suppress criticism than to meet it. Persecution is the direct, logical, and primitive expression of the herd. We take the first step away from the herd when we try to protect society against its own urge to destroy, by throwing the protection of law and custom around the malcontent, the lonely thinker, the passionate few, the minority group. When we do this, we make as great an advance in human culture as was made when mankind discovered the wheel.
>
> Unlike mechanical invention, however, intellectual liberty is not automatically self-evident. Now that we have the wheel, we are not likely to revert to the stone-boat. But society is continually under the pressure of numbers to revert to the herd. [*Primer of Intellectual Freedom* (1949), p. xiv].

the decline of civilization, the values they have celebrated in the saints and sages whom they have agreed to canonize. They are the values that readily lend themselves to rational justification, yet need no justification. No one ever yet found it necessary to justify a humane and friendly act by saying that it was really a form of brutality and oppression; but the resort to coercion in civil government, in war and revolution, in the exploitation of the poor or the liquidation of the rich, has always to be justified by saying that the apparent evil is an indirect means of achieving the greater or the ultimate good. Even the Hitlers and the Stalins, in order to win the support of their own people, find it necessary to do lip service to the humane values, thus paying the customary tribute of hypocrisy which virtue exacts from vice.

Whatever the limitations of reason may be, it is folly to renounce it, since it is the only guide we have—the only available means of enlarging the realm of scientific knowledge, the only means of discriminating the social value of the various uses to which such knowledge may be put. Whatever the limitations of reason may be, they are not so great that the civilized man cannot recognize the existence and the necessity of naked force and coercion in an imperfect social world, without attributing to them the creation of those humane and rational values which by their very nature affirm that naked force and coercion are at best necessary evils.

The case for democracy is that it accepts the rational and humane values as ends, and proposes as the means of realizing them the minimum of coercion and the maximum of voluntary assent.[1]

---

[1] *EDITOR'S NOTE*: This enlightenment ideal which Professor Becker reaffirmed in 1940 was eloquently stated by John Stuart Mill in his 1859 essay *On Liberty of Thought and Discussion*. Mill argued as follows:

There is the greatest difference between presuming an opinion to be true, because, with every opportunity for contesting it, it has not been refuted, and assuming its truth for the purpose of not permitting its refutation. Complete liberty of contradicting and disproving our opinion is the very condition which justifies us in assuming its truth for purposes of action; and on no other terms can a being with human faculties have any rational assurance of being right. Opinions which someone seeks to silence:

1. May be true. To deny this is to assume our own infallibility;
2. May contain a portion of truth needed to perfect the accepted (but not wholly sound) position;
3. May stimulate thought, may change prejudices into rationally based beliefs, and may replace formal professions, which are inefficacious for good, with heartfelt convictions.

Whether by Locke in the seventeenth century, Voltaire in the eighteenth, Mill in the nineteenth, or Fellman and Becker in the twentieth, the liberal spirit is characterized by an openness of mind, a passion for truth wherever it may lead, and an insistence on the free and unrestricted communication and criticism of ideas and institutions.

# 5.8 THE NEW NATURALISM
## Daniel Yankelovich

"Great ideas often enter reality in strange guises and with disgusting alliances." This phrase, from Whitehead's *Adventures of Ideas*, raises an intriguing question about the college youth movement. Whitehead was referring to the emergence in Western civilization of the idea of the essential equality of men, and to the vicissitudes of this idea over three millennia as our civilization moved from the presumption of slavery to the presumption of equality. Might the college student movement conceivably harbor an idea of comparable importance? Should its claim to transform our moral sensibilities and national life styles be taken seriously? Are we witnessing the growth of an authentic and, in the European sense of the word, *serious* movement in American history, or merely a nervous spasm elicited in response to the nervous-making events of our time?

In the course of our research with college students over the past seven years, I have gradually come to regard these questions as the most crucial ones that can be raised about the student movement. Critics of student protest have often let their prejudices and emotions interfere with their judgment. Those who are offended by the long hair, the rioting, the open sexuality, and the challenge to authority see only strange guises and disgusting alliances. Devotees of the counterculture, on the other hand, romanticize the movement and greet each strange new guise it assumes as the inspired expression of a great idea. But is it not possible that such judgments—on both sides—are half-truths which, even though they seem to contradict each other, actually form a single truth? Is it not likely, as Whitehead implies, that an important new idea struggling to gain clarity of expression will assume various transitional forms, some of them disturbing or even ugly and others contaminated by the circumstances of the moment? Indeed, do not *all* great ideas that find expression in mass movements first enter history in strange, transitional guises? . . .

Daniel Yankelovich, "The New Naturalism," excerpts from Part III (pp. 167–185) of *The Changing Values on Campus: Political and Personal Attitudes of Today's College Students*: A survey for the John D. Rockefeller 3rd Fund by Daniel Yankelovich, Inc., New York: Simon & Schuster (Washington Square Press edition), 1972. Copyright © 1972 by JDR 3rd Fund, Inc. Reprinted by permission of Pocket Books, a division of Simon & Schuster, Inc. Footnote references here omitted.

Author [with William Barrett] of *Ego and Instinct* (New York: Vintage Press, 1971), Daniel Yankelovich is Professor of Psychology at New York University and president of the social-attitudes research firm which bears his name.

This excerpt deals with only the positive or constructive aspects of the New Naturalism, and omits aspects which Dr. Yankelovich calls "not authentic."

The idea energizing the student movement . . . offers a banner around which young people, hungry for a new moral faith, can rally; and it promises to fulfill inherent human needs which are now being frustrated. Conceptually, the idea is neither wholly original nor yet a platitude. It has, in fact, been a recurring theme of our civilization for hundreds of years, though it has probably not been urged in so compelling and novel a form since the time of Rousseau.

The essence of the idea is that we must initiate a new stage in man's relatedness to nature and the natural. In the hierarchy of values that constitute man's conception of the *summum bonum*, the student-led cultural revolution elevates nature and the natural to the highest position. Whatever is "natural" is deemed to be good; whatever is artificial and opposed to the natural is bad. But what is natural and what is opposed to nature? The answer is by no means self-evident. . . .

Here are some of the varied aspects of "nature" and the "natural" which reside either implicitly in the student movement's philosophy of nature:

1. Moving the Darwinian concept of nature as "survival of the fittest" into the background; placing emphasis instead on the interdependence of all things and species in nature.
2. Placing emphasis on sensory experience rather than on conceptual knowledge.
3. Living physically close to nature, in the open, off the land.
4. Living in groups rather than as isolated individuals or in "artificial" social units such as the nuclear family.
5. Rejecting hypocrisy, "white lies," and other social artifices.
6. Deemphasizing realms of knowledge illuminated by science; instead, celebrating the unknown, the mystical, and the mysterious elements of nature.
7. Emphasizing cooperation rather than competition.
8. Embracing the existentialist emphasis on being rather than doing or planning.
9. Deemphasizing detachment, objectivity, and noninvolvement as methods for finding truth; arriving at truth by direct experience, participation, and involvement.
10. Looking and feeling natural, hence rejecting makeup, bras, suits, ties, artificially groomed hairstyles.
11. Expressing one's experience nonverbally; avoiding the literary and the stylized as artificial and unnatural; relying instead on exclamations, silence, vibrations, and various nonverbal forms of expression to communicate and respond.
12. Rejecting "official" and hence artificial forms of authority; authority is to be gained by winning respect and is not a matter of automatic entitlement by virtue of position or official title.
13. Rejecting mastery over nature, emphasizing harmony with nature.
14. Deemphasizing organization, rationalization, cost-effectiveness.

15. Emphasizing self-knowledge, introspection, discovery of one's natural self.
16. Emphasizing the community rather than the individual.
17. Rejecting mores and rules that interfere with natural expression and function (e.g., conventional sexual morality).
18. Emphasizing the preservation of the natural environment at the expense of economic growth and technology.

These varying conceptions of nature and the natural grow out of, and are a reaction against, the dominant modes of thinking in American culture as represented by technology, rationalism, and traditional middle-class sensibility. Here is a random concatenation of words and phrases that capture as well as any formal definition the sensibility which the student's cultural revolution rejects:

Professional . . . system . . . planning for the future . . . conceptual framework . . . experiment . . . organization . . . detachment . . . management . . . verification . . . facts . . . technology . . . cost-effectiveness . . . theory . . . rationalization . . . efficiency . . . measurement . . . statistical controls . . . manipulate . . . mechanization . . . institutions . . . power . . . determinism . . . intelligence testing . . . abstract thought . . . programming . . . calculate . . . objectify . . . . . . behaviorism . . . modification of the human environment . . . liberal . . . molded to specification . . . genetic planning . . . achievement.

The counterculture is well named: it defines itself, at least in part, in terms of what it opposes. And what it opposes constitutes a huge part of our culture. Yet, as the varied definitions of nature and the natural listed above suggest, the positive side of the counterculture, though often submerged beneath its oppositional tendencies, is the more signficant one. We would like to call special attention to three themes in the new naturalism of the student movement—the stress on community rather than on the individual, the apparent anti-intellectualism and emphasis on the nonrational, and the search for sacredness in nature.

## The Community vs. the Individual . . . .

["Community," says Robert A. Nisbet,] "encompasses all forms of relationships which are characterized by a high degree of personal intimacy, emotional depth, moral commitment, social cohesion, and continuity in time. Community is founded on man conceived in his wholeness rather than in one or another of the roles, taken separately, that he may hold in a social order. It draws its psychological strength from levels of motivation deeper than those of mere volition or interest, and it achieves its fulfillment in a submergence of individual will that is not possible in unions of mere convenience or rational assent. Community is a fusion of feeling and thought, of tradition and commitment, of membership and volition. It may be found in, or be given symbolic expression by, locality, religion, nation, race, occupation or crusade. . . ."

[Today's youth] identify the desire for power as destructive of the sense of community they deem so important. They see it as anti-egalitarian and unnatural.

Their deep mistrust of power draws on a long tradition. Psychologist Alfred Adler, writing in Germany in the early 1920's spoke of "this poison of craving for power." Anticipating the counterculture, he saw the quest for power as responsible for the destruction of all spontaneous human relationships. For Adler, the striving for power, especially personal power, is a "disastrous delusion." The simplest means to everything seems to be by way of power, but this "simplest means" always leads to destruction. All too often, the ideal of our times is the isolated hero for whom fellowmen are mere objects. The sickness of our civilization, in Adler's view, flows directly from the high valuation we place on power and on individualism at the expense of community. Power, in other words, belongs with the despised and rejected idea system: individualism/egoism/manipulation-of-others/isolation/power. It is antithetical to the system: community/service/care-for-other/preservation-of-nature. . . .

The task of restoring, preserving, and creating new forms of community has, in fact, haunted the Western mind ever since the Middle Ages. It is as if the great victories in succeeding centuries won by Protestantism, individualism, rationalism, science, and industrialization all were gained at a terrible cost—the sacrifice of community. The cost was minimized in the headiness of newly won freedom, democracy, and material progress. Yet, as our history unfolds, the élan of our technological/materialist society wears down. A terrible loneliness and sense of isolation breaks through at the society's greatest points of vulnerability. In our present type of society, many of the human bonds of community—bonds seen as so necessary to the spirit as to be constitutive of all that is humanly natural—have come apart. Ordinary human decency, repose, and stability depend on restoring them.

Some such notion of community—its roots in human nature, its pivotal importance, its opposition to individualism, and its terrible absence in our society—lies at the very heart of the student conception of nature and the natural. Hume was the first of the modern philosophers to stress as inherent and "natural" human characteristics the qualities of goodness, giving, and cooperation—qualities implied by the student use of community. In our day, society is seen by the student movement as suppressing these qualities as ruthlessly as the cramping moral codes of the Victorian era suppressed sexuality.

## The Nonrational

Perhaps no other aspect of the cultural revolution is as poorly understood—and as widely misinterpreted—as student mistrust of rational, conceptual, calculative, and abstract modes of thought. Faculty scholars, in particular, are appalled at the seeming anti-intellectualism of the counterculture with its stress on sense experience and what often seems to be an ideological commitment to inarticulateness.

The scholarly professor of English Literature begins to wonder about his own sanity after a long day's experience with the glories of the English language being reduced to a repetitive series of "like," "you know," "freaked out," etc. The historian questions his own commitment to the past after spending months with students for whom only the present and the future seem to exist. Time itself loses its ordered sequence, becoming a patternless series of quantum leaps from one sensory immersion to another.

The student movement reserves its most brutal shock, however, for those logically minded managers, technologists, engineers, professors of business administration, planners, accountants, experimenters, and quantifiers for whom rational, orderly, and logical methods are the royal road to truth. For these professionals—and they are the men who keep our society running—student disdain for rational procedures is incomprehensible. In such attitudes, should they be generalized, they see the destruction of all they have built. And they are probably correct. . . . [because, as] our society is presently constituted, service to one's fellowman, offered with compassion but without knowledge, can be a menace to both giver and recipient. Carried to its extreme, rejection of concepts, technique, professionalism, know-how, and methods of rationalization can be sloppy and self-defeating. Unless the cultural revolution is to be confined to enclaves of elitist dropouts with well-heeled parents, it must learn to coexist with the technological thrust of our society.

If the new naturalism as an idea system is to have a constructive impact on the society, it must presuppose the existence of an affluent economy with a technological base. Charles Reich to the contrary, Consciousness III cannot thrive unless Consciousness II also thrives. The relationship between them is symbiotic, not mutually exclusive.

With these qualifications registered, we come to our main point which is that the student critique of the rational, the technical and the abstract is not mainly negative; indeed, it is not a *vote against* but a *quest for* other modes of understanding. Some of the greatest philosophers of our century, notably Wittgenstein, Heidegger, Whitehead, and others, have performed their own critique of so-called rational thought and have arrived at conclusions not that different from those embraced by the counterculture. Coming from widely divergent traditions of philosophy, these seminal thinkers concur on one central conclusion; namely, that our equation of abstract logical thinking with knowing, with truth, and with rationality itself is based on a profound misunderstanding created by fallacies built into the epistemological assumptions of the past three hundred years of Western philosophy and science.

The marriage of abstract thought with quantitative methods—what might be called "McNamaraism" even though McNamara himself has now transcended his own methodology—creates a remarkably restricted mentality.

When applied to certain narrow problems of logistics or of conditioning pigeons in the laboratory it can be excellent. But it fails utterly when social/ political reality is to be grasped, Vietnam being an example. An argument can be made that rigid adherence to McNamaraism, far from being the essence of rationality, is itself a virulent form of irrationalism. There is something irrational about the evangelical dogmatism of the B. F. Skinners and the other Dr. Strangeloves of our era who, skimming the surface of reality and imposing upon it the most doctrinaire of *a priori* premises, insist upon their approach as the one and only True Method. Let us not make the mistake of equating what they are doing with reason itself.

The mathematician Marston Morse once said, "The creative scientist lives in 'the wildness of logic' where reason is the handmaiden and not the master . . . I believe that it is only as an artist that man knows reality."

Morse's conclusions, shared by many creative scientists often after long agony of introspection about how their discoveries were actually made, is that the logical, orderly, abstract processes of explicit reasoning are merely the surface manifestations of rationality. They presuppose other, less well-organized forms of experience which arise out of an immediacy of involvement, a total engagement of the mind and senses with the subject being studied. This type of involvement is the opposite of detachment and sequential logic. Without it, technical reason is doomed to perform its sterile operations in a vacuum. Reason is trivial when cut off from its grounds in direct experience.

The counterculture grasps this important truth, even though it chooses to ignore the complementary truth that direct experience undisciplined by technical reason can also be a treacherous master leading to slovenly mysticism and ultimately to a breakdown of communication. Both forms of thought are as necessary to create understanding of reality as both sexes are needed to create new life. . . .

## The Sacred

The search for the sacred in nature—the third major theme in the cultural revolution's system of ideas—shares many of the same characteristics as the concern with reason and the nonrational. There is the same partial truth, the same unrealistic turning of one's back on what has already been accomplished—but also the same unerring aim at one of the most dangerous and critical imbalances in our American culture.

The point can be conveyed by contrasting a windmill with a bulldozer. The windmill has to accommodate itself to the wind and the terrain. To fulfill its function as a windmill it has to fit into a part of nature; it makes use of this region even as it accommodates itself to it. It also makes use of the wind. But it uses the wind in such a way as not to consume it. The wind continues on and remains the wind. The windmill can use the wind only by giving itself to it; it lets the wind be wind. In putting the wind to use, it does not suppress, repress, or otherwise level or convert the wind into something else.

The bulldozer is a human artifact of a very different kind. Its name conveys appropriately the idea of power: it does not accommodate itself to the objects of nature, but overpowers them. It bursts through obstacles, pushes them aside, levels them. The word "leveling" is significant here: as it levels, the bulldozer reduces trees, hills, and terrain into a uniform rubble. This rubble, of course, can become the side on which roads and houses are built. The human habitat is thus extended a little farther over the earth. All of this we unquestioningly call progress. The bulldozer has powers of transforming the conditions of life quite beyond the feeble achievements of the old-fashioned windmill.

But power is accompanied by responsibility. The uprooting of trees leads to soil erosion, inadequate drainage and easy flooding. A superhighway becomes a congested procession of automobiles and trucks belching fumes and noise. Nearby communities, which once had a life of their own, are transformed into mere traffic intersections. The bulldozer has the power to create new conditions of life, but also to disrupt the whole fabric of life which already has a balance of its own. A fateful burden weighs upon the wisdom of the men who make use of it.

By contrast, a mistaken windmill has no such frightening possibilities. Perhaps the windmill has been put up in the wrong place to catch enough of the wind, or it is too far from the convenience of the neighboring farmers. But no permanent damage has been done. The mistakenly built windmill has not disrupted irreparably the life of the community around it. It need not even be taken down. It may be left where it is, an attractive though not very useful edifice gracing a landscape. On the other hand, the consequences of the misuse of the bulldozer are not so easily amended. In some cases, indeed, they might be irreparable. The windmill may well be a symbol of an archaic past—gentle, old-fashioned, and somewhat ineffectual; but the bulldozer is not necessarily a mark of progress in human evolution. . . . Just as we should never use people merely as tools but regard them as ends in themselves, so now we must extend this moral imperative to nature. If human life is to be regarded as sacred, so is nature itself sacred. It cannot and must not be bulldozed into oblivion. Our very survival depends upon it not being bulldozed.

In summary, then, a preoccupation with nature and the natural, a tendency to romanticize nature, a striving to live in harmony with nature, an invidious contrasting of the virtues of natural man and the natural life with the corrupting influences of civilization—these are constant and recurring themes in Western intellectual history. But the stress on nature as it occurs in the student movement adds a vital new dimension to this tradition, one that cannot be dismissed as a mere romantic reaction to technological/materialist culture. It represents a basic shift in man's conception of himself and his place in the universe. . . . [It represents a] changing conception of man's relationship to a nature that is no longer seen as infinite, brutish, and something to be mastered with the bulldozer, but as finite, precious, fragile, and essentially good. We are being asked to stop our frantic rush to bend nature to the human will and instead to restore a vital, more harmonious—and more humble—balance with nature.

# 5.9 SOME AMERICAN INDIAN VALUES
## Harold Cardinal

From the beginning, the Indian accepted the white man . . . [and] helped him overcome his weaknesses in trying to make his way in our environment. We taught him to know our world, to avoid the pitfalls and deadfalls, how to trap and hunt and fish, how to live in a strange environment. Is it too much to ask the white man to reciprocate?

An Indian looks at nature and sees beauty—the woods, the marshes, the mountains, the grasses and berries, the moose and the field mouse, the soaring eagle and the flitting hummingbird, the gaudy flowers and the succulent bulbs. He sees an overall fitness, an overall collective beauty, but he looks deeper. He sees the beauty of the individual components of the big picture. He sees the diversity of the various elements of the entire scene. He admires the grace of a leaping deer, the straight-line simplicity of the pines the deer leaps through, the jagged, three-dimensional thrust into the sky of the rugged peaks, the quick silver flash of a trout on the surface of a wind-rippled lake. He turns a sensitive ear to the faraway eerie wail of the loon and the nearer snuffling grunt of a bear pawing at a ground squirrel's den, and he blends them into the whispering of grasses and the bolder talk of the tall pines. He feels the touch of wind against his cheek and the coolness of the mist above the rapids. He surveys the diversities of nature and finds them good.

Harold Cardinal, *The Unjust Society*, Edmonton, Canada: M. G. Hurtig, Ltd., 1969. Excerpts from pp. 78–89, 132, 51, 61, 1–3. By permission. Harold Cardinal, born in 1945, is president of the Indian Association of Alberta, and a member of the board of the National Indian Brotherhood of Canada.

The reader may wonder why a Canadian author is included in an anthology on American education. The reason is that, with respect to the Indians at least, the two nations are quite similar. To verify this point, read Lehman L. Brightman, "Mental Genocide: Some Notes on Federal Boarding Schools for Indians," *Inequality in Education*, No. 7, February 10, 1971, pp. 15–19. See also Vine Deloria, Jr., *Custer Died for Your Sins*, New York, 1969, especially Chapter 3 "Laws and Treaties" and Chapter 5, "Missionaries and the Religious Vacuum."

An Indian thinks this might be the way of people. He knows that whites and Indians are different. He knows that there are differences even within these larger groups, differences between Scot and Ukrainian, between Cree and Iroquois. He knows there are differences between man and his brother, red or white.

To the Indian this is the natural way of things, the way things should be, as it is in nature. As the stream needs the woods, as the flowers need the breeze, as the deer needs the grasses, so do peoples have need of each other, and so can peoples find good in each other. Indians are close to nature, so it is natural for them to see the bigger world in terms of the small world they do know. They know that men of different cultures and races have much to offer one another. We offer our culture; we offer our heritage. We know it is different from yours. We are interested in your culture and your heritage; we want you to discover ours. . . .

Long before the white man came to the new world, Indians held ceremonies of thanksgiving and of spring's coming. There were sacrifices and offerings and prayers to win favour or appease the spirits. There was the shared suffering with the Great Spirit that came with the self-torture of the sundance and other religious ceremonies.

True, not all Indians were monotheistic; many attributed spirit or soul to everything animate and many things inanimate, but nearly all shared concepts of a Great Spirit dominating all other spirits. Whether he was called Manito, Orenda or Wakanda, the Great Spirit of the Indian was much like the Mana of the Polynesian or the God of the white man.

The Indian believed in the spirit of brotherly love, in the principle of sharing, in the purification of giving, in the good sense of forgiving.

The Indians developed prophets and seers who were akin to holy men, who served their people as healers and sorcerers, who were both good and evil. These were the medicine men.

The medicine man held great power in the Indian society. A medicine man of strong character quickly became a social and political leader of his people as well as a spiritual advisor. In a modern white village he would be a combination of the mayor, the local general practitioner and the local minister of the only church in town. He was the renaissance man of the Indian society. . . .

The first missionaries found the way almost prepared for them. They received a warm reception from the heathens and savages who weren't, after all, so heathenish or savage that they didn't welcome the message of a loving Jesus. The Indian was the first member of the ecumenical movement. He was willing to accept the white missionary's message of love for his fellow men, because it came as a complement to rather than a contradiction of the Indian way of life. The fact that the missionary lived with the people, shared their hardships, learned their language, suffered with them when the hunt was unsuccessful and rejoiced with them when things went well proved a tremendous asset in his work of conversion. Because he lived as one of them, the early missionary was able to move easily into the position of medicine man and was able to take over most of his roles. The new values brought by the white man seemed similar to their own and the Indians trusted their new teachers, put great faith in their message. The missionary became the new social and moral conscience of the Indian.

Because of the missionary's position in the band, he was able to ease the way for the coming of the fur trader, the settler, the white police, the new law bringers. Since he was part of the new force, the missionary gradually took over the medicine man's role as law enforcer. With his cachet of medical aids, more sophisticated than those of the medicine man, he took over the final stronghold of the now-deposed tribal leader.

Certainly for the first generation of converts, the switchover from indigenous beliefs to those of Christianity was relatively smooth. The advance work by the missionaries enabled the churches to move in and carry on what amounted to immersion courses in their respective faiths. The transition was smooth for the Indians since none of their beliefs were stretched too far in the new direction. They dovetailed rather than clashed.

But the white missionary did not come, pure and simple, in the spirit of brotherhood. He came stealthily in the spirit of Christian brotherhood, a different concept. He came to preach his way and to convert, and he cared little even when he understood that his way disrupted the savage society.

As the missionary gradually pushed his only rival, the medicine man, out of the teepees and lodges, he began to introduce his own European value system. The missionary and the trappers and settlers who followed him laughed at the Indian version of religion, scoffed at the all-important visions and dreams, defied the ancient taboos without visible harm and brought with them dread new illnesses like smallpox, measles and influenza, which no combination of medicine-man herbs, roots and berries could cure.

The white religion was a religion of concern with the hereafter; the Indian way was more concerned with the practical everyday interplay of action between man and his familiar spirits. Slowly the Indian found the new faith perverting his ancient beliefs from a religion of action in everyday life to a religion of thou-shalt-nots. The new religion focussed on abstractions; the old religion had been oriented toward people. The old religion of the Indians' forefathers slowly was twisted into moral positions that had little relevance to his environment, twisted to fit seemingly senseless white concepts of good and bad. Pragmatic ethics and the morality enshrined in the Indian's code by his environment were replaced with a concern for good and evil that was foreign to the Indian.

The missionaries, either Roman Catholic or Anglican in the early days, were horrified when they learned that the medicine men were dispensers of birth control means. And they found other pagan practices to preach against. They scoffed at Indian offerings to lesser gods; they mocked propitiation of the spirits of animals killed for food or fur; they scorned the medicine man's posturing and costumes.

Some Indians felt that their old gods were better for Indians and the new ones better for white men but, generally, the Indian who clung to the old ways was left behind. He was denied the medicine of the old ways because the medicine man, once all-powerful, was stripped of his authority. An Indian's refusal to accept the new, stronger medicine of the white man left him, too, naked and defenceless.

The Indian was forced to put his trust in the new white medicine man. But when the missionary shoved the old medicine man aside he failed to fill all of the void left. He disrupted Indian society by removing from it the checks and balances that had been maintained under the old system. The missionaries' treatment of the second generation of Indian converts began to show a marked difference.

The missionary was there to convert the Indian. To convert him he had to care for him. To care for him in modern terms meant to educate the illiterate, leaderless Indian youth. The government shrugged aside responsibility for Indian education, quite content to let the church do the job. So it happened that the early spiritual goal was translated into educational objectives that proved disastrous to the Indian. The church's idea of education never progressed far beyond simply training the Indian to make him an easier convert.

The church, following the missionary into the Indian community, worked hand in hand with existing government officials in plotting the life of the Indian. There was a state of interdependence between the forces of church and government. The government needed the church to control the Indians by persuading them to live peacefully on reservations and encouraged the church to assume full leadership responsibilities. The church needed the power of the government to ensure that law enforcement powers would be at their disposal to force children to attend the residential schools churches were setting up. The churches further persuaded the government to pass legislation outlawing remnants of surviving Indian religious ceremonies, thus speeding conversion. The *Indian Act* of the 1920s and 1930s thus contained legislation forbidding some aspects of the sundance and the potlatch.

Collusion of church and state was supposed to facilitate the development of good Christian brown white men. The churches' perverted interest in education resulted in the neglect of the spiritual needs of the Indian communities. The development of the residential school system eroded the vital Indian family unit. Propagation of Christian beliefs rather than the dispersal of knowledge aimed at teaching the Indian to adjust to the new non-Indian society became the educational goal of the church schools.

Residential school was no bed of sweet balsam for the young Indian student. Often as early as the age of five, he was yanked forcibly from his parents' arms and taken scores of miles away to the residential school, where a system of harsh discipline combined with an utterly foreign environment quite literally left him in a state of shock. . . .

The children were not allowed to speak in their own language. Their teachers, unlike the early missionaries, made no attempt to understand the native tongue. They couldn't even be bothered to learn the children's names and gave them instead easier-to-pronounce Christian names. . . .

Let it be acknowledged that the missionary teacher acted (usually) out of the best of motives but brought about the worst of all results: a Christian without character. By taking the child through his formative years, the church school deprived him of the social training he would have received at home and needed in order to fulfill his responsibilities to his kin and to members of his society. He was deprived of the opportunity to learn his role and his relationship to members of his community. He was turned toward a life that was foreign to him and one that he could not be a part of. But he was a stranger to his people upon his return. The child went to school an Indian. The young man emerged a nothing. . . .

Whether or not the churches today have the honesty to admit their responsibility for many of the social problems that exist in the native world, the Indian still accuses them. . . . If the Great Spirit is dead the Indian knows who killed him. It was the missionary. If the church is not dead it most certainly is dying, and the Indian knows what poison worked here, too— the missionary.

If there is still a place in modern-day Indian society for the church, that place must be found and designated by the Indian. The church is so discredited in native society that quite possibly its smartest move in the long run would be to cease all its activities on behalf of native peoples. After a time, provided a new approach relates to the spiritual and moral needs of our people, the church might be able to find a new purpose and acceptance. . . . Many authorities foolishly believe that genuine integration can be imposed upon the Indian people from the top, through means which can only be termed unscrupulous and devious. To the Indian mind, integration—or assimilation —has no more rightful place in government programming than would an attempt to integrate Roman Catholics and Jehovah's Witnesses. And about as much chance of succeeding.

The whole question of education has to be rethought in the light of the total needs of the Indian people. The obvious first step is the transfer of power from the people responsible for the administration of education to the people whose lives will be determined by it. No educational programme can be successful and, it follows, no society can be successful, where the people most directly concerned and affected have no voice whatever in their own education. . . .

Many bureaucrats feel that Indians are not yet ready to assume control of the education of their children but, we ask, how could even the most stupid Indian create a worse mess than has been handed him by the missionaries and bureaucrats over the past one hundred years? As long as the government persists in using education for its own designs, education will continue to be an unpleasant, frightening and painful experience for Indian children who have little reason to like or be interested in school anyhow. . . .

It sometimes seems to [Canadian] Indians that Canada shows more interest in preserving its rare whooping cranes than its Indians. And Canada, the Indian notes, does not ask its cranes to become Canada geese. It just wants to preserve them as whooping cranes. Indians hold no grudge against the big, beautiful, nearly extinct birds, but we would like to know how they managed their deal. Whooping cranes can remain whooping cranes, but Indians are to become brown white men. The contrast in the situation is an insult to our people. Indians have aspirations, hopes and dreams, but becoming white men is not one of them. . . .

For Indians . . . [the nineteenth century slogan] "The only good Indian is a dead Indian" . . . [is not very different from the twentieth century attitude that] "The only good Indian is a non-Indian."[1]

---

[1] *EDITOR'S NOTE*: With respect to cultural assimilation, the contrast between the American Negro and some American Indians is quite significant. In an article on "The Right not to Assimilate" (*Social Science Review* 35: 135–143, June 1961, by permission of the University of Chicago Press and of the Phelps-Stokes Fund) Alexander Lesser shows that accommodations and adjustments to our industrial society by many Indian communities is not accompanied by correlated changes in their basic Indian attitudes of mind and personality: ". . . They choose principally what we call material culture and technology and little of our sentiments and values and our philosophy of life. . . . [Many Indians] want and need the freedom to be Indians within the framework of America. . . The disappearance of our Indian communities by assimilation has a crucial finality that assimilation can never have for other American minorities. Irish, or German, or Scandinavian, or Italian immigrants who become assimilated can still look toward a homeland from which they came, a viable tradition and culture which dignifies their origins. For the Indian, the tribal community is the only carrier of his tradition; if it disintegrates and disappears, his tradition becomes a matter of history, and he loses part of his identity. We are coming to know the importance of this sense of identification with a viable tradition in the meaning of Israel for many American Jews, or of the emergence of free African nations for many American Negroes. . . . [The white man's policy toward the Indians should be] to stop hampering their efforts to work out their own destiny, and especially to stop trying to make them give up their Indian identity. In a world which may be moving toward greater internationalism, in which we hope that peoples, however diverse, will choose the way of democracy, we cannot avoid the responsibility for a democratic resolution of the American Indian situation. Our attitude toward the Indians, the stubbornest non-conformists among us, may be the touchstone of our tolerance of diversity anywhere."

For an excellent discussion of the conflict between traditional Indian values and the economic values of those using Indian territory for strip mining, read Alvin M. Josephy, Jr., "The Murder of the Southwest," *Audubon* 72: 52–67, July

1971. For recent attempts to free Christian theology from the imperialism which characterized the Constantinian era of Church history, and from the economic and cultural imperialism which has characterized modern missionary Christianity, read Joseph Sittler, "Two Temptations—Two Corrections," *National Parks* 45: 21, December 1971. There are dozens of excellent books on ecology which deal with these problems in great detail.

---

# 5.10 ECUMENISM AND THE CULTURAL REVOLUTION
## M. M. Thomas and Gregory Baum

---

### THOMAS

All over the world, the necessity of modernization of traditional societies, and the search for the higher reaches of development by modernized societies, have led to the breakdown of the traditional integration between religion, society and state and to the assertion of the autonomy of culture from religious control. . . . [The] societies which are today emerging everywhere are secular, technical, and pluralistic, in their main features; and broadly speaking, the role of religions has to be exercised at the level of inspiring and moulding the mind and spirit of men and cultural institutions, without controlling them. At least this is the direction in which all societies seem to be moving. . . .

I would like to affirm that through the revolutions of our time, men are seeking a fuller and richer human life, a greater fulfillment of their humanity. We may discern this struggle of men for their fuller humanity at four levels.

*First*, there is everywhere the search for human freedom understood as creativity. Men want the freedom to create new things, new societies, new

This selection consists of two excerpts. The first is from M. M. Thomas, "Ecumenism and the Cultural Revolution," *Religious Education* 42: 93–97, March–April 1967. Used by permission of the publisher, the Religious Education Association, New York City.

M. M. Thomas is Director, Christian Institute for the Study of Religion and Society, Bangelore, India. He was Henry W. Luce Visiting Professor of World Christianity at Union Theological Seminary, New York, 1966–1967.

The second portion consists of two statements by Gregory Baum, O.S.P., editor of *The Ecumenist*, and professor of Theology, St. Michael's College, University of Toronto.

The two statements by Father Baum are from *The Ecumenist: A Journal for Promoting Christian Unity* 5: 33–36, March–April 1967, and 1: 73–75, June–July 1963. By permission of *The Ecumenist*.

cultures and new purposes. In fact if we look at the last three to four hundred years of modern history, men have revolted against religions primarily because in the name of a fixed divinely ordained order they prevented men's creativity in science, arts, and morality. In fact, many doctrines of the creator-God have been so defined as to give no room for the creativity of men, so that men had to revolt against God himself to affirm human creativity. In a sense, the process of secularization in the modern world and a good deal even of militant secularism have been primarily an affirmation of man's humanity as essentially creative.

*Secondly*, today everywhere there is the search for freedom as the awareness of a responsible selfhood. Self-determination, self-development and self-identity are phrases charged with great meaning in the life of individuals as well as groups in the modern world. Men and women ask for their fundamental rights of responsibility as human persons. Nations and races and cultures are in the struggle for their self-identity and for the power and responsibility to exercise their selfhood.

*Thirdly*, there is among all people the search for a love which is different from paternalism. Paternalism is a form of love, no doubt. But today, it appears to men and women in all situations to be lacking in true reverence for the dignity of the person. Young people revolt against paternalism in the family; and there is revolt against paternalism of caste, class and race. In fact we shall misinterpret even the struggle of the poorer classes, races and nations against poverty, if it is seen only as a search for bread to satisfy hunger. Of course it is that, but it is the search for bread as the expression of justice to man's manhood.

*Fourthly*, men everywhere have become conscious of a sense of history. On the one hand, there is the awareness of a universal history of mankind, and, on the other, every nation, race and group is becoming conscious of its own historical mission and vocation in the world, and is struggling to define it.

In this seeking for creativity, selfhood, love and historical mission, men are driven in the deepest levels of their spirit by the vision of new dimensions of human existence; and this new humanism is the spiritual ferment within the cultural revolutions of our contemporary world.

## BAUM

Religious convictions are regarded as fanatical when they prevent a man from being open to others, block his ears, and always make him misunderstand what others are saying. . . .

Man comes to be a person through dialogue with others. Man is a listener summoned to respond, and his responses constitute him in his personal being. . . .

Man is an open-ended being. He is involved in an unending dialogue which makes him to be who he is. Man is forever led into new situations, he listens to a summons that does not come from himself, and by responding to it he determines his existence as a person. . . .

Man is not an individual who grows by focussing on himself. Man does not achieve well-being by straining narcissistically after self-fulfillment. Man is a person, and hence he becomes more truly himself through communion with others. The center of man is outside of himself. . . .

Since institutions are made to promote man's life in society, they inevitably reflect the understanding of man that is current at the time they are created. The institutions in the Church—seminaries, monasteries, convents, ecclesiastical government and law courts—embody and promote the ideal of man as it was conceived at the time when they received their definitive shape. What is happening today is that with a new self-understanding many Christians find that these institutions no longer adequately promote human life. This is the deep cause for the restlessness in the Catholic Church. The present institutions of the Church operate on an anthropology that is no longer ours. . . .

Vatican Council II attempted to modify ecclesiastical institutions by making them correspond to the new anthropology. The liturgy (in the vernacular) was to make men into listeners and brothers. Participation was the key concept that inspired all the changes in institutions, whether these had to do with worship, ministry, religious life, or ecclesiastical government. Institutions in the Church must allow Christians to participate; and it is through the very process of participation that men are renewed, made sensitive to the Spirit, and open to one another. This ideal of participation in ecclesiastical institutions exists, so far, mainly on paper.

Protestant leaders and spokesmen of other religions have repeatedly expressed their hope that the Second Vatican Council define the Church's position on religious liberty. They realize that two distinct views on this matter are taught by Catholic theologians in our century. Some theologians, the representatives of the older school, assert that error has no rights, and therefore in "Catholic" countries governments should not tolerate Churches teaching erroneous doctrines. In such countries, they teach, the government should protect and advance the true religion. Only when Catholics are in a minority is religious liberty a good to be striven for, since in that situation it will favor the true Church. Other theologians, belonging to the new school, the majority position today, teach that religious liberty is a good promised by the gospel, to be announced and defended by the Church in whatever situation she finds herself. These theologians reject the idea that "error has no rights," since error is an abstraction and since people who err do have rights. These theologians derive their understanding of religious liberty from the notion of man and the notion of faith revealed in the Scriptures and taught by the Church. Man is created by God to seek him with his mind and heart and this requires freedom; and the very notion of faith, through which man is reconciled and united to his God, implies a free search and a free surrender. Man can be faithful to his destiny only if he follows his good conscience. From this understanding of the gospel, these authors would say that interference and pressure by governments in the area of religion is never legitimate, except temporarily in unusual circumstances, when the exercise of a religion should interfere with the public welfare of society.[1]

---

[1] *EDITOR'S NOTE:* To more fully appreciate the meaning of Father Baum's theological position, consider the Catholic position of 1948 as it appeared in Rome in the Jesuit fortnightly *La Civiltà Cattolica:*

"The Roman Catholic Church, convinced, through its divine prerogatives, of being the only true church, must demand the right to freedom for herself alone, because such a right can only be possessed by truth, never by error. As to other religions, the church will certainly never draw the sword, but she will require that by legitimate means they shall not be allowed to propagate false doctrine. Consequently, in a state where the majority of the people are Catholic, the church will require that legal existence be denied to error, and that if religious minorities actually exist, they shall have only a *de facto* existence without opportunity to spread their beliefs. If, however, actual circumstances. . . . make the complete application of this principle impossible, then the church will require for herself all possible concessions. . . .

"In some countries, Catholics will be obliged to ask full religious freedom for all, resigned at being forced to cohabitate where they alone should rightfully be allowed to live. But in doing this the Church does not renounce her thesis. . . . but merely adapts herself. . . . Hence arises the great scandal among Protestants. . . . We ask Protestants to understand that the Catholic church would betray her trust if she were to proclaim . . . that error can have the same rights as truth. . . . The church cannot blush for her own want of tolerance, as she asserts it in principle and applies it in practice." *Time* 51: 70, June 28, 1948.

Such intolerance of Catholic toward Protestant, and of Protestant toward Catholic, still survives in Northern Ireland in the year 1973. But such intolerance—and such inhumanity—are as nothing compared to the treatment of the American Indian by the Catholic Hernando Cortez in Mexico or by the Protestant Andrew Jackson in the United States. If the Christian religion is an integral element of Western Civilization, then a revision of Christian theology is a most urgent need. For an excellent discussion of this problem, read René Dubos, *The God Within,* New York: Scribners, 1972.

For expositions of related theological viewpoints, read Gregory Baum: *Man Becoming: God in Secular Experience,* New York: Herder and Herder, 1970, especially pp. 185–238; Jurgen Moltmann, *Theology of Hope,* London: SCM Press, 1967, especially pp. 230–238; H. Richard Niebuhr, *Radical Monotheism and Western Civilization,* Lincoln: University of Nebraska Press, 1960, especially pp. 87–99; M. M. Marty and D. J. Peerman, eds., *New Theology No. 5,* New York: Macmillan, 1968, especially pp. 79–89.

# 5.11 TOWARD A WORLD CIVILIZATION
## Huston Smith

About the middle of the century, Arnold Toynbee predicted that for another hundred years historians would still be interested primarily in the continuing impact of the West upon Asia, but that two hundred years down the line they would be more involved with the answering impact of Asia upon the West; and two thousand years down the line (only Toynbee could venture to look that far ahead) historians would look back on the twentieth century as the one in which mankind took its first concerted steps toward the creation of a genuine world civilization.

Of course, it is too early to anticipate in any detail what the contours of this emerging world civilization will be, but not too early, I think, to ask what the great enduring civilizations have to contribute to it.

I take as my basic assumption that man is inescapably engaged in three basic conflicts: 1) with nature, 2) with his fellow-men, and 3) with himself. Roughly, these may be identified as man's natural, social, and psychological problems. The great surviving cultural civilizations are also three—the Chinese, the Indian, and the Western. It helps us to understand and relate the unique perspectives of these three civilizations if we think of each as accenting one of man's basic problems. For, generally speaking, the West has attended more assiduously and with higher expectations to the problem with nature, China with the social, and India with the psychological.

Beginning with the West, I think what distinguishes Western civilization has been its conviction that human fulfillment is to be sought naturalistically. By this is meant not only *in* nature but *through* nature. Three ideas arose indigenously in the West and nowhere else: the individual, faith in historical progress, and modern science. Each of these is related to one of nature's three components: space, time, and matter. If anything has no location in space, or cannot be identified in time, or has no material component, then we are inclined in the West to say that if it exists, it is not part of nature; it is supernatural.

There is a connection between each of the great discoveries of the West and each of the components of nature. Science bears an obvious correlation with matter. Scrutinize the material world carefully enough and sooner or

Huston Smith, "Toward A World Civilization." Reprinted with permission from the March/April 1967 *Center Diary*, a publication of the Center for the Study of Democratic Institutions in Santa Barbara, California.

Huston Smith teaches philosophy at Massachusetts Institute of Technology. He was previously professor of philosophy at Washington University, St. Louis, and has been visiting lecturer at the University of Colorado and visiting professor of theology at the Iliff School of Theology.

later the patterns of connection and correlation begin to emerge, and one finds the way to modern science. [Similarly with space and time.][1] . . .

Why the West turned in the direction of nature we shall never fully know, for its origins, like all origins, are veiled in the twilight of early history. But its basic interest in and high regard for nature seem traceable to the hospitality of its cradle environment, significantly christened the "Fertile Crescent." Here nature almost coaxes inquiry and certainly rewards advances. Western man accepted her overtures; from the first, his primary curiosity was directed outward, toward nature. His growing feeling was that everything is orderly, exact, measurable, impartial.

Perhaps the most important factor, however, was not geography but theology. For, of the three great civilizations, the West is the only one that regarded nature or the cosmos as the deliberate creation of a being perfect both in will and in power. The very first verse of the West's Bible proclaims that "in the beginning God created the heaven *and the earth*," and when at the close of the chapter he looks upon "every thing that he had made," earth included, "behold it was very good." Furthermore, the goodness of earth lies not only in beholding it but in working with it: man is commissioned to "have dominion over . . . the earth." The incarnation pays matter its highest conceivable compliment—it can become divine. The Kingdom of Heaven, from Jewish and early Christian revelation down to the social gospel, is to come on earth. Even in death, the West will not desert the body. If there is to be life after death, it, too, must be in some sense physical: "I believe . . . in the resurrection of the body." All of this, then, invests the natural world with a dignity not really to be found to the same extent in the attitudes of other civilizations.

What gave the West its interest in time, or progress—here we are clear-

---

[1] *EDITOR'S NOTE*: Significantly different from other cultures of ancient times, the Hebraic and the Hellenic world views were also radically different from one another. The dynamism of western thought may be a result of the tension between these two powerful, yet rival, points of view. The anthropologist Robert Redfield has written:

> The mutual involvement of God and nature is . . . pretty plainly a common characteristic of most primitive or ancient world views. Sky and god, rain and deity are somehow together, aspects of the same thing. The radical achievement of the Hebrews in putting God entirely outside of the physical universe and attaching all value to God is recognized as an immense and unique achievement. And the fresh beginning of Greek science in conceiving a universe in which order was immanent without any reference to God at all is also recognized as exceptional and extraordinary. These two tremendous transformations in world view within our own heritage . . . are opposite and complementary transformations of earlier world views. The one, by the Hebrew, made God all important. The other, by Greek and modern, made God unnecessary.

—Robert Redfield, *The Primitive World and Its Transformations*, Ithaca, New York: © 1953 by Cornell University. By permission of Cornell University Press, 1953, 1957, p. 102.

est—is that one of its major components, namely the Hebraic perspective, arose through the concrete historical event of the exodus. The exodus gathered the milling tribe together and gave them a sense of peoplehood and destiny. One looks in vain in either Indian history or Chinese history for a single historical event that initiated a perspective comparable to the exodus. But there is another point about time in the West. The West is the only civilization whose perspective continues to be molded by a people—the Jews —who in their formative period were for the most part either displaced or oppressed persons. This experience made of the Jews a people in waiting. The Jews were always waiting for something—to cross over into Jordan, to get back to the Promised Land, to throw off the yoke of the oppressor. This waiting quality gives to the Jewish mind a future orientation which eventuates in the idea of the prophet. The idea's specifically Jewish form is messianism, its Christian form is the Second Coming, its secular form is the idea of historical progress, and its heretical form is the Marxist dream of a classless society.

Finally, . . . [of] the three great civilizations, the Western is the one that has been historically the frontier civilization, moving first from the eastern shores of the Mediterranean around towards the western shores and then up into the largely uninhabited swamps and marshes of Europe, and finally skipping across the ocean to the New World.

Now let us swing across the huge Eurasian land mass over into China. . . . [The Chinese] had a different racial stock, the Mongolian; a different mode of writing, digraphs rather than an alphabet; a different mode of eating, chopsticks instead of fingers as in Southeast Asia or utensils as in Europe. But those are surface features. What is interesting is the distinctive fundamental option of these people in their search for human fulfillment.

I think that the Chinese option was to build the good life through building the good society. Nature, for some reason, never appeared to the Chinese mind as lending itself to alteration for improvement. Against nature the most that could be hoped was a holding operation. It never occurred to the Chinese mind that life could be improved by changing the basic relationship between man and nature. So they turned toward society, where they had a wonderful opportunity. They were a homogeneous racial stock, because Mongolians were all very much alike, and so these black-haired sons of Khan set themselves to perfecting human relationships. Their basic technique was to identify those values they felt would be most worth developing in human relations and then to turn all the powers of education, formal and informal, toward internalizing these values in every Chinese citizen.

One of the most important principles that guided the Chinese in their social relations was that the group had priority over the individual. Whereas in the West we think of the individual as the basic unit of social reality and of groups as relations into which individuals enter and out of which they may pass, the Chinese turn this around. For them the basic unit of social reality is the group. For certain purposes individuals may be abstracted in thought but these abstractions have no reality apart from the concrete whole. The individual has no more viability in his own rights than an eye when plucked out of its orbit.

When the Chinese went on to ask which group is most important, they didn't hesitate to answer "the family." To move beyond the family to society, they thought it had to be a class society. . . .

When the Chinese asked how the classes should be layered in regard to prestige and emoluments, they put the scholar-administrator at the top; he was the most valuable person because he orchestrates, as it were, the human resources. The West, of course, has the ideal of the philosopher-king, but it has not made as concerted an effort as China did to realize that ideal— not that it was fully realized in China either, but it was at least more of a practical working ideal than it has been in the West.

Following in the order, next, were the producers, first the farmers and then the artisans, and under them the merchants. This meant that production was more important than distribution. In the West, since industrialization, this has not been so; hence, the sales force in our modern corporation occupies an importance at least equal to that of the production force: We can produce as much as we want to—the problem is to get it distributed. But in traditional China the ever-present problem was to get enough, not how to get it around.

Last in the class scale was the soldier; the man of violence seems to be necessary somewhere, but his role is never really creative. Part of all this was the belief that education was central in the social system, and the heart of education was not merely intellectual education but moral education.

Turning last to the third great civilization—the Indian—we find neither the natural nor the social environment looking promising to her. India's natural environment is different from but no more friendly than China's. The tropical region of the Ganges with its thick vegetation, unbearable humidity, and burning heat, the parching dryness of other regions, where for ten months of the year there is nothing but the nightly dew to quench the thirst of the ground—the Indian environment is one of fierce extremes. Discouraged by the overpowering forces of nature, Indian man surrendered his initiative and turned away from nature. His outlook became unrealistic in the technical sense. The desert, particularly, must have discouraged him. Facing nature in this form, gaunt, bleak, desiccated, dangling its haunting mirages—no wonder the Indian began to think: Nature is ungovernable and, in some strange way, unreal. She is shadowy, ever-shifting, mysterious, horrible if you will, but what is the use of trying to find out her laws. It is all *maya*. It is all magic, a trick, the play of a mysterious cosmic illusion.

Faced with a seemingly intractable nature, China turned her attention to society. But in this area India found herself facing the most devilish of social problems—a color-culture barrier. The distinction between Aryan and Dravidian was clear, and to this day—3500 years later—the line persists. No Indian ingenuity was adequate to break this curse. Caste tried to do so, but instead of caste's remedying the evil, in the end the evil took over caste, turning it into a device for perpetuating social distance. Relatively early, then, India lost hope of solving life's problems on the social frontier. Instead, she turned inward, centering her attention on the psychological problem. If we could only understand who we truly are we might win an inner freedom beyond the opposites that block both nature and society.

Thus, the Indians became introspective psychologists, perhaps the world's greatest. . . . [For example,] Indians have seen far more clearly than we have that the subconscious, besides being pathological, can also be healthy. When it is, it works for us beyond the powers of the conscious mind, balancing to a degree the damage it can do if it is pathologic. The West has tended to forget that doctors deal with sick patients; as a doctor, Freud dealt mainly with sick subconscious minds and he gave us a brilliant typology of the ways in which the pathological subconscious can create trouble. But what is equally true, that the subconscious can work in our behalf when it is healthy, perhaps only the frontier scientist and the really creative artist in the West understand. . . .

Gordon Allport of Harvard has noted that Indian psychology is alive to four goals of life: pleasure, worldly success, duty, and liberation. Allport goes on to say that Western psychology has a lot on the first goal—pleasure for pleasure's sake. The psychology of worldly success we also know pretty well; we are able to motivate people toward worldly achievement. But when it comes to duty, the West has only a nickel's worth in its concept of the super-ego. And with regard to liberation, virtually nothing in Western psychology speaks profoundly to that goal. . . .

Each of the three great civilizations has achieved notable results with one of man's basic problems, but each also has been brought to the brink of ruin by not attending sufficiently to the other two problems. The obvious conclusion is that an adequate world civilization must strike all three notes as a chord.

# 5.12 THE CARE AND FEEDING OF A SMALL PLANET
## Barbara Ward and René Dubos

The astonishing thing about our deepened understanding of reality over the last four or five decades is the degree to which it confirms and reinforces so many of the older moral insights of man. The philosophers told us we were one, part of a greater unity which transcends our local drives and needs. They told us that all living things are held together in a most intricate web of interdependence. They told us that aggression and violence, blindly breaking down the delicate relationships of existence, could lead to destruction and death. These were, if you like, intuitions drawn in the main from the study of human societies and behavior. What we now learn is that they are factual descriptions of the way in which our universe actually works.

Both the development of atomic science and the piecing together of the planet's and of man's evolution—master intellectual achievements of modern times—have provided a solid basis for a completely new appreciation of the unity, interdependence and precariousness of the human condition. And since this reality comes to us with all the weight of scientific proof and cogency, we can hope that it will be more convincing than was the earlier, less scientifically substantiated knowledge. The unraveling of atomic structure and the unfolding of our biological history thus offer a remarkable paradox. On the one hand, nuclear power gives man the means of self-annihilation. On the other, the delicacy and balance of the evolutionary process offers him the perspective he needs to avoid planetary suicide.

This warning and this hope echo in the ancient wisdom of all the earth's great cultures. But perhaps because Western man has been largely responsible for opening up the furnaces of nuclear power and for penetrating to the most intimate mechanism of life, it is in Western tradition that we find the most urgent warnings against arrogant and unheeding power. For the Greeks it is Prometheus, stealer of fire, who is chained to the rock. Nemesis in the shape of shrieking, destroying harpies follows the footsteps of the overmighty. In the Bible, it is the proud who are put down from their seats; the exalted are those of humble spirit. At the very beginnings of the scientific age, in the Faustian legend, it is the man of science who sells his soul to secure all knowledge and all power.

Reprinted from *Only One Earth* by Barbara Ward and René Dubos by permission of W. W. Norton and Co., Inc. © 1972 by Report on the Human Environment, Inc.

Barbara Ward (Lady Robert Jackson) is at the School of International Affairs, Columbia University. René Dubos is Professor of Biology at Rockefeller University, New York. Both writers have authored many books.

All this does not imply a retreat from the fantastic achievements of science or scepticism concerning its immense possibilities for future use. The scientific method employed now to decipher not the separation but the inter-connections of material things can provide men with better, more reliable and wiser means of working with his environment. Nature has so many unstable, unpredictable and violent facets that man needs all his probing intelligence and enormous potentiality for understanding to enhance and stabilize its capricious bounties. In fact, in Goethe's retelling of the Faustian legend, the end is not torment but redemption—when Faust at last uses his powers not for aggrandizement but to drain a marsh and feed the people.

But the warning remains. Powers on such a scale require the furthest reach of wisdom, detachment and human respect in their exercise. If man continues to let his behavior be dominated by separation, antagonism and greed, he will destroy the delicate balances of his planetary environment. And if they were once destroyed, there would be no more life for him.

It is sometimes said of those who try to persuade man of his environmental predicament that they paint a picture so gloomy and irreversible that the average citizen's response is to go out and buy a can of beer. If nothing can be done to escape the onward rush of some irresistible eco-doom, then why take the trouble even to return the can? But indeed over a vast range of environmental problems, action *is* possible, policies *are* available, reversals can take place, water run clean, the sun shine over clear cities, the oceans cleanse "Earth's human shores" and harvests ripen in uncontaminated fields.

Indeed, some nations and other jurisdictions already are launched on effective planning and pollution control programs. Already some cities enjoy cleaner air than they knew three or four decades ago. Rivers are being cleaned up and fish are returning to them. There are places where rangelands are managed properly, where soil erosion, has been stopped, wildlife is preserved and timberland carefully reforested. There are even examples of reversing the deterioration of inner cities. And all this has been done within the limits of existing knowledge, known techniques, and institutional capabilities.

If men have not hitherto realized the full extent of their planetary inter-dependence, it was in part at least because, in clear, precise, physical, and scientific fact, it did not yet exist. The new insights of our fundamental condition can also become the insights of our survival. We may be learning just in time. . . .

The first step toward devising a strategy for Planet Earth is for the nations to accept a *collective* responsibility for discovering more—much more —about the natural system and how it is affected by man's activities and vice versa. This implies cooperative monitoring, research and study on an unprecedented scale. It implies an intensive worldwide network for the systematic exchange of knowledge and experience. It implies a quite new readiness to take research wherever it is needed, with the backing of international financing. It means the fullest cooperation in converting knowledge into action—whether it be placing research satellites in orbit or reaching agreements on fishing, or introducing a new control for snail-borne disease.

But it is important not to make so much of our state of ignorance that we are inhibited from vigorous action now. For while there is much that we do not yet understand, there are fundamental things that we *do* know. Above all, we know that there are limits to the burdens that the natural system and its components can bear, limits to the levels of toxic substances the human body can tolerate, limits to the amount of manipulation that man can exert upon natural balances without causing a breakdown in the system, limits to the psychic shock that men and societies can absorb from relentlessly accelerating social change—or social degradation. In many cases we cannot yet define these limits. But wherever the danger signals are appearing—inland seas losing oxygen, pesticides producing resistant strains of pest, laterite replacing tropical forests, carbon dioxide in the air, poisons in the ocean, the ills of the inner cities—we must be ready to set in motion the cooperative international efforts of directed research which make available, with all possible speed, solutions for those most intimately concerned with the immediate problem and wider knowledge for all men of how our natural systems actually work. To go blindly on, sharing, inadvertently, the risks and keeping to ourselves the knowledge needed for solutions can only mean more agonies than we can cope with and more danger than future generations deserve.

A full and open sharing of new knowledge about the interdependence of the planetary systems on which we all depend can also help us, as it were, to creep up on the infinitely sensitive issues of divisive economic and political sovereignty.

Given our millennial habits of separate decision-making and the recent tremendous explosion of *national* power, how can any perception of the biosphere's essential unity and interdependence be combined with the acutely self-conscious separate sovereignty of more than 130 national governments?

Yet, in fact, for at least a century, some habits of cooperation have been accepted by states simply through recognition of their own self-interests. Ever since the world economy began to increase in extent and interdependence in the eighteenth and nineteenth centuries, sovereign states have shared some of their authority either by binding themselves to certain forms of cooperative behavior or by delegating limited power to other bodies. Despite rhetorical insistence on absolute sovereignty, governments have recognized in practice that this is impossible in some cases and inordinately foolish in many more. It is no use claiming the sovereign right not to deliver other people's letters if they use their sovereign right to refuse yours. The alternative to international allocation of radio frequencies would be chaos in world communications to the disadvantage and danger of all states. In brief, when governments are faced with such realities, they have exercised their inherent sovereign right to share voluntarily their sovereignty with others in limited and agreed areas of activity.

In the twentieth century, as a consequence of an ever greater overlap between supposedly sovereign national interests, the number of international treaties, conventions, organizations, consultative forums and cooperative programs has multiplied rapidly. The growth of an intergovernmental community finds its most concrete expression in the United Nations and its family of specialized functional agencies and regional commissions. Outside the United Nations system, there has been an analogous growth of international organizations, governmental and non-governmental, especially on the regional level.

All intergovernmental institutions are still, ultimately, creatures of national governments, but a large amount of their day-to-day work is sufficiently and obviously useful that a measure of authority and initiative comes to rest with them . . . [until] literal definition of sovereignty gets blurred in practice and the existence of continuous forums for debate and bargaining helps instill the habit of cooperation into the affairs of reluctant governments.

It is onto this scene of ultimate national sovereignty and proliferating intermediate institutions that the new environmental imperatives have broken in the last few years. . . . A rash of environmental councils and commissions is now appearing round the world to coordinate the activities of hitherto separate ministries. Several countries have taken the bolder step of bringing relevant ministries — housing, transport, technology — together in single Departments of the Environment. The various experiments are mostly not yet two years old, and it is too soon to say how well they may succeed in introducing an integrative view of man-environment relations into the national decision-making processes. Certainly it will not be easy.

And certainly it will be still more difficult at the international than at national levels of decision-making. So locked are we within our tribal units, so possessive over national rights, so suspicious of any extension of international authority that we may fail to sense the need for dedicated and committed action over the whole field of planetary necessities. Nonetheless there are jobs to be done which perhaps require at this stage no more than a limited, special and basically self-interested application of the global point of view. For instance, it is only by forthright cooperation and action at the global level that nations can protect mankind from inadvertent and potentially disastrous modification in the planetary weather system over which no nation can assert sovereignty. Again, no sovereignty can hold sway over the single, interconnected global ocean system which is nature's ultimate sink and man's favorite sewer.

Where pretensions to national sovereignty have no relevance to perceived problems, nations have no choice but to follow the course of common policy and coordinated action. In three vital, related areas this is now the undeniable case—the global atmosphere, the global oceans, and the global weather system. All require the adoption of a planetary approach by the leaders of nations, no matter how parochial their point of view toward matters that lie within national jurisdiction. A strategy for Planet Earth, undergirded by a sense of collective responsibility to discover more about man-environment relations, could well move, then, into operation on these three fronts: atmosphere, oceans and climate. It is no small undertaking, but quite possibly the very minimum required in defense of the future of the human race.

But it is not only the pollutions and degradations of the atmosphere and the oceans that threaten the quality of life at the planetary level. There are threats, too, of disease spreading among undernourished children, of protein deficiency maiming the intelligence of millions, of spreading illiteracy combined with rising numbers of unemployed intellectuals, of landless workers streaming to the squalid cities and worklessness growing there to engulf a quarter of the working force. An acceptable strategy for Planet Earth must, then, explicitly take account of the fact that the "natural resource" most threatened with pollution, most exposed to degradation, most liable to irreversible damage is not this or that species, not this or that plant or biome or habitat, not even the free airs or the great oceans. It is man himself.

Here again, no one nation, not even groups of nations, can, acting separately, avoid the tragedy of increasing divisions between wealthy "North" and poverty-stricken "South" in our planet. No nations, on their own, can offset the risk of deepening disorder. No nations, acting singly or only with their own kind, rich or poor, can stave off the risk of unacceptable paternalism on the one hand or resentful rejection on the other. International policies are, in fact, within sight of the point reached by *internal* development in the mid-nineteenth century. Either they will move on to a community based upon a more systematic sharing of wealth—through progressive income tax, through general policies for education, shelter, health and housing —or they will break down in revolt and anarchy. Many of today's proposals for development aid, through international channels, are a first sketch of such a system.

But at this point, if gloom is the psychological risk of all too many ecological forecasts, may we not go to the opposite extreme of Pollyanna optimism in forecasting any such growth of a sense of community in our troubled and divided planet? With war as mankind's oldest habit and divided sovereignty as his most treasured inheritance, where are the energies, the psychic force, the profound commitment needed for a wider loyalty?

Loyalty may, however, be the key. It is the view of many modern psychologists that man is a killer not because of any biological imperative but because of his capacity for misplaced loyalty. He will do in the name of a wider allegiance what he would shrink to do in his own nature. His massive, organized killings—the kind that distinguishes him from all other animals— are invariably done in the name of faith and group or people or clan. And here it is not wholly irrational to hope that the full realization of planetary interdependence—in biosphere and technosphere alike—may begin to affect man in the depths of his capacity for psychic commitment. All loyalty is based on two elements—the hope of protection and the hope of enhancement. On either count, the new ecological imperative can give a new vision of where man belongs in his final security and his final sense of dignity and identity.

At the most down-to-earth level of self-interest, it is the realization of the planet's totally continuous and interdependent systems of air, land and water that helps to keep a check on the ultimate lunacies of nuclear weaponry. When after the Chinese and French nuclear tests in 1969, the air above Britain was found to contain 20 percent more Strontium 90 and Cesium 137, it is not a very sophisticated guess that the air above France and China contained no less. It is the force of such recognitions that lay behind the first global environmental agreement—the Test Ban Treaty negotiated in 1963—which has kept the other major powers out of competitive air testing and saved unnumbered children from leukemia. Similar calculations of enlightened self-interest underlie the treaty to keep nuclear weapons out of space, off the seabeds and away from Antarctica.

Even where success is in doubt—as in the treaty to prevent the spread of nuclear weapons, or the Soviet-American negotiations for a mutual limitation of strategic arms—the underlying rationale is still the same. As the airs and oceans flow round our little planet, there is not much difference between your Strontium 90 and my Strontium 90. They are lethal to us both.

It is even possible that recognition of our environmental interdependence can do more than save us, negatively, from the final folly of war. It could, positively, give us that sense of community, of belonging and living together, without which no human society can be built up, survive and prosper. Our links of blood and history, our sense of shared culture and achievement, our traditions, our faiths are all precious and enrich the world with the variety of scale and function required for every vital ecosystem. But we have lacked a wider rationale of unity. Our prophets have sought it. Our poets have dreamed of it. But it is only in our own day that astronomers, physicists, geologists, chemists, biologists, anthropologists, ethnologists and archaeologists have all combined in a single witness of advance science to tell us that, in every alphabet of our being, we do indeed belong to a single system, powered by a single energy, manifesting a fundamental unity under all its variations, depending for its survival on the balance and health of the total system.

If this vision of unity—which is not a vision only but a hard and inescapable scientific fact—can become part of the common insight of all the inhabitants of Planet Earth, then we may find that, beyond all our inevitable pluralisms, we can achieve just enough unity of purpose to build a human world.

# 5.13 TRANSCENDENCE— A UNIFYING CONCEPT
## Philip H. Phenix

### The Meaning of Transcendence

The term "transcendence" refers to the experience of limitless going beyond any given state or realization of being. It is an inherent property of conscious being to be aware that every concrete entity is experienced within a context of wider relationships and possibilities. Conscious life is always open to a never-ending web of entailments and unfoldings. No content of experience is just what it appears to be here and now without any further prospects or associations. All experience is characterized by an intrinsic dynamism that in principle breaks every bound that rational patterning or practical convenience may establish.

The sense of this fundamental category can perhaps be made clearer by referring to some of the cognate terms that have been employed in the theological tradition to point to it. The one most akin is "infinitude," which expresses the never-finished enlargement of contexts within which every bounded entity is enmeshed. To affirm the finiteness of anything is to presuppose a participation in infinitude that makes it possible to acknowledge the finite. Finitude is thus a specification of limitation within the ambience of infinitude—a deliberate stemming of transcendence for purposes of conceptual or active control.

A second allied concept is "spirit." Spirit is the name given to the property of limitless going beyond. To have a spiritual nature is to participate in infinitude. Reason refers to the capacity for the rational ordering of experience through categories of finitude. Spirit makes one aware of the finiteness of the structures imposed by reason. To say that persons are beings with spirit is to point to their perennial discontent and dissatisfaction with any and every finite realization. Thus it is sometimes said that spirit finds its exemplification more in the yearning impulses of feeling and the innovative projects of will than in the settled conclusions of intellect.

The essential quality of transcendence is manifest also in the secular concept of idealization, which is central, for example, in the nontheistic, naturalistic thought of John Dewey. Every actuality is set within a context of ideal possibility. Every end realized becomes the means for the fulfillment of further projected ideals, and this is a process that is generic to human experi-

Philip H. Phenix, "Transcendence and the Curriculum," *Teachers College Record* 73: 271–283, December 1971. Excerpts used by permission.

Professor Philip H. Phenix teaches philosophy at Teachers College, Columbia University.

ence. Much the same idea is implicit in Dewey's concept of continuous growth —of that valuable growth that leads to further growth. The qualitative test of growth is whether it is consistent with a limitless enrichment of realizations through the progressive actualization of ideal possibilities. This vision of continuous, progressive reconstruction of experience as the norm of human existence is a nontheological interpretation of the fundamental religious concept of transcendence.

## Dimensions of Transcendence

The general concept of transcendence may be analyzed into at least three principal dimensions: temporal, extensive, and qualitative. Temporal transcendence refers to infinitude of process. The experience of temporal passage in its essence is a consciousness of transcendence, for it manifests an ineluctable going beyond. Heraclitus was the first among Western thinkers to point to the primordial character of temporal flux, within which the logos of reason was a subordinate principle of order. In modern philosophy Bergson was perhaps the foremost exponent of the basic dynamism of reality, which he called the *élan vital,* apprehended by an act of intuition that yields profounder insight than the static conceptions of discursive reason. Whitehead also made "creative advances into novelty," i.e. continuous temporal transcendence, the most fundamental presupposition of his system of categories for describing reality.

To be humanly alive is to experience each moment as a new creation, to know that this moment, though continuous with the past, is yet a distinct and fresh emergence, which will in turn yield to still further novel realizations. Every human present, retrospectively regarded, is perceived as created, and prospectively regarded, as a destiny. These two terms—creation and destiny—are the two temporal poles between which transcendence ranges. As such, they are perennially important theological categories. The experiential meaning of creation—of being created—is the consciousness of retrospective temporal transcendence of prior states of being. The experiential meaning of destiny, and of participating in creative activity, is the consciousness of prospective actualizations beyond every particular attainment. The various ideas in the religions of mankind referring to the preexistence or immortality of the soul aim to symbolize the temporal dimension of transcendence both in its retrospective and prospective modes.

A second dimension of transcendence is extension. Limitless going beyond is experienced not only with reference to time but also in respect to inclusiveness. The classic philosophical statement of this dimension of transcendence is supplied by the doctrine of internal relations, which is the central idea and the key to philosophical idealism, though not exclusively wedded to that way of thinking. According to this doctrine, any entity is constituted by the set of relationships that it has with all other entities. Thus nothing exists in isolation, but always in relation. Reality is a single interconnected whole, such that the complete description of any entity would require the comprehension of every other entity. . . . [Thus, in Whitehead's philosophy,] every actual occasion or event is a particular mirroring of the whole universe.

Something of the same idea is implicit in modern field theories and in the ideas of contextualism and ecology. An electron, a magnet, a chunk of matter, or a person is never an isolated, separate entity, but exists in a context of electrostatic, magnetic, gravitational, or personal field relationships. In the last analysis, every being is a being-in-relation, and is what it is and behaves as it does by virtue of its participation with other beings.

The theological expression of the principle of extensive transcendence is supplied by the doctrine of monotheism and of the divine omnipresence. There is a single ultimate ground of all being, and all beings are mutually related in that common unitary reality. Hence, every particular experience contains the possibility of evincing the limitless wealth of participations to which it is heir, thereby bearing witness to a principle of transcendence toward wholeness that is one hallmark of religious orientation.

To the temporal and extensive dimensions of transcendence a third may be added, namely the qualitative. This dimension refers to the consciousness of limitless possibility of going beyond in degrees of excellence. It is the source of the principle of criticism that levies judgments of relative worth on concrete actualizations. What this principle affirms is that no actual occasion or finite grouping of occasions constitutes a complete qualitative achievement, but that beyond all such realizations higher fulfillments are possible.

This dimension of qualitative transcendence is well exemplified in one of the central concepts in Tillich's theology, that is, in what he terms the "Protestant Principle." By this term he does not refer primarily to the historic movement called Protestantism, but rather to the principle of protest that denies qualitative ultimacy to any actuality, be it institution, person, belief, or cultural norm. According to this principle, the religious consciousness is manifest in the refusal to accord supreme worth to any and every realization of nature or humanity. Implicit in such refusal is commitment to an inexhaustible ideality that renders a judgment of partiality and insufficiency on whatever exists.

The theological expression of qualitative transcendence is also contained in such concepts as divine holiness, righteousness, and perfection. That God is holy, righteous, and perfect experientially signifies the persuasion of the human consciousness that no finite reality is of supreme worth, the creative restlessness of the human spirit that never remains content with any historic attainment, and the perennial protest of the prophetic conscience against the absolutizing of limited goods.

*Universality and Negation of Transcendence.* It has been suggested that transcendence is a primordial category for the interpretation of human experience in the sense that it is an elemental and ineluctable aspect of the human condition. That is to say that transcendence is universal. It is phenomenologically not the case that some persons, called "religious" or "spiritual" types, experience it while others do not. I am arguing that human consciousness is rooted in transcendence, and that analysis of all human consciousness discloses the reality of transcendence as a fundamental presupposition of the human condition. To be sure, this same human consciousness also discloses aspects of finitude. Acts of demarcation, of limitation, and of closure are manifestly present in human behavior. What I maintain is that all such finite determinations are imbedded in and are specifications of an indeterminate ground of creative advance into novelty, of contextual relations, and of qualitative gradations.

The relation of finite and infinite in man has the paradoxical property that boundless creative lures, outreachings for wider relations, and strivings for ideality, all of which transcendent tensions challenge the status quo of finite realizations, cause persons to negate transcendence in order to save themselves from the threatened dissolution of actual attainments. The denial of spirituality in the name of individual self-sufficiency or various forms of absolutism, of institution, race, class, nation, tradition, or doctrine, is evidence of this flight from transcendence. This negative self-protective movement is what the Judaic and Christian traditions have called sin. As theologians in these traditions have regularly pointed out, the pervasive and persistent denial of transcendence is, in fact, prime evidence for the presence and power of transcendence. This is the meaning of the myth that portrays the devil as a fallen angel, that is, as a spiritual agent employing his creative transcendence to generate an illusion of self-sufficing autonomy.

## General Dispositions

We are now in a position to proceed with a discussion of the significance of the experience of transcendence for the enterprise of education. Certain qualities of life are associated with transcendence, and at the same time play a decisive role in teaching and learning. I submit that these general human dispositions provide a set of criteria for a transcendence-oriented curriculum as contrasted with one that is predicated upon the neglect or denial of transcendence.

*Hope.* The first disposition engendered by the experience of transcendence is hope. Hope is the mainspring of human existence. As existentialist thinkers remind us, conscious life is a continual projection into the future. Even though the adventure may project one into the unknown, it is animated by an affirmation of the movement forward in time. Without hope, there is no incentive for learning, for the impulse to learn presupposes confidence in the possibility of improving one's existence. It can be argued that widespread loss of hope is one of the principal causes of educational problems that beset contemporary America. When widespread social dislocations, dissolution of customary norms, dehumanization, and other malaises of social and cultural life cause people to feel impotent, no technical improvements in the content or methods of instruction will induce people to learn well. On the other hand, those who are buoyed by strong hope can overcome substantial formal deficiencies in program or technique. The explicit acknowledgment of transcendence as a ground for hope may therefore contribute significantly to the efficacy of education.

Few recent thinkers have so persuasively argued that a transcendent hope is the driving force for personal and collective achievement as Teilhard de Chardin. He saw the cultural and educational crisis of our time primarily as a faltering of hope; by presenting a cosmological vision in which man's conscious responsible striving for progress is viewed as continuous with the upward drive toward coordination that has powered the entire evolutionary ascent, he endeavored to provide intellectual warrant for an animating hope that can give mankind the heart to continue learning.

*Creativity.* The recognition of transcendence as inseparable from the human condition lends special emphasis to the disposition toward creativity. To be human is to create. The fashioning of new constructs is not an exceptional activity reserved for a minority of gifted persons; it is rather the normal mode of behavior for everyone. Dull repetitiveness and routinism are evidences of dehumanization. In this respect the institutions and practices of education have often inhibited, rather than fostered, humaneness, by inculcating habits of automatic conformity instead of imaginative origination.

The prime enemy of creativity is the flight from transcendence which in the theological tradition of the West has been termed sin. Insofar as educators function as agents for transmitting and confirming cultural traditions unchanged, they are ministers of sin. When they presume to act as authorities dispensing to the young knowledge and values that are to be accepted without question, they act as enemies of transcendence. On the other hand, the educator who affirms transcendence is characterized by a fundamental humility manifest in expectant openness to fresh creative possibilities. To be sure, he does not ignore or discount the funded wisdom of the past. He does not regard it as a fixed patrimony to be preserved, but as a working capital for investment in the projects of an unfolding destiny.

Creativity is fostered by having due regard both for transcendence and for immanence. By the experience of immanence I mean the sense of importance in what is actualized in existence. Immanence and transcendence are intimately related. Immanence is the treasure deposited by the creative activity of transcendence. Existential realizations lose their savor when the freshness of transcendent impulse that ushered in their birth is forgotten, and projected enterprises degenerate into quixotic gestures when the sustaining and ennobling structures of past actualizations are rejected. The educator thus fosters creativity when he loves and respects the traditional learning, conceived as immanence, to be transformed and rejuvenated in the service of transcendence.

*Awareness.* The dispositions of hope and creativity correspond to the temporal dimension of transcendence. Corresponding to the extensive dimension are the dispositions of awareness: sympathy, empathy, hospitality, and tolerance, that is to say, openness outwards, as well as toward the future. In acknowledging transcendence, one adopts a positive attitude toward all other persons, other cultures, and other social groups, in fact, toward all other beings, including the objects of nature. Accepting transcendence frees one from the self-protecting isolation that regards the different or the unfamiliar as a threat to be avoided. Alienation is evidence of the flight from transcendence, and separation and exclusion are manifestations of the primary sin of striving for self-sufficient autonomy.

No teaching can occur without a predisposition toward relation on the part of the teacher who seeks to shape the life of the student and to mediate to the students his (the teacher's) life of relation with the circumambient world. Nor will the student learn effectively in the absence of a hospitable openness to that world and to those who assist him in establishing satisfying relationships with it. This factor of sensitivity is the main theme in Buber's pedagogical theory. For him, the clue to significant education does not reside in the specific methods or contents of instruction, but in the presupposition of the primacy and the power of the elemental relation, which is the source of all being. He sees the primordial relation as a reality in which one may confidently dwell, and within which the particular categories and connections of reason and practice are secondarily discriminated. This assumed indwelling by the teacher in transcendence can help to release the student's powers of awareness, thus providing strong catalysis for learning. In turn, teachers who are inured to self-defensive closedness may be liberated to wider sympathies by sharing in the relatively unspoiled freshness of young people who affirm the world and celebrate the possibilities of ever-deepening relationships within it.

*Doubt and Faith.* Corresponding to the qualitative dimension of transcendence are the twin dispositions of constructive doubt and faith or, combining the two, faithful doubt. A central insight of Tillich's thought is this intimate linkage of doubt and faith within the context of transcendence. Tillich argues that really serious doubt—the radical questioning of any and every alleged finality—is only possible to one who is grasped by a transcendent faith, that is, who enjoys a confidence that wells up from the creative grounds of being and does not rest on any objectified security structures. This position is summarized in Tillich's reformulation of Luther's doctrine of justification by faith in the state of sin to read justification by faith in the state of doubt. The serious doubter is justified by his faith in the unconditioned ground of being manifest in the very seriousness of his activity of doubting.

The educator rooted in transcendence helps to foster a constructive disposition toward doubt, that is, a spirit of criticism. Such a spirit is to be distinguished sharply from the destructive doubt of the cynic or skeptic or from the attitude of indifference engendered by dilettante sophistication. The latter dispositions are essentially faithless, in the sense that they presuppose the futility of any sustained quest for truth or right on the grounds that the perennial struggle of mankind to achieve demonstrable securities has proven unsuccessful. Abandoning the search for ultimate certainties, the skeptic unwittingly cuts the ground from under serious inquiry itself, thus discrediting even his own activity of doubting. The Cartesian insight still holds, though in modified form: I doubt, therefore I am. The secure foundation of the human condition as a spiritual being is the faith-evidencing activity of concerned and responsible doubting.

The teacher who is spiritually aware does not seek to protect himself from the insecurity of uncertainty, perplexity, and irremediable ignorance. He does not try to hide behind a screen of academic presumption and professional expertise, embellished with mystifying jargon. Nor does he confuse the role of teacher with that of authoritative oracle. He does not expect or encourage his students supinely to accept his beliefs or directions. On the other hand, he shares with conviction and enthusiasm the light that he believes he possesses, and encourages his students to do the same, resolutely resisting in himself and in his students the paralysis and sense of futility associated with skepticism and indifference.

*Wonder, Awe and Reverence.*   Consummating the dispositions associated with the experience of transcendence are the attitudes of wonder, awe, and reverence. Consciousness of infinitude entails a sense of the manifold powers and possibilities of the reality in which one's existence is embedded. This sense is the root of the impulse to learn. Dewey spoke of the unsolved problem as the stimulus for thought. I believe his concept of the problem as basically the blocking of organic drives was too narrowly biological, and that a sounder, more positive, and more distinctly human formulation would be that thought grows out of wonder, which in turn is rooted in the spiritual act of projecting ideal possibilities. Thus instead of regarding human learning primarily as a means of biological adaptation, it may be thought of as a response to the lure of transcendence. Indeed, the very notion of adaptation appears to be meaningful only in terms of the process of creative invention for the purpose of realizing specific ideal harmonies.

Wonder refers to the suspenseful tension of consciousness toward the unknown future in response to the attraction of unrealized potentialities. It includes the vague adumbration of enriching relationships yet unestablished but beckoning. It is the hovering shadow of an answer resident in every question seriously asked. Awe is the sense of momentousness excited by the experience of transcendence. It is the source of persistent interest in learning and of patient efforts toward realization, born of the sense that the human career, as well as the cosmic enterprise of which it is a part, is an affair of capital importance. Reverence betokens a recognition of one's participation in transcendence as a surprising and continually renewed gift, in contrast to the view of one's existence as a secure possession and as an autonomous achievement. The reverent disposition saves one from the arrogance of self-sufficiency which interferes with openness to creative possibilities in learning, and issues in a spirit of thankfulness for the gift of life that makes study a welcome opportunity and not a chore and an obligation.

## Consequences for the Curriculum

The acknowledgment of transcendence suggests a curriculum that has due regard for the uniqueness of the human personality. If a person is a creative subject, then the core of his selfhood can never be defined in terms of objective formative patterns that are common to a social group. To be sure, for practical purposes provision must be made to enable the young to participate effectively in the common life. But it makes a great difference whether the patterns of culture are regarded as essentially constitutive of the personality or as resources for use by a personality whose springs of being lie at a deeper level than any social norm, that is to say, in transcendence.

A curriculum of transcendence provides a context for engendering, gestating, expecting, and celebrating the moments of singular awareness and of inner illumination when each person comes into the consciousness of his inimitable personal being. It is not characterized so much by the objective content of studies as by the atmosphere created by those who comprise the learning community. Its opposite is the engineering outlook that regards the learner as material to be formed by means of a variety of technical procedures. In contrast, the curriculum of transcendence requires a context of essential freedom, though not of anarchy, which is the correlate of indifference and of skepticism about the structures of being. Freedom in the school of transcendence is based on openness to fresh possibilities of insight and invention and provision of ample cultural and interpersonal resources for the formation of unique structures of existence.

*Concern for Wholeness.* The lure of transcendence is toward wholeness. It follows that the educator in responding to that incitement creates a curriculum that fosters comprehensiveness of experience. The argument for education of the whole person in the last analysis rests on the consciousness of transcendence. In a technical, success oriented society the payoff is found in specialized competence. From the standpoint of personal and social efficiency, the arguments for breadth of knowledge and skill are few and unconvincing. To be sure, there must be some with sufficient scope of understanding to be able to coordinate the parts of the social mechanism. Yet even their comprehensiveness can be conceived in narrow managerial terms. The case for general education for all rests finally on the nature of persons as essentially constituted by the hunger for wholeness.

A curriculum designed to respond to this hunger is obviously multidisciplinary. It affords opportunities for the enrichment of understanding in diverse areas of human experience, as, for example, in the theoretical, the practical, and the affective domains. Narrowness and exclusivity of concentration are incompatible with the demands of transcendence.

On the other hand, it is important not to be misled into the advocacy of superficial generality in the plan of studies. Since transcendence has a qualitative as well as an extensive dimension, it is just as essential to provide opportunities for intensive understanding as for extensive range of studies. That is why the curriculum of transcendence is multi-*disciplinary* in nature. The disciplinary character insures depth of penetration—a progressive enlargement of insight within the framework of methods and categories that has proven fruitful in inquiry. It cannot be overemphasized that transcendence is not simply openness-in-general. It presupposes that being has structures. These structures are the immanent patterns of transcendence. Hence the necessity for discipline. Transcendence is not an invitation to anarchy but to glad obedience to the structures or logos of being. These patterns are the objective norms for knowledge and for conduct, and they are what the various disciplines aim to disclose. Productiveness of insight in any discipline is evidence that the categories and procedures that define it in some degree reflect the logos of being.

The criterion of wholeness, then, is not incompatible with specialized inquiry. It does, however, require that each specialized mode of investigation be understood in relation to other such modes. Each discipline is founded upon certain deliberate limitations and simplifications which make it possible to advance understanding of inexhaustibly complex realities. What consciousness of transcendence does is to make one aware of the partiality of each disciplined outlook and sensitive to the many-sidedness of the reality that one confronts. . . . In this sense, the curriculum in the light of transcendence is *inter*-disciplinary as well as *multi*-disciplinary. . . .

Furthermore, though the various disciplines are conceived as channels of insight into the structures of being, it is not assumed that any standard or traditional set of disciplines provides the full and final disclosure of the nature of things. Hence consciousness of transcendence encourages an open-textured orientation toward the very enterprise of discipline-making, hospitality toward the emergence of fresh discipline perspectives, and willingness to replace partial outlooks that have served well in the past with more comprehensive or penetrating ones as they emerge in the successive transformations in the evolution of culture. On these grounds, the transcendence-oriented educator helps his students to be alert to the realities of intellectual mutations, revolutions, and inventions, and endeavors to create an atmosphere and an expectation in which his students may share in the construction of new and more illuminating patterns of thought.

*Education for Inquiry.* The recognition of transcendence suggests a characteristic perception of the central task of teaching and learning as dedication to the practice of inquiry. The transcendent perspective is opposed to all outlooks that presuppose a fixed content of knowledge, beliefs, or skills that the learner is meant to acquire. The assumption that anything is knowable with completeness and certainty arrests inquiry and closes the channels that lead on to deeper and wider insight.

On the other hand, transcendence is compatible with confident acceptance of the possibility of valid knowledge, once its partial, limited, and contingent character is acknowledged. . . . Commitment to inquiry is thus opposed to two polar positions: dogmatic finality or certainty and nihilistic skepticism about the possibility of warranted knowledge. The confident practice of inquiry rests on faith in the intelligibility of reality together with an acknowledgment of the boundless depth and the interconnections of the structures of intelligibility. . . .

*The Practice of Dialogue.* Inherent also in education carried on according to the norms of transcendence is the practice of dialogue. The extensive dimension of transcendence presupposes a lure toward ever wider associations of complementarity and of enriching relatedness. It is incompatible with all self-sufficient isolation and exclusiveness of perspective. Hence growth in understanding is to be sought by engaging in the activity of open-ended, continuing communication. The indissoluble unity between teaching and learning is affirmed in the recognition that enlargement and refinement of insight are possible only through the mutual stimulation of conjoint inquiry. One learns effectively only as he seeks to make his perspectives intelligible to others and in turn seeks to enter into their perceptions. . . .

*The Cultivation of Transcendence* . . . is possible . . . [By] living hopefully and creatively, with faith and reverence, by experiencing the joys of responsible freedom, by seeking for wholeness of disciplined understanding, and by engaging in continual dialogic inquiry, one tacitly acknowledges the presence and power of transcendence. . . .

[An] important factor in the cultivation of transcendence is the witness of those who consciously celebrate it in their own existence. When fearful and self-protecting tendencies tend to obscure the light of infinitude and doubts tend to annihilate rather than transform, one may bolster flagging faith by turning to others in strong grasp of transcendence. In this respect the teacher by his own mute witness may play a central role in the maintenance of the primordial grounds of learning morale.

# INDEX OF NAMES

Italic page numbers indicate that the author cited is quoted in the text.

# INDEX OF SUBJECTS